EXTREME UNCTION

A DISSERTATION

Submitted to the Faculty of Canon Law of the Catholic University of America in partial fulfillment of the requirements for the Degree of Doctor of Canon Law

By the

REV. ADRIAN JEROME KILKER, J. C. L.

Of the Archdiocese of Philadelphia

WASHINGTON, D. C.

1926

Nihil Obstat:

✠Thomas J. Shahan, S. T. D.,

Censor Deputatus.

Washingtonii, D. C., die XVII Maii, 1926.

Imprimatur:

✠D. Card. Dougherty,

Archiepiscopus Philadelphiensis.

Philadelphiae, die XXVII Maii, 1926.

TABLE OF CONTENTS

FOREWORD

The bestowal of Extreme Unction is one of the paramount features of a priest's career. The time of its administration is fraught with significance. Given, as it always is, when the patient is in danger of death from sickness, it is a momentous event, a crisis in the life of the recipient.

It is well then that a priest should be thoroughly cognizant of the laws of the Church which regulate the administration of this great gift of a munificent God. Only thru a thorough realization of their terms can he hope to discharge an intelligent ministry.

The promulgation of the Code has given us very succinctly the norm of action for the exercise of this phase of sacerdotal duty. Within eleven canons are summed up the directions which should rule the activities of priests in administering the oil of the unction to sick souls. No radical changes of legislation have been made from the old law, but there are some alterations of primary importance. Yet no book, at least in English, has undertaken the consideration *ex professo* of this sacrament from a juridical standpoint. For this reason alone, a work on the subject does not seem untimely.

Deep and weighty problems lie beneath the simple terminology of the canons. The intertwining of theological subjects makes an escape from this impossible. Canonical problems extend their ramifications into dogma, history and liturgy. They are indeed manifold and perplexing, but their mastery connotes a deeper understanding of the law. Hence they have a great interest for the jurist.

As a consequence the various theological, historical and liturgical problems have been investigated. No exhaustive treatment of them has been attempted, but in every case they have been noted and a summary survey presented.

The writer cannot let the opportunity pass without expressing his thanks to the Faculty of Canon Law of the Catholic University for their many practical suggestions to him in the preparation of this work.

CHAPTER I.

A DOGMATICO-HISTORICAL INTRODUCTION

CHAPTER I.

There are few laws of the Church that have not a foundation in dogma. No matter how purely disciplinary they seem, they can generally be found to have their support from some dogmatic substratum.

Sacramental legislation is essentially of this kind. There, if anywhere, the commentator must understand the fundamental tenets involved, lest by injudicious daring he trespass beyond the limits that revelation has defined.

For this purpose he must be conversant with the practices of preceding centuries. In matters sacramental, history goes far toward a proper conception of dogma. It is a useful corrective that saves the judgment from *a priori* conclusions that are often fatally erroneous. Dogma is applied practically thru laws; and these too have a history of their own. Born of the exigencies of time and place, they give us an insight into the viewpoint of their day. They have changed often, yet dogma remains the same. Thus the dogmatic foundation allows great scope in the choice of material for the superstructure of law to be erected upon it. But if the wrong material is used, if the legal edifice projects beyond the boundaries of the foundation, the structure thus built will topple and tumble and crash of its own inherent weakness.

Accordingly in treating with Extreme Unction, it is not only advisable, but positively imperative, to take a short excursion into the realms of dogma and of history. Such a sally, by refreshing our minds with thoughts theological, will furnish the correct setting of stage, will produce the proper perspective for a consideration of the canonical legislation on the subject. Thereby the terminology of the canons will assume a deeper, fuller meaning. Thereby interpretation of them will be clarified, facilitated.

Who, for instance, understands thoroughly the force of the word "infirmitatem" in Canon 940, except he who realizes the power of ἀσθενεῖ in the text of St. James? The sufficiency of a single unction, the prohibition of iteration, and numerous other points, are almost unexplainable without the light of their dogmatic and historical background.

Hence the reader is led, in preparation for the canonical treatment of the subject, in a somewhat hasty fashion thru the territories of dogma and history—to dally for a moment here and there at points of paramount interest, but on the whole, to gain only fleeting glimpses of provinces traversed before.

I. The Name

This sacrament received in the course of the centuries many titles. The Greeks and the Latins, though one in dogmatic belief, were widely dissentient when it came to naming this channel of grace. Even within each rite it was given a host of names, by reason of its various effects, or of the multiple ritualistic differences of administration, or of its remote and proximate matter. Thus in the Latin Church it was designated as: "sanctum oleum infirmorum," "unctio sacrati olei," "sacra olei unctio," "sacra unctio Dei," "unctio infirmorum," "unctionis officium," etc. In Milan at the time of St. Ambrose it was known as "the imposition of hands upon the infirm."[1] Innocent I in his epistle to Decentius[2] called it "chrisma." The second Council of Aachen[3] spoke of it as "oleum sanctificatum;" while the Council of Trent[4] termed it the "sacramentum exeuntium."

Equally as numerous is the array of names given by the Greeks to this sacrament. The most common name is εὐχέλαιους[5] (i. e. oil of prayers). Goar in his Euchologion[6] recounts other names, such as ἐλαίου χρῖσις, χρῖσμα, χρῖσμα δι ἐλαίου, καθιέρωσις δι ἐλαίου.

Benedict XIV in his encyclical *"Ex quo"* (March 1, 1756)[7] witnesses to the fact that the Greeks occasionally called this

1 Magistretti, *Manuale Ambrosianum*, pp. 74 sqq., 94 sqq.

2 Denziger-Bannwart, *Enchiridion*, n. 99; M. P. L., 20, 559B; Mansi, III, 1030-31; C.I.C. Fontes, n. 19.

3 Cap. II, *"De Vita Inf. Ord.,"* can. 5—Harduin IV, 1397A.

4 Sess. XIV, *De Ext. Unct.*, cap. 3.

5 Goar, *Euchologion*, p. 346, n. 42; p. 349, n. 1.

6 Goar, *op. cit.*, p. 349; cf. Ralli, Περὶ τῶν μυστηρίων τῆς μετανοίας καὶ τοῦ εὐχελαίου, p. 110.

7 C. I. C. Fontes, n. 438, paragr. 45.

sacrament of the sick "Heptapapadum," i. e., the office of seven priests. Thus in 1277 at the Synod of Constantinople the patriarch, John Vecco, in his acceptance of the confession of faith of the Council of Lyons, wrote to John XX: "Extremam Unctionem etiam ipsam recipimus similiter cum aliis sacramentis, quae a nobis celebrata, 'Heptapapadum' nominatur."[8]

The present name of "Extreme Unction" has been in general use since the twelfth century. As far back as the ninth there are evidences of its employment. The virgin Maura, who lived at that time, asked Prudentius, the Bishop of Troyes, to administer to her the sacrament of "Extreme Unction."[9] The term became hallowed by the constant use of the Scholastics. Peter Lombard, for instance, titles the twenty-third distinction of the fourth Book of Sentences *"De Sacramento Extremae Unctionis."*[10] In like manner a rubric of the Decretals of Gregory IX reads: "Alex. III—Solus Sacerdos potest sacramentum *unctionis extremae* infirmo conferre."[11] Its official enshrinement in the declarations and canons of the Council of Trent[12] ensured its permanency as the name of this sacrament.

The reason for the name, "Extreme Unction," has ever been an unsettled question. Estius[13] ascribes it to the fact that it is the last in point of time of all the unctions of the several sacramental rites. The first is that given to catechumens before Baptism. The second follows close on the heels of the actual baptismal ablution. The bishop performs the third at Confirmation. Priestly hands are hallowed with a fourth unction in ordination. A fifth, though not sacramental, unction is given to secular princes.[14] The sixth—and the last, because no other follows it—is that of our sacrament. Other theologians, like Kern, say that the sacrament has its name, not because it is the last unction, but because it is administered only to those "in extremis." It is the "sacramentum exeuntium," as Trent

---

8 Harduin, VII, 758B.

9 M. P. L., 115, 1374C.

10 M. P. L., 192, 899.

11 c. 14, X, *de verb. signif.*, V, 40.

12 Sess. XIV, *De Ext. Unct.*, c. 3.

13 *In Quattuor Lib. Sent. Comm.*, ad dist. xxiii libri quarti, n. 1—tom. IV, p. 285; cf. also Catalano, *Rit. Rom.*, tom. I, p. 300.

14 Pontificale Romanum, Pars I, *"De Benedictione et Coronatione Regis."*

aptly calls it. This certainly seems to be the viewpoint of most of the faithful—with the result that they defer too often the sacred unction until the patient is beyond the pale of recovery.[15] Chardon complains bitterly of the unfortunate suggestiveness of the name: "Ce sacrament n'a pas toujours porté le nom d'Extrême Onction. Ce nom lui est venu de l'abus qui s'est introduit, et qui n'est que trop commun depuis quelque temps, d'attendre a l'extrémité pour le recevoir."[16]

II. The Sacramentality

The first question of dogmatic import in regard to Extreme Unction is that of its sacramentality. To Catholics ordinarily the mere statement of the Church is sufficient; but to the canonist, who is to look at the sacramental canons from every focus, a rather searching treatment of the proofs is most desirable. The very Scriptural texts on which the proof rests determine to an appreciable degree the wording of the canonical legislation. Consequently there is no irrelevancy in a consideration of the question, for it will save burdening the canons' exegesis with many cumbersome explanations.

It is a matter of Catholic belief, of course, that Extreme Unction is a sacrament. The Council of Trent[1] decided that authoritatively by fulminating an anathema against those denying this truth. In the century preceding, Eugene IV, in his instructions to the Armenians,[2] had mentioned it among the seven sacraments. These were not the first official documents on the subject. As far back as 1208 the belief of the Waldensians on this matter was questioned by the Pope.[3] The profession of faith subscribed to by Michael Paleologus in the Council of Lyons[4] enumerated it among the sacraments. Suspicion of contemning Extreme Unction rested on the Wicliffites

15 Kern, *Tract. de Ext. Unct.*, p. 3.
16 Migne, *Theol. Cursus Compl.*, vol. XX, col. 747.

1 Sess. XIV, *de Ext. Unct.*, c. 1.
2 Const. "*Exultate Deo,*" 22 Nov. 1439, paragr. 14—C. I. C. Fontes, n. 52; Denziger-Bannwart, *Enchiridion*, n. 700.
3 Innocent III, ep. "*Ejus exemplo,*" Dec. 18, 1208—C. I. C. Fontes, n. 30.
4 Anno 1274—C. I. C. Fontes, n. 35; Denziger-Bannwart, *Enchiridion*, n. 465.

and Hussites to such an extent that Martin V ordered a special investigation into their dogmatic beliefs on the subject.[5]

The batteries of Trent were levelled chiefly against the so-called reformers. Luther[6] with much pretense of erudition had denied the sacramentality of the sacred Unction. With impious impudence Calvin declared it to be "histrionic hypocrisy,"[7] asserting that it has been *passé* since the cessation of charismatic healing. Previous to these reformers there was no definite heresy regarding Extreme Unction. The Albigensians may be said to have rejected it in their principles, and the Waldensians actually did denounce it as the "ultima superbia"—but no direct dogmatic denial is recorded before Luther's day.[8]

A) *Proof from Scripture*

The bulwark of the Catholic argument is one very conclusive Scriptural text—James, V, 14. Protestant theologians pretend to be astounded that the Catholic Church can exegete from the words of St. James the sacrament of Extreme Unction. On the other hand Catholics are equally amazed at the vagaries they in turn are guilty of, in a frantic effort to escape the real meaning of the text. They are unanimous only in the rejection of the Catholic interpretation. There is no accord as to what meaning should be substituted—"quot capita tot sententiae." They attack the text at every point. They dispute about the author of this rite, about its duration, about its ministers, about the subject, about the matter, about the "prayer of faith," about the end and effects. Small wonder that Catholics are stupefied that such unanimity in the rejection of revealed truth can be coupled with such diversity in asserting error.

The Council of Trent lays specific stress on the Jacobean text. Hear its own words: "Now, this sacred unction of the sick was instituted by Christ our Lord, as truly and properly a sacrament of the new law, insinuated indeed in Mark, but recommended and promulgated to the faithful by James the

---

5 Const. "*Inter Cunctas,*" 22 Feb. 1418—C. I. C. Fontes, n. 43; Denziger-Bannwart, *Enchiridion*, n. 669.

6 *De Captivitate Babylonica*, cap. "*de Ext. Unct.*"

7 *Inst.*, IV, xix, 18.

8 Cf. De Sainte-Beuve, *De Ext. Unct.*, disp. I, art. II, in Migne, *Curs. Theol. Comp.*, vol. xxiv, 10, sqq.; Bellarmine, *De Sac. Ext. Unct.*, Liber unicus, c. I.

Apostle and brother of the Lord. 'Is any man,' he saith, 'sick among you? Let him bring in the priests of the Church, and let them pray over him, anointing him with oil in the name of the Lord: and the prayer of faith shall save the sick man; and the Lord shall raise him up; and if he be in sins, they shall be forgiven him.' In which words, as the Church has learned from apostolic tradition, received from hand to hand, he teaches the matter, the form, the proper minister, and the effect of this salutary sacrament.''[9] Thus the Council infallibly instructs us of the sacramental nature of the Jacobean prayer-unction and gives us incidentally the correct exegesis of the Jacobean text.

An analysis of this text of St. James will convince one of the potency of this proposition. In verse 13 of the fifth chapter of his Epistle St. James wrote: "Is any of you sad? Let him pray. Is he cheerful of mind? Let him sing." Prayer is thus prescribed as a general remedy against every affliction. But to persons in a special state of affliction, the apostle proposes the use of a special prayer. Thus he continues: 'Ασθενεῖ τις ἐν ὑμῖω; προσκαλεσάσθω τοὺς πρεσ Βυτέρους τῆς ἐκκλησίας, καὶ προσευξάσθωσαν ἐπ' αὐτὸν ἀλείψαντες ἐλαίῳ ἐν τῳ ὀνόματι κυρίου. Καὶ ἡ εὐχὴ τῆς πίστεως σώσει τὸν κάμνοντα, καὶ ἐγερεῖ αὐτὸν ὁ κύριος· κἂν ἁμαρτίας ᾖ πεποιηώς, ἀφεθήσεται αὐτῷ.

The opposition of the words ἀσθενεῖ and κάμνοντα to the word used in verse 13—κακοπαθεῖ—brings into prominence the notion that not any one sick is meant here, but only those who are truly "aegroti." The hesitancy of Protestant exegetes[10] to extend the meaning of this word to all sick lends much presumption to the truth of the Catholic interpretation. The correct meaning of this word is of paramount importance in determining the true subject of this sacrament, and thus explaining the force of the term "infirmitatem" in Canon 940. An inspection of its full significance now will save retracing our steps when treating the canon just mentioned.

Cornelius a Lapide comments: "Quod ait 'infirmatur,' intellige graviter et periculose ad mortem; hic enim ἀσθενεῖ,

[9] Sess. XIV, *De Extr. Unct.*, cap. I—Translation by Waterworth, *Canons and Decrees of the Council of Trent*, p. 105.

[10] Cf. e.g., Ropes, *Epistle of St. James* (International Critical Commentary), p. 308.

i. e., viribus et robore plane destituitur, quem proinde mox vocat τὸν κάμνοντα, i. e., periculose laborantem.'"[11] Suarez also notes: "Verbum κάμνοντα deficientem et pene morientem significat.'"[12] By a comparison with other verses in Scripture, it will be found that the restriction of the meaning of ἀσθενεῖ to those alone who are seriously sick is undoubtedly warrantable. St. Paul, in writing to the Philippians (II, 26) mentions the report that reached them about the sickness of Epaphroditus, his co-worker and "fellow-soldier" διότι ἠκούσατε ὅτι ἠσθένησεν). The seriousness of the sickness was emphasized by the saint in the following verse: "Nam et infirmatus est usque ad mortem"—καὶ γὰρ ἠσθένεσεν παραπλήσιον θανάτῳ. In the Gospel of St. John there are several clear examples. In chapter 4, verse 46, there is found the account of the ruler "cujus filius infirmabatur Capharnaum"—οὗ ὁ υἱὸς ἠσθένει ἐν Καπερναούμ. The gravity of the case is evidenced by the plea of the ruler to Christ: "Lord, come down, before that my son die" (v. 49). In the eleventh chapter of St. John the word ἀσθενεῖν is used three times to describe the condition of Lazarus. That Lazarus was "sick unto death" is certainly clear from the Gospel story. Again the term is found in the Gospel of St. Matthew, when he recounts the words of Christ to the twelve sent forth by Jesus with the power of miracles: Ασθενοῦντας, θεραπεύετε, λεπροὺς καθαρίζετε, νεκρους ἐγείρετε, δαιμόνια ἐκβάλλετε, &c. (X, 8). Finally in the Acts of the Apostles (IX, 37) the Greek text ἀσθενήσασαν ἀποθανεῖν ("Ut infirmata moreretur") makes it manifest that it is a question of the more serious bodily infirmities.[13] This meaning of ἀσθενεῖ is made all the more certain by its connection with κάμνοντα in the following verse: "Et oratio fidei salvabit infirmum." Κάμνω is equivalent to "deficio, lacesso et graviore infirmitate laboro." It ceases then to be surprising that theologians define ἀσθενεῖν to mean "periculoso morbo laborare," and κάμνειν to signify "morti propinquum esse."

Examples of this identical meaning of ἀσθενεῖν can also be found in classical Greek. Thus Demosthenes, in his

11 *Commentar. in Ep. S. Jac.*, ad cap. V, 14.
12 Disp. 42, sect. 2, n. 3.
13 Cf. Berti, *De Theol. Discipl.*, tom. VIII, l. 35, de Extr. Unct., c. 9.

first Oration against Philip, speaks of the relief the Athenians felt when they heard of the sickness of Philip because they expected him to die: *Τέθνηκε Φίλιππος· Οὐ μὰ Δί, ἀλλ' ἀσθενεῖς.* Similarly in the first paragraph of the first chapter of the Anabasis: *ἐπεὶ δὲ ἠσθένει Δαρεῖος καὶ ὑπώπτευε τελευτὴν τοῦ βίου, ἐβούλετο τὼ παῖδε ἀμφοτέρω παρεῖναι.*

These arguments are certainly at first blush quite convincing. Yet it is not to be denied nor concealed that they become startlingly less convincing when one looks in a lexicon, there to learn that neither *ἀσθενεῖν* nor *κάμνειν* signify solely or primarily or even commonly "aegrotum esse," much less "periculose aegrotum esse." Nor is the argument valid that they are used exclusively in the Scriptures in such a sense so that their signification in Holy Writ has become hallowed. The word *κάμνειν* appears in the Scriptures but five times, and nowhere outside of James V, 14 does it signify "aegrotum esse."[14] *Ἀσθενεῖν* is more often used in the Bible, but not infrequently does it mean a deficiency in natural or supernatural forces necessary for a particular end. An example of this is to be had in the book of Judges (XVI, 7-11). There Samson deceived Delilah repeatedly, telling her that if she resorted to several expedients, *καὶ ἀσθενήσω καὶ ἔσομαι ὡς εἷς τῶν ἀνθρώπων.* Add to this the fact that the force *ἀσθενεῖν* of in these comparisons is learned more from the context than from the inherent significance of the word—and it will be seen that too much stress cannot be laid on the grammatical import of the terms.

The true force of *ἀσθενεῖν* can be gathered best from a study of its setting in the text of St. James. In verse 13 there is mentioned a general remedy against all afflictions, viz., prayer (*προσευχέσθω*). In the very next verse a special kind of prayer is prescribed for a particular kind of affliction. The meaning of *ἀσθενεῖ* can be gauged from *προσκαλεσάσθω τοὺς πρεσβυτέρους τῆς ἐκκλησίας.* The sick man is advised to call the priests of the Church. He is therefore considered to be weighed down by his sickness to such an extent that he cannot approach the priests himself—a thing *per se* required by courtesy.[15] Then St.

---

14 Ropes (*Epistle of St. James—Internat'l Critical Commentary*—p. 308) notes that the use of *κάμνειν* in the sense of this verse is common in secular Greek.

15 Bord, *L'Extrême Onction*, p. 56.

James talks of a certain ritualistic function—a prayer-unction—which must be done by the "presbyteri" and by no others; thus connoting some very unusual status of the ἀσθενῶν i. e., his serious sickness. Moreover the presence of no slight indisposition in the sick man was in the mind of the apostle when he wrote of the wonderful effects of this "prayer-unction." The man is to be "saved," to be "raised up," and if necessary, his sins are to be remitted. There is an unmistakable innuendo of the incompetency of the natural powers to obtain this result—for it is the Lord Who "saves" and "raises up" the sick person. Whenever divine aid of such a nature is regarded as necessary for an invalid, his affliction must surely be grave.

One objection may be raised to this explanation. Primarily, it is true, the "prayer-unction" was instituted for the seriously sick; but may not its application be extended to those who are burdened with grief and other afflictions of the soul? The answer is decidedly, "No." Such an extension is in no way permissible. In verse 13 St. James expressly provides a remedy for the other afflictions of man, viz., personal prayer—"Tristatur aliquis vestrum? Oret."

Προσκαλεσάσθω τοὺς πρεσβυτέρους τῆς ἐκκλησίας.

In classical Greek the word πρεσβύτεροι surely means "provecti aetate." In the New Testament, if used without further determination or qualification, it generally has the force of "praepositi Ecclesiae." Thus in the Acts of the Apostles (XIV, 22), the pastoral Epistles (I Tim., V, 17 & 19; Tit. I, 5) and in Peter's first epistle (V, 1) they are surely the officers of the Church, "episcopi et sacerdotes secundi ordinis." There are many places in the epistles that "presbyteri" is translated to mean "the ancients." The verse of St. Peter's Epistle just quoted will explain to some extent the question whether "the ancients" were the presiding priests or simply the laymen in charge of a community. "The ancients, therefore," writes the Prince of the Apostles, "that are among you, I beseech, who am myself also an ancient," &c. Here it is hard to construe "presbyteri" in any other sense than "praepositi Ecclesiae." This amounts to practical certainty when we read further. "Feed the flock of God," he tells them, . . . "taking care of it, not by constraint but willingly according to God, not for filthy lucre's sake, but voluntarily: neither as *lording it over the clergy,* but being made a pattern of the flock from the heart. And when the Prince of *pastors* shall appear, you shall receive a never-fading crown of glory." Surely priestly, and even episcopal duties, such as these could not be commanded of the laymen of the community, no matter how venerable they might be. Similar interpretations may be deduced from the context in other places of the New Testament where "presbyteri" is rendered as "the ancients."[16]

It cannot be contended however that there is no place in the New Testament where "presbyter" cannot be rationally interpreted except as "priest." St. John calls himself ὁ πρεβύτερος at the beginning of his second and third Epistles. This is rendered in the Vulgate as "Senior" and in the English translation as *"The ancient."* Whether St. John is speaking of himself as an apostle, or as a very old man, or as the last of the apostles, cannot be settled with certainty. A second instance is found in 1 Tim., V, 1 sqq.: "An ancient man (πρεσβυτέρῳ) rebuke not, but entreat him as a father; young men, as brethren; old women, as mothers; young women, as sisters, in all chastity. Honor widows that are widows indeed." Here the absolute possibility of construing πρεσβύτερος in any other sense than "provectus aetate" is quite evident. The result must be consequently that the words τοὺς πρεσβυτέρους do not finally close the question that priests only are meant in the text of St. James.

When used, however, with the determining clause τῆς ἐκκλησίας the argument gains immense strength. It is hard to see how the complete phrase could signify any other personages than those who perform the sacred ministry, those who are called "priests" in the Church. In this very sense St. Luke used this term in the Acts of the Apostles: "A Mileto autem mittens Ephesum, vocavit τοὺς πρεσβυτέρους τῆς ἐκκλησίας."[17]

---

16 Cf. A. A., XI, 30; XV, 4, 6, 22, 23; XVI, 4; XXI, 18; &c.

17 Act. App., XX, 17. Strangely enough, the Vulgate renders this "Majores natu ecclesiae"; but it is rightly interpreted by St. Irenaeus (*Adv. Haereticos,* lib. III, cap. 14, n. 2—M. P. L., 7, 914) to mean bishops and priests. Modern exegetes accept this meaning. Cf. e.g., Knabenbauer, *Comm. in Act. App.*, ad cap. XX, v. 17—*Cursus Script. Sac.*

Καὶ προσευξάσθωσαν ἐπ' αὐτὸν ἀλείψαντες (αὐτὸν) ἐλαίῳ ἐν τῷ ὀνόματι (τοῦ) Κυρίου.

This contains clear mention of the necessary elements of the sacrament: oil, the remote matter; unction, the proximate matter; prayer in the name of the Lord, the form. The phrase προσευξάσθωαν ἐπ' αὐτόν is an additional proof that the subject is considered "*decumbens.*" It is to be noted that the aorist participle ἀλείψαντες signifies a simultaneous action with that expressed in προσευξάσθωσαν.[18] Thus the praying and the anointing are to be done at the same time, as is required for the valid confection of any sacrament that the matter and form be present at one and the same time. The apostle does not prescribe the form of unction nor the prayer to be employed. This is due to the fact that he was instructing the faithful, and not the priests[19]—and also, and perhaps more truly, because a set form of prayer and a particular mode of unction are not essential. Priests, however, must do the anointing in the name of the Lord, that is, by His order and command, as His legates and ministers.[20] It cannot mean a mere invocation of the Lord's name, because this is already implied in the mandate "orent super eum"—and the assumption of tautology is unwarrantable. We are led then to no other conclusion than that the Apostle is inculculating here the divine institution of this rite. Its perpetuity is secured because it is not given to charismatics, but is placed as one of the functions of the priestly office. Since the priesthood is perpetual, so is this power.

Καὶ ἡ εὐχὴ τῆς πίστεως σώσει τὸν κάμνοντα, καὶ εγερεῖ αὐτὸν ὁ Κύριος· κἂν ἁμαρτίας ᾖ πεποιηκὼς ἀφεθήσεται αὐτῷ (James V, 15).

This verse asserts the existence of the only other necessary element to make Extreme Unction a sacrament, viz., its effects. First of all, the health or safety of the sick man is generally

---

18 Bord, *L'Extrême Onction*, p. 45.

19 Bord, l.c.

20 Ven. Bede, *Exp. sup. Jac. Epist.* (M. P. L., 93, 43), is of the opinion that the phrase, ἐν τῷ ὀνόματι κυρίου, should be taken with ἐλαίῳ not with ἀλείψαντες The majority of theologians and exegetes do not agree with him. They hold that it applies to the action, the proximate matter, rather than to the material or remote matter. Cf. Bord, *op. cit.*, pp. 45-46.

ascribed to the rite, i. e. to the work performed. But since this rite is simply an instrumental cause—as all sacramental rites are—the health or safety is more accurately attributed to the Lord—*"et alleviabit eum Dominus."* Finally the sequel of such an effect in a sin-burdened subject is mentioned—*"et si in peccatis sit, remittentur, ei."*

A close inspection of the text reveals much. "Oratio *fidei* salvabit infirmum." This prayer is not pronounced by the penitent but by the priests. They are commanded to do the praying—"orent super eum." It is the prayer of faith because a) objective faith teaches us the Divine institution and efficacy of the rite and because b) subjective faith moves the priest to perform this rite in the sincere belief that it is more efficacious than a simple deprecation.

"Salvabit"—is equivalent to *"servabit, liberabit a malis quae eum premunt."*[21] Yet what are these evils which the seriously sick usually suffer? In general they are physical pains and weakness, which produce sorrow of soul, affliction of mind, ineptitude to salutary impulses of grace, fear of death, dread of judgment, horror of the punishments of the other life, remorse of conscience, diffidence, impatience, temptations to despair, etc. Not everybody, it is true, is afflicted in the same degree. Yet the text uses the word "salvabit," connoting that Extreme Unction destroys, or at least impairs, that which physical evils cause in man. It directs its batteries first against spiritual evils, which are always evils *simpliciter* to men; but its effects overflow against physical evils when such an exuberance is expedient for the welfare of the soul.

The text next reveals the mode employed by the Lord in the "saving" of the sick man. "Et alleviabit eum Dominus"—He will "raise him up"—*ἐγερεῖ αὐτόν*—i. e., *sustentabit, eriget, animabit, confortabit.*[22] The infirm will receive powers that will make him superior to the evils that oppress him; he will be able to rise above the depressions of nature, the diffidence, the cowardice that possesses him. He will become capable of all salutary acts conformable to his status, so that he may be disposed for the perfect healing of the soul, and, if

21 Kern, *Tract. de Ext. Unct.*, p. 68.
22 Kern, *Tract. de Ext. Unct.*, p. 69.

expedient, also for the healing of the body. Such an alleviation is effected by actual graces. When, however, the illness is long, there is granted habitual aid, sanctifying grace conferring a right to such actual graces that the sick man needs.

Many Protestant theologians have endeavored to restrict the meaning of the words "saved" and "raised up" to bodily effects. Puller[23] defends this view with especial vehemence. Yet this would involve an arbitrary and violent construction of the text and does not supply a reasonable explanation of the universal and perpetual character of the apostle's prescription. "A few verses further on," says Toner,[24] "the predominating spiritual and eschatological connotation of 'saving' in St. James' mind emerges clearly in the expression, 'shall save his soul from death.'" Neither can we reasonably suppose that the apostle endeavored to inculcate that every anointed Christian would be the recipient of bodily alleviation and cure; yet he orders the unction for all, insinuating that the "saving" and "raising up" are at least the normal, if not the infallible, effects of the prayer-unction. "Are we to suppose, therefore," asks Toner[25] "that St. James thus solemnly recommends universal recourse to a rite which, after all, will be efficacious for the purpose intended only by way of a comparatively rare exception?" As a consequence it is not hard to see that these elaborate and even clever attempts to explain away the meaning of the Jacobean text are doomed to failure.

"Et si in peccatis sit"—κἂν ἁμαρτίας ᾖ πεποιηκώς

In an effort to defend their opinion that the principal effect of Extreme Unction is the remission of venial sin, many Catholic theologians say that this last effect is not conditionally promised. For example, Estius writes: "Scire enim oportet conjunctionem illam *'si'* saepe sic usurpari, ut non tam conditionem incertae ac dubiae rei significet, quam concessionem rei certae et indubitatae, quemadmodum Mal. I dicitur: *'Si* pater

[23] Puller, *The Anointing of the Sick in Scripture and Tradition,* (London, 1904), p. 289 sqq.

[24] Catholic Encyc., art. *"Extreme Unction."* Toner has reference to verse 20: "Scire debet quoniam qui converti fecerit peccatorem ab errore viae suae, salvabit animam ejus a morte et cooperiet multitudinem peccatorum."

[25] L. c.

ego sum, ubi est honor meus? et *si* Dominus ego sum, ubi est timor meus?' i. e., cum constet me Patrem esse et Dominum vestrum, cur non ut Patrem honoratis et ut Dominum timetis? Sic Paulus ait II Thes. I: '*Si* tamen justus est apud Deum retribuere;' etc. Et ipse Jacobus alibi in hac epistola (c. 1): '*Si* quis vestrum indiget sapientia;' etc.? Quis enim vestrum non indiget sapientia?''[26]

Though supported by many, this interpretation is false. An examination of the Greek texts cited by Estius reveals the employment of the particle εἰ with the indicative—a grammatical form always signifying a thing certain. But James V, 15 contains the particle κἂν It is a true conditional promise, unqualified by any limitation to venial sins. Indeed mortal sins are first thought of in such a connection, for a man with only venial sins is hardly spoken of as a "man in sin."

A point not to be overlooked is that the Apostle does not attribute this remission of sins either to the prayer of faith or to the Lord. As a result, it is a licit conclusion that this remission follows from the alleviation, that it is a secondary effect. This is a further warrant for the inference that alleviation includes the infusion of sanctifying grace.

This elaborate analysis of the Jacobean text establishes beyond doubt the sacramentality of Extreme Unction. We have a sensible sign, efficacious of grace, permanently established by Christ. We have shown that the sacred unction with prayer signifies an internal supernatural unction, alleviation and exhilaration—and effects this, even thru the infusion of first grace when necessary. The permanency of institution by Christ is seen by its place among the priestly functions, by its annexation to the priestly character, whose existence is guaranteed by its author, Christ.[27]

This analysis is not without a canonical bearing. It elucidates paragraph 1 of Canon 938; it enlightens us as the true meaning of various terms in 940 and 943; it explains the insistence of the legislator in Canon 941 in regard to conferring

---

26 *Comm. in quart. Lib. Sent.*, dist. xxiii, s. 4, p. 287E.

27 Cf. S. C. S. Off., "*Lamentabili*," July 3, 1907, *Errores Modernistarum*, n. 48—A. S. S., XL, 476.

the sacrament at least conditionally although it is not *de necessitate medii.*

It would hardly be wise to pass over without a word the reference in the Council of Trent to the Gospel of St. Mark. The words of the decree 'apud Marcum quidem insinuatum'' refer to the thirteenth verse of the sixth chapter of his gospel: ''Et exeuntes praedicabant ut poenitentiam agerent: et daemonia multa ejiciebant et ungebant oleo multos aegros et sanabant.'' Many theologians, both before and after the Council of Trent have held that the institution of Extreme Unction is found in these words. Among these are found such names as Victor of Antioch,[28] Theophylactus,[29] Amulo, bishop of London (841),[30] Huymo, bishop of Halberstadt,[31] Euthymus,[32] Maldonatus,[33] De Sainte-Beuve,[34] Berti[35] and Schell.[36] The main line of argument of these theologians is substantially this: it cannot be admitted that the Lord wished the Apostles to cure all sick persons indiscriminately. Such a charisma came to the Apostles after the coming of the Paraclete—and consequently its exercise was a rare event. It must be concluded then that, as the end of the Messiah's mission, so the purpose of the unction of the sick was primarily spiritual, viz., the conversion to true penance. To the anointed sick a pledge was given of participation in the goods and graces which the Messiah offered to mankind—a pledge confirmed by the corporal cure of many. Accordingly the words of the Evangelist refer primarily to a spiritual healing; whence the deduction that the unction of the sick was the sacramentum ''exeuntium.''

This argumentation is by no means satisfying. First of all, the purpose of the Apostles' mission is clearly announced

---

28 *Comment. ad Marc. VI, 13*—Cramer, *Catena Graec. Patrum,* I, p. 324.
29 *Enarratio in Evangelium Marci, c. VI, vv. 12, 13*—M. P. G., 123, 550C.
30 *Epistola ad Theobaldum, ep. Lingoniensis*—M. P. L., 116, 82D.
31 *Homilia CV in Verba Evangelii, Feria V Pentecostes*—M. P. L., 118, 573C.
32 *Comm. in Marc. c. VI, vv. 12, 13*—M. P. G., 129, 807B.
33 *Comment. in Marc. VI, v. 13,* vol. I, p. 517.
34 *Tract. de Sacr. Unct. Infirm.,* disp. II, a. 1—Migne, *Cursus Theol. Comp.,* xxiv, 19 sqq.
35 *De Theol. Discip.,* Tom VIII, l. 35, ''*De Ext. Unct.*'' c. 2.
36 *Katholische Dogmatik,* 3 Bd. II Teil, p. 616 s.

in Matt. X, 1 [37] and Luke IX, 1-2.[38] There it is seen that the Lord gave them the power to cure only as a criterion of the truth they were teaching. There is no indication of the remission of sins or of any sacramental rite. The Gospel writers, when speaking of the mission of the Apostles, do not tell what rule the Lord prescribed for the use of the power in their hands. How the command was executed can be seen by Luke IX, 6: "Egressi autem circuibant per castella, evangelizantes et curantes ubique." St. Mark adds that many demons were exorcised and many sick healed by unction.[39] The words of St. Luke (θεραπεύοντες πανταχοῦ) and of St. Mark (ἤλειφον . . . καὶ ἐθεράπευον) must be understood of corporal cures. It then becomes manifest that no conclusive exegesis of the sacramentality of Extreme Unction can be found in the Marcian text. The Council of Trent cautiously inserted that the sacrament was "insinuated" therein, i. e., prefigured or hinted at, but it took care not to advance it as a Spiritual text supporting the credibility of the doctrine.

Other powerful reasons can be adduced against the probability of the institution of this sacrament in the account of St. Mark: 1) The effect of the Apostolic Unction was complete corporal sanation primarily, and probably in a miraculous manner; that of Extreme Unction is complete spiritual cure primarily, and possible corporal cure secondarily: 2) The subject of Extreme Unction is a baptized sick person; there is no mention made of the necessity of Baptism in the subject when the Apostles exercised their gifts of healing: 3) The minister of Extreme Unction is a priest; the Apostles, at the time they received their power, were not yet priests: 4) Extreme Unction is the complement of Penance; yet Penance had not yet been instituted.[40] These additional reasons serve to establish

---

37 "Et convocatis duodecim discipulis suis dedit illis potestatem spirituum immundorum ut eicerent eos et curarent omnem languorem et omnem infirmitatem."

38 "Convocatis autem duodecim apostolis, dedit illis virtutem et potestatem super omnia daemonia, et ut languores curarent. Et misit illos praedicare regnum Dei et sanare infirmos."

39 VI, 13.

40 Cf. Alb. a Bulsano, *Inst. Theol. Dog.*, vol. III, p. 197; Kern, *Tract. de Ext. Unct.*, p. 78-9; *Bellarmine, De Ext. Unct.*, lib. unicus, c. 1-2; Suarez, disp. 39, sect. 1, n. 4, Benedict XIV, *De Syn. Dioc.*, l. 8, c. l. n. 2.

more firmly the utter untenability of the assertion that the Gospel of St. Mark demonstrates the sacramentality of Extreme Unction.

B) *Proof from Tradition.*

The argument from Tradition, though of paramount importance, cannot here be entered into with the same detailed analysis as that of the Scriptural proof. A worthy presentation of it would assume huge proportions and would require the use of too much space. Besides, much of it will be found scattered thruout the commentaries on the several canons.

It is sufficient to remark that there is a comparative paucity of extant testimonies from the early centuries—and that as a result Catholics have recourse to a general argument from prescription. The Eastern Church, although separated since 869, has never ceased to regard the Jacobean rite as a sacrament. Moreover, the Monophysites and the Nestorians, who broke away from Rome in the fifth century, retained in their rituals the unction of the sick. This is positive evidence that these churches have been in possession of a common and undivided tradition as far back at least as the beginning of the fourth century. On the other hand, no evidence is forthcoming from that or any earlier time that would tend to enervate the legitimate presumption that the tradition is apostolic.[41]

The reason of the scarcity of testimonies is hard to find. Binterim[42] ascribes it to the fact that it came under the "*disciplina arcani.*" He has evidently forgotten that this very regulation did not prevent the ecclesiastics of those ages from making frequent references to other sacraments which fell under the scope of the same discipline. It is refreshing, too, to realize that Launoi is rash in his contention that recourse to this sacrament was much rarer in earlier centuries.[43]

---

41 Cf. Liber Sacramentorum Gregorii Magni—"*Oratio ad infirmum ungendum*"—M. P. L., 78, 233C; The Euchologion of Serapio; Wobbermin, "*Altchristliche Stücke aus de Kirche Agyptens*" in Zietschrift fur Kirchengeschichte, t. xx, p. 291 sqq., 451 sqq. Cf. words of Jeremias, schismatic Greek patriarch—apud Schelstrate, Acta Orient. Eccl., I, 202; Denziger, *Rit Orient.*, II, 483.

42 Die Vorzuglichsten Denkwürdigkeiten der Christkathol. Kirche, vol. VI, pt. III, p. 241. This view is also held by Billot, "*De Ecclesiae Sacramentis,*" (*De Extrema Unctione*), thesis xxiv, parag. 2, p. 230.

43 *Op. Omnia,* t. 1, p. 455 sqq., also p. 561.

There are better explanations available. In the first place, several early commentaries on St. James' Epistle (by Clement of Alexandria, Didymus, St. Augustine and Cyril of Alexandria) have been almost totally lost, leaving as the earliest accurately preserved treatment that of St. Bede's (735). Furthermore it is to be remembered that Extreme Unction is the supplementary sacrament of Penance, and that in the early days it was administered before Viaticum. The Fathers had no systematic sacramental theology. They treated of various dogmas as the interests of public instruction required. When they spoke of Penance, they had reference usually to public confessions, and not to private confessions made in danger of death. About the administration of Penance privately the Fathers rarely spoke. Since Extreme Unction followed such secret confessions, it can be understood that the silence of the Fathers on the administration of Penance privately goes far in explaining their silence on Extreme Unction.

In conclusion it may be remarked that Catholics must be on their guard against endeavoring to prove too much from patristic writings. Protestant controversialists insist that the Fathers speak in terms of Trent; they demand that we prove that Extreme Unction was recognized as a sacrament in the strict sense long before the definition of sacrament in the strict sense was drawn up. We are not bound to accede to their unreasonable exactions. We have done enough when we have shown that St. James permanently prescribed this anointing in terms that imply its sacramental efficacy; that the Church was content for many centuries with the plain words of the Epistle—and simply went on fulfilling the Apostolic prescription: and that, finally, when need of an exact definition did arise, the Church defined infallibly and forever "the true meaning and the proper efficacy of the Jacobean prayer-unction."[44]

III. The End

The clear conception of the end of a thing is conducive to a more perfect knowledge of its ultimate nature, its efficacy and its attributes. As a consequence theologians, after demon-

[44] J. P. Toner—Cath. Encycl., art. "Extreme Unction."

strating the sacramentality of Extreme Unction, address themselves to the question of its end and purpose. They all agree that this divine aid enriches the soul with all helps necessary to put it in the state of grace. Since the Council of Trent, however, theologians have been busied with the necessity of insisting on the existence of Purgatory, which the Reformers denied. Jansenistic rigorism tainted the works of others; with the result that they have seemingly refused or neglected to attribute to this sacrament all of its rightful powers.

But later theologians, especially those of the present day, like Kern,[1] have recalled that the benign Redeemer wishes not only that His faithful should escape the fires of hell, but also that they should escape purgatory's painful punishment by an immediate entrance into glory. This is accomplished only by a complete sanation of the soul, by freeing it from all *reatus* of sin or of punishment, and by reenforcing it against all spiritual weakness from past sins or present bodily afflictions. Mortal man, weakened by disease and pain, would hardly be capable of doing this alone. He needs some aid, an external help to fill the place of his dwindling powers. This help, we know, is found in the sacrament of Extreme Unction. The proximate end of Extreme Unction—the end for which all effects concur—is then the perfect sanation of the soul. This end is always intended by the Lord, and therefore is always obtained if the sacred rite is impeded by no obstacle.

Among the particular effects of this sacrament is the restoration of health, if it be expedient to the salvation of the soul. Not rarely is the perfect sanation of the soul more benefited by a corporal alleviation than by a prolonged continuance of pain even to death. In this case the sacrament exercises its "vis sanativa." Often, too, the disease is of such a nature that thru medical skill the patient will naturally recover. The means of salvation are certainly not destined to kill any one. Accordingly in such cases the ultimate end of the sacrament viewed *secundum se,* viz., immediate entrance into glory, is deferred—only to be more happily attained if the subject uses well the spiritual goods he has received.

---

1 *Tract. de Ext. Unct.,* pp. 81-85.

The end of Extreme Unction then can be said to be the complete sanation of the soul together with its immediate entrance into glory, unless the restitution of bodily health is more expedient. In defense of this, theologians mobilize a host of irrefragable arguments. They adduce reasons of congruity,—to show how becoming it was to the benignity and goodness of Christ to attach to the sacrament of the "exeuntium" the power and efficacy to wipe away all barriers to an immediate entrance into heaven.[2] They array a series of quotations from patristic writings[3] and ancient liturgies[4] to support their claim. They draw up a battle-line of scintillating Scholastics, geniuses without peer in the realms of theological intellectuality. Blessed Albertus Magnus,[5] the Seraphic Bonaventure,[6] Angelic Thomas,[7] the subtle Scotus,[8] Peter of Tarantasia (afterwards Innocent V),[9] the dogged Durandus[10] are the leaders of this army. Besides these shining lights, there are adduced the reserves, such as Richard Middleton,[11] Aureolus—the prince of Scotists,[12] Peter de Palude—an esteemed Thomist,[13] Gersonius,[14] Dionysius of Carthage,[15] and Capreolus—prince of Thomists.[16]

The realms of the East have been invaded for testimony to

---

2 Kern, *Tract. de Ext. Unct.*, p. 82.

3 E.g., S. Chrysostom., *De Sacerdotio*, lib. III, n. 6—M. P. G., 48, 644; S. Hilarius, *Tract. in Ps. CXXI*, n. 12—M. P. G., 9, 665D, 666A; Procopius, *Comm. in Levit., c. II, v. 1*—M. P. G., 87, 702; Hieronymus, *In cap. XLV Ezechielis*, v. 24—M. P. L., 25, 456C; S. Greg. Nyssa, *In Cant. Cantic. Hom. III*—M. P. G., 44, 826; S. Augustinus, *Quaest. Evang.*,—M. P. L., 35, 1340.

4 Martene, *De Antiq. Ecc. Rit.*, l. 1, c. 7, a. 4—Ordines II, IX, XII; cf. also *Missa pro Infirmis* (*Absolutio cum Impositione Manuum*)—Martene, l. c., Ordo XII.

5 *Comm. in lib. quartum Sent.*, ad dist. xxiii, dis. I, a. 2.

6 *Breviloq.*, pars. VI, c. 11.

7 *Suppl.*, q. 29, a. 1; III, q. 65, a. 1: *Summa Philos.*, l. IV, c. 73.

8 *Reportata Parisiana, Comm. in lib. quartum Sent.*, ad dist. xxiii qu. unic.

9 *Comm. in lib. quartum Sent.*, q. II, a. 2.

10 *Comm. in lib. quartum Sent.*, ad dist. xxiii, dis. II, q. 2, n. II.

11 *Comm. in lib. quartum Sent.*, ad dist. xxiii, a. 1, q. 3.

12 *Comm. in lib. quartum Sent.*, ad dist. xxiii, a. 2.

13 *Comm. in lib. quartum Sent.*, ad dist. xxiii, q. 4.

14 *Regulae Morales*, r. 155.

15 *Summa fidei orthodoxae*, l. IV, a. 146 (*Opera Omnia*, vol. XVIII, p. 197A).

16 *Comm. in IV lib. Sent.*, q. 1, a. 3, ad. 5.

this claim. Oriental church documents and theologians[17] are investigated with searching scrutiny and reveal with a marvelous unanimity the reasonableness and genuineness of the contention of present day theologians in regard to the end of Extreme Unction. The Council of Trent presents another bulwark of defense. For "it hath also seemed good to the holy Synod to subjoin to the preceding doctrine on Penance the following on the sacrament of Extreme Unction, which by the Fathers was regarded as being the completion, not only of Penance, but also of the whole Christian life, which ought to be a perpetual penance."[18] Now if Extreme Unction is the complement of Penance, it accomplishes what Penance leaves undone, it perfects what Penance leaves incomplete in the full remission of sins. It must remove all our disabilities and restore to our anemic souls the ruddy glow of grace that shone in them immediately after Baptism. In Penance the stain of sin is washed from us and we are garbed in the robe of sanctifying grace. But the justice of God exacts that some temporal punishment be undergone in satisfaction for the affront to His Majesty. Extreme Unction however is a revelation of the ineffable mercy of Him Who willeth not the death of a sinner. In his sacrament God's justice is swallowed up in His mercy. The mercy of Him Who died for us cannot brook the delay which His justice demands, and accordingly He has invented this wonderful way of circumventing—as it were—His very Self.

With this alignment of evidence and authority, the proposition seems proven. A thorough realization of this will reveal the importance of the sacrament of Extreme Unction. It should be a spur to zeal for priests and people to spend every effort to take advantage of this veritable sesame to the treasures of God.

---

17 Symeon Thessalonicenses, *De Sacro Euchelaei Ritu*—M. P. G. 155, 527C & 530D; M. Calcas, Περὶ πίστεως καὶ περῖ τῶν ἀρχῶν τῆς καθολικῆς πίστεως, c. 6,—M. P. G., 152, 607A; *Ordo Lampadis Syrorum Jacobitarum*—Denziger, *Ritus Orient.*, t. II, p. 509; ibid., p. 515; *Antiquus Ritus apud Armenos*—ibid, p. 522; *Ordo Lampadis Alexandrinus*, ibid., p. 500; *Officium S. Olei*,—Goar, *Euchologium*, p. 337 sqq.

18 Sess. XIV, *De Ext. Unct.*, proem.—Translation by Waterworth, *Canons and Decrees of the Counc. Trent*, p. 104.

IV. The Essence

1. *The Matter of Extreme Unction.*

The remote matter of Extreme Unction is oil of olives. This the Council of Trent definitely defined: "Intellexit enim Ecclesia materiam esse oleum ab episcopo benedictum."[1] There has been no doubt that the oil meant by St. James is the oil of olives.[2] Every heretic who has insisted on belief in this sacrament at all has insisted on olive oil as the remote matter.

The congruity of oil as the matter of this sacrament is very striking, for the effects produced by oil on the physical body bear a singular analogy to those produced by Extreme Unction on the soul. St. Gregory of Nyssa expresses beautifully the effect of oil: [Oleum est] "lucis materia, recreat lassitudinem, relaxat laborem, caput exhilarat et ad certamina opem fert iis qui legitime certant."[3] Other very expressive testimonies are those of Gregory the Great[4] and Theophylactus.[5] St. Thomas adduces further reasons for the aptitude of oil: "The spiritual healing, which is given at the end of life, ought to be complete, since there is no other to follow; it ought also to be gentle, lest hope, of which the dying stand in utmost need, be shattered rather than fostered. Now oil has a softening effect, it penetrates to the very heart of a thing, and spreads over it. Hence in both the foregoing respects, it is suitable matter for this sacrament. And since oil is, above all, the name of the liquid extract of olives, for other liquids are only called oil from their likeness to it, it follows that olive oil is the matter which should be employed in this sacrament."[6]

In the Latin Church it has ever been the custom to employ pure, unadulterated olive oil. In some Eastern rites the practice of adding a little water as a symbol of Baptism, or a little

---

1 Sess. XIV, *De Extr. Unct.*, cap. 1.

2 St. Cyril of Alexandria, *Comm. in Marc., VI, 13* (apud *Catena Graecorum Patrum*, edited by Cramer, vol. 1, 324).

3 *Hom. IX in Cant. Cant.*, M. P. G., 44, 963A.

4 *Expositionum in lib. I Regum, l. 4, c. 5*—M. P. L., 79, 278B.

5 *Enarratio in Ev. S. Marci, c. VI, 12-13*—M. P. G., 123, 550B-C.

6 *The "Summa Theologica"* (transl. by Fathers of Eng. Domin. Prov.), *Suppl.*, q. 29, a. 4.

wine in memory of the Good Samaritan, or even of the dust of the sepulchre of some saint, has long been in vogue.[7]

There is no doubt that some blessing of the oil is befitting, for this sacrament is administered to baptized people who are members of Christ's mystical body and are holy with at least an ontological sanctity. Neither is there any doubt that a blessing of the oil is required by precept, for all rituals demand this. Some theologians, however, have denied that there is any need of blessing for the valid confection of the sacrament. Among these the chief names are Victoria,[8] Juenin,[9] De Sainte-Beuve,[10] Berti[11] and Natalis Alexander.[12]

St. Thomas advances a triple argument against these theologians. 1st, all sacramental efficacy descends from Christ; consequently those sacraments which He Himself made use of, have their efficacy from His very use. E. g., by corporal touch He gave the efficacy of spiritual regeneration to water, so that the blessing of baptismal water is not essential. However, Christ did not use this sacrament of Extreme Unction, nor any corporal unction.[13] 2nd, a blessing of the matter is required from the plenitude of the grace received, which causes not only the forgiveness of the sins themselves, but also of their effects, and at times of the bodily infirmity. 3rd, the corporal effects are not caused from the natural properties of the oil; hence it is eminently fitting that such efficacy be given to it thru a blessing.[14]

These reasons seem to be reasons of congruity—and do not convince beyond the shadow of doubt. A few facts from tradition will suffice to prove our point. The question whether the

---

7 Cf. Symeon of Thessalonica, *De Sacro Euchelaei Ritu*, cap. CCLXXXVIII—M. P. G., 155, 523C; Arhangelskij, "Izsledovanije ob istoriceskom razvitii cinosoversenija Jeleosvjascenija ot ustanovlenija sego tainstva do izdanija nynesnjago jego Posledovanija, s podrobnym izjasnenijem sego poslednjago," p. 113, sqq.

8 *Summa Sacramentorum*, "*De Ext. Unct.*," n. 217.

9 *Comm. Hist. et Dog. de Sac.*, diss. VII, q. 3, c. 1, concl. 3.

10 *De Ext. Unct.*, disp. III, a. 1, apud Migne, *Curs. Theol. Comp.*, XXIV, 87.

11 *De Theol. Discipl.*, Tom. VIII, lib. 35, c. 4, prop. 4.

12 *Th. D. et M.*, lib. II, "*De Ext. Unct.*," c. 1, a. 2.

13 Soto explains away the unctions of Christ by Magdalen (Luc. VII) and Nicodemus (Joan. XXIX) by saying "Nullam habebant sacramenti rationem" (*Comm. in lib. quart. Sent.*, dist. 23, q. 1, a. 3).

14 *Suppl.*, q. 29, a. 5.

oil needs any blessing at all is the only question considered here. The exact nature and quality of the required blessing is left to the consideration of Canon 945—a procedure which seems more proper.

The testimony of tradition in favor of the necessity of some preconsecration of the oil is overwhelming. Everywhere it is found that in the administration of this sacrament blessed oil has been employed. The writings of Cassiodorus,[15] Innocent I,[16] Dynamius Patritius,[17] Callinicius,[18] Isaac Antiochenus[19] and many others are clear and decisive, and witness conclusively to the practices of apostolic times. Furthermore, the Fathers, while speaking often of the blessing of Baptismal water, never failed to insist that such blessing was by no means essential for the valid use of the water. They make no such statements in regard to the dispensability of blessing the oil.

The Scholastics taught unanimously the need of some blessing.[20] Their disciples faithfully followed the teaching until the time of the Council of Trent. The words of the Council, "oleum . . . . benedictum" seem to be final. This seems to be corroborated by the determination of the matter of Baptism by the Council (Sess. VII, *de Baptismo,* can. 10), and by its unwillingness to decide the vehement disputes of theologians in regard to the matter of Confirmation and Holy Orders.

The proximate matter of Extreme Unction is the anointing with blessed oil. The treatment of this will come naturally under Canon 947, and is accordingly passed over here.

2. *The Form of Extreme Unction.*

The greatest variety of forms have been used in the administration of Extreme Unction. Some are deprecative, some opta-

---

15 *Complexiones in Epp. Apostolorum*—ep. S. Jac. ad dispersos, n. 11—M. P. L., 70, 1380C.

16 *Epistolae et Decreta*—ep. xxv, c. 8—M. P. L., 20, 559-60; C. I. C. Fontes, n. 19.

17 *Vita S. Marii,* c. I, n. 3—M. P. L., 80, 27C-D.

18 *Vita S. Hypatii—Acta Sanctorum,* 17 Jun., vol. IV, p. 251.

19 Bickell, *S. Isaaci Antiocheni Opera Omnia,* p. 1, p. 187 sqq.

20 E. g., Petrus Lombardus, *Libri IV Sent.,* lib. quart., dist. 23, "*De Sac. E. U.,*" n. 1—M. P. L., 192, 899; Albertus Magnus, *Comm. in Lib. quart. Sent.,* dist. 23, a, 2 ad q. 1; S. Thomas, *Suppl.* q. 29, a. 5; S. Bonaventure, *Comm. in Lib. quart. Sent.,* dist. 23, a. 1, q. 3 ad 4; Durandus, *Comm. in Lib. quart. Sent.,* dist. 23, qu. 2, ad 2.

tive, others indicative, still others imperative, and some mixed.[21] Controversies have waged, and still wage, as to the precise nature of the form required for the valid confection of the sacrament. Among the various forms theologians have found it extremely difficult to single out a common element which they say is divinely revealed and consequently essential. It is not a question whether the present-day Oriental or Occidental forms are valid. Such is admitted by all. The problem is whether the wording of the formula must contain a real prayer —the "*oratio fidei*" of St. James' text.

All the scholastics asserted that some kind of form was positively essential for the validity of the sacrament. Most of them demanded a formula of deprecation. St. Thomas[22] and Launoi,[23] though tenaciously holding the theory that only a deprecative form was admissible, were chary of condemning the practice of the ancient rites; and, to explain away surmounting difficulties, tried to transform by the alchemy of the minister's intention a form held by themselves to be *per se* invalid into one which was eminently permissible. Not a few other theologians, especially those who prefer positive arguments, have striven to make theology and history agree. They realize that the indicative form was widely in use in the West and to some extent in the East, and they see the absurdity of denying that the sacrament was validly confected for centuries in those churches. As a result they insist on the absolute validity of the indicative form.[24]

Kern[25] and Pohle-Preuss[26] have suggested a compromise, by maintaining on the one hand that the deprecatory form is required by the Jacobean text, and on the other hand that the indicative forms which have been employed were virtually deprecatory.[27] They offer an analogy from Scripture:[28] "Lord, he whom Thou lovest is sick"—a very apt illustration, for it

---

21 Cf. *Infra*, chap. II, p. 73 sqq.
22 *Suppl.*, qu. 29, a. 8.
23 *Op. Omnia*, t. I, p. 543.
24 E. g., Benedict XIV, *De Syn. Dioc.*, l. VIII, c. 2, n. 2-3.
25 *Tract. de Ext. Unct.*, pp. 152-166.
26 *The Sacraments*—vol. IV, p. 23.
27 De Sainte-Beuve, *De Ext. Unct.*, disp. 4, a. 2—apud Migne, *Curs. Theol. Compl.*, XXIV, col. 94-7; Martene, *De Antiq. Rit. Eccl.*, l. 1, c. 7, a. 3, paragr. 9.
28 John XI, 3.

breathes a prayer as truly as if couched in unmistakable terms of impetration. Toner, writing in the Catholic Encyclopedia,[29] admits the reasonable construability of some indicative forms in the way pointed out by Kern and Pohle-Preuss, but he emphatically denies it in regard to other forms. He declares that the prayer used in the blessing of the oil will suffice, if prayer be needed at all for the form of the sacrament.

When the form is deprecative, the question arises whether a voluntary distraction of the priest would nullify the sacrament. Augustine Reding, the Prince-Abbot of Einsiedeln, did some very subtle reasoning to prove that the essence of vocal prayer would not be destroyed by the presence of voluntary distractions.[30] Consequently the prayer would be real in the form and the Sacrament validly confected by ministers who deliberately induced distractions. Gonet[31] and Billuart[32] proffer a better explanation. The validity of the sacrament does not depend on the prayer of the priest as a private person. The efficacy of the rite flows from the merits of Christ, in Whose person this prayer is made. Consequently, when the priest says the words of the form, no matter how distracted he is, provided (we are assuming) that he has the intention "faciendi quod facit Ecclesia," the sacrament will have its effect. It is the Church which prays thru its minister.

V. The Effects

The effects of Extreme Unction are as varied as they are potent. As has been said, its end is the perfect healing of the soul—and it surely has the inherent power to attain its end in those who present no obstacle. There is a certain terseness about the description of effects in the decree of Eugene IV to the Armenians,[1] viz., "the healing of the mind, and so far as it is expedient, of the body also." The Council of Trent explains the effects somewhat more at length:[2] "This effect is

29 art. "*Extreme Unction.*"
30 *Theol. Scholast.*, tom. 5, q. 11, a. 2.
31 *Clyp. Theol. Thomist.*, tom. 6, "*De Ext. Unct.*," disp. proem., a. 2, paragr. 4, page 704.
32 *Summa S. Thom.*, "*Tr. de Ext. Unct.*," disp. unic., a. III.

1 Const. "*Exultate Deo*" (in Conc. Florentin.) 22 Nov. 1439, paragr. 14; C. I. C. Fontes, n. 52; Denziger-Bannwart, *Enchiridion*, n. 700.
2 Sess. XIV, *De Ext. Unct.*, cap. 2.

the grace of the Holy Ghost, Whose unction blots out sins, if any remain to be expiated, and the consequences (*reliquias*) of sin, and alleviates and strengthens the soul of the sick person, by exciting in him a great confidence in the divine mercy, sustained by which he bears more lightly the troubles and sufferings of disease, and more easily resists the temptations of the demon lying in wait for his heel; and sometimes, when it is expedient for the soul's salvation, recovers bodily health." All these effects are contained within the scope of "*salvabit,*" "*alleviabit,*" and "*remittentur peccata*" of the Jacobean text.

1. *The Remission of Sins.*

"Si quis dixerit, sacram infirmorum Unctionem non conferre gratiam, nec remittere peccata, nec alleviare infirmos: sed jam cessasse, quasi olim tantum fuerit gratia curationum, A. S."[3]

This effect is plainly enunciated by St. James—"et si in peccatis sit, remittentur ei." It is clearly supported by tradition, and has been taught by all theologians. All formulae of consecration explicitly or equivalently ask for the sanctification of the oil in order that it may become a means of salvation.[4] In the Western Church today the very form of the sacrament proclaims this one effect—"Indulgeat tibi Dominus . . . quidquid deliquisti."

Consequently it is a doctrine of Catholic teaching that sins are remitted by Extreme Unction. There are no qualifications made by the sacred text or by Catholic tradition as to what kind of sins is forgiven. As a result it is quite certain that mortal sins come within the scope of the remissory power of the sacrament. This follows logically from the *raison d'etre* of the Sacrament, which was instituted by a benign Savior to furnish the Christian in danger of death with every needful help. It is not unusual that a sick man cannot confess, yet he places no obstacle to the infusion of grace into his soul thru a sacrament. To such a one Extreme Unction becomes the pillar of salvation.[5]

---

3 Ibid, can. 2.

4 Cf. Euchologion of Serapio, pp. 53 & 118; Sacramentarium Gelasianum, "*Missa Chrismalis in Feria V Maj. Hebdom.,*" apud M. P. L., 74, 1100.

5 Cf. Suarez, disp. XLI, s. 1, n. 16.

It is the more common opinion that one unable to receive Penance should, if physically possible, prepare himself for Extreme Unction by a perfect act of contrition. It is argued that this Sacrament is the complement of Penance, which puts one in the state of grace; and consequently every effort must be spent to attain as nearly as possible the state of soul ordinarily resulting from the reception of Penance. Yet though remission of sins is not the primary purpose of Extreme Unction—and this is evident from the conditional way that St. James speaks about it—nevertheless this effect is attributed *per se* and directly to the Unction. This means nothing less than that Extreme Unction is from direct institution, although secondarily, a sacrament of the dead, capable not only of increasing but also of conferring sacramental sanctifying grace. This is not an entrenchment on the sacrament of Penance, as Pohle-Preuss[6] would have it. The obligation of submitting all grievous sins to the power of the keys still holds, if the patient recovers sufficiently to make his confession.

Consequently, if the subject is for any reason at all excused from confession or from eliciting an act of contrition, Extreme Unction will bestow first grace, provided he is actually or at least habitually attrite. Habitual attrition is nothing more than an act of sorrow for sins committed, elicited after their commission and not revoked. Billot[7] is somewhat less exacting in his requirements of the sick man. He contends that there is no obligation to elicit an act of perfect contrition, but that attrition *cum voto Poenitentiae* suffices. He bases his contention on the fact that Extreme Unction *per se* and *ex proprio suo fine* acts in the same fashion as the other two sacraments of the dead. Schell[8] goes even further, saying that a sinner no longer capable of an act of contrition or attrition, can validly receive Extreme Unction, provided he places no obstacle to grace by final impenitence. It is enough to have a general purpose and intention—a purpose that can be had even while sinning—of afterwards formally repenting and dying in the friendship of God. These two opinions are singular, and are not

6 *The Sacraments,* vol. IV, p. 32.

7 *De Eccl. Sacramentis, "De Ext. Unct.,"* thesis XXVI, t. II, p. 240, nota.

8 *Katholische Dogmatik,* III, p. 629 sqq.

supported by the vast majority of theological minds. It seems only too reasonable that the subject be required to take at least ordinary means to dispose himself by an act of perfect contrition for a sacrament primarily of the living. It is to be noted, however, that the subject is not bound to confess before receiving Extreme Unction. There is no divine or ecclesiastical precept exacting this. It is only required that one should place himself in the state of grace.[9]

It is none the less true that if a man is unable or is too ignorant to elicit an act of perfect contrition or mistakes attrition for perfect contrition, he is justified thru Extreme Unction, provided he is at least habitually attrite. Yet there is no remission without attrition, despite Schell's opinion, for the Council of Trent[10] explicitly demands sorrow for all forgiveness of sin.

If Extreme Unction remits mortal sins, a fortiori it remits venial sins. *Qui potest plus, potest etiam et minus in eadem specie.* There has been no doubt of its efficacy in this regard in the minds of theologians, but there has been much discussion regarding the dispositions of the subject necessary for such remission.

Clericatus[11] claims that venial sins are remitted *ex opere operato* without any needful cooperation on the part of the sick person. According to him, it is quite sufficient to have no formal complacency in them. Vasquez[12] requires in the subject formal or virtual attrition. Suarez[13] is content with requiring non-complacency in the sin and a desire of receiving this sacrament and its effects. Gonet,[14] St. Bonaventure,[15] and not a few Thomists and Scotists teach a mediate remission of sins thru the excitation of acts of devotion, love, etc. From the maze

---

9 Cf. *Infra*, chap. VII, p. 232 sqq.

10 Sess. XIV, *De Poenitent.*, can. 4.

11 *Decisiones Sacramentales*, De Extr. Unct., decis. 82, n. 5: "Sicut Baptismus ex opere operato et ex sui institutione delet culpam originalem in pueris absque ulla dispositione subjecti tunc existentis in infantili aetate, ita servata proportione [facit] . . . hoc Sacramentum Extremae Unctionis."

12 *Comm. in III p. D. Thom.*, q. 87, a. 3, dub. 3, n. 8.

13 Disp. XLI, s. 1, n. 21.

14 *Clypeus Theol. Thomisticae*, tom. VI, tr. 5, disp. 4, n. 59.

15 *Comm. in Lib. Quartum Sent.*, dist. 23, a. 1, q. 1, concl. 3.

of conflicting claims, Kern[16] culls three very reasonable conclusions, which seem to rest on firm reasons:

1. The venial sins of a man who also is in mortal sin are remitted immediately *vi sacramenti,* if the subject have at least habitual attrition;

2. The venial sins of a just man are immediately remitted, if he elicited for them a certain attrition which *per se* may not measure up to that required for obtaining their pardon without a sacrament;

3. If Extreme Unction does not remove venial sins immediately *ob defectum dispositionis,* nevertheless it forgives them indirectly by producing the necessary dispositions.

2. *The Remission of Temporal Punishment.*

An investigation into the end of Extreme Unction leaves no doubt that Extreme Unction remits temporal punishment. It was instituted for the perfect healing of the soul with a view to its immediate entrance into glory, unless indeed the all-knowing Master of Life and Death should deem the restoration of bodily health more expedient. Consequently it must accomplish the removal of all disabilities, it must render us fit to enter our heavenly home without delay. Were this not so, it would be absurd to say that the sacrament is "*consummativum spiritualis curationis.*"[17] Nor could it be said with any more truth that this sacrament is the complement of Penance. Since Penance usually leaves unforgiven some of the *reatus poenae,* and since Extreme Unction completes and rounds out the purging of Penance, it is beyond the pale of doubt that the guilt left unforgiven by Penance must be obliterated by Unction. Every obstacle to eternal glory not removed by Penance must be destroyed by the potent graces of Extreme Unction in the march of the soul towards heaven.

Many theologians are loath to admit this effect at all. They fear that it will do away with the *raison d'etre* of Purgatory and of suffrages for the dead. But there is not a single solid argument that can be advanced against this view, if the exigencies of polemical controversies are subordinated to the Catholic

---

16 *Tract. de Ext. Unct.,* pp. 186-7.

17 St. Thomas, *Summa Contra Gent.,* lib. 4, c. 73, *de Ext. Unct.*

theory. The truth of the matter is that it was only under the enervating influence of the Protestant Reformation that the doctrine began to wane. It was clearly propounded in earlier rituals and in the writings of the pre-Tridentine theologians up to Richard Tapper.[18] The insistence of post-Reformation Catholic theologians on the existence of Purgatory had the drastic effect of an attenuation of the traditional teaching on this point. The Jansenistic spirit that infected many with rigoristic views of divine justice and vengeance aided to stifle for a time this older and truer view. Theologians forgot that Extreme Unction remitted temporal punishment and preserved the soul from Purgatory, and as a consequence many authors do not even mention the question. At last, however, the tradition is arising from the lamentable desuetude into which it had unfortunately fallen. Kern[19] in his remarkable treatise successfully vindicates to this sacrament its glorious prerogative. Schmitz,[20] who wrote twenty years earlier, had barely mentioned this effect, but today theologians are allying themselves in huge numbers with Fr. Kern.[21]

This doctrine must not be construed to mean that infallibly the remission of the entire temporal debt occurs when Extreme Unction is received. Often the subject blocks the completeness of the effect by defective and impeding dispositions. But if the subject has in every way the correct disposition and devotion[22] it must be conceded that he receives "*plenissimam poenarum relaxationem.*" Furthermore, this view does not militate against the utility of indulgences or of Masses for the dead; nor does it usurp the prerogative of martyrdom. The uncertainty of our knowledge concerning the real dispositions of the sick man leave little escape from the obligation in charity to

18 Buchberger, *Kirchliches Handlexicon,* S. v.

19 *Tract. de Ext. Unct.,* pp. 189-91.

20 *De Effect. Ext. Unct.,* p. 80.

21 Cf. Toner—Catholic Encycl., art. "Extreme Unction;" Pohle-Preuss, *The Sacraments,* vol. IV, p. 27; Vermeersch, *Th. M.,* III, 650.

22 Pierrot (*Theologie Morale,* col. 1075) recommends the following dispositions for the fruitful reception of Extreme Unction:

1. Une foi ferme et une confiance entière en Jésus Christ—"oratio fidei salvabit infirmum."
2. Un amour ardent pour Dieu.
3. La contrition au moins imparfaite.
4. Enfin une grande résignation en la volenté de Dieu, voit qu'il donne la mort.

pray for him. Besides, it is positively wrong to assert that temporal punishment can be remitted only thru indulgences. Again Extreme Unction differs from martyrdom in so far as martyrdom does not depend for its blessed effect on the dispositions of the subject. It is the peculiar privilege of martyrs to go straightway to bliss, no matter how imperfect the dispositions have been.[23]

It is truly consoling to have this truth restored to its proper eminence in theology. A realization of its immense consequences should sharpen the clergy to zeal in the ministration and reception of this channel of grace. It should become a sweet solace to sorrowing survivors to have this further assurance that their departed friends have been spared the painful purgatorial punishments. It should be a spur to those in charge of the sick to summon the priest in opportune time, just as it should be a reproach to those who delay the call until the death-rattle has been heard. It should stimulate us to pray for its worthy and devotional reception, since we know that its object is "ut anima aeque pura sit post obitum ac infantis qui statim post baptismum moritur."[24]

3. *The Confortatio Animae.*

The approach of death with its distressing pains, its physical prostration and mental disquietude, is truly an appalling time. A thousand perplexities beset the sick man; a thousand temptations assail him.[25] The devil empties his resources in

23 Kern, *Tract. de Ext. Unct.*, p. 191.

24 *Poenit. Egberti Eborac., lib. I, cap. 4*—M. P. L., 89, 416.

25 St. Gregory the Great describes this very graphically (Moral., l. XXIV, c. 11, "In cap. xxiii Beati Job"—M. P. L., 76, 305): "Saepe electis etiam nolentibus in cogitatione subrepitur, quod in se quidem solerter inspiciunt et ante Dei oculos, quanti sit reatus, attendunt; et cum de his omnibus semper judicia districta pertimescant, tunc tamen haec vehementer metuunt, cum ad solvendum humanae conditionis debitum venientes districto judici appropinquare se cernunt. Et fit tanto timor acrior, quanto et retributio aeterna vicinior. Ante oculos autem cordis nihil inane tunc transvolat de phantasmate cogitationis, quia subductis e medio omnibus se et illum tantum considerant cui appropinquant. Crescit pavor vicina retributione justitiae, et urgente solutione carnis, quanto magis districtum judicium jamjamque quasi tangitur tanto vehementius formidatur. Et si ea, quae sciunt se nunquam praetermisisse, meminerunt, formidant tamen illa, quae nesciunt, quia videlicet semetipsos dijudicare et comprehendere omnino non possunt, atque urgente exitu subtiliori terrentur metu. Unde Redemptor noster solutioni carnis appropinquans et

an effort to snare his weakened victim. Reason itself declares the appropriateness of a heavenly antidote against the evils and the horrors of that fearful hour.

Not only reason, however, but Scripture also assures us of the existence of this opportune aid. "Et alleviabit eum Dominus," St. James wrote. In the face of the tremendous issue, Extreme Unction becomes our firm protection. It renders us secure from mortal sin, it remits all venial sin, it comforts and strengthens the soul in its trust of God's mercy, it saves the soul from the traps of the tempter, it sustains the sick person with solace and soothing, it fortifies him in the last assaults that he must withstand in his warfare for eternal salvation—in a word, it carries him thru the "valley of the shadow of death" into the kingdom of God.

4. *The Restitution of Bodily Health.*

It is a doctrine of our faith that one of the effects of Extreme Unction is the restoration of bodily health, if recovery is expedient for the soul's welfare. It is embodied in the fol-

---

membrorum suorum servans speciem factus in agonia prolixius orabat. Quid enim pro se ille, cum in agonia esset, peteret, qui in terris positus caelestia cum potestate tribuebat? Sed appropinquante morte nostrae mentis in se certamen expressit, qui vim quamdam terroris ac formidinis patimur, cum per solutionem carnis aeterno propinquamus judicio. Neque enim tunc cujuslibet anima immerito terretur, quando post pusillum hoc invenit, quod in aeternum non possit. Consideramus quippe quod viam vitae praesentis nequaquam sine culpa transire potuimus, consideramus etiam, quia nec hoc quidem sine aliquo reatu nostro est, quod laudabiliter gessimus, si remota pietate judicemur. Quis enim nostrum vitam praecedentium Patrum valeat vel superare vel assequi? Et tamen David dicit: 'Ne intres in judicium cum servo tuo, quia non justificabitur in conspectu tuo omnis vivens' (Ps. 142, 2). Paulus cum diceret: 'Nihil mihi conscius sum,' caute subjunxit: 'Sed non in hoc justificatus sum' (I Cor. IV, 4). Jacobus dicit: 'In multis enim offendimus omnes' (Jac. III, 2). Joannes dicit: 'Si dixerimus quia peccatum non habemus, ipsi nos seducimus et veritas in nobis non est' (I Joan. I, 8). Quid ergo facient tabulae, si tremunt columnae? Aut quomodo virgulta immobilia stabunt, si hujus pavoris turbine etiam cedri quatiuntur? Solutioni ergo carnis appropinquans nonnumquam terrore vindictae etiam justi anima turbatur."

In the proemium (Sess. XIV, *De Ext. Unct.*) the Council of Trent wrote: "Nam etsi adversarius noster occasiones per omnem viam quaeret et captet, ut devorare animas nostras quoquo modo possit; nullum tamen tempus est quo vehementius ille omnes suae versutiae nervos intendat ad perdendos nos penitus et a fiducia etiam, si possit, divinae misericordiae deturbandos, quam cum impendere nobis exitum vitae perspicit."

lowing words of the Council of Trent: "The thing here signified is the grace of the Holy Ghost; Whose anointing..... raises up and strengthens the soul of the sick person, by exciting in him a great confidence in the divine mercy; whereby the sick being supported...... at times obtains bodily health, when expedient for the welfare of the soul."[26]

As usual theologians, though unanimous in their teaching of the actuality of the effect, are widely divided in their opinions regarding the conditions on which this effect depends and the mode in which it is produced. Not a few,[27] influenced by the language of the Council, hold that health will not be restored unless it is foreseen that a longer life will lead to a greater degree of glory, thus making recovery a sign of predestination. It is hard to admit this. It would imply that a real revelation of predestination has been made by God to the subject; it would release him from the injunction of the Apostle to work out his salvation in fear and trembling. It would also insinuate that those who died after Unction would have become worse and might have even perished eternally, had they been returned to health. Moreover it makes the fruit of the sacrament dependent, not upon the actual state of the recipient's soul at the time of Unction, but upon his doings at some time in the future—an inadmissible hypothesis, for the sacraments act "ad modum causarum necessariarum."[28]

Another opinion is advanced by Suarez,[29] Tanner,[30] Sylvester Maurus[31] and others. They hold that restitution of bodily health does not infallibly follow even when expedient for the soul's salvation, but only when God wills it *juxta ordinem divinae sapientiae et providentiae.* They stress especially the word "*interdum*" in the sentence of the Council of Trent quoted above. Yet their contention seems foundless, for their claim would take this effect from the realms of "ex opere operato" and reduce Extreme Unction to a sacramental.

---

26 Sess. XIV, *De Ext. Unct.*, cap. 2 (Translation by Waterworth, *The Canons and Decrees of the Council of Trent*, p. 105-06).

27 Cf. Gregory of Valencia, *Comment. Theol.*, t. IV, disp. 8, q. 1, p. 3; Ballerini-Palmieri, *Opus Theol. Moral.*, t. V, tr. X, sect. VI, n. 57.

28 Tract. de Ext. Unct., p. 196-7.

29 Disp. 41, s. 4, n. 5.

30 *De Ext. Unct.*, q. 1, dub. 2, n. 48.

31 *Opus Theol.*, t. III, l. 13, q. 255, n. 5.

Indeed, there are not wanting theologians who claim that this effect is not *ex opere operato,* but simply that of a sacramental.[32] Yet such an opinion ceases to be tenable when it is remembered that sacramentals are of ecclesiastical institution, sacraments of divine institution. Moreover, such a doctrine is absolutely alien to all patristic traditions.

An odd theory was proposed by Dominic Soto.[33] He held that corporal sanation was not an immediate effect of the sacrament, but that the sick man receives thru the sacrament some supernatural aid for recovering health. This aid is given in some certain quantity and proportion always and infallibly. When, therefore, health does not follow, it must be ascribed to the fact that the aid given was not sufficient to produce its effect on account of the virulence of the disease. Though Soto is not to be condemned so strongly as Suarez[34] imagines, nevertheless he is wrong when he attaches to Extreme Unction a certain determined amount of sanative power which is always imparted to the body regardless of its expediency or inexpediency for the health of the soul.

Still another opinion holds that Extreme Unction liberates from a disease, if such liberation is "ad animae salutem et sine miraculo fieri potest."[35] It seems, however, that it is a little too much to assert the utter inability of Extreme Unction to liberate from a disease which would otherwise result in death, if such liberation were for the soul's salvation.

Kern[36] gives a quite logical explanation of the matter. According to him, the alleviation of the soul exercises an influence on the body, whence a corporal alleviation follows, which can be so great that health is restored. Since, however, Extreme Unction has a principal effect, viz., the comforting of the soul, it can reasonably be concluded that corporal alleviation thru Extreme Unction takes place when and in so far as it is expedient for the perfect healing of the soul. This alleviation and

32 Cf. Estius, *Comm. in Lib. Quartum Sent.,* dist. 23, paragr. 5, tom. IV, page 289B.

33 *Comm. in Lib. Quartum Sent.,* dist. 23, q. 1, a. 2, concl. 5.

34 Disp. 41, s. 4, n. 4.

35 Tournely, *Praelect. Theol. De Septem Sac.,* "*De Extr. Unct.,*" qu. ultima, a. 1, quaestiunc. 7.

36 *Tract. de Extr. Unct.,* pp. 205-15.

the consequent cure never occurs when the sickness is not a punishment for sin.

5. *The Principal Effect of Extreme Unction.*

Since the days of Scholasticism it has been hotly debated which of the above mentioned effects is the principal one. Thomists, treading the trail of their Angelic Master,[37] say that the *confortatio animae* is the principal effect. Allied with them are Gregory of Valencia,[38] Suarez,[39] Becanus,[40] Tanner,[41] Abelly,[42] Alphonsus de Liguori,[43] Lehmkuhl,[44] Simar[45] and Schmitz.[46] The Scotists, on the other hand, cling tenaciously to the doctrines of the *Doctor Subtilis,* viz., that the principal effect of Extreme Unction is the final remission of venial sins. De Sainte-Beuve,[47] Sambovius,[48] Tournely,[49] St. Bonaventure,[50] Frassen[51] and Mastrius[52] accede to this view of the Master. Still other theologians, like Estius,[53] Berti[54] and Herman,[55] say that all the above-mentioned effects are equally principal and primary. Oriental theologians[56] surprisingly give corporal cure as the chief effect of this sacrament. The conflict of opinions has been so involved that many theologians have refused to attempt a decision and have contented themselves with merely recounting the opinions of the disputants.[57]

---

37 *Suppl.*, q. xxx, a. 1.
38 *Comment. Theol.*, t. IV, disp. 8.
39 Disp. 41, s. 1, n. 11, sqq.
40 *Theol. Scholast.*, P. 5, t. 2, cap. 27 (*de Extr. Unct.*), q. 6.
41 *Theol. Scholast.*, t. IV, disp. VII, q. 1, dub. 2.
42 *Medulla Theol.*, P. 2, tract. 1, cap. 6, (*de Extr. Unct.*), sect. 3.
43 *Th. M.*, VI, 731.
44 *Th. M.*, II, 713.
45 *Lehrbuch de Dogmatik,* (3 Aufl), S. 790.
46 *De Eff. E. U.*, pp. 64-9.
47 *De Sac. Ext. Unct.*, disput. V, a. 1—apud Migne, *Cursus Theol. Compl.* vol. 24, col. 98 sqq.
48 *Tract. de Sacr. Ext. Unct.*, disp. 5, a. 1.
49 *Praelectiones Theol.*, "De Ext. Unct.," q. 4.
50 *Comm. in lib. Quartum Sent.*, dist. 23, a. 2, q. 2; *Breviloquium*, P. VI, cap. xi.
51 *De Sac. Ext. Unct.*, dis. 4, q. 4, n. 4.
52 *Th. M.* disp. 22, q. 4, a. 1, n. 52.
53 *Comm. in Lib. Quartum Sent.*, ad dist. 23, paragr. 4, tom. 4, p. 288A.
54 *De Theol. Discipl.*, t. VIII, l. 35, c. 10.
55 *Tractatus Theologici in IV Librum Sent.*, tr. 8, q. 4.
56 Makarij, "Pravoslavno-dogmaticeskoje bogoslovije," n. 232; Stefan, "Tainstva i obrjady pravoslavnoj cerkvi," p. 18.
57 Benedict XIV, *De Synod. Dioc.*, l. 8, c. 7, n. 3; Clericatus, *Decisiones Sacramentales*, "De Ext. Unct.," dec. 82, n. 1.

The cause of such a diversity of teaching seems to lie in the fact that theologians looked at the sacrament in connection with certain adjuncts present in the subject. It is easily seen that, due to peculiar conditions of various patients, one man would be benefited especially by one effect while another would be aided principally by another and different effect. For instance, an unconscious sick man has mortal sins for which he is at least habitually attrite. For such a one the remission of sins is undoubtedly the most necessary and beneficial effect. Again, if God knows that a sick man, when restored to health, would collect for himself a wealth of merit, then surely corporal sanation would be for him most expedient. For some, the remission of venial sins; for others, the remission of the temporal punishment; for still others, the comforting of the soul would best avail. Thus an imperfect understanding of what was really meant by the principal effect can and actually has led to interminable disputing and confusion.

Much progress can be made toward a solution by remembering that the principal effect is that which by the help of sanctifying grace is *per se* induced and thru which all other fruits of the sacrament are bestowed. In the light of this fundamental definition, the untenability of some of the opinions becomes evident. For example, the principal effect of Extreme Unction cannot be corporal cure, because health follows from a redundancy of spiritual grace. This is more apparent when it is realized that the principal effect of one and the same sacrament cannot be specifically different in one subject than in another. Each sacrament acts *ad modum causarum naturalium,* and each sacrament is instituted principally for one effect, although other effects may be obtained thru it. However, the degree of dispositions of the subject go far in the determination of how well the principal effect is produced. This difference of dispositions likewise explains why one secondary effect is coupled more intimately with the principal effect in one subject rather than in another. But unless the primary effect is the same in every subject, the concept of sacrament is destroyed.

Consequently it is clear that the final remission of venial sins is not the principal effect nor the primary end of the sacrament. In the first place, only those actually dying, not those in danger of death, would be fit subjects for this sacrament; because the subject must be beyond the capability of sinning. Yet such a postponement of the administration of this sacrament has been proscribed by many ecclesiastical decrees.[58] Moreover, this opinion would hold the reception of Extreme Unction as inefficacious in those whose venial sins had been deleted by Penance or Viaticum, since one incapable of the principal effect of a sacrament is *"incapax sacramenti."* A third reason for condemnation might be advanced from the fact that those about to receive would be bound to procure in themselves the disposition necessary to produce the primary effect, in other words, they would be bound *sub gravi* to elicit sorrow for slight sins. The absurdity of such a demand is patent. No divine nor ecclesiastical law can be produced demanding that all complacence in venial sin be removed for the valid reception of any sacrament.

With equal clarity it can be seen that the principal effect of Extreme Unction is not the remission of mortal sins. To assert this is to assert that Extreme Unction is primarily a sacrament of the dead. Moreover St. James spoke of the remission of sins in a conditional sense—evidencing the validity of administration to those who had no sins.

Again, the principal effect of Unction is not the remission of temporal punishment. Otherwise saints, those who have no purgatorial expiation to make, are absolutely incapable of validly receiving the sacrament.

To defend the equality of all effects is quite as preposterous, for it entails the production thru one sacramental action of several specifically different effects. Extreme Unction would then be specificated by at least four different objects.

It remains to say that the principal effect of this sacrament must be the comforting of the soul of the sick man, by which it is strengthened against the perils of spiritual debility consequent upon a disease. This becomes clearer from a consideration of the subject of the sacrament. A man approaching death may be in need of many things. If he is an object of

58 Cf. e. g., Benedict XV, litt. apost. *"Sodalitatem,"* May 31, 1921 (A. A. S., XIII, 342); Pius XI—litt. ap. *"Explorata res est"*—Feb. 2, 1923, (A. A. S., XV, 103).

divine ire, he needs above all else the remission of his mortal sins. He usually needs the remission of his venial sins, lest he appear before his Judge in a nuptial garment not wholly spotless. He may need condonation of temporal punishment, for otherwise, he must be shut from the vision of God, while purgatory's fires purge the dross from his soul. He may need something to conquer the horror of human nature at the approaching dissolution, to elude the wily traps of the enemy so unmercifully annoying him, to stifle the temptations to inordinate grief, cowardice and desperation, and to face the supreme hour with trust and resignation in the divine will. All who are nearing death need these aids—yet not all the faithful about to die can be helped by Extreme Unction. This Sacrament can be given only to those in danger of death from *sickness.* Hence its institution must have been made for the purpose of overcoming the evils which are conjoined with grave bodily sickness and for conferring the benefits which all those in grave illness require.[59]

Experience reveals one marked difference between those in danger of death from sickness and those in danger of death *ab extrinseco.* The bodily sick manifest a spiritual debility from their affliction, a complete prostration of the mental forces as a result of the collapse of the inferior powers. From this weakness there arises an especial difficulty in cooperating with graces conferred thru other supernatural means, a marked remissness in rejecting temptation, a multiple danger of losing salvation. Extreme Unction, then, must be a medicine, a celestial antidote, against that spiritual weakness that comes with bodily infirmity. It must furnish from its very nature an extraordinary spiritual fortitude, a vigor of mind and an exhilaration of soul which will be eminently suitable to expeditious cooperation with grace. As a consequence, every man who has at least a passive potency of receiving comfort against that spiritual weakness which is conjoined with grave sickness, is capable of a valid reception of this sacrament, even if he have no need at all of the other fruits or effects. Truly it seems most reasonable to say that the principal effect of the Sacrament of Extreme Unction is "confortatio animae infirmi."

---

59 Cf. Suarez, disp. 42, sect. 2, n. 6.

The specific signification of the sacrament corroborates this contention. Sacraments effect what they signify. The Unction of the sick, then, must effect enlightment of the intellect, and consequently consolation, exhilaration, alleviation, strength and courage; in a word, all that is included in the meaning of "confortatio animae." An examination of patristic quotations is all that is required to show the force of this argument.[60]

VI. The Properties.

This discussion of Extreme Unction has passed logically from a discussion of the basic point, viz., its sacramentality, to a consideration of its end, its essence and its effects. An investigation of its properties, i. e., the questions of its unity, its reviviscence and its iterability, should next engross our attention. These problems are so intimately interwoven with canonical legislation that no treatment of them from a juridical point of view can be thorough without a discussion of the dogmatic aspects. To these three problems could be added the question of the *necessity* of Extreme Unction, but this can be fully and more properly discussed in the commentary on Canon 944.

1. *The Unity of Extreme Unction.*

Extreme Unction is, of course, one sacrament. For many centuries, however, it has been mooted as to the precise nature of this unity. Does it possess a unity of indivisibility, i. e., does its sacramental efficacy follow only from the completed rite —or does it possess the unity of integrity, i. e., are the single unctions partial sacraments, as it were, whose sum total constitutes one whole sacrament? Intimately and inseparably connected with this question is also the problem of when the sacrament produces its effects.

In the discussion of these two problems there is no recourse to Scripture or to Tradition or to dogmatic definitions.

---

60 Cf. Eusebius Caesareensis, *Demon. Evangel., l. IV, c. 15*—M. P. G., 22, 294A; S. Maximus Taurinensis, *Expositiones de Capit. Evangel. III*—M. P. L., 57, 811B; Procopius Gazaeus, *In Levit. xxix,* 31—M. P. G., 87, 702; St. Fulgentius, *Ep. 14,* n. 42—M. P. L., 65, 430 B-C; St. Gregory of Nyssa, *In Cant. Cant., Hom. IX*—M. P. G., 44, 963A; St. Augustine, *Quaest. Evang., l. II, n. 19*—M. P. L., 35, 1340; Euthymius, *In textum S. Marci, cap. VI, vers. 12*—M. P. G., 129, 807; St. Isadore of Spain, *Quaest. in V. T., in Levit., c. 5*—M. P. L., 83, 323A.

It is necessary to depend for the solution to a great extent upon theological reasoning.

There were two great divisions of thought on the matter among the ancient theologians. Albertus Magnus, the leader on one side, wrote: "Plures sunt ibi unctiones quae omnes uniuntur in uno effectu quem complent; et ideo omnes sunt unum sacramentum. Et quod dicitur quod quaelibet est sacramentum, dicendum quod omnes sunt unum sacramentum, quia quaelibet est signum et causa reliquiarum, non secundum partem, sed secundum totum omnes simul."[1] St. Thomas,[2] Suarez[3] and many others concur in this view, and the Sixth Council of Beneventano[4] included it in its synodal enactments.

On the other hand the Scotist school held the opposite opinion. The *Doctor Subtilis* himself wrote: "Est sacramentum unum quia habet tam unam materiam quam unam formam totalem, quae sunt unum signum totale unius effectus totalis, sc. plenariae innocentiae restitutae per remissionem totalem omnium peccatorum venialium. Licet enim plures sint formae partiales et multi partiales effectus, ut remissiones peccatorum venialium commissorum in parte tali vel tali, ut ore vel manu, tamen una est totalis materia et totalis forma, quae sunt signum totale

---

1 *Comm. ad Lib. IV Sent.*, a. 17 ad 2 (apud *Opera Omnia*, vol. XXX, p. 24).

2 *Suppl.*, q. 30, a. 1 ad 3: "Quando sunt multae actiones ordinatae ad unum effectum, ultima est formalis respectu omnium praecedentium, et agit in virtute earum; et ideo in ultima unctione gratia infunditur, quae effectum sacramento praebet."

Yet, strangely enough, the Angelic Doctor seems to be inconsistent, for in the question preceding he writes: "Quamvis in Eucharistia, si post consecrationem panis moritur sacerdos, alius sacerdos possit procedere ad consecrationem vini, incipiens ubi ille dimisit, vel etiam incipere a capite supra aliam materiam, tamen in extrema unctione non potest a capite incipere, sed debet semper procedere, quia unctio in eadem parte facta tantum valet, ac si consecraretur bis eadem hostia, quod nullo modo faciendum est" (*Suppl.*, q. 29, a. 2 ad 3). Why would the repetition of the unction be ineffective, if it is not impeded by a sacramental effect already present?

3 Disp. 41, s. 2, n. 12: "Vera sententia est, effectum hujus sacramenti dari in eo instanti, in quo consummatur essentialiter hoc sacramentum, consummatur autem, cum primum quinque actiones cum quinque formulis perficiuntur."

4 Tit. 8, c. 3, anno 1374 (apud Catalano, *Rit. Rom.*, t. I, p. 319): "Licet multae fiant ibi inunctiones, ultima tamen est ibi formalis respectu omnium praecedentium, et agit in virtute earum, et ideo in ultima inunctione gratia infunditur, quae effectum praebet sacramenti. Et ideo unum sacramentum dicitur unitate perfectionis, quae est per finem."

totalis remissionis et plenariae justificationis ab omni peccato veniali."[5] Mastrio writes even more clearly: "Fundamentum praecipuum est, quia quaelibet unctio cum sua forma propria effectui proprio respondente, et ad singulas unctiones completur sensu substantiali formae; ergo quaevis unctio cum sua propria forma est proprium sacramentum gratiam conferens . . . . Ergo si quaevis unctio cum sua propria forma habet proprium significatum partiale ab aliis distinctum, habebit etiam suum effectum proprium partialem ab aliis condistinctum."[6]

With one or the other of these opinions by far the majority of theologians agree. There is no doubt that some of them supposed that the five unctions with their respective forms were essential for the validity of the sacrament. Yet if this supposition were true, the question could never be solved. For if Christ constituted the essence of this sacrament in five unctions, it would be impossible to determine with our lack of Scriptural or traditional arguments just what kind of unity He wished to attribute to this sacrament. In consequence of Canon 947 such a view in regard to the necessity of the five-fold form and the five-fold unction is no longer tenable.

Dominico Soto[7] held that a third element played a part in the determination of the time of the effects of the sacrament, viz., the intention of the minister. According to his theory, the Unction has its effect at the time of the completion of the last unction, whether such an unction pertain to the sacrament essentially or only integrally. The essence of the Sacrament consists, by divine law, in the unction of the five senses. The Church has added to these the unction of the feet and (in his day) the unction of the reins. These two latter anointings become integral parts of the Sacrament, and the intention of the minister must accordingly be directed to all seven unctions. The consequence will be that the conferring of grace will be delayed until the seventh anointing is complete.

This theory is generally rejected—and deservedly, too; for a minister cannot bring it to pass by his intention that grace

---

5 *Report. Paris.*, l. IV, dist. 23, q. unic.
6 *Th. M.*, disp. 22, q. 4, a. 2, n. 64.
7 *Comm. in quart. lib. Sent.*, t. I, ad dist. xxiii, q. 2, a. 3.

will not be conferred after the whole essential rite has been completed, but that, instead, it will be induced at some future moment selected by him either arbitrarily or from a supposed command of the Church. If such an intention prevailed, nothing at all would be effected, for an intention in regard to the sacraments may not be *"de futuro"* (except in Matrimony).

Other opinions, termed by Kern[8] as "singular," teach that the *whole* effect takes place after the first unction; or that it follows ordinarily the fifth unction, except in such cases where the subject died during the anointment, and then after the last unction performed; or that, in case of necessity *only,* one unction with a general form can *validly* confer the grace and fruits of the sacrament, while in all other cases the five unctions were absolutely necessary, etc.

Father Kern[9] proposes another solution of the question. The essence of the sacrament demands neither the unction of the five senses nor the five-fold repetition of the form. It is necessary and sufficient that the sick man be anointed and that the effect which the rite has been divinely intended to produce be sought by the prayer of the priest. There is not an iota of evidence to prove that Christ instituted five partial sacraments which singly cause different grades of grace. The sacrament of the *"exeuntium"* is as much one sacrament as that of the *"intrantium,"* Baptism, where a triple ablution is prescribed. Moreover the practice of the Greek Church, by which a priest performs all the unctions under a single form, weighs strongly against the probability of the institution by Christ of a five-fold form with a five-fold unction.[10]

With this premise established, Father Kern makes use of the third element that Soto brought into the solution of the case. Now it is one thing *to anoint the sick man, let us say, upon the breast,* and quite a different thing *to anoint the breast of the sick man.* The former implies that the unction is the primary consideration and the place of unction something secondary;

8 *Tract. De Ext. Unct.,* p. 327.

9 *Op. cit.,* pp. 328-9.

10 Neither this custom nor Canon 947 clinches the question finally. There is still the possibility that the Church used its prerogative of changing the matter and form of the sacraments. In fact, this very solution is proposed by Dr. Walter McDonald in the Irish Theological Quarterly, vol. II, (1907), p. 333.

while the latter connotes the importance of the specific part of the body anointed. Consequently, if a priest intends that the unction prescribed by St. James is to be performed by a single unction (joined, of course, with a general form), then the effect of the sacrament is produced after such an unction just as certainly as in those Churches,[11] where only one form and one unction were required. However, if it is the intention of the minister to perform the Jacobean rite by anointing the organs designated by his ritual book, and using the particular forms prescribed therein, then by his intention such a priest groups all these sacramental and sacerdotal actions "*sub aspectu unius*" —and grace follows from the completed rite.

Applying this theory to the mode of unction defined by the Western Church, we get the following conclusions. Each form refers, not to the remission of sins as such, but only to the forgiveness of sins committed by one particular sense. Therefore such an anointment *per se* is not the rite promulgated by St. James. Moreover, the sins of one sense cannot be forgiven while those of another sense are retained. All serious sins must be erased at once. Consequently, the Jacobean prescription is not fulfilled until those unctions and forms are performed which would refer to the remission of all sin. If the minister did not intend to anoint the feet, then the sacrament is conferred after the fifth unction, on the grounds that, broadly speaking, the senses are the source of every sin. But if the priest does not include in any one of these anointments a reference to the sins committed "*per gressum,*" because of the fact that he intends to perform subsequently a particular unction upon the feet, it is only after this additional unction that the rite is complete, and the effect is produced. If the minister does not advert to these distinctions, but merely intends to do as the Church does, Father Kern thinks it probable that the sacrament is conferred after the fifth unction, because the anointments of the five senses include sufficiently within their remissory scope all the sins committed by the subject.

Rites other than the western procedure must be viewed

---

11 As e. g., in the Coptic rite—Denziger, *Rit. Orient.*, t. I, p. 186 and similarly in the ancient Mozarabic rite—apud *Monumenta Eccl. Liturgica* (ed. Cabrol et Leclerq), vol. v, p. 71.

in a similar way. Unless the minister intended to confer the sacrament in the first (or in any other) unction, the effect of the sacrament does not take place until the very last unction is performed. If the minister elicits no specific intention in the matter, the discipline of the Church settles the question when the essential unctions, necessary to signify the remission of all sins contemplated by the Jacobean rite, have been performed.

It is easy to see by this theory how the sacrament can be confected in case of necessity with a single unction. It leads to this consequence, however, (as shall be seen in treating Canon 947): all the ceremonies which are "supplied" after the short form has been used are not of a sacramental nature. They are simply *"sacramentalia,"* with no effect *"ex opere operato."*

Father Kern's theory has not met with universal, wholehearted acceptance. Quinn[12] thinks it open to the same objection as Soto's opinion. "It is hard to see," he writes, "how the intention of the minister (if sacramental at all) can suspend the effect which the unction signifies." Yet in strictness Father Kern does not claim this. What he asserts is that the unction of a particular organ with a form which does not refer to forgiveness of all sins cannot be *per se* the rite prescribed by St. James. It is the wording of the form which circumscribes the effect of the rite, not the intention of the minister. When the various unctions together with the several forms cumulatively refer to the forgiveness of all sins, then and only then is the Jacobean prescription fulfilled. What Father Kern claims that the minister's intention does effect is this, viz., that even if the forgiveness of all the sins would be amply referred to by any series of unctions, as, for example, those of the five senses, nevertheless, if the priest specifically excepts the sins committed by any other particular part of the body, then the unction of such a particular part is essential to complete the rite of St. James.

Dr. McDonald[13] is not at all pleased with this theory of Kern's. He holds the Scotist view, claiming the Sacrament to be composed of five partial sacraments. The breaking up of

12 *Some Aspects of the Dogma of Extreme Unction,* p. 76.
13 Irish Theological Quarterly, vol. II (1907), p. 333.

the Jacobean rite into these partial unctions was done by the authority of the Church, who can change to some extent the matter and form of the sacraments. Either the exercise of this power must be allowed here, or, he says, "you must fall back on the intention of the minister, empowering him to alter the signification of the words he utters, and thereby make certain rites sacramental or merely ceremonial according as he intends. the form to cover and remit all sins or only those of a certain class . . . I cannot help regarding it as much more probable that it was by Church authority the character of Order was divided . . . and according to the same analogy each of the seven unctions should be regarded as a distinct sacrament, all combining to form a generic whole, which once constituted in its fulness, cannot any more than the sacrament of Order be repeated while its lasts."

In answer to Kern's argument that the form of a particular unction is deficient because its refers to the sins committed by a single organ and no species of sin can be remitted separately, Dr. McDonald argues that, since the form of each of the unctions signifies some remission of sin, each unction must be "capable of infusing grace, which is the test of true sacramental efficacy.". The naming of special sins in these forms is done simply because of the actual graces infused for help against temptations to these particular sins, and for the remission of the temporal punishment due to such transgressions.

The promulgation of Canon 947 made Noldin alter his opinion in regard to this question. Prior to the Code, he insisted that the last unction brought with it the sacramental grace.[14] In his latest edition of the Moral Theology, he reveals his reversal of viewpoint. Now he thinks that the essential graces of the sacrament are given in the first anointment. The subsequent unctions supplement and perfect this effect by the infusion of actual graces and by the increase of sanctifying grace, if the dispositions of the patient become better thru the stimulation of the unction or unctions already received.[15]

This view is very popular with present-day theologians.

---

[14] *Th. M.*, De Sac., n. 446 (editio septima—1908).

[15] *Th. M.*, De Sac., n. 431 (editio quarta decima—1921).

Lehmkuhl,[16] Tanquerey-Quevastre,[17] Vermeersch-Creusen[18] subscribe to it heartily. Its practical application lies in the value of repeating or "supplying" the unctions in a case where the short form is used. Logically this question falls under the treatment of Canon 947, and will be dealt with at that time.[19]

The time when the special effects occur presents some difficulties. A) Mortal sins are immediately remitted with the infusion of sanctifying grace whether this happen after the first unction or after the last. This also accomplishes the pardon of venial sins and condones temporal punishment, according to the disposition of the penitent. B) If the use of reason has not been snatched away by unconsciousness or insanity, supernatural aids are also imparted immediately, which bestow comfort and alleviation and induce a feasibility of co-operation with the impulses of grace. C) These comforting and sustaining graces perdure thru sickness until death or recovery. D) Since corporal health arises from the redundancy of spiritual comfort—and since much depends on the nature and the seriousness of the disease—the effect is obtained differently in different subjects. That some alleviation very often instantly appears, is a fact of experience.

2. *Reviviscence.*

The problem of reviviscence confronts us when a sacrament has been validly received, but remains "*informe*" because of the lack of due dispositions in the recipient. When rightly administered, Extreme Unction confers a title to sanctifying grace and to all other aids expedient for the sick man. But it happens sadly enough that sometimes the recipient places an obstacle to one or more of the special graces that the sacrament confers, or even to the infusion of first grace itself. It then becomes of paramount importance to look into the powers of reviviscence of this potent sacrament.

The "*obex*" or "*fictio*" which impedes the effects of the sacraments is either formal or material. The former is present when a man, conscious of his improper dispositions, know-

16 *Th. M.*, II, 718.
17 *Brev. Syn. Th. M.*, n. 1260B.
18 *Epitome*, II, 231.
19 Cf. *Infra*, chapter xii, p. 386 sqq.

ingly receives the sacrament. The latter occurs when the "obex" is inculpable—a case easily imaginable, as, for example, when the subject has been suddenly struck down to unconsciousness.

Theologians propound it as the more probable opinion that, "remoto obice," Extreme Unction does revive, whether the "fiction" be material or formal.[20] The moral dispositions of a subject affect the validity of no sacrament except Penance. Moreover, the valid administration of a sacrament surely accomplishes *something* in the recipient. Surely, too, that "something" can be nothing else than the title to sanctifying grace and the right to the other fruits, on the condition that the defective disposition be removed. Were this not true, there would be no difference between the valid and the invalid reception of a sacrament.

On the other hand, there is no valid reason for denying the reviviscence of Extreme Unction. It is admitted in the Sacraments of Baptism, of Confirmation, and of Orders. It is the more probable opinion in regard to Matrimony because of the permanence of the sacrament. Certainly one who has been validly anointed needs the effects of the sacrament thru reviviscence. He cannot be, as a general rule, licitly reanointed—and yet it seems alien to the divine benignity to deprive him of such benefits because of his former temerity, or perhaps only misfortune or ignorance. Such a subject is far more in need of Extreme Unction's effects than one who has prepared himself well for its worthy reception. Since Extreme Unction cannot be repeated in the same illness unless it is a prolonged one,[21] such deprivation of the effects otherwise obtainable thru reviviscence would be disastrous.

Some theologians have gone to fanciful excesses in granting this reviving efficacy to Extreme Unction. De Lugo[22] attributed to it the power of remitting venial sins after death. Suarez[23] thought it probable that the efficacy of the anointing extended beyond the restoration of health. Didacus Nugnus, O. P.,[24] asserted it to be certain that, even after health had

20 Cf. Hurter, *Th. D. Comp.*, III, n. 306; Tanquerey, *Th. D.*, III, n. 321.
21 Cf. *Rit. Rom.*, tit. V, cap. I, n. 8; cf. *infra*, chap. V, p. 192 sqq.
22 *De Sacramentis in Genere*, disp. IX, sect. 6, vers. finem (n. III).
23 Disp. 41, s. 1, n. 24.
24 *Expositio in III p. D. Thomae, suppl.*, q. 30, a. I.

been regained, if the *obex* were not until then removed, sanctifying grace—and also the other spiritual effects—would follow. Surely this seems stretching the powers of reviviscence too far. A healthy man is incapable of receiving grace *"qua alleviatio;"* and since this is the sacrament's principal effect, he is incapable of every other effect.

What is required for reviviscence in the several cases may be summed up as follows:

a) If the fiction is material and no new grave sin is committed since the reception of Extreme Unction, it suffices that the sick man do what should *per se* have been before unction. There is no defect present other than *"defectus dispositionis ab initio."*

b) If the fiction is material and a grave sin has been committed since the anointing, attrition with sacramental absolution or perfect contrition is required.

c) If the fiction is formal, the sacrament of Penance or perfect contrition is necessary. If the *obex* is removed by Penance, then the infusion of grace occurs "ex duplici fonte," i. e., directly from the sacrament of Penance and by reviviscence in the sacrament of Extreme Unction.[25]

3. *The Iterability.*

Theologians all agree on the permissibility of repeating Extreme Unction in the following circumstances:

1. When the infirm man has been restored to health and falls again into a mortal disease, no matter how short the period of time between the sicknesses;

2. In the same sickness, if the danger of death passes after the Unction has once been given and the sick man relapses into a new danger of death. The reason alleged is that, just as a person whose sickness is not at least probably fatal has no right to the sacrament, so a man whose danger of death has receded completely does not retain any title to the benefits that the sacred unction confers. For verification of this recession and recurrence of a dangerous state, many theologians demand the lapse of some period of time—a not unreasonable exaction,

25 Cf. Kern. *Tract. de Ext. Unct.*, p. 377-8; Tanquerey, *Th. D.*, III, n. 323; Aertnys, *Th. M.* II, n. 354.

if too much strictness is not insisted upon in the measurement of that time. St. Bonaventure wisely observed: "Absurdum valde videtur sacramenta regulari secundum motum astrorum."[26]

Some theologians, as shall be seen in the discussion of Canon 940, 2, teach that if a man is anointed in imminent danger of death which subsequently passes away, whereby the man is somewhat relieved although not beyond the remote danger of death, another anointing may be made if the crisis again appears.[27]

By far the great majority of theologians deny the validity of Extreme Unction when repeated in the same danger of death. Among contemporary writers, however, Kern[28] holds as probable the opinion maintaining the validity of repeated unction in the same danger of death. He is not alone in his contention, but is rather one of the more recent adherents to an authoritative band of positive sacramental theologians. The most eminent members of this group are Menardus,[29] Launoi,[30] Martene,[31] Juenin,[32] Drouven,[33] Bouget,[34] Catalano,[35] Pellicia,[36] Binterim,[37] Telch[38] and Vermeersch.[39] Other theologians[40] were convinced by the practices of the ancient Greeks that repetition of the Unction in the same danger of death was undoubtedly valid. Some, like Billuart,[41] Gerbert[42] and Schanz,[43] did not dare to brand as invalid the ancient custom. Finally,

26 *Comm. in IV lib. Sent.*, ad dist. xxiii, a. 2, q. 4 ad 2.
27 Cf. *infra*, chapter V, p. 192.
28 *Tract. de Ext. Unct.*, pp. 338-63.
29 *In Notis ad Lib. Sacr. S. Greg.*—M. P. L., 78, 523C.
30 *Op. Omnia*, t. I, p. 548 sqq.
31 *De Antiq. Eccl. Rit.*, l. I, cap. 7, art. 2, n. 15.
32 *Comm. Hist. et Dog. de Sacr.*, d. 7, q. 9, c. I.
33 *De Re Sacramentaria*, l. vii, q. 5, c. 2.
34 *Instit. Cathol. in modum Catecheseos*, c. VII, paragr. 3.
35 *Rit. Rom.*, t. I, pp. 303-4.
36 *De Christ. Ecc. Politia*, t. II, l. 6, s. 2, c. 3, paragr. 2, p. 479.
37 *Denkwürdigkeiten*, 6 B, 3 T., 3 K., paragr. 9.
38 *Epit. Th. M.*, "*Sententiae Probabiles*"—de E. U.—p. 415-6.
39 *Th. M.*, III, 666.
40 Wirceburgenses, *De Ext. Unct.*, c. 2, a. 3, "Dico" 3; Tournely, *Prael. Dog.*, De E. U., qu. ult., a. 2, "quaeres" 2.
41 *Summa S. Thomae*, De Ext. Unct., disp. unic, a. 7, "Petes" tertio.
42 *Principia Th. Sac.*, c. VI, paragr. 78.
43 *Die Lehre von der Sakramenten*, p. 661.

since the days of Benedict XIV,[44] moralists[45] have counselled against over-strictness in the refusal to repeat the sacrament in lingering illnesses.

Convincing texts from old rituals, such as the Gregorian Sacramentary,[46] the Ordo of Rheims,[47] the Codex of the Monastery of St. Remigius,[48] the Codex Tilianus[49] and many others,[50] show that it was the custom from the early ages down to twelfth century to confer Extreme Unction on seven successive days. Instances of the actual fulfillment of this ritualistic prescription are also extant.[51]

Kern adduces authorities to show that the Greek ceremony of Extreme Unction, wherein seven priests anoint by going thru the entire formula, is but a development of the pristine practice of anointing on seven different days.[52] Surely the ceremony given in the Euchologion [53] does not seem arranged for a single visitation to the sick. For example, in the beginning of the ceremony a very solemn blessing of the oil is performed by the first priest who is to anoint—and that very same oil is used in the unctions by all the priests. Yet the second and the third and the fourth and the fifth and the sixth and the seventh priests bless it again individually, as though it were profane, before they proceed in turn to anoint the sick man. It does not seem that such could be the original practice. It is more logical to view this as a development of the custom in the early church to anoint for seven successive days. According to Maltzew,[54] the Coptic liturgy witnesses to this practice even today. Denziger,[55] however, speaks of a single unction made by a

---

44 *De Syn. Dioc.*, l. 8, c. 8, n. 4, in fine.

45 St. Alph., *Th. M.*, VI, 715; AErtnys, *Th. M.*, II, 368 ad III; Lehmkuhl, *Th. M.*, II, 725; Scavini, *Th M.*, III, 442; Gury, *Th. M.*, II, 691.

46 M. P. L., 78, 537.

47 Martene, *op. cit.*, l. 1, c. 7, a. 4, Ordo 8.

48 M. P. L., 78, 537B.

49 M. P. L., 78, 528C—cf. *ibid.*, 20, 22.

50 E. g., Pont. of Salisburgo (Salzburg), apud Martene, *l.c.*, Ordo XII: *Codex Victorinus*, Ordo XIX; *Codex Turonensis*, Ordo IV; etc.

51 E. g., Vita S. Remberti, *Acta SS.*, Feb. 4, p. 571.

52 *Tract. de Ext. Unct.*, pp. 345-50.

53 A Latin translation of the Greek ceremony is given in Martene, "*De Antiq. Ecc. Rit.*," l. 1, c. 7, a. 4, Ordo XXX.

54 *Die Sacramente*, p. CCCXXXII.

55 *Rit. Orient.*, t. II, p. 501 ss.—cf. t. I, p. 187 ss.

priest, and the unctions on the following days made by the sick man himself.

The declaration of the Council of Trent seems at first face to militate very strongly against this proposition. The words of the Council are: "Quod si infirmi, post susceptam hanc unctionem, convaluerint, iterum hujus sacramento subsidio juvari poterunt, cum in aliud simile vitae discrimen inciderint."[56] Yet Kern[57] shows ably enough the possibility of construing the Tridentine text in a positive sense, rather than in an exclusive sense, i. e., the Council intended to assert the validity of Extreme Unction repeated in the specific circumstances it mentions rather than propose a taxative enumeration of the cases of its valid repetition.

Neither is the present practice an argument against Kern's contention. It can be said to be of a disciplinary rather than of a dogmatic nature. Churchmen were only too human in the Middle Ages—and simony and sacrilege had to be expugned by determined legislation. This was the course chosen by the Church to end forever the avarice of pastors who demanded exorbitant stipends for the administration of the sacrament.[58]

It is the theological reasons of Kern—the *"argumenta ex ratione theologica"*—which meet most opposition. Putting his terms in the language of the school, he notes that the external rite (sacramentum tantum) causes to be produced in the soul a *reality* (res et sacramentum); and with this reality as their proximate cause, sanctifying grace and the other gifts of the sacrament result (res tantum). Hence it is to the "effect and sacrament" (which seems to be the best translation of "res et sacramentum"), rather than to the mere sacrament that the sacramental effect is due. Now in Extreme Unction the "effect and sacrament" consists in a right or title to the spiritual comfort and other aids given by this sacrament. As Kern himself puts it: "In Extrema Unctione res et sacramentum consistit in titulo sive jure remoto ad confortationem spiritualem et alia auxilia cum illa conjuncta; quod jus in subjecto oritur ex efficaci repositione in manu misericordiae divinae."[59] The

---

56 Sess. XIV, *de Ext. Unct.*, c. 3.
57 *Tract. de Ext. Unct.*, pp. 359-60.
58 Cf. *infra*, chap. v, p. 151 sqq.
59 Kern, *Tract. de Ext. Unct.*, pp. 350-2.

question then becomes: Can the *right* to spiritual comfort and the other aids be increased or intensified? There is no reason why it cannot, because, unlike in the case of Order, Baptism and Confirmation, the *"jus ad confortationem spiritualem"* is the very "res et sacramentum" of Extreme Unction. The only possible thing to hinder this increase of right would be an intrinsic incapability of the spiritual comfort itself allowing of increase. The question now resolves itself further. Can spiritual comfort (confortatio), when once conferred, be increased? It is quite evident that such a thing is possible, since it consists especially in acts of faith, hope, love, spiritual joy, etc. Moreover, since no sacrament takes away the potency of falling into future sins, it is also plain that if any appreciable period of time intervenes between the man's anointment and his death, he will likely have committed several venial sins. Hence a repetition would be effective for this very reason.

Kern's reasoning was attacked with very great violence by Dr. Walter McDonald, the dean of Dunboyne Establishment at Maynooth. Writing in the Irish Theological Quarterly [60] shortly after the appearance of Kern's work, he defends the common belief with great mastery. He denies in the first place that "the effect and sacrament" of Extreme Unction, as well as that of Penance, is a right. He says that it is rather a basis of right, which may be intensified or not. The character of Baptism, Confirmation or Order is a basis of right to certain sacramental graces. It is intrinsically capable of increase (why not?), somewhat in the same fashion as sanctifying grace itself. Yet no second repetition of these sacraments actually intensify this basis of right. The question arises then how a mere repetition of Extreme Unction—while the "effect and sacrament" is already in the soul—produces any intensification of sacramental efficacy. Pursuing this same thought, Quinn[61] also argues: "Father Kern tells us that helps given by the sacrament are capable of increase. But how can they be increased by the repetition of a rite which merely signifies something that has already been effected? The rite should be ineffective, because its normal effect has already been produced and remains. Even

60 Vol. II (1907), p. 339-42.
61 *Some Aspects of the Dogma of Extreme Unction*, pp. 131.

if it were effective, its effect (*res et sacramentum*) would establish no stronger claim on God for sacramental graces. For, as a mere repetition the rite would cover no new ground. The reality produced by it in the soul could be the moral cause of only the selfsame graces or helps, already due to the sacrament conferred."

It is no escape from this conclusion to draw a parity with the Penance or the Eucharist, which may be repeated very often. The "effect and sacrament" of Penance (at least, according to the best opinion) is transient, while that of Extreme Unction has a quasi-permanency, lasting, as all admit, thruout the whole duration of the danger of death. Whenever the "effect and sacrament" have been produced by a prior administration and are continuing in the soul thruout a period of time, there is neither room nor need of the selfsame "res et sacramentum" as long as the former one continues. In the case of the Eucharist, the "effect and sacrament" lasts only as long as the species remain incorrupt in the stomach. During that time a new reception has no sacramental efficacy.[62] "Why is this," Dr. McDonald asks, "if not because the effect and sacrament is already there—produced by the first reception?"[63]

Drouven,[64] in defending the validity of repetition, offers as one of the reasons: "Nec quidquam obstat quominus et peccatorum remissio, et restitutio corporalis sanitatis, qui duo ejus effectus sunt, saepe a Deo iteratis unctionibus et mysticis precibus postulentur." The flaw in this is that he assumes that the remission of sins, &c., are asked for by the external rite (sacramentum tantum), whereas it is only thru the mediation of the "effect and sacrament" (res et sacramentum) that this petitioning is done. And in the case of Extreme Unction—since the effect and sacrament continue—the impetration of these effects from God is continuous, so that there is no need of subsequent administrations of the sacrament for this purpose. Indeed the effect and sacrament are more truly petition-

62 We are not dealing here with the question of the production of accidental grace by the consumption of the second species. This case regards the reception a second time in the same fashion as the first reception, whether that was done under both species or only under a single species.

63 Irish Theological Quarterly, vol. II, (1907), p. 341.

64 *De Re Sacramentaria*, l. 7, q. 5, cap. 2.

ing God for the helps and graces of the sacrament than the valid external rites (sacramentum tantum) can be said to do so.[65]

The consequence is that the arguments in favor of repetition from theological reason are not very impressive. But what of the positive arguments? How can we explain the existence of a practice which was so widespread that it could hardly have existed without the knowledge of Rome, nor even without official approbation? Dr. McDonald has recourse to the Scotist theory of partial sacraments. The full grace of the sacrament is not received until the last unction of the rite is done. The essential graces are conferred in the first unction, and these are increased and perfected by the subsequent anointings. This increase and perfection are accomplished by the infusion of actual graces into the soul, having generally a particular relation with the transgressions of the sense or organ anointed. The theory is intelligible in regard to the anointments made on various distinct parts of the body. But how is it possible to extend this theory to the case where the very rite is repeated thru the performance of the identical unctions on the selfsame parts of the body seven times? For instance, what does the subject receive from a second and third unction of the eyes that he has not received in the first anointment? How can two unctions of the same organ increase and perfect a particular effect when the repetition of the entire rite does not increase the general and essential effect of the sacrament?[66]

It seems more logical to have recourse to the explanation given by Quinn[67] and by Bishop MacDonald[68] that these practices were nothing else than abuses. Yet besides the respon-

---

65 Cf. Quinn, *Some Aspects of the Dogma of Extreme Unction,* p. 131.

66 Kern (*Tract. de Ext. Unct.,* p. 343-4) says that it is impossible to separate the sacrament into so many partial administrations because the interval between them is too long; and the intention of the minister would have to be "*de futuro.*" The force of this is weakened by the promulgation of Canon 947. It shall be seen (cf. *infra,* chap. xii, p.) that many claim that the unctions can be supplied at any time throughout the same danger of death when the sacrament has been conferred by the short form. In other words, while the "effect and sacrament" remains in the soul, it is permissible to perfect the sacrament by the performance of these additional unctions, whereby actual graces are conferred.

67 *Some Aspects of the Dogma of Extreme Unction,* p. 131.

68 Amer. Eccl. Review, vol. XLII (1910), pp. 23-6.

sibility which this sweeping condemnation imposes, these authors have to proffer an explanation of the Greek practice of blessing the oil so often. They must explain too, the value of the action of the second and third and other priests in the performance of the same anointings as the first priest. In the Greek ceremony, when would the essential effect occur? Would it be after the first unction of the first priest? This can easily be claimed, and with just as much reason it can be claimed that actual graces are infused by the subsequent unctions of the first priest, so that thereby the sacrament is perfected and made integral.[69] But what of the unctions of the second priest? He anoints the very parts of the body which the first priest has done. Is the "effect and sacrament" intensified in such a way that more actual graces result, especially in favor of that sense or source of sin anointed twice? Yet how can the sacrament be perfected by a re-unction of the same parts of the body? The purpose in distributing the unctions among the various sources of sin is to express more fully the effects of the sacrament. But there is no fuller expression of the effect thru a repetition of the unction of the same parts twice or oftener.

The only outlet is a contention that the unction by the first priest in the Greek ceremony is a sacrament and all the other unctions merely ceremonial, as Arcudius claims,[70] or that the actions of the seven priests unite into one sacramental action. Both of these contentions are open to attack in several vital spots. Goar[71] rebuked Arcudius for his opinion in this regard, and offered in its stead the alternative that the one sacrament was confected seven times with sacramental fruits. It is indeed hard to see what difference there is between the confection of seven different sacraments (different *numero*) or one sacrament confected seven times with sacramental fruit. If it is held that the seven priests are but one moral minister, the question again revives: when is the essential effect of the sacrament conferred? Is it after the unctions have been completed by the seventh priest—or after the first unction of the first priest? If the former, how can the effect of the

---

69 Quinn actually does espouse this theory in the question of the unity of Extreme Unction. (Cf. *opus cit.*, pp. 80-1).

70 *De Concord. Eccl. Occid. et Orient.*, l. v, c. 6.

71 *Euchologion*, p. 354, n. 37.

sacrament be suspended after its full significance has been expressed fully by the first priest? It would be quite a different problem, perhaps, if the subsequent anointments were made on parts of the body distinct from those anointed by the first priest. But where the six other priests anoint the selfsame organs, once more it must be asked, what further signification of the effects of the sacrament, what fuller expression of the outward sign of the sacrament is made? On the other hand, if the essential grace is conferred after the first unction, and this is increased and perfected by the later ones, we fall into the selfsame difficulty as to how a second unction of the eyes produces a second and increased partial effect, when an increase of the general and essential effect is impossible.

The argument from positive theology in support of validity of repetition in the same danger seems to rest on solidly probable grounds. It can be more easily avoided and ignored than refuted. On the other hand the argument from theological reason is not so cogent. However, we must not forget how fallible theologians were in their argumentations about the "supplying" of the unctions after the decree of the Holy Office in 1906.[72] Not one of them seemed to hit the exact truth. The statement of Pallavicini is very appropriate in this connection: "Ma specialmente ne soggetto che allora si maneggiava, de' sacramenti; vedevasi depender il tutto dall' arbitraria instituzione di Dio, senza che vi rimanesse quasi alcun opera all' umano discorso per trarne conclusioni infallibili."[73] At any rate, adherence to the view which holds validity of repetition has some advantages. In the first place it gives a logical explanation of the Greeks in their seven-fold unction. Secondly, it saves us from the temerity of asserting, at least implicitly, a sweeping condemnation of a one-time widespread practice—a course which the wise theologian hesitates to take.

72 Cf. *infra*, chap. xii, p. 385.

73 *Istoria del Concilio di Trento*, t. II, l. XII, cap. 12, n. 18.

CHAPTER II.

THE ELEMENTS OF EXTREME UNCTION

CANON 937.

"Extremae unctionis sacramentum conferri debet per sacras unctiones, adhibito oleo olivarum rite benedicto, et per verba in ritualibus libris ab Ecclesia probatis praescripta.

CHAPTER II.

The titles of the first part of Book III of the Code treat of the sacraments in the order of enumeration made by the Council of Trent.[1] Consequently the fifth title of this part is inscribed "De Extrema Unctione." It is divided into three chapters and eleven canons. The first chapter deals with the minister of this sacrament, and contains two canons. The second chapter disposes of the subject of Extreme Unction in five canons. Chapter Three treats of the rites and ceremonies of the sacrament, and comprises three canons. Canon 937 stands alone, an introduction to the ten which follow.

Though couched in general terms befitting an introduction, it embodies the doctrines of Trent and the Popes. There is explicit mention of its sacramental nature, of its remote and proximate matter and of the form. It omits all mention of the minister and of the subject, for they are external to the sacrament and also because they are treated specifically in the later canons.

"Extremae Unctionis sacramentum."

Unlike in the case of matrimony,[2] the Code does not formulate a distinct canon stating the sacramentality of Extreme Unction. It takes this for granted by employing the phrase "the sacrament of Extreme Unction." Yet denials of this fundamental truth by heretics have led the Church to proclaim over and over again the true doctrine in this matter.[3] Even as late as 1907 Pius X condemned the modernistic view:[4] "Jacobus in sua epistola non intendit promulgare aliquod sacramentum Christi, sed commendare pium aliquem morem, et si in hoc more forte cernit medium aliquod gratiae, id non accipit eo rigore, quo acceperunt theologi, qui rationem et numerem sacramentorum statuerunt."

1 Sess. VII, *De Sac. in genere*, can. 1.
2 can. 1012.
3 Cf. *supra*, chap. I, sect. II, p. 6 sqq.
4 S. C. S. Off., *"Lamentabili,"* 3 Jul. 1907 *Errores Modernistarum*, n. 48, A.S.S., XL, 476.

The Code continues:

"Conferri debet per sacras unctiones."

The announcement of the proximate matter of the sacrament is contained in these words. The plural "unctiones" is used, not because more than one unction is essential, but because in the ordinary mode of administration several anointings are required by Ritual.

Suarez[5] tells of an opinion which held that this sacrament consisted in the "oleum ab episcopo benedictum;" and that the unctions were but the application of a sacrament already confected. Those who proposed this were probably influenced by a comparison of this sacrament with the Eucharist, which has a permanent "esse." Yet this opinion can have no basis in fact. Its proponents failed to recognize that thru the consecration of the Eucharist the very Author of grace is not only signified but actually becomes present, while in the blessing of the oil, grace is neither given nor signified. Moreover the essential form of the sacrament would be the prayer used in the blessing of the oil, not that used when anointing the body. The essential form of the Eucharist is not the prayer "Corpus Domini" &c. said in the administration of Holy Communion. With no less certainty "Per istam sanctam unctionem" &c. would not be the form of Extreme Unction. This is certainly contrary to the doctrines of the Church on this point.[6]

Moreover, if Extreme Unction consists in blessed oil, then blessed water, and not the ablution, is the sacrament of Baptism. Yet from the very words of Christ, "baptizantes eos," we learn that the proximate matter of baptism consists in an action. Similarly we can deduce what the proximate matter of Extreme Unction is from the words of the Apostle, "ungentes eum."

In the third place, if such were the case, the proper minister of Extreme Unction would be the bishop—and not the priest, unless he had an Apostolic faculty.[7] A priest, when an-

---

5 Disp. 40, sect. 2, n. 1.

6 Cf. Conc. Trid., Sess. XIV, *De Ext. Unct.*, cap. 1, in fine.; Eugene IV, const. *"Exultate Deo"* (in Conc. Florentin.) 22 Nov. 1439, paragr. 14, C. I. C. Fontes, n. 52.

7 Can. 945.

ointing, would simply be a dispenser of the mystery, in the same fashion as a deacon can distribute the Eucharist.

Finally the valid reception of the sacrament would not depend upon its application by a priest any more than that of the Eucharist does. Even a layman would be able to apply it validly, and in case of extreme necessity would probably be allowed to do this licitly.

It can be seen how absolutely foundless such a doctrine is. And more—it is in positive discord with the teachings of the Council of Trent: "Intellexit enim Ecclesia materiam esse oleum ab Episcopo benedictum; nam unctio aptissime Spiritus Sancti gratiam qua invisibiliter aegrotantis anima inungitur, repraesentat."[8] Here oil blessed by a bishop is said to be the *matter* of the sacrament, not the sacrament itself. From this it follows that the form of the sacrament is not the prayer used in the blessing of the oil, for this has already been said. It consists of the words spoken at the very moment that the matter is applied to the subject. The prayer of blessing simply constitutes the oil valid matter of the sacrament.

The number and places of the unctions is the first consideration proposed by this canon. The Scriptural text furnishes no definite enlightenment, for St. James simply wrote "ungentes eum oleo." Hence the Scholastics had to deal with the question as to whether the whole body must be anointed. St. Bonaventure[9] gives the reasons for and against this problem, and decides that only seven parts of the body are to be anointed, viz., the five senses, the feet and the reins, because these represent fully the sources of sins, whose deletion is the purpose of Extreme Unction. Similarly the Angelic Doctor solves the question: "The sacrament is shown to us under the form of a healing. Now bodily healing has to be effected, by applying the remedy, not to the whole body, but to the parts where the root of the disease is seated. Consequently the sacramental unction also ought to be applied to those parts only in which the spiritual sickness is rooted."[10]

---

8 Sess. XIV, *De Ext. Unct.*, cap. 1.

9 *Comm. in quart. lib. Sent.*, dist. 23, a. 2, q. 3.

10 *The Summa Theologica of St. Thom. Aquin., Suppl.*, q. 32, a. 5 (Translated by the Fathers of the Eng. Dom. Province).

It is certain today that the unction of the whole body is not required. Such an extensive application of oil is no more necessary in this sacrament than the ablution of the entire body in Baptism. Nor has such ever been the practice of the Church. All the rituals are content with defining certain prominent parts of the body to be anointed. Yet there is no unanimity in this regard among the various Rituals, either of the East or of the West. The places of unction prescribed by them, as well as the number of anointings to be made, have differed immensely thru the course of time.

Theodulf, the bishop of Orleans in the ninth century, testifies in his *Capitulare*:

> "Apostoli, ungentes oleo infirmos, non amplius quam tres cruces cum oleo super eos faciebant. Unde Graeci, qui ipsam Traditionem apostolorum imitantur, similiter tres tantum cruces cum oleo faciunt, fundentes cum ampulla oleum infirmorum in crucis modum super caput et vestimenta et totum corpus infirmi, incipientes crucem a capite usque ad pedes, in transverso a manu dextra usque ad brachia et pectus usque ad sinistram manum, semel dicentes ad ipsas tres cruces: 'Ungo te in nomine Patris et Filii et Spiritus Sancti ut oratio fidei salvet te et alleviet te Dominus et si in peccatis sis, remittantur tibi.' "[11]

Yet if this ritual was universal at all, its universality was short-lived, for Goar produces in his "Euchologion[12]" a Greek ritual of the ninth century which ordered unctions on the forehead, the ears and the hands.

In interesting contrast to these, there is the ritual prescribed by Symeon, the Orthodox archbishop of Thessalonica in the fifteenth century:

> "Ungit oleo ad modum crucis ipsius frontem ob contentas in eo cogitationes; faciem quoque inungit propter sensuum organa, postremo manus a pravis cogitationibus et operibus eum expians, sanctoque oleo et signo crucis muniens et perfecte sanctificans."[13]

Two centuries later Arcudius gives a still different rite, making apparent how very little fixity there has been in the

---

11 M. P. L., 105, 221.
12 p. 348.
13 *Liber de Sacramentis*, "*De Sacro Ritu S. Olei.*"—M. P. G., 155, 515 & 527.

Oriental procedure:

> "Graecorum sacerdotes ungunt aegri frontem, mentum, ambas genas, ita ut fieri videatur unctio in capite ad modum crucis; deinde pectus, tum manus idque ex utraque parte, postremo pedes."[14]

Yet a contemporary, Metrophanes Critopulus,[15] speaks of a rite wherein unctions were made only on the forehead, breast, hands and feet.

Today some of the Uniats anoint in the same fashion as the Roman Church. Others retain the order of unctions mentioned by Arcudius. The schismatics also differ among themselves in regard to the parts of the body anointed, but none of them accept the Roman custom.[16]

The same, if not more, diversity of ritualistic observance marks the Latin Church in regard to the number and places of unctions.

The Gregorian Sacramentary, which has come from the hands of Gregory the Great, prescribes unctions "on the neck and throat and between the shoulders; and on the breast or in the place of pain."[17] A note is added to the effect that many priests anoint the sick "insuper in quinque sensus corporis, i. e., in superciliis oculorum et in naribus deintus et in narium summitate sive exterius et in labiis exterius, et in manibus exterius, i. e., deforis."[18]

It is clear that unction of the senses is considered altogether supererogatory. An old Pontifical of the Library of the Parisian Dominicans "*ad portam Sanjacobaeam*"[19] orders, even for cases of necessity, unctions upon the crown of the head, the forehead, the ears, the eyes, the nose, the lips, the

---

14 *De Concord. Eccl. Occident. et Orient. in Septem Sacram. Admininst.*, l. 5, cap. 7.

15 *Confessio*, c. 13.

16 Cf. Kern, *Tract. de Ext. Unct.*, p. 134, footnote.

17 M. P. L., 78, 235.

18 L. c. N. B. Although the anointing of the five senses is mentioned in this note, nevertheless the enumeration of the organs, according to the text of Migne, includes the nose twice and omits the ears altogether. "Naribus" is evidently a misprint for "auribus"; and is translated "ears" by Quinn (*Some Aspects of the Dogma of Extreme Unction*, p. 65). This is further confirmed by the sentence which follows the above text in the Sacramentary: "Hoc enim faciunt ut si in *quinque* sensus mentis et corporis aliqua macula inhaesit hac medicina Dei sanetur."

19 Launoi, *Op. Omnia*, t. I, p. 575.

breast, the shoulder-blades, the hands and the feet. In direct antithesis to this rite which demanded so many unctions, the ancient mozarabic ritual prescribed but one single anointment, and that "in capite."[20]

The old Code of Ratoldi[21] gives unctions for the ears, nose, lips, breast, shoulder-blades, hands and feet. The omission of the eyes is noteworthy.

An ancient *Ordo* of the Church of Tours decreed four unctions: "in collo, in gutture, et inter scapulas, et in pectore seu loco ubi dolor imminet."[22]

A ritual of Rheims, just as old, ordered anointings "in vertice capitis, in superciliis oculorum, in auribus deintus, in narium summitate, in labiis exterius, in planta pedum."[23] Here the unction of the hands is omitted, a rare thing when the anointments of the other senses are prescribed.

Few of the ancient *Ordines* were content with the unction of the senses only. Thus the *Codex Arremarensis*[24] adds to the unctions of the senses the anointing of the feet, throat, neck, shoulder-blades, and navel or place of pain. Similarly, the *Codex Tilianus*[25] prescribed the oil to be applied "in collo et gutture et pectore et inter scapulas, seu in loco ubi dolor plus imminet et in quinque sensibus corporis" &c. The unctions

> "In dextro tempore et sinistro, non in fronte nec in vertice . . . item in superciliis et sublicíis juxta angulos oculorum. . . . Item aures intus et foris in summitate crucis signa recipiunt. . . . Item nares in summitate et subtus inungantur crucis modo. . . . Item labia, dicendo, &c. . . . et exterius super mentum et guttur faciendum . . . item super humeros duos, hoc est, scapulas, non in pectore, neque inter scapulas. . . . Item super manus; et si presbyter est, non infra: sin aliter et infra. . . . Et super pedes et sub plantis cruces fiunt."

---

20 "*Ordo ad vistitandum vel perungendum infirmum*"—apud *Monumenta Ecclesiae Liturgica* (ed. Cabrol et Leclerq), vol. V: "*Le liber Ordinum en usage dans l'eglise Wisigothique et Mozarabe d'Espagne du 5—II siècle*, p. 71.

21 Launoi, *Op. Omnia*, t. 1, p. 574.

22 Martene, *De Antiq. Eccl. Rit.*, l. 1, c. 7, a. 4, Ordo IV.

23 Martene, l.c., Ordo VIII (tenth century).

24 De Sainte-Beuve, *De Sac. Ext. Unct.*, disp. III, a. II, apud Migne, *Curs. Theol. Comp.*, vol. xxiv, 89.

25 M. P. L., 78, 22.

decreed by the *Codex Remigio-Remensis*[26] are very numerous and interesting. The oil was to be applied
A still greater number of unctions was prescribed by the *Codex Siculus,* the ancient *ordo* of Salzburg. Not only the five senses were designated, but also the head, neck, throat, breast, heart, shoulder-blades, feet, the place of pain and all joints.[27] A huge number of anointings was also commanded by the "Liber Sacramentorum" of St. Gatian of Tours.[28] Crosses of oil were to be made "in collo, in gutture, et inter scapulas, et in pectore, et in quinque sensibus corporis, in genibus quoque, et in cruribus, suris, pedibus ac plantis, et pene in omnibus membris, seu in illo loco ubi dolor plus imminet."

In the Church of Noyon[29] nine unctions were made, viz., upon the five senses, the neck, the throat, the shoulders and the breast. To these nine the *Codex Ecclesiae Floriacensis*[30] added another unction, "ad cerebrum." All ten plus an additional unction of the place of pain are given by the *Codex Cl. V. Domini Desmarais.*[31]

In Soissons the five senses were anointed together with the breast, shoulder-blades and feet; and the unction of the ears preceded that of the eyes.[32]

The very same places of unction were noted in the *Missale Romaricense*[33] but the order in which the unctions were to be made was slightly different. To these unctions the Pontifical of Sens[34] adds that of the throat, while the Ritual of Beauvais[35] adds both the neck and the throat.

The Pontifical of Amiens[36] omits the unction of the lips, but adds to those of the other four senses the anointments of the throat, breast and feet. The Ritual of the Church of St. Mary of Rheims[37] prescribed crosses of oil for the crown of the head,

---

26 Launoi, *Op. Omnia,* t. I, p. 575.
27 Martene, *De Antiq. Eccl. Rit.*, l. 1, c. 7, a. 4, Ordo XII.
28 Martene, l.c., Ordo III.
29 Martene, l.c., Ordo X.
30 Martene, l.c., Ordo XXI.
31 Martene, l.c., Ordo XXIII.
32 Martene, l.c., Ordo XIII.
33 Martene, l.c., Ordo XIV.
34 Martene, l.c., Ordo XV.
35 Martene, l.c., Ordo XVII.
36 Martene, l.c., Ordo XXIV.
37 Martene, l.c., Ordo VIII.

the eyes, ears, nose, lips and feet, thus omitting the hands; whereas the Church of St. Mary Magdalen near Le Mans[38] ordered, besides the unction of the five senses, an unction of the feet and of the navel. In Cambrai the lips were not mentioned, but there were many unctions none the less. Here the crown of the head, the forehead, both temples, the face, the eyes, the ears, the nose, the throat, the neck, between the shoulder-blades, between the breasts, the hands, the feet and the navel or place of pain, were assigned for unction.[39]

The Pontifical of Emesa in Syria[40] ordered the unction of the five senses, then added the announcement: "Juxta consuetudinem quorundum ungitur in pectore . . . similiter et in umbilico," and finally directs the unction of the feet. Priests in Châlons-sur-Marne were instructed by their Ritual[41] to anoint the eyes, the ears, the nose, the shoulder-blades ("super scapulas, non in pectore neque inter scapulas") the hands and the feet. Yet those who followed the Ritual of the Monastery of *Moisacensis*[42] anointed, in addition to the five senses and the neck and the throat, the very places which the Ritual of Châlons forbade, viz., the breast and *"inter scapulas."*

The Ritual of Verdun[43] surprisingly omits the unction of the nose, and prescribes anointments for the neck, the throat, the place of pain and the head. A very old Ordo of the Roman Church directs the oil to be applied to the five senses and leaves optional the anointing of the feet and reins.[44]

This investigation into the positive practice of the administration of Extreme Unction is advantageous. The wide variance of rite before the sixteenth century goes far to explain the Church's power, exemplified in Canon 947, to declare that one single unction is eminently sufficient to confer the sacrament. When the unction of the five senses became universal in the West toward the end of the sixteenth century, theological opinion bcame so fixed that up until 1906 the validity of a single unction was represented in most theological text-books as ex-

---

38 Martene, l.c., Ordo XXVI.
39 Martene, l.c., Ordo XVI.
40 Martene, l.c., Ordo XX.
41 Martene, l.c., Ordo XXVII.
42 Martene, l.c., Ordo IX.
43 Launoi, *Op. Omnia*, t. I, p. 578.
44 Launoi, op. cit., p. 575.

tremely dubious. Yet history proves decisively that the places of unction are not of necessity unalterably determined. They have varied more or less according as they seemed to express most fittingly the inward significance of the sacrament in the eyes of those who composed the rituals of the respective Churches.

This proves that the canon, in ordering the sacrament to be conferred "per sacras unctiones," had good reason not to become too specific in its statement of the places of unction. Even today additional unctions are made in the various dioceses which do not use the Roman Ritual. The last edition of the Roman Ritual gives but six places of unction, omitting, as it does, all mention of the reins. By this canon a priest is commanded to follow his own ritual. Hence he who omits an unction prescribed by his own ritual, though not directed by the Roman Ritual, is guilty of a serious sin of disobedience against the prescriptions of this canon.[45]

The amount of oil to be used in an unction and the extent or size of the unctions have hardly been questioned. Any application of oil which verifies the common estimation of unction suffices.

It has been debated, however, whether a single drop of oil would be sufficient to confer the sacrament. Though of little practical value, many authors have discussed the question. Suarez denies the possibility of considering the use of only one drop of oil as a true unction. He writes: "Non enim erit satis unicam guttam olei stillare, quia id vel non est ungere vel certe est res aliquo modo dubia, sed oportet partem corporis oleo linere, aliquid per illam diffundendo; hoc enim est proprie et in rigore ungere."[46]

Other great theologians have taken the opposite view. La Croix,[47] Diana[48] and Kenrick[49] think such an application of oil a sufficient unction. St. Alphonsus[50] calls the affirmative opinion the more probable one, provided that the five senses are

45 Cf. also Can. 947, § 1.
46 D. 40, s. 2, n. 4.
47 *Th. M.*, lib. VI, p. II, n. 2094.
48 *Op. Coord.*, tom. II, tr. IV, res. VI.
49 *Th. M.*, III, de E. U., cap. unic., n. 3.
50 *Th. M.*, VI, 709, dub. 4; cf. St. Alph., *Prax. Conf.*, n. 275, 1.

touched. Gury,[51] Aertnys[52] and Ferreres[53] agree with St. Alphonsus, but Konings[54] refuses to concede the opinion more than mere probability.

In practice consequently it is necessary—as the "pars tutior"—to make a real unction by spreading with the thumb (or virgula) the holy oil upon the organs anointed. It would seem, speculatively, that if all the senses were touched even with the same drop, there would be a true diffusion. However De Herdt[55] advises that the thumb be dipped anew into the oil before the unction of each individual sense. Since no extent of the unction is prescribed, the priest may make it any reasonable size, remembering all the while that the very least "diffusio" suffices.

"Adhibito oleo olivarum"

The remote matter of our sacrament is stated here. This has been treated at some length in Chapter I[56] and little could be said that is not repetition.

In all rites in union with the Church olive oil is used.[57] A writer in the *Kirchelexicon,*[58] speaks of a report that cottonseed oil was used in quite recent times in North America. Such a practice, if it ever really existed, was certainly an abuse. It may have occurred from a falsification of the oils by manufacturers. At any rate bishops and priests must be careful in this regard. The Second Plenary Council of Baltimore[59] laid

51 *Comp. Th. M.*, II, 681.
52 *Th. M.*, II, n. 357.
53 *Comp. Th. M.*, II, 835, quaer. 10.
54 *Th. M.*, n. 1502, q. 11.
55 *Lit. Prax.*, III, 200.
56 Cf. *supra*, p. 24 sqq.
57 Denziger notes that the Armenians seem to use butter in place of oil at times. "Oleum olivae idque benedictum ad unctionem extremam adhibendum esse, nisi Armenos forsan excipias, qui aliquando butyrum loco olei usurpasse videntur." (*Rit. Orient.*, t. I, p. 185.)
58 Vol. IX, col. 712; cf. Ephem. Lit., V, (1891), 443.
59 Tit. V. cap. 7, n. 311: "Oleum ex oliva ad hoc sacramentum administrandum requiri constat. Curandum igitur est omni studio, ne olea adulterina, quae circumferuntur hoc nomine falso insignita, ad ungendos infirmos adhibeantur. Quum vero manifesta res sit, id quod tanquam oleum ex oliva fere ubique venditatur, ita callida arte confici, vel aliis oleis ex cetis aut larido ita misceri et obrui, ut olivi nil nisi nomen habeat; excitanda est Episcoporum sollicitudo et diligentia, ut per Catholicos optimae fidei mercatores verum et purum olivum ab Europa quotannis advehendum curent, ea saltem quantitate, quae omnium dioeceseon necessitatibus pro hujus et aliorum sacramentorum administratione sufficere possit."

down a very serious warning in the matter, and some years later the Holy Office called attention to a very widespread adulteration of the oil intended for the sacraments.[60]

"Rite benedicto."

It has already been shown that some blessing is needed to make the oil valid matter for Extreme Unction.[61] The words of this phrase are in keeping with the general terminology of the canon. The oil is to be blessed *"rite,"* i. e., according to the rite prescribed. A fuller discussion of this rite and of the exact quality of the blessing must be reserved to the treatment of Canon 945.

"Per verba in ritualibus libris ab Ecclesia probatis praescripta"

The number and variety of the forms that have been employed in Extreme Unction are extremely divergent. A speculative treatment of their validity has already been given in Chapter I.[62] An excursion into the realms of their history is interesting and of great value in arriving at a true judgment of what is really essential in them after all.

Greek forms have been consistently deprecative in nature,[63] but in the Latin Rite the variance has been most marked. Some are indicative, others optative, others deprecatory, others imperative; while still others are a combination of two or more of these. Some express one effect, some another, while some try to express all the effects of the sacrament.

In the thirty Ordines given by Martene,[64] fifteen[65] are indicative, seven [66] are optative, two [67] are deprecative, one [68] is

---

60 S. C. S. Off., 9 Jul. 1881—Coll., n. 1556.

61 Cf. *supra*, chapter I, sect. p.

62 Sect. IV, p. .

63 Theodulf of Arles gives an exception to this rule in regard to the rite of the Greeks before the schism. The form then used by them was indicative: "Ungo te in nomine Patris et Filii et Spiritus Sancti, ut oratio fidei salvet te et alleviet te Dominus et si in peccatis sis, remittantur tibi." (M. P. L., 105, 221.)

64 *De Antiq. Rit. Eccl.*, lib. 1, cap. 7, a. 4.

65 Ordines I, III, IV, V, VII, XI, XII, XIV, XVI, XVII, XIX, XX, XXV, XXVII.

66 Ordines VIII, XIII, XV, XXII, XXIV, XXVI, XXIX.

67 Ordines VI et IX.

68 Ordo XXVIII.

imperative, while four[69] are mixed, i. e., a combination of two or more of these.

An equal divergence can be noted in the multitude of Rituals quoted by Launoi.[70] Thus indicative forms are found in the Pontifical of Cambrai,[71] the Manual of Lyons,[72] the Manual of Châlons-sur-Marne,[73] the Manual of Amiens,[74] the Manual of Verdun[75] and the Manual of Metz.[76] The Pontifical of Laon[77] contains an optative form practically the same as the present Roman form: "Per istam sanctam unctionen et suam piissimam misericordiam parcat tibi Dominis quidquid oculorum vitio deliquisti. Amen."

Other rituals give indicative forms for some unctions and optative ones for others. Thus in the Manual of the Church of Vienna[78] all the anointings are done with an indicative form except that of the place of pain, which has an optative accompaniment. The very same occurrence is found in the Manual of Toul,[79] except that the form for the place of pain was deprecative. In the Ritual of Le-Puy-en-Velay[80] all the forms are indicative except that of the throat, which is optative. A very old Pontifical, dating back to the ninth year of the reign of Charlemagne, uses an indicative form for all the anointings except the lips, where it prescribes an optative formula.[81]

Some liturgies give partial indicative forms, but add a prayer, optative in nature to these forms, making the combination practically one complete form. In the Manual of Arras,[82] for instance, the form to be used outside of necessity[83] is indi-

69 Ordines II, X, XVIII, XXIII.
70 *Opera Omnia*, t. I, pp. 464-568.
71 Launoi, op. cit., p. 496-7.
72 anno 1548, Launoi, op. cit., p. 507.
73 anno 1529, Launoi, op. cit., p. 511-2.
74 anno 1541, Launoi, op. cit., p. 516.
75 anno 1554, Launoi, op. cit., p. 524.
76 anno 1542, Launoi, op. cit., p. 526.
77 Launoi, op. cit., p. 501.
78 anno 1500, Launoi, op. cit., p. 503-4.
79 anno 1529, Launoi, op. cit., p. 521.
80 anno 1527, Launoi, op. cit., p. 529.
81 Launoi calls this the *Pontificale Bibliothecae Tilianae*—op. cit., p. 467-8.
82 anno 1563, Launoi, op. cit., p. 517-8.
83 It is well worth while noticing that this Ritual prescribed a form to be used in case of necessity. Its forms were optative; and the unction of the senses and of the feet were all prescribed. (Launoi, op. cit., p. 517-8.)

cative, and is immediately followed by this oration:

> "Per istam sacratissimam unctionem et suam piissimam misericordiam et benedictionem indulgeat tibi Dominus quidquid peccasti per visum, per auditum, per odoratum, per gustum, per tactum, per gressum pedum, et absolvat te ab omnibus peccatis tuis confessis, contritis et negligenter oblitis, in nomine Patris et Filii et Spiritus Sancti. Amen."

A similar oration can be found at the end of the indicative forms prescribed by the Manual of Vannes.[84] A very early Sacramentary, compiled by order of the Abbot Ratholdus, about the year 986, uses an indicative form with an optative oration as the complement.[85] A similar occurrence is found in the famous *Codex Remigio-Remensis*.[86]

Mixed forms occur in several of the rituals. Thus the Sacramentary of Gregory[87] has an indicative and an optative element in the composition of its form. The Ritual of Soissons[88] prescribes a form partly indicative, partly imperative. A thirteenth century rite, used in the Church of St. Lawrence at Milan,[89] reveals a form partly indicative, partly imperative and partly optative. The Pontifical of Prudentius of Troyes[90] has a form whose character is partly indicative, partly optative and partly deprecatory.

These are but a few of the different forms which actually have been used in the course of the centuries. They are enough, however, to prove that the forms have differed as much as the places of unction.

The present canon does not declare the validity or invalidity of any of them. It simply binds every priest to the use of his own ritual, be it Roman, Ambrosian, diocesan or monastic. On the point Benedict XIV wrote: "Injungendum est parochis ut formam adhibeant in Rituali praescriptam, quae certe sine gravi flagitio, non potest privata auctoritate immutari."[91]

Whether a Greek priest, guilty of using a valid form other than that prescribed by his rite, would violate this canon is

84 anno 1596, Launoi, op. cit., p. 519.
85 Launoi, op. cit., p. 483-4.
86 Launoi, op. cit., p. 489-90.
87 M. P. L., 78, 235.
88 anno 1530, Launoi, op. cit., p. 513.
89 Magistretti, *Manuale Ambrosianum*, t. I, p. 147 s.
90 Martene, *De Antiq. Rit. Eccl.*, lib. 1, c. 7, a. 4.
91 *De Syn. Dioc.*, l. 8, c. 2.

hard to say. It might possibly be argued that this canon treats of a matter which of its nature affects Orientals.[92] The different terminology used in this canon and in Canon 2 is also worthy of note. Canon 2 speaks of "libri liturgici ab *Ecclesia Latina* probati;" whereas this canon uses the phrase "in ritualibus libris ab *Ecclesia* probatis." It is evident that the latter phrase is wider in scope, at least *prima facie,* than the former.

---

92 Canon 1.

CHAPTER III.

THE MINISTER OF EXTREME UNCTION

CANON 938.

1. Hoc sacramentum valide administrat omnis et solus sacerdos.

2. Salvo praescripto can. 397, n. 3, 514, 1-3, minister ordinarius est parochus loci, in quo degit infirmus; in casu autem necessitatis, vel de licentia saltem rationabiliter praesumpta ejusdem parochi vel Ordinarii loci, alius quilibet sacerdos hoc sacramentum ministrare potest.

CHAPTER III.

I. The Valid Minister

Hoc sacramentum valide administrat omnis et solus sacerdos.

This paragraph enshrines a dogma of our faith. The Council of Trent has anathematized those who teach any other doctrine. In Sess. XIV, *De Ext. Unct.*, can. 4, the Sacred Synod declared: "Si quis dixerit presbyteros Ecclesiae, quos B. Jacobus adducendos esse ad infirmum ungendum hortatur, non esse sacerdotes ab episcopo ordinatos, sed aetate seniores in quavis communitate; ob idque proprium Extremae Unctionis ministrum non esse solum sacerdotem, A. S."

Even as early as the year 416 there was some doubt as to the capability of priests to administer this sacrament. Pope Innocent I dispelled this doubt in his letter to Decentius, the Bishop of Eugubinus.[1] "Ceterum illud," he wrote, "superfluum videmus adjectum ut de episcopo ambigatur; quod presbyteris licere non dubium est. Nam idcirco de presbyteris dictum est, quia episcopi occupationibus aliis impediti, ad omnes languidos ire non possunt." Origen had even before that ancient date borne witness to the very same interpretation of St. James' "*presbyteri;*"[2] and the identical exegesis was rendered also by St. Chrysostom.[3]

In the early centuries the controversy waged about whether the rite of unction was solely an episcopal function or not. Such questions probably arose from the fact that in those ages Bishops very often did confer the last rites of the Church. Many historical documents tell of actual anointings by Bishops. E. g., Charlemagne was anointed by a bishop; St. Adalard was likewise honored (as St. Gerard wrote in the Life of that saint); the Empress Mathilda received Extreme Unction from Archbishop Willelmus; Ferdinand the King of Spain (Castile) was

1 Ep., "*Si instituta ecclesiastica,*" cap. 8—C. I. C. Fontes, No. 19.
2 *Homilia II in Leviticum*, M. P. G., 12, 418B.
3 *De Sacerdotio*, lib. III, sect. 6—M. P. G., 48, 644.

attended by a Bishop, etc.[4] Moreover the ancient rituals declared that if a Bishop were present, the rite of unction was his privilege.[5] Durandus [6] discusses the impropriety of being later anointed by a priest, when one has been anointed by a Bishop.

Several particular Councils vindicated to priests the power to anoint. E. g., the Council of Châlons-sur-Saone (813) prescribed: "Secundum beati Jacobi apostoli documentum, cui etiam documenta patrum consentiunt, infirmi oleo, quod ab episcopis benedicitur, a presbyteris ungi debent."[7] Other councils, as those of Aachen, (836),[8] Magonza (847),[9] and Pavia (850),[10] legislated in a similar vein.[11]

In later years the pendulum swung dangerously near the heretical end of the arc of theological thought, when Thomas Netter, a Carmelite of Walden,[12] denied the necessity of the presence of Orders in the minister for the valid confection of this sacrament. Launoi[13] trespassed beyond the hedge-rows of Catholic dogma in his contention that deacons, in case of necessity could, with the Bishop's permission, administer this sacrament. He defended his opinion on the ground that, since a deacon could administer Viaticum and, as was widely thought in the Middle Ages, receive confessions, he could also administer Extreme Unction. However the constant and insistent declarations of the Church, demanding the sacerdotality of the minister, and the remarkable clarity of the text of St. James [14] effected the prevention of any notable discussion on this important matter.

Church legislation and instruction in this regard abounds. The Corpus Juris Canonici contained not only the letter of Innocent I,[15] but also a decision of Alexander III[16] which

4 Cf. Catalano, *Rit. Rom.*, t. I, p. 323.
5 Martene, *De Antiq. Ecc. Rit.*, l. I, c. 7, a. 4 (Ordo XII).
6 *Rationale Div. Officiorum*, l. I, c. 8, n. 25.
7 Can. 48—Harduin IV, 1040.
8 Cap. II, can. 5—Harduin IV, 1397.
9 Harduin V, 13.
10 Harduin V, 27.
11 Cf. Hurter, *Th. D. Comp.*, III, p. 479.
12 *Doct. Antiq. Fidei*, t. II, c. 163, n. 3.
13 *Op. Omnia*, t. I, p. 569, observ. II.
14 Cf. *supra*, chap. I, sect. II, p. 8 sqq.
15 C. 3, D, XCV.
16 C. 14, X, *de verb. signif.*, V, 40.

teaches, at least implicitly, the necessity of ministry by a priest. Eugene IV, in his Constitution "*Exultate Deo,*"[17] stated: "Minister hujus sacramentum est sacerdos." Soon after came the declaration of the Council of Trent, only to be followed by an order of Benedict XIV[18] forbidding pastors to send the holy oils to the sick for self-unction.

Despite such an imposing array of decisions and definitions, D. A. Boudinhon, as late as 1905, was bold enough to declare in the "Revue Catholique des Églises"[19] that lay people could not only anoint one another but also their very selves, on the alleged ground that such was the custom of the patristic ages. He seems to have overlooked entirely the definition of Trent, declaring "*proprium* Ext. Unct. ministrum esse solum sacerdotem." The force of "proprium" here has been held by positive and scholastic theologians[20] to be equivalent to "solum;" and consequently that it is *de fide* that priests alone can administer this sacrament. Their conclusion is reënforced by a comparison of the language of the Council of Trent on the minister of Confirmation. The Council[21] did not call the bishop the minister "proprius" of Confirmation, but the minister "ordinarius." Thus allowance was made for the delegation to a priest of the power to administer that sacrament. No such deduction is possible from the language of the Council with regard to the minister of Extreme Unction.

Neither has the argument much weight which holds that, since Extreme Unction has matter already consecrated, it can like the Eucharist be validly administered by anybody. In the first place, administration of the Eucharist is not its confection, whereas administration of Extreme Unction includes its confection. Indeed, many theologians have held that the very fact

17 Nov. 22, 1439, paragr. 14—C. I. C. Fontes, No. 52.

18 Const. "*Ex quo,*" March 1, 1756, paragr. 47—C. I. C. Fontes, No. 438.

19 July, 1905, vol. II, p. 401, sqq.; cf. also "*Canoniste Contemp.,*" vol. XXX (1907), p. 643 sqq.

20 E.g., cf. Suarez, disp. 43, s. 1, n. 2; Nugnus, in *Suppl. S. Thom.*, q. 31, a. 2; Gonet, *Clyp. Theol. Thomist.*, t. VI, *de Ext. Unct.*, dis. 3, a. 2, paragr. 14, p. 716; Mastrius, *Th. M.*, disp. 22, qu. 6, a. I; Frassen, *De Sac. E. U.*, disp. 3, q. 3, con. 2; Sylv. Maurus, t. III, q. 260; Drouven, *De Re Sacr.*, l. 7, q. 4, c. 2; Sasse, *De Sacr.*, t. II, p. 264; Gihr, *Die hl. Sakramente*, t. II, p. 294; Pohle-Preuss, *The Sacraments*, vol. IV, p. 38; Heimbucher, *Die hl. Olung*, p. 240; Tanquerey, *Th. D.*, III, p. 545.

21 Sess. VII, *De Confirmatione*, can. 3.

that the matter has been consecrated is a reason for the need of a consecrated minister.[22]

There are three patristic texts which on first face seem to afford a basis for Boudinhon's contention. The first is from the much-quoted letter of Innocent I: "Non est dubium quod de fidelibus aegrotantibus accipi vel intelligi debere, qui sancto oleo chrismatis perungi possunt; quo ab episcopo confecto, non solum sacerdotibus sed *omnibus uti* Christianis licet in sua aut suorum necessitate inungendo."[23]

Divorced from its context, this quotation seems rather convincing; but a review of the entire epistle will furnish the correct impression that the doubt decided by Innocent was not whether or not the ministration of this sacrament might be extended to the laity, but rather whether it was an exclusively episcopal function or not. Decentius questioned even the validity of priestly unction, and hence there was no query at all about the capability of laymen in the matter. The word "uti" is used in a passive sense, i. e., "uti licet," *sed ministerio sacerdotum.*[24] Some authors[25] maintain that an official and a private use of the oil has been distinguished by the Pope—and that, consequently, the unction, when private, was merely a sacramental, while the official unction was a sacrament whose administration was reserved to bishops and priests. The Pope in no way—as is deducible from the mention of "priests" in the passage—considered the unction by laymen as identical with that of the Jacobean rite, but at most he regarded it as a devotional use of the oil, probably for charismatic purposes. To understand this text in a causative way, i. e., that the laity should have the oil at hand so as to insure anointment by priests is not impossible, nor altogether irrational. It does seem however to have a forced, unnatural meaning; for we have an abundance of evidence declaring the charismatic and devotional use of the holy oils by the laity in the early centuries.[26] Schell

---

22 Cf. St. Bonaventure, *Comm. in. lib. quarti Sent.*, dist. xxiii, a. II, qu. I.

23 Ep. "*Si instituta ecclesiastica,*" 19 Mar. 416, cap. 8, M. P. L., 20, 559; also C. I. C. Fontes, No. 19.

24 Cf. Hurter, *Th. D. Comp.*, III, p. 478, footnote 1.

25 Cf. Pohle-Preuss, *The Sacraments*, IV, p. 14; Bord, *L'Extrême Onction*, p. 102.

26 Cf. S. Thom. Aquin., *Suppl.*, q. 31, a. 1 ad 2.

suggests another explanation:[27] The Pope's decision is probably to be understood as applying to a sort of unction by desire in case if necessity (an analogue of lay confession), manifesting the patient's good will to do what is in his power.[28]

St. Eligius, bishop of Noyon (640-59), in his treatise "*De Rectitudine Catholicae Conversationis,*" wrote: "Qui aegrotat in sola Dei misericordia confidat, et Eucharistiam corporis et sanguinis Christi cum fide et devotione accipiat, oleumque benedictum fideliter ab Ecclesia petat, unde *corpus suum* in nomine Christi *ungat* et secundum Apostolum oratio fidei salvabit infirmum et alleviabit eum Dominus," etc.[29]

This text loses all corroboration of Boudinhon's contention when it realized not only that many manuscripts read "*ungatur*" instead of "*ungat,*" but also that the custom of the Greek language often allowed the use of the active form in a passive sense. St. Eligius was speaking of the anointment "in nomine Christi" and "secundum Apostolum." Hence he referred to the unction performed as the Apostle prescribed, i. e., by priests. Moreover, it was not infrequent for the Greeks to speak of the subject in the active voice (ὁ ποιῶν, ὁ ποήσας τὸ εὐχέλαιον) or in the middle voice (ὁ ἐπαλειψάμενος). All these conspire to show that St. Eligius was speaking of the reception rather than of the administration of this sacrament.[30]

The third text is a very ancient one whose author was probably St. Caesar of Arles. It reads thus:[31] "Quoties aliqua infirmitas supervenerit, corpus et sanguinem Christi ille qui aegrotat accipiat; et inde *corpusculum suum ungat* ut illud, quod scriptum est, impletur in eo: 'Infirmatur aliquis, inducat presbyteros et orent super eum, ungentes eum oleo' . . . Videte fratres, quia qui in infirmitate ad Ecclesiam cucurrerit, et corporis sanitatem recipere et peccatorum indulgentiam merebitur obtinere."

The very arguments that have been advanced against the other texts are of the same avail here. It is clear that a passive

---

27 *Kath. Dogmatik,* III (II Teil), 623.

28 Cf. Pohle-Preuss, *The Sacraments,* IV, p. 41-42.

29 n. 5—M. P. L., 40, 1178.

30 Cf. Kern, *Tract. de Ext. Unct.,* pp. 16-17.

31 *Serm. CCLXV, in app. Serm. S. August.*—M. P. L., 39, 2238; cfr. Revue Benedictine, vol. XIII (1898), p. 209; Revue d'histoire et de litterature religieuses, vol. X (1905), p. 606.

sense must be given to "ungat" in this quotation. How could an unction by one's own self fulfill in anyway the precept, "Infirmatur aliquis . . . inducat presbyteros . . . et orent *super eum, ungentes eum* oleo?"

It is inescapable therefore that the sacerdotality of the minister in Extreme Unction is absolutely essential for the valid confection of this sacrament. "Hoc sacramentum valide administrat . . . solus sacerdos."

The Canon reads however—"*omnis* et solus sacerdos." The scope of "omnis" is in no way circumscribed or qualified. Hence it follows that excommunicated, suspended, interdicted and degraded priests are included. The valid administration of the sacrament is a function of Orders—and the power of Orders is not destroyed by any fulminations of the Church.

A priest, however, cannot anoint himself, as Clericatus holds.[32] His stand is based mainly on three arguments: 1) Since it is not repugnant in a case of necessity for a physician to cure himself of a bodily illness, neither is it repugnant for the priest, as spiritual physician, to apply this spiritual medicine to his own soul when it is sick. 2) *Qui potest plus, potest etiam et minus.* It is permitted to a priest to administer to himself, outside of Mass, the Holy Eucharist, when there is no other priest or deacon present, even for devotion's sake. Consequently it is lawful for a priest to administer to himself Extreme Unction, especially in case of extreme necessity. 3) In Matrimony the ministers and the subjects are the same persons. Hence, since there is no repugnance in the fact that the ministers are identical with the subjects, in case of Extreme Unction he who administers can be he who receives.

These arguments are groundless. In the first place, ecclesiastical history adduces few, if any, examples of a priest administering the sacrament to himself. This is a clear indication that there is in the Church a firm persuasion, derived from Tradition, that a priest cannot impart to himself the aids of Unction any more than he can give himself sacramental absolution. Furthermore, since Extreme Unction is the complement of Penance, and since a priest cannot administer Penance

[32] *Decisiones Sacramentales,* "De Ext. Unct.," dec. 75.

to himself, the presumption is against his capability of anointing himself.

Again, it is not true to assert that the administration of Communion is a greater thing than to anoint, for in the administration of Communion there is no confection of a sacrament. There is simply the application of a sacrament already confected, an application permitted even to lay people in the times of the persecutions. With regard to Matrimony, it can be replied that the spouses do not administer the sacrament to themselves, but rather to one another.

There is a certain incongruity in the case of one anointing himself. There does not seem to be the fulfillment of the circumstances that the Jacobean text considers. One can hardly summon himself, pray over himself, and do the various other things connoted or presupposed by the Jacobean text.[33] Moreover, Baptism, though of maximum importance, cannot be administered to one's self; and finally the sacrament of orders is not *in bonum privatum,* but rather *propter utilitatem fidelium* —it is a grace *gratis data* not for one's own sanctification, but for co-operation in the justification of others.

There has been a specific decree of the Congregation for the Propagation of the Faith on this very point. On March 23, 1844, it declared "inspectis ipsis divini eloquii verbis, vel facile patet, sacramentum Extremae Unctionis etiam in casu necessitatis, absente nimirum alio presbytero, non posse missionarium aegrotantem sibi metipsi ministrare."[34]

"Omnis *sacerdos.*"

An inspection of the rituals of the Greek and Western Churches will reveal a difference in regard to the number of the priests required for the administration of this sacrament. Likewise the text of St. James speaks of "priests" while this canon uses the singular number. How are these seeming essential discrepancies to be explained?

The solution of the problem lies in the interpretation of the words "inducat presbyteros ecclesiae." Many explanations have been attempted. Berti[35] argues that the expression is

33 Cf. Diana, *Op. Coord.*, t. II, tr. IV, res. 39.
34 Ferraris, *Prompta Biblioth.*, Suppl., v. "*Ext. Unctio,*" n. 4.
35 *De Theol. Discip.*, t. VIII, "*De Ext. Unct.,*" l. 35, c. 8.

figurative (enallage) and hence in reality only one priest is meant. The objection to such a solution is not only that it is difficult to show from the context but also that it would involve the condemnation of the Oriental mode of administration. Peter Dens[36] and Tanquerey[37] improve somewhat on the explanation of Berti by holding that the plural is used here so as to include the singular number—an idiom not too rare in Scripture. E. g., Luke xvii, 14: "Ite, ostendite vos sacerdotibus," whereas by Leviticus, xiv, 2, we know that presentation of one's self to one priest was sufficient.[38] Similarly, these theologians assert, St. James did not wish to exclude the administration of the unction by a single priest, if more priests were not obtainable.

A better explanation can be given by examining the original text. When St. James wrote "*προσκαλεσάσθω τοὺς πρεσβυτέρους τῆς ἐκκλησίας*," he was speaking to men of his own time. Side by side with larger cities, where a bishop was encircled by many priests to aid him in his duties, there lay small towns, where the bishop alone, or even a presbyter, discharged personally all the sacerdotal functions. James wrote his epistle to the Catholic world, not to any particular city, or nation or people. Hence when he advised the sick to call in "the priests of the church," he meant the priests of the sick man's own parish church, whether it be the bishop alone or the presbyter alone or the bishop with his priests. Suppose, e. g., that St. James had said, "Inducat medicos loci." It would be immediately clear that the apostle was recommending the use of the medical art, and therefore was insinuating that according to the locality one or several physicians were to be summoned. Thus, too, the apostolic mandate of summoning spiritual physicians can be regarded.

There is no solid basis to the contention that the text demands that several priests be summoned in every case. It does not read *προσκαλεσάσθω ἐνίους πρεσβυτέρους* but *τοὺς πρεσβυτέρους τῆς εκκλησίας*. Accordingly the sacrament would be rightly administered by a bishop, by a priest or by several priests. The number of priests "*non spectat ad valorem*"—and one priest

---

36 *Theol. Mech., De Ext. Unct.*, n. 7, p. 45.

37 *Th. D.*, III, 792a.

38 Cf. also Matt. ii, 20; xxvii, 44 & 48; Marc., xv, 36; Joan. xix, 29, for similar examples.

is eminently sufficient. Hence it is within the power of the Church to define "*pro diversitate temporum et locorum*" the number of priests to be employed in this sacramental function. In fact the Church actually exercised this right when she defined the Western practice of using but one priest in the administration of Extreme Unction.[39]

This view is confirmed by a clear and consistent Tradition. From the days of the great Fathers there has been in the Church a firm persuasion that one priest could validly and licitly administer this sacrament. For instance, Callinicius, in relating the life of St. Hypatius (366-446),[40] after a description of the charity of the saint toward the sick, continues: "Si vero necessitas suaderet, infirmum oleo inungi debere monebat abbatem, qui presbyter erat (ἦν λὰρ πρεσβυτέρος) et curabat ab ipso perfici unctionem." Cassiodorus[41] and Isaac of Antioch[42] also speak of the minister in the singular number. Similarly a large number of the rituals of antiquity make provision for but one minister, certifying by actual practice the belief of that time.[43] In the year 1175, Alexander III made an official pronouncement, afterwards incorporated into the decretals of Gregory IX:[44] "Sacerdos, uno praesenti clerico, et etiam solus, potest infirmum ungere." Later Benedict XIV declared:[45] "Nec refert utrum eadem Extrema Unctio per unum vel plures presbyteros fiat, ubi hujusmodi viget consuetudo; dummodo

39 Cfr. Kern, *Tract. De Ext. Unct.*, p. 256; Toner, in the *Cath. Encyc.*, art., "Ext. Unction"; Pohle-Preuss, *The Sacraments*, vol. IV, p. 42.

40 Acta SS., 17 June, t. IV, p. 251.

41 *Complex. in Epp. App.*, "*Ep. S. Jacobi ad Dispersos*," *n. II;* "Si quis alterius praegravatur injuria vel corporis imbecillitate quassatur, presbyterum dicit adhibendum, qui oratione fideli et olei sancti perunctione concessa salvet eum." (M. P. L., 70, 1380.)

42 "Sacerdotem visitatorem non probatum habent stultae ideoque signationem contemnunt . . . At potius, o mulier, donum quidem tribue recluso, sed signationem a sacerdote tuo accipe, Servi Christi . . . afferre solent aegrotos et infirmos ad sanctum altare, non autem ipsi oleum conficere audent . . . sed ubi sacerdos regens est plebem, observant ordines justitiae" (Bickell, *S. Isaaci Antiocheni Opera Omnia,* p. I, page 187).

43 Cf. Martene, *De Antiq. Ecc. Rit.*, l. 1, cap. VII, a. 4 (Ordines XII, XXVIII, XXIX); *Sacramentarium Gregorianum* (ed. by Menard)—M. P. L., 78, 225D; "*Ordo ad visitandum vel Perungendum Infirmum*" (Mozarabic rite)—*Monumenta Ecclesiae Liturgiae* (ed. by Cabrol et Leclerq), vol. V, p. 71.

44 C. 14, X, *de verb. signif.*, V, 40.

45 Const. "*Etsi pastoralis,*" 26 Maii, 1742, paragr. V, n. III—C. I. C. Fontes, n. 328.

credant et asserant illud sacramentum, servata debita forma et materia, ab uno presbytero valide et licite confici."

On the other hand, there is nothing to prevent the valid and licit administration of this sacrament by several priests. Since St. James used the plural, it is manifestly commendable that all the priests of the sick man's church perform the sacramental rite. Hence where there is no positive law on the subject promulgated by the Church for special exigencies, several priests may validly and licitly perform the unction.

This is the unswerving conviction of tradition. Old sacramentaries of the Latin Church reveal the plurality of ministers for this sacrament.[46] Martene's collection[47] furnishes striking corroboration of this fact. Some Greek theologians[48] have so insisted on a plurality of ministers as to declare that an administration by less than three priests was positively invalid.

The antiquity of the rite can be deduced from the practice of the Orientals who separated from the Church in the fifth and sixth centuries. Denziger write: "Orientales septem sacerdotes regulariter huic officio impendere solent vel, si non adsint, quinque vel tres, vel si opus sit, etiam unum."[49]

The ritual of the Greeks united with Rome has not been without the sanction of ecclesiastical authority. The provincial council of the Ruthenians, held in 1720 at Zamos, enacted this decree: "Quamquam in graeca Ecclesia receptum fuerit, prout aliquando etiam in Latina, ut septem sacerdotes, iisque deficientibus tres saltem advocarentur ad ministrandum hoc sacramentum, iique omnes et materiam subministrarent et formam proferrent, sciant tamen pastores, plures ea de causa adhiberi solitos sacerdotes, tum ob reverentiam ejusdem ac gratiae copiam, quam confert, tum ut plurium sacerdotum preces effectum sacramenti coadjuvent. Qua de causa S. Synodus statuendum censet, ut si septem aut tres sacerdotes haberi commode non possint, unus, qui totius Ecclesiae personam gerit,

46 Cf. Catalano, *Rit. Rom.*, t. I, p. 325; *Sacramentarium Gregorianum*, l.c.; *Acta S. Chrotildis*, cap. iii, n. 19—*Acta SS.*, June 3, vol. I, p. 291; *Vita S. Hunegundi*, cap. iii, n. 20—Acta. SS., Aug. 25, vol. V, p. 232.

47 Martene, *l.c.*, Ordines XII, XIX.

48 Cf. Symeon of Thess., "*De Sacro Ritu Sancti Olei,*" c. 288—M. P. G., 155, 518B.

49 *Rit. Orient.*, t. I, p. 188.

ex cujus virtute hoc sacramentum perficit, illud conferat ac infirmo ministret.''[50] A few years later this legislation was ratified by Benedict XIII in his constitution *''Apostolatus officium.''*[51] The quotation given on the preceding page from the constitution *''Etsi pastoralis''* of Benedict XIV asserts this in similar fashion. Hence it becomes obvious that the difference in number of priests administering this sacrament is merely disciplinary, and can be regulated by legislation of the Church.

Today one priest is used in the Latin Church. The Roman Ritual leaves place for but a single minister.[52] The Greeks demand seven priests, if so many are obtainable. Otherwise they are content with five, three or one. The reason why seven are generally employed is said by some to be on account of Extreme Unction's destructive powers against the seven capital sins, by others because of the mystic meaning of the number seven in Scripture, by still others because it corresponds to the number of organs anointed in the Greek ceremony. Many other fanciful reasons have been adduced by Greek devotional writers. For instance, Mesoloras tell us:[53] 'O *ἀριθμός ἕπτα ἀνέχαθεν ἦτο ἰεπός - - ἕπτα ἡμέραι, ἕπτα ἑβδομάδες, ἑπτάρωτος λυχνία, ἕπτα μυστήρια,* etc. Symeon of Thessalonica[54] gives as the reason the analogy between the effect of Extreme Unction and the command of God, in the prophecy of Isaias, that seven priests should stand before the walls of Jericho and blow a trumpet seven times. When this was done, the walls of that city fell to the ground. In Extreme Unction seven priests anoint seven times, the walls of sin fall down, and make possible the entrance of the anointed into the holy city.

The reason why the Latin Church restricts the office of Unction to only one priest is no mystical one. Benedict XIV,[55] sorrowfully ascribes it to the sacrilegious avarice of priests of the Middle Ages. They demanded a high stipend for their work, with the result that many poor died without the sacrament. Yet others are not so harsh against the memory of these

---

50 Tit. III, paragr. 6, *De Ext. Unct.*—Coll. Lac., t. II, p. 38.
51 July 19, 1724—Coll. Lac. t. II, p. 2 sqq.
52 Tit. V, cap. 2.
53 'Εγχειρίδιον p. 220.
54 *De Sacro Ritu Sancti Olei,* c. 288—M. P. G., 155, 515, 518.
55 *De Syn. Dioc.* l. viii, c. 4, n. 6.

priests. Kern[56] attributes it to a rather widespread custom in the Western Church. In testimony of this he points to Martene, who found in thirty old Ordines only three which require the sacramental co-operation of several priests. The origin of such a custom can be assigned to many causes: the lack of priests in rural districts; cases of necessity which frequently occurred and usually demanded an exception; the frequent interference of other business, thus preventing the attendance of some of the priests at the ceremony; the desire of uniformity in ministering to the sick; and perhaps even the cooling of fervor. The consequence was the gradual vanishment of the practice of having several ministers when administering the last rites.

Just a few words need be said about the rite when administered by several priests. There are many possible ways. All may anoint each member at the same time and say the form in unison; all may anoint the same member at one time, while only one says the form; all may say the form while only one anoints; all may simultaneously anoint, each anointing a separate member and saying the proper form for that particular member. Without a doubt all these methods of unction are valid, for the essentials have been placed by the priests as by one moral person.

There are however two questionable modes of unction. First, the sacramental rite may be so divided that, while some anoint silently, the others recite the form without anointing. Menard[57] and Martene[58] hold that this manner of anointing the sick has been prescribed in some ancient rituals. To confer the sacrament in this way has been denounced by Benedict XIV[59] very vehemently. Many theologians[60] consequently think that this procedure is invalid. Nevertheless a more benign view would admit a distinction in this case. It is too cruel to hold that for centuries several rites, perhaps even the Roman Church, did not validly confer Extreme Unction. Since the several

56 *Tract. de Ext. Unct.*, p. 254.
57 M. P. L., 78, 235 sqq.
58 *De Ant. Ecc. Rit.*, l. I, cap. 7, a. 4, Ord. III, IV, V; also cf. l.c., a. 3, paragr. 4; Catalano, *Rit. Rom.*, t. I, p. 333.
59 Const. "*Etsi pastoralis,*" May 26, 1742—Coll. Lac., t. II, p. 511 or C. I. C. Fontes, No. 328.
60 P. Dens, *Theol. Mech.*, "*De Ext. Unct.,*" p. 44.

priests are morally one person constituting in the name of Christ and the Church the sacramental minister of the Unction, it is hard to prove beyond the possibility of doubt that the sacrament is thus invalidly confected—provided, of course, the form be not given a false meaning. Whence it can be concluded that in the absolutely extraordinary case, where only two priests are present, one without hands, the other without speech, it is not prohibited that they should administer Extreme Unction, at least *sub conditione,* by having one priest say the form while the other anoints with oil.[61]

The second mode of unction called into question is that used in some places by the Greeks of today. In conferring the Euchelaion each priest separately and successively goes thru the various unctions, with their corresponding forms. Such a formula is, of course, certainly valid, but the question arises: What does the second, third, fourth, fifth, sixth, and seventh priests' actions avail? Is the sacrament conferred seven times or only once? Since this involves the question of iterability in the same danger of death, the reader is referred to the discussion on that point which has been considered in the first Chapter (cf. page 51 sqq.). This will also be treated later under Canon 940, § 2.

In the Roman Church today it is generally held that one priest alone must be employed in the performance of the actual sacramental rite in the administration of Extreme Unction, except in case of necessity. Such a contingency would arise if the patient were so near to death that the unctions could not be completed by one priest before the sick man's demise. In such a case it would indeed be allowable to proceed under Canon 947, paragraph 1, and to use a single unction with a general form, but such a procedure is not obligatory, if several priests are present who can perform by simultaneous actions the sacramental rite completely.[62] Another case of necessity would occur if a priest swooned, was stricken with paralysis or died after

61 Cf. Kern, *Tract. de Ext. Unct.*, p. 264.

62 Diana, *Op. Coord.*, t. II, tr. IV, res. 22; Suarez, disp. 43, s. 2, n. 5; S. Alph., *Th. M.*, VI, 724; D'Annibale, *Summ. Th. M.*, III, 417; Elbel-Bierbaum, *Th. M.*, Pars VIII, conf. X, n. 217; Kenrick, *Th. M.*, III, "*De Ext. Unct.*," cap. unic., n. 8; Noldin, *De Sac.*, 438 b; Tanquerey, *Th. D.*, III, 792.

commencing the unctions and before their completion. A second priest may then finish the rite, provided that there be a moral unity between the breaking off and the continuance of the unctions. Hence if a space of fifteen minutes or more has elapsed, the safer way is to repeat the entire sacrament.[63]

II. The Licit Minister

2. "*Salvo praescripto can.* 397, *n.* 3, 514, 1-3, *minister ordinarius est parochus loci in quo degit infirmus; in casu autem necessitatis, vel de licentia saltem rationabiliter praesumpta ejusdem parochi vel Ordinarii loci, alius quilibet sacerdos hoc sacramentum ministrare potest.*"

Logically enough the Code proceeds within the confines of the same Canon from a consideration of the valid minister of this sacrament to that of its lawful minister. This paragraph definitely determines whose right and whose obligation it is to administer the sacrament of the dying. It is a corroboration and repetition of n. 3 of Canon 462, where the ministration of Extreme Unction is enumerated among the functions reserved to the pastor.

This legislative insistence on the pastor's right in this regard is well-warranted. As far back as the Council of Vienne, official legislation was necessary to stop the encroachments of religious on pastoral rights.[64] This did not successfully end their trespasses—and again the rights of the pastor were held up as sacred by Leo X.[65] One hundred years later Innocent X[66] vindicated a third time to pastors their rights in this matter. In the constitution "Apostolicae Sedis"[67] of Pius IX, an excommunication, reserved *simpliciter* to the Pope, was directed against religious who anointed without due permission.

As a consequence it is clearly a parochial function. The pastor is the ordinary minister of the sacrament. To him its

---

63 Tamburini, *Moral. Explic.*, t. II, l. VI, *De Ext. Unct.*, cap. I, paragr. III, n. 4; S. Alph., l.c.; Voit, *Th. M.*, n. 906-07; *Analecta Eccl.*, vol. VIII, p. 428 sq.; Noldin, l.c.; Augustine, *A Commentary*, IV, 407-8; Gury-Ferreres, *Casus Consc.*, II, 786.

64 C. 1, *de privilegiis et excessibus privilegiatorum*, V, 7, in Clem.

65 Const. "*Dum Intra,*" 19 Dec. 1516, paragr. 7; C. I. C. Fontes, n. 72.

66 Const. "*Cum Sicut,*" 14 Maii 1648, paragr. 4, I, ad 17; C. I. C. Fontes, n. 232.

67 12 Oct. 1869, paragr. II, n. 14—Collectanea, n. 1348.

administration belongs *vi officii.*[68] Since he has this power ordinarily, he may delegate it either *in toto* or *ex parte,* either in general or in particular.[69]

The pastor meant in this canon is the pastor of the territory where the man lies ill, not the pastor *proprius* of the sick man. The wording of the Canon is very explicit on this score: "Parochus loci in quo degit infirmus." His claim extends over all the sick within the limits of his parish whether they be his own subjects (by Canon 94) or "peregrini" or "vagi" (by Canon 91).

Several exceptions are made by law. In the first instance, the administration of the last sacraments to the bishop of the diocese is reserved by Canon 397, n. 3, to the dignitaries and the canons of the cathedral chapter according to their order of precedence. The precedence of dignitaries and canons is determined by Canon 408. There it is decreed that, unless particular statutes or legitimate customs provide otherwise, the dignitaries shall have precedence over the canons, the senior canons over the junior, titular canons over the honorary, the honorary canons over the beneficiaries. Dignitaries or capitularies endowed with episcopacy take precedence over all other dignitaries or canons who are only priests. Dignitaries take rank from the nobility of their dignity or according to the common law of precedence.[70]

Canon 514 also exempts certain classes from the pastor's jurisdiction. "In every clerical institute," the Canon reads, "the superiors have the right and duty to administer either personally or thru another Viaticum and Extreme Unction to sick professed members and novices, and to others who dwell day and night in the religious house by reason of service or education or hospitality or sickness."[71]

Hence every clerical institute, whether exempt or non-exempt, whether papal or diocesan, has the privilege of attend-

68 "Sacerdoti igitur hujus sacramenti administratio commissa est. Neque tamen ex sanctae ecclesiae decreto cuivis sacerdoti, sed proprio pastore qui jurisdictionem habeat, sive alteri, cui ille ejus muneris fungendi potestatem fecerit, hoc sacramentum administrare licet." (Cat. Conc. Trident., *De Ext. Unct.*, n. 13.)

69 Cf. Can. 199, par. 1.

70 Can. 106, nn. 3 & 5.

71 Cf. Augustine, *A Commentary,* III, p. 141.

ing to the spiritual needs of its own sick. By clerical institutes are understood those orders and congregations, the majority of whose members are, or by their constitutions are destined to be, in sacerdotal rank.[72]

The first class of sick exempted by this paragraph of Canon 514 are the professed and the novices. Naturally enough, if any exemption were to be made, these should be the principal beneficiaries.

The "aliive" enumerated under this same canon are divided into several groups, according to the reason or capacity as a resident of the monastery. They must actually dwell, i. e., have board and lodging, in the religious house or at least within the premises. The term "domus religiosa" is taken in the sense of the entire premises of the religious house (*intra septa monasterii*).[73] Accordingly a number of buildings may compose a *domus religiosa,* if the religious actually dwell in them. Nor is it required that they be joined to the monastery *per modum unius.* No matter how distinct they are from the building itself, provided they form part and parcel of the place, they are said to be included in the term "domus religiosa." Hence hospitals, hostelries, schools, etc., actually within the precincts of the monastery are included in the exemption. Finally it makes no difference whether the house is subject in other ways to the pastor. This exemption in regard to administering Extreme Unction still holds.[74]

The first group of non-religious exempt from the jurisdiction of the pastor are servants who work for the religious and dwell within the precincts of the monastery. It is not essential that they live within the monastery building itself, but simply that they dwell within the confines of the monastery (*intra septa monasterii*). Whether they work for pay or from charity makes no difference in regard to this privilege. Postulants are also included within this group.[75] They are said to be in the monastery "causa famulatus."

The second exempt group are boarding students, those who receive not only education but also board and lodging at the

---

[72] Cf. can. 488, 4.

[73] Augustine, *A Commentary,* III, p. 142.

[74] Blat, *Comm. Text.,* l. II, p. 562, n. 573, paragr. 1, 2.

[75] Fanfani, *De Jure Religiosorum,* n. 415.

religious house. It excludes "day-students," but not those who live at school except during the vacation period.[76]

The third group are guests, not alone those who, live in the religious house habitually,[77] but even those visiting "ad tempus," transients, as pilgrims, travellers, wayfarers, etc.[78] Furthermore, people who come to visit their religious friends with the intention of staying one full day and night come within the scope of the privilege.[79]

The last class is that of sick persons who are cared for by religious in their own monasteries. This would hold *a fortiori* if the religious had a hospital on the premises. Augustine[80] notes that workingmen, etc., who would not otherwise come under this exemption, if nursed in the religious house, are forthwith included.

"Diu noctuque" signifies the actual commoration for one entire day, or at least the actual entrance and reception into the monastery with the intention of remaining that length of time.[81] Genicot is not nearly so liberal. He demands of "guests" a stay of "aliquot dies."[82] The former opinion seems more probable. Otherwise the pastor would be compelled to exercise his functions in a territory that is really, after a fashion, not his own. Furthermore "guests" who may satisfy in a private oratory the Sunday precept of hearing Mass are those who have been received by the "*privilegiatus*" for one day.[83] The argument seems to be "*a pari*" in regard to the meaning of "guests" intended by this canon.

The obligation to attend any and all of the above-mentioned groups of sick persons falls primarily on the superior of the institute. He is not bound to consult or to inform the parish priest in the matter, because on him alone devolves the obligation of attending these sick. The discharge of this obligation

---

76 Augustine, *A Commentary,* III, p. 143; Genicot-Salsmans, *Inst. Th. M.*, II, 338.
77 Cf. S. C. EE. et RR., July 21, 1848—Bizzarri, *Coll.*, p. 564 sqq.
78 Augustine, *op. cit.*, p. 144; Blat, *Comm. Text.*, lib. II, n. 573.
79 Cf. Fanfani, *l.c.;* Vermeersch-Creusen, *Epit., I,* 581, 4.
80 *Op. cit.*, p. 144.
81 Cf. Vermeersch-Creusen, *Epit.*, I, 581, 4; Augustine, *A Commentary,* III, p. 142; Fanfani, *De Jure Religiosorum,* n. 415.
82 *Inst. Th. M.*, II, 338.
83 *De Locis Sacris,* n. 90.

however does not require a personal fulfillment. Another priest may be delegated to perform it, as the Canon allows.

The second paragraph of Canon 514 vindicates to the confessor (and his "vices gerens") the right and the duty of administering the last sacraments to nuns with solemn vows.[84] This is due to the fact that these nuns live in papal cloister—and the number of persons who may penetrate the sacred precincts is strictly limited.[85] The confessor's right extends also to all classes of non-religious persons mentioned under the first paragraph of Canon 514, provided of course that they reside within the precincts of the convent. Consequently female servants, alumnae, guests and the sick are to be anointed by the confessor, and not by the parish priest.[86]

The confessor here meant is the ordinary confessor, appointed in conformance with Canon 520, paragraph 1. The extraordinary confessor is consequently excluded. If there are several ordinary confessors, any one of them is competent.[87] The "vices gerens" is the confessor temporarily substituting during the absence (for any cause whatsoever) of the ordinary confessor. If neither the confessor nor his substitute is at hand, any other priest may enter the cloister to anoint.[88]

A still further exemption from the pastor's jurisdiction is made of seminarians. According to Canon 1368 the seminary is altogether exempt from parochial jurisdiction; and the rector receives the rights of a pastor with regard to everything but the administration of matrimony. Consequently it is the right and duty of the rector or his delegate to administer Extreme Unction to all in the seminary. "*All*" includes the several classes mentioned in canon 514.[89]

In every other case the pastor is the minister ordinary. The exceptions above noted are taxative—and any attempt to extend them has met with a rebuff from the Apostolic See. The Sacred Congregation of Rites forbade regulars to anoint tertiaries

---

84 Only nuns with solemn vows are "moniales"—cf. Can. 488, 7.

85 Canon 600; S. C. de Rel., 6 Feb., 1924, III, 2, f—A.A.S. XVI, 99; cf. Schaaf, *The Cloister*, p. 116 sqq.

86 S. C. EE. et RR., May 1788—Bizarri, *Coll.*, p. 348; S. C. de Rel., *ibid.*

87 Blat, *Comm. Text.*, lib. II, n. 573.

88 S. C. de Rel., *ibid.*

89 Cf. Fanfani, *De Jure Parochorum*, nn. 293, B, and 289.

of their own order.[90] On March 17, 1663, the same Congregation vindicated to the pastor the right to anoint collegiate canons residing within his parish.[91] In 1756 a decision declared that it was the function of the pastor, and not of the archpriest, to bring Viaticum and Extreme Unction to Dignitaries, canons and abbots "beneficiati" who had a residence within the parish.[92] Moreover the Congregation of the Propaganda justified the action of Dutch pastors in placing obstacles in the path of Capuchin missionaries in Holland who were administering without permission sacraments whose ministration was reserved to the pastor.[93] Even Cardinals and titular bishops are not exempt from the jurisdiction of the pastor in this regard.[94] It is evident from the above how loath the legislative authority is to invade parochial rights on this matter.

In virtue of paragraph 3 of Canon 514, the pastor receives the right of conferring this sacrament in all lay institutes within his parish which the Ordinary has not subjected to any special chaplain. Consequently all religious of these institutes, together with their servants, guests and sick persons must be attended by the pastor in whose parish the house is erected. There are no exemptions made from this canon. It affects, e. g., the Christian Brothers, the Brothers Hospitallers of St. John of God, etc., for these are lay institutes. It probably includes the Brothers of Mary, for, although some of these are priests, yet by far the majority are lay brothers, and it is consequently a lay institute.

Difficulty might arise as to who is competent to anoint in an institute of this kind when two parishes overlap because of linguistic divisions. According to Augustine,[95] the solution depends, primarily, upon the will of the founder or foundress, and, secondarily, upon the custom of the place. If neither of these affords a solution, the Ordinary should be called upon to decide.

It is within the power of the bishop to subject such lay

90 S. R. C., *Spoletana Terrae de Visso,* 20 Jun. 1609, ad 1—D. A., n. 271.
91 S. C. R., *Montis Regalis,* 17 Mar. 1663, ad 4—D. A., n. 1255.
92 S. C. R., *S. Severi Praeëminent.,* 18 Dec. 1756, ad 7—D. A., n. 2441.
93 S. C. P. F., (C. G.), 13 Jun. 1633—*Collectanea,* n. 73.
94 Fanfani, *De Jure Parochorum,* n. 293, B.
95 *A Commentary,* III, p. 145.

institutes to the jurisdiction of a special chaplain.[96] He may also exempt from parochial jurisdiction "*domus piae,*" of any nature whatsoever. Hence hospitals, asylums, orphanages, hostelries, or any other institution destined for pious or charitable purposes may for a just and serious reason be confided to a special chaplain.[97] It is to be noted however that the appointment of a chaplain does not *per se* exempt these places from the pastor's jurisdiction. It is necessary that the bishop make specific provision for such exemption.[98] When this is done, the spiritual duties devolve upon the chaplain. The pastor should be notified of this quasi-exemption in order to avoid possible friction. Once the chaplain is appointed, the pastor may not licitly interfere.[99] It would be quite as unlawful for him to confer Extreme Unction in such a place without permission as it would be for the chaplain to confer it in the parish.

In the case of sisters with simple vows, the pastor of the parish is the competent minister, even if they have their own confessor. Such sisters are lay religious and have not solemn vows or papal cloister. Hence they have not the privileges of "moniales." If however they are subject to a special chaplain, he alone is competent.

With regard to Viaticum, Vermeersch[100] holds that its repetition is not reserved to the pastor in the same danger of death. This cannot be argued of Extreme Unction, for Extreme Unction may not licitly be repeated in the same danger of death.[101] Hence each and every administration is reserved to the pastor.

Finally, attention may be called to the fact that quasi-pastors, and, if they are endowed with full powers, parochial vicars enjoy the same rights as *parochi.*[102] Accordingly what has been said in regard to the pastor's right of administering

96 Can. 464, 2.

97 Cocchi, *Comm. in Cod.*, Lib. II, Pars I, Sect. II, n. 344; Augustine, *op. cit.*, II, p. 544; Blat, *Comm. Text.*, lib. II, n. 511.

98 Cf. Fanfani, *De Jure Parochorum*, n. 477.

99 Blat, *op. cit.*, n. 573, paragr. 3; cf. S. C. C., *Ravennaten.* 27 Jun. 1789, dub. I—Ferraris, *Bibliotheca*, v. "Ext. Unctio," t. III (Romae, 1886).

100 *Summa Novi Codicis*, n. 336; Genicot-Salsmans, *Inst. Th. M.*, II, 181; Fanfani, *op. cit.*, n. 189.

101 Can. 940, 2.

102 Can. 451, 2.

Extreme Unction to all the sick in his parish applies with equal force to those who are equiparated to pastors in law.

"In casu autem necessitatis."

In case of necessity any priest may lawfully administer Extreme Unction. The necessary faculty for the licit confection of this sacrament in such circumstances is obtained from the Code itself. The necessity can be physical or moral.[103] The former is present when the pastor cannot possibly reach the sick person. The latter arises when he cannot be called or cannot administer it without most serious inconvenience. A moral necessity would be verified also in the case where the pastor has incurred excommunication or suspension. Tantamount to a moral necessity is the situation wherein the pastor unreasonably refuses to anoint personally and to give permission to another.[104] In this case, a priest may with a safe conscience proceed, not only because he may presume reasonably on the permission of the Ordinary, but also because a priest has from this very canon the actual permission of the Pope.[105] Such a priest is made by law the extraordinary minister of the sacrament.[106]

"Vel de licentia saltem rationabiliter praesumpta ejusdem parochi vel Ordinarii loci, alius quilibet sacerdos hoc sacramentum ministrare potest."

Since the pastor is the ordinary minister of the sacrament, he may delegate any other priest to perform this function.[107] The vicar *oeconomus,* or temporary administrator of a parish, enjoys full parochial rights, and can, therefore, delegate in like manner.[108] The Ordinary of the place where the man lies sick can also grant permission, "etiam contradicente parocho."[109] Because of the fact that he can delegate, the Ordinary himself

103 Blat, *Comm. Text.,* lib. III, p. I, n. 281, paragr. 2.

104 Blat, *l.c.*

105 Diana, *Op. Coord.,* tom. II, tr. IV, res. 25; Laymann, *Th. M.,* lib. V, tr. 8, c. 6, n. 2; Benedict XIV, *De Syn. Dioc.,* l. 8, c. 4, n. 7; S. Alph., *Th. M.,* VI, 723; Elbel-Bierbaum, *Th. M.,* Pars VIII, Conf., IX, tom. II, n. 360; Babenstuber, *Ethica Supernat.,* Tract. de Ext. Unct., a. IV, n. 6.

106 Blat, *l.c.*

107 Can. 199, 1.

108 Can. 473; cf. S. C. C., 12 Sept., 1874—A. S. S., VIII, 1298; Augustine, *A Commentary,* IV, p. 399.

109 Blat, *Comm. Text.,* lib. III, p. I, n. 281.

has the right to administer personally this sacrament within his own territory. Delegation of a power presupposes possession of that same power by the delegator.

Curates do not need their pastor's permission, for they supply the pastor's place in the entire parochial ministry. However, the pastor can reserve this function to himself, with the result that any administration on the part of the curate against his will would be unlawful.[110] If the faculties or diocesan statutes give curates the right of administration, they can bestow the sacrament licitly, even against the reasonable will of the pastor. In such a case they have the "licentia Ordinarii."[111]

Delegation or permission can be made to any priest. However, excommunicated or suspended or personally interdicted priests are ordinarily not desirable subjects for delegation.[112] Nevertheless, if the sacrament were sought for a just reason from an *excommunicatus toleratus,* not yet denounced by a condemnatory or a declaratory sentence—or from a suspended or personally interdicted priest—license might licitly be given him, according to Canon 2261, paragraph 2. Indeed it may also be given to a *vitandus* if no other ministers are present and a personal administration by the pastor or Ordinary is impossible. The subject of Extreme Unction must, of course, be in danger of death—and in such a case a *vitandus* becomes a lawful minister.[113]

License can be given expressly—in writing, orally or by signs—or tacitly, i. e., when permission can be reasonably gathered from the circumstances. It may also be legitimately presumed where, e. g., it is foreseen that it would be readily granted or that the pastor would be pleased if he were spared the inconvenience of personal administration. This presumption is allowable even when there is no canonical reason present for the granting of the permission, but a more intimate knowledge of the pastor personally is undoubtedly required to justify such a presumption.

Under all these cases a priest becomes the lawful, extraordinary minister of the sacrament.[114] A priest who admin-

110 Cf. can. 476, 6 and 462, 3.
111 Augustine, *l.c.*
112 Cf. can. 2261, 1; 2284, 2275, 2.
113 Can. 2261, 3.
114 Blat, *Comm. Text.*, l. III, p. I, n. 281, page 341.

isters Extreme Unction in any other case commits a grievous sin, because he invades the right of the pastor "*in re gravi.*" Before the Code regulars who dared this incurred excommunication simply reserved to the Holy See.[115] Since this censure is not included in the present legislation, it is now obsolete.[116]

115 Const. "*Apostolicae Sedis,*" 12 Oct. 1869—Coll. S.C.P.F., n. 1348.
116 Cf. Can. 6, n. 5.

CHAPTER IV.

THE OBLIGATION OF THE MINISTER

CANON 939.

"Minister ordinarius ex justitia tenetur hoc sacramentum per se ipse vel per alium administrare, et in casu necessitatis ex caritate quilibet sacerdos.

CHAPTER IV.

Minister ordinarius ex justitia tenetur.

Laymen have the right to receive from the clergy, in as far as ecclesiastical regulation permits, spiritual benefits and especially the means necessary to salvation.[1] All who belong to the Church have a title to the wondrous well-springs of sanctification she possesses; and on the legitimately constituted dispensers of these treasures the obligation of imparting them is imposed.

This canon divides the clergy's obligation according to the minister, and binds the ordinary minister from justice and the extraordinary minister from charity.

The ordinary minister of Extreme Unction is the pastor of the place where the subject lies sick.[2] He is bound to administer the sacraments to all who seek them reasonably. He has a contract with his people, in virtue of which he receives the sustenance, or at least the honor, of a pastor with the obligation of performing "ea quae pastoris sunt." Among the duties of a pastor the administration of the sacraments in preëminent.[3]

It need hardly be noted that the obligation on the Dignitaries and Canons of the Cathedral Chapter (from Canon 397) and on the various priests mentioned in Canon 514, arises likewise from justice—for they are really ordinary ministers of the sacrament in regard to certain particular subjects.

Hence all priests who are charged with the care of souls are bound under pain of sin to succor all committed to their charge and to administer to them the last sacraments, if they are in grave need of them.[4] Ordinarily, then, they are bound *sub mortali* to administer Extreme Unction to those who seek it unless a just cause excuses. If such a priest does not, he

1 Can. 682.
2 Can. 938, 2.
3 Can. 467.
4 Fanfani, *De Jure Parochorum*, n. 229.

has refused to furnish what he is bound *ex justitia* to do.[5] The consequence is certainly mortal sin. The gravity of the sin, of course, is measured by the spiritual loss arising from it; and in the sacrament of Extreme Unction the loss sustained thru a failure to receive it is almost incalculable.[6]

The question arises: Under what *incommodum* is the pastor bound to administer Extreme Unction? Theologians commonly hold that pastors are bound "cum periculo sanitatis aut vitae" to administer the sacraments absolutely necessary for eternal salvation. Hence since the only *absolutely* necessary sacraments are Baptism and, for those in mortal sin, Penance, it can hardly be said that the pastor is obliged to such a serious risk to confer Extreme Unction. Extreme Unction is ordinarily bestowed after Penance and Viaticum, i. e., after the man's salvation has been morally assured.[7]

In the time of the plague at Milan, Gregory XIII decided that the parish priests of Milan and their curates were obliged *sub gravi* only in regard to the administration of Baptism and Penance in the case of plague-stricken patients. Fagnani[8] says that this declaration was never published. Some time later a decision of St. Antoninus, archbishop of Florence (1459), was discovered, which ordered pastors to administer all the sacraments even during times of plague. The question was again referred to the Holy See by St. Charles Borromeo. This time the Congregation of the Council decided that no general rule should be made, but that the saintly archbishop was to be advised that pastors were obliged in conscience to remain at their posts, ready to administer Baptism and Penance.[9] Benedict XIV[10] notes that the countersignature of this document at Rome and its reception at Milan have not been recorded. Consequently an argument from this document, such as that employed by Noldin[11] and Genicot,[12] is quite questionable. The

5 Vermeersch-Creusen, *Epit.*, II, 224; St. Alph., *Th. M.*, VI, 729 &c.
6 Noldin, *De Sac.*, n. 34.
7 *Rit. Rom.*, tit. V, cap. 1, n. 2.
8 *Jus Canon., seu Comm. Absolut. in Quinque Lib. Decret.*, lib. III, in cap. "Clericos," tit. IV, n. 45, "*De Clericis non residentibus.*"
9 S. C. C., 12 Oct. 1576, probante Greg. XIII, S. C. C., 6 Dec. 1576—cf. Noldin, *De Sac.*, n. 34; also cf. "The Casuist," vol. IV, 81.
10 *De Syn. Dioc.*, l. 13, c. 19, nn. 6-7.
11 Noldin, *De Sac.*, n. 34.
12 Genicot-Salsmans, *Inst. Th. M.*, II, 119.

learned Pope holds the very opposite opinion. He maintains that it is obligatory upon the pastor, even with danger of death, to administer Extreme Unction to his subjects.[13] He bases his principal argument upon the Apostolic confirmation given to the decrees of the Fifth Provincial Council of Milan. In the acts of this Council are found two chapters of synodal legislation concerning the cautions to be taken by priests while they are ministering Extreme Unction and after they have ministered it.[14] From the context it can be reasonably deduced that the legislator presupposes an obligation on the pastor in this instance. Consequently, even though the official approbation of the Council's proceedings by the Holy See do not give them any binding force beyond the territory of its jurisdiction, nevertheless they may be taken as an indication of the Holy See's attitude on the subject.

However, it is by far the more common view that the pastor is not bound to administer Extreme Unction "cum periculo vitae" when Penance has been provided.[15] Even theologians, like Suarez[16] and Sylvius,[17] who insist that it is seriously incumbent on the pastor to administer Viaticum, excuse him from the duty of bestowing Extreme Unction at the peril of his life. Although it is dear to the heart of the Good Shepherd for a pastor to dare all that his flock may obtain the salutary graces of this sacrament of the "exeuntium," nevertheless he is bound in justice to risk his life for his sheep only when their spiritual lives are seriously endangered. This is surely not the case when the sick person has already been confessed and absolved.

It is to be noted, however, that when the danger of death can be removed or reduced to a negligible quantity by the use of disinfectants and the like, a pastor is bound to employ these and to confer the sacrament.[18] The advantages are so enormous that special inconveniences must be suffered in these un-

13 Op. cit., l.c., nn. 8-11.

14 Apud *Acta Eccl. Mediol.*, pars I, tom. I, pp. 246-8.

15 Barbosa, *De Pot. Parochi*, cap. xxii, n. 17; St. Alph., *Th. M.*, VI, 729; Vermeersch-Creusen, *Epit.*, II, 224; Concina, *Th. Chr.*, Lib. I, *De E. U.*, diss. I, cap. 3, q. 4; Ferreres, *Comp. Th. M.*, II, 280; Lehmkuhl, *Th. M.*, II, 51; Noldin, *De Sac.*, n. 441; &c.

16 Disp. 44, sec. 3, nn. 17-20.

17 *In Suppl. ad III p. D. Thom.*, q. 32, a. 3, conclus. 3.

18 Barbosa, *De Off. et Pot. Parochi*, cap. xxii, n. 17; Suarez, d. 44, sect. 3, n. 20.

usual circumstances. The employment of preventive measures is not too much to expect of the one who has an *obligation* to care for the spiritual needs of his parish. He must cope with the contingencies of extraordinary situations in a reasonable fashion. When too much is not demanded to overcome the dangers on these occasions, he is required to put himself to inconveniences which are proportionate to the benefits which the souls under his charge will receive as a result of his trouble. The immense advantages that accrue to the sick person thru the potent graces of Extreme Unction certainly demand that no slight pains be taken by those in charge of souls to remove the causes which excuse them from bestowing the sacrament.

There is also the common opinion that if Extreme Unction is the only hope of salvation, e. g., if the dying man has not been to confession for a long time and can be absolved only conditionally now because unconscious, there is then a grave obligation on the pastor to give Extreme Unction even at the peril of his life.[19] The Synod of Namur (1639) passed the following enactment: "Qui autem peste affectus non est confessus, nec potest confiteri, pastor teneatur illi extremam unctionem, etiam cum periculo vitae, dare.[20]" The reason is, of course, that Extreme Unction gives sanctifying grace to those who have only attrition for their sins and cannot make a confession. Since the acts of the penitent are at least the quasi-matter in the sacrament of Penance, the value of an absolution imparted conditionally to an unconscious man without previous confession is very dubious indeed. Extreme Unction is left as the sole sure means of assisting the dying man.

In order that a priest be strictly bound to endanger his life in the behalf of a soul under his care, it is quite necessary that all the conditions demanding such heroism be verified *adamussim.* In the first place it must be required that the subject be truly in grave peril of his eternal salvation. Secondly, the means which the priest has at his command must be certainly sufficient to relieve the patient from his necessity. Moreover the

---

19 Fanfani, *De Jure Paroch.*, n. 229; Noldin, *De Sac.*, n. 34; Genicot-Salsmans, *Inst. Th. M.*, II, 119 & 421; Sebastiani, *Summ. Th. M.*, n. 398D; Konings, *Th. M.*, n. 1505, q. 3; Vermeersch, *Th. M.*, III, n. 190, &c.

20 Tit. xiv, c. x; cf. Kenrick, *Th. M.*, III, *de Ext. Unct.*, cap. unic., n. 14.

hope of rescuing the sick man must be morally assured; and finally no graver evils must result from the fulfillment of this obligation. If any of these conditions is lacking, the severity of the obligation is relaxed.

Accordingly, if the priest is morally certain that the sick man is in the state of grace, either because he has not sinned since his last confession or because of his ability to make an act of perfect contrition, he is excused from risking his life to administer Extreme Unction. If he knows nothing or is in doubt about the state of conscience of the sick man, Suarez holds that a priest is obligated to hazard certain danger of death in order to anoint the sick man. "Adverto non satis esse," he writes,[21] "quod parochus negative se habeat, ignorans statum infirmi, ut (ex generali regula) praesumat illum esse in bono statu, quem non scit esse in malo; hujusmodi enim praesumptio postulatur ad ea quae sunt favorabilia alteri; non vero licet illa uti ad negandum illi debitum ministerium, et exponendum eum periculo saltem dubio aeternae damnationis . . . . Requiritur ergo ut positive constet moraliter de bono statu bonaque dispositione poenitentis." Later authors are not so exacting as Suarez. They demand simple probability, not moral certainty, of the state of grace in the sick man. "Non teneretur Parochus," Cappello[22] declares, "aliusve *certo periculo vitae* se exponere, si *probabiliter* putaret, ex gr., moribundum . . . non reperiri in statu culpae mortalis vel sibimet consulere posse per contritionem perfectam." Fanfani[23] similarly speaks of the pastor's obligation as absolute only when the subject is *certainly* in mortal sin. Vermeersch[24] is equally as liberal in his application of the general principle, and he notes further that the strict obligation can never be laid upon a priest in regard to anointing a sick man who has become unconscious. The uncertainty of the sick man's dispositions, he avers, excuses the priest from walking into a certain danger of death. There is certainly enough authority for a pastor to follow the milder opinion. He can refuse to enter a *certain* danger of death for the purpose of anointing under every cir-

21 D. 44, s. 3, n. 15.
22 *De Sacramentis*, I, 67.
23 *De Jure Paroch.*, n. 229.
24 *Th. M.*, III, nn. 190, 658.

cumstance where the absolute need of his attendance upon the sick man is not evident. The deduction of Vermeersch, asserting the uncertainty of the sick man's dispositions in every case where the sick man is unconscious, seems too sweeping. A fair indication of the internal dispositions can be obtained at least sometimes, and especially in such cases as contemplated by Canon 943.

Moreover, the success of the *auxilium* proffered by the pastor must be morally certain. Hence, if the priest sees that he will probably be hindered from administering the sacrament, he is not bound to undergo a *certain* imperilling of his life. Similarly, if he feels that he may not reach the sick person on time, yet such attempt on his part will result fatally for him (as in times of persecutions), he is released from the strict obligation of attendance.[25]

Finally, if it is foreseen that graver evils will result from the fulfillment of his office in this regard, the priest is not bound to submit himself to such an inevitable jeopardy of life. Private good must cede to the common good. Hence if the pastor knows that, by his death, the salvation of the community will no longer be sufficiently provided for because of lack of priests, he is excused from hazarding himself at such a price.[26] This problem may arise often in missionary lands, where the harvest is great and the laborers few. In times of persecution a similar question may arise. In 1899 the Holy Office was asked about the duties of missionaries in the kingdom of Buganda, a land where the faithful were compelled to conceal their faith. Attendance by the missionaries upon the sick meant imminent danger for the sick man, his family, and indeed the whole Christian community. Hence the question was put: "utrum ad hoc periculum praecavendum missionarii possint ac debeant infirmos non visitare, an, spreto quolibet periculo sive privatorum sive communitatis Christianae, aegrotos in gravi moriendi periculo constitutos visitare possint aut debeant ut illos sacramentis Ecclesiae reficiant?" The query was not directly answered, but there is undoubtedly an insinuation that the missionaries are not *bound,* at least, to render spiritual

---

25 Cf. Fanfani, *De Jure Parochorum*, n. 229; Cappello, *De Sac.*, I, 67.
26 Suarez, D. 44, sec. 3, n. 15; Vermeersch, *Th. M.*, III, 190; Fanfani, *l.c.*

assistance to the sick. The words of the reply were: "R. Ad mentem: mens autem est a missionariis fideles monendos ut, attenta difficultate habendi missionarii adsistentiam in mortis articulo, omni studio satagant peccata vitare, et in mortis periculo mutuam sibi adsistentiam praebeant; ac insuper missionarii bene instruant catechistas, qui in expositis casibus missionarii vices aliqua ratione fungantur."[27]

Just as the certain and complete fulfillment of every condition is necessary to impose a strict obligation on the pastor when the danger is serious and certain, so a solidly probable realization of these identical conditions is needed to create a rigid responsibility of anointing a sick man when it entails probable danger of death to the priest. "Eadem regula," writes Cappello[28] " . . . . valet quoque, congrua congruis referendo, ubi agitur de gravi necessitate, ob quam sacramenta ministranda sunt cum periculo gravi et probabili sanitatis aut vitae." In order, then, that the pastor must risk a probable danger of death, it is necessary that the subject be probably in grave peril of losing eternal salvation and that success of the venture be probably assured. "Si solummodo *probabilis* sit successus vel necessitas, obligatio pro pastore manet quidem cum probabili vitae periculo."[29]

The obligations of the pastor when Extreme Unction is the sole means of salvation can be briefly summed up. If it is morally certain that the patient will not attain salvation except thru the ministration of the priest and if there is moral certainty of the successful outcome of the priest's attempt to confer the sacrament, a priest in charge of souls is bound in justice to brave certain danger of death, and even death itself, to confer the sacrament upon the dying man. However, if the common good will subsequently suffer thru the loss of the priest, the advantage that will accrue to the particular individual must be regarded in relation to the greater good that will be gained by the community. Hence in such a case a priest is released from this severe obligation. Indeed he may often be bound not to attend a sick person, as, for example, when he is sure

27 S. C. S. Off., 3 Apr. 1899; cf. Bucceroni, *Casus Consc.*, II, n. 138, p. 218.
28 *De Sacr.*, I, 67.
29 Vermeersch, *Th. M.*, III, 190.

that his demise will seriously imperil the eternal salvation of many others in the community. In this case it is a question of the lesser evil.

When the subject is in grave necessity, i. e., when he is in probable need of the sacrament and there is probability of its successful bestowal, the pastor is required *ex justitia* to expose his life to a probable danger of death. In this he differs from those who have not the charge of souls, as will be seen shortly, for they are bound gravely to attend a sick man only when he is in extreme necessity.[30]

The question of the priest's obligation in the cases contemplated by Canon 941 is also worthy of consideration. The general principles announced hitherto must be put into play in the determination of these solutions also. The pastor by virtue of his office is bound to give the sacraments to those reasonably seeking them. His flock have a right to the reception of these gifts absolutely if they are absolutely capable, and conditionally if they are doubtfully capable of benefitting by them. They are entitled to everything which will morally assure them of salvation and which at the same time is within the bounds of reason.

Consequently a pastor is bound to anoint conditionally a child who has only doubtfully attained the use of reason. Such a child cannot make a confession and, since the conditional absolution is of very questionable efficacy, the eternal safety of the child is not properly secured except by an administration of Extreme Unction. By virtue of his office the pastor then has the duty of conferring the sacrament. This obligation is certainly grave,[31] and only a very serious inconvenience excuses from it. Blat[32] says the measure of the obligation is to be gauged according to the terminology of our Canon. It stands to reason, however, that a priest is not bound to enter the same degree of peril to give this sacrament to a child who needs it *only probably* as he would be obliged in the case where an adult would *surely* need it for salavtion.

---

30 St. Alph., *Th. M.*, II, 30; Collet, *Decal.*, cap. 1; Gury, *Th. M.*, II, n. 215; Ferreres, *Comp. Th. M.*, II, 281.

31 Lehmkuhl, *Th. M.*, II, 723; Gury-Ferreres, *Casus*, II, n. 799; Lebherz, in The Casuist, vol. II, p. 176; Cf. St. Alph., *Th. M.*, VI, 719.

32 *Comm. Text.*, lib. III, p. I, n. 285.

A distinction must be drawn here which will be of use very soon. A child has more than a probable right to the sacrament. He has a certain right to a conditional administration of it. Only thuswise is he sure of salvation; and his title to the means which will ensure his salvation is not only probable but certain. Accordingly since the child's claim upon the parish priest is certain, he will be obligated under serious inconvenience to do all for the salvation of this soul in his charge.

The second case for consideration is the obligation upon the pastor to anoint in cases of apparent death. For these men, unable, of course, to confess, the sacrament of Extreme Unction will be the only sacrament of avail—if indeed any sacrament at all will be of avail. As has been said often before, the value of conditional absolution is too problematical. Extreme Unction becomes *per accidens* necessary *necessitate medii*, if these subjects are in mortal sin.

The solution would be easy if the patient were certainly known to be but apparently dead. Dissolution would not have yet truly occurred; the subject would still be a "viator," having a claim upon the pastor's services as much as the rest of the Church militant under such a priest's care. But there is no certainty in this case—and consequently the solution of the case must depend upon the principles of probability. One of the most important considerations that must be noted in gauging the priest's obligation is the length of time since the first appearance of apparent death. Naturally the duty of the pastor dwindles in proportion to the distance from the seeming cessation of life. The manner of death must also be investigated. As shall be seen in the treatment of Canon 941, the occurrence of somatic death in lingering sicknesses is much quicker than in sudden cases of accident. In the former instances the soul probably takes its departure within an hour after the greater vital functions cease; in the latter several hours or even a day may elapse before the real separation of the soul from the body.

While the man is probably alive, he has a right to the sacraments, provided that all the other conditions necessary are present. Consequently the pastor is bound to administer them to the souls in his care, for they have a claim to his attention especially in these urgent cases. Their title to a conditional administration is reasserted by the Code in Canon 941. The law says "*ministretur sub conditione,*" not "potest ministrari sub conditione." Accordingly there is an obligation in justice upon the ordinary ministers to perform this conditional administration; and similarly a duty in charity upon the extraordinary ministers.[33] Where there is solid probability that the man is not yet dead, the obligation is seriously binding on the ordinary minister to give this sacrament even at the cost of grave inconvenience.

The consensus of theological opinion is that a man is very probably alive for a half-hour after apparent demise in lingering illnesses, and at least an hour in sudden accidents. Consequently within these times a priest in care of souls is bound *sub gravi* to administer this necessary sacrament.[34] O'Malley,[35] claiming strenuously that somatic death does not occur for at least an hour in every instance after seeming dissolution, feels that the priest who does not anoint within that time is just as guilty as if he refused to anoint a man evidently alive. Many extend the obligation of the pastor in cases of sudden death to two hours and even longer.[36] Genicot,[37] on the other hand, restricts it to a half-hour; and Ferreres, in his appendix to the *Casus*,[38] binds the priest strictly only for that same period of time. The opinion which obligates a priest for one-half hour in lingering diseases and an hour for sudden accidents seems very reasonable. In the first place a distinction should be made between the two modes of meeting death; and secondly, the priest must not be bound beyond the dictates of reason to an unseemly lengthy period after the appearance of death. After

33 Blat, *Comm. Text.*, lib. III, p. I, n. 285.

34 Sabetti-Barrett, *Th. M.*, n. 828, q. 6; Gury-Ferreres, *Casus*, II, 1213; Ferreres, *Comp. Th. M.*, II, 856; Noldin, *De Sac.*, n. 294, nota 1; Villada, *Casus*, p. 235; Kern, *Tract. de Ext. Unct.*, p. 322; O'Neill, in the Irish Eccl. Record, Fifth Series, vol. 26, (1925), pp. 515-17 and 630-31.

35 *The Ethics of Medical Homicide*, p. 88.

36 E.g., Noldin, *De Sac.*, n. 294, nota 1; Kern, *Tract. de Ext. Unct.*, p. 322; Antonelli, *Medicina Pastoralis*, II, 1026; &c.

37 *Inst. Th. M.*, II, 422.

38 Gury-Ferreres, *Casus Conc.*, II, n. 1213; Cf. Synod of Madrid, lib. 2, tit. 3, const. 6, p. 194; Synod of Orense, const. 78, p. 48 (Orense, 1908); Prov. Council of Saragossa, c. 6, tit. 2, pag. 92 (Caesaraugust., 1908).

such time the obligation of the priest lessens as the approach of certain signs of death become evident. It is quite enough that he *may* confer the sacrament after this period of strict obligation. Zeal will dictate more than justice; but, on the other hand, works of supererogation are not to be made to spring from duty. Consequently, although it is slightly probable that men snatched away thru unforeseen accidents may have latent life even for several days, the proportion of chances to the contrary is so overwhelming that it smothers all obligation of conferring the sacraments on the part of the pastor.

The obligation of the pastor in the case of those who are doubtfully in danger of death[39] can be dismissed without much difficulty. If there is any danger that the spiritual welfare of the patient will not be sufficiently secured by a conditional administration while the danger is still doubtful, the pastor is bound *sub gravi* to give the sacrament. If, however, the delay required to determine the exact status of the sick person will not be of any great detriment to the sick person, there cannot be said to be a grave obligation on the minister ordinary until certain danger of death does appear.

In the treatment of Canon 940 cognizance is taken of the opinion allowing the administration of Extreme Unction to non-Catholics. Probability—at least, external—must be admitted of this opinion. However the question of the pastor's obligation in justice to confer Extreme Unction upon these persons presents no problem. The ordinary minister is bound *ex justitia* only to the souls under his charge. The prescription of Canon 1350, 1, ordering him to consider the non-Catholics in his district as "commendatos sibi in Domino" certainly does not extend to this case. At most, non-Catholics have a tenuously probable right to a conditional administration—if indeed they can be said to have any right at all. Thus they differ from Catholics who have doubtfully attained the use of reason, &c., for these have a certain right to a conditional administration.[39] The title of those not in the Church to these aids of salvation is very hazy and befogged. Otherwise there would be no need to safeguard the reverence due the sacrament thru the attachment of so many conditions to the administration as is required

39 Cf. *supra*, p. 112 sq.

when the Unction is imparted to non-Catholics. Moreover, those who claim that there is any obligation at all are careful to stress that it arises from charity and not from justice. Consequently a pastor is not bound *vi sui muneris* to administer Extreme Unction to the non-Catholics of his district.

The question of the pastor's obligation of repeating Extreme Unction will best be considered in the treatment of Canon 940, 2. Accordingly it is passed over here, with the remark that if the danger is new and distinct, the obligation on the pastor is new and distinct. These cases present no difficulty; but problems can arise in instances where the patient is afflicted with a lingering disease. Since several contingencies must be taken into consideration in connection with these cases, the treatment of the strict duty of the pastor is best discussed at that time.

The pastor is bound to give Extreme Unction to all the sick—not to the rich alone, nor to the plague-stricken alone, but to all sick Christians in his care. This was inculcated time after time by Clement XII,[40] while Benedict XIV[41] denounced with scorching scorn the hypocritical heroism of some missionaries in the Indies who, though giving their life in the service of the vineyard, thought it too menial to attend the "pariahs."

Tantamount to a refusal to administer the sacrament (and, therefore, mortally sinful) is a serious delay, if such delay puts the sick man in probable danger of dying without the sacraments.[42] The Roman Catechism[43] states that it is a serious sin for the pastor to defer anointing until the "ultimum vitae tempus"—and even to the time when "mors proxime instat." Such a delay deprives the sick man of several special effects, e. g., help in the last agony, possibility of corporal sanation, &c., which would have been to him of paramount importance. Hence as Canon 944 says: "Omni studio et diligentia curandum ut infirmi dum sui plene compotes sunt, illud recipiant."[44]

---

40 Litt. ap., "*Compertum,*" 24 Aug. 1734, dub. XII, C. I. C. Fontes, n. 296; litt. ap., "*Concredita Nobis,*" 13 Maii, 1739, C. I. C. Fontes, n. 300.

41 Const., *Omnium sollicitudinum,*" 12 Sept. 1744, paragr. 14, dub. XII, paragr. 26, 33 sqq.—C. I. C. Fontes, n. 348.

42 Genicot-Salsmans, *Inst. Th. M.*, II, 119; Fanfani, *De Jure Parochorum*, n. 229; Kenrick, *Th. M.*, III, *De Ext. Unct.*, cap. unic., n. 20; &c.

43 *Cat. Conc. Trid.*, De Ext. Unct., n. 9.

44 Cf. treatment of this question *infra*, chap. viii, p. .

"Per se vel per alium"

A pastor can fulfill his obligation thru his curate or thru any priest who accepts the permission (*licentia*) of the pastor.[45] Consequently though bound to formal residence in his parish in times of plague, yet he is not bound to the personal administration. Noldin[46] and others[47] hold that if the dying man asks for the pastor expressly, he is obligated to attend him personally unless impeded by more serious business. Since however the strict letter of the law allows a fulfillment of the obligation "per alium," it is hard to see how he is bound in justice to a personal administration of this sacrament.[48] It is, of course, most desirable that the pastor should go if personally summoned; but to bind him in justice to this is quite a different thing. Rule 72 of the *Regulae Juris* seems very apt: "Qui facit per alium, est perinde ac si faciat per seipsum."[49]

"Et in casu necessitatis ex caritate quilibet sacerdos."

In case of necessity any priest is bound to administer Extreme Unction. His obligation arises from charity, for by charity we are bound to succor our neighbor when he is in great need.[50] All theologians hold that such aid must be proffered even with the peril of life if the neighbor is in extreme necessity. Hence it would follow that a priest is bound—and *sub gravi*—to administer the necessary sacraments to those in extreme spiritual need.[51]

A man is said to be in spiritual necessity when he is in danger of losing his eternal salvation. He is in *extreme* necessity when he cannot help himself, and hence without outside aid is in peril *simpliciter* or *moraliter* of eternal damnation. Practically tantamount to this extreme case is that of *quasi-extreme* necessity, i. e., where without external assistance, peril of losing salvation is very imminent. In *grave* necessity are

45 Blat, *Comm. Text.*, l. III, p. I, n. 282.

46 *De Sacr.*, n. 34, 3.

47 Wernz-Vidal, *Jus Canon.*, II, *De Personis*, n. 736; Cappello, *De Sac.*, I, 68; Vermeersch, *Th. M.*, III, 190.

48 Suarez, d. 44, s. 3, n. 12; Genicot-Salsmans, *Inst. Th. M.*, II, 119; Ferreres, *Comp. Th. M.*, II, n. 841; Woywod, *A Practical Commentary*, I, n. 860; Blat, *Comm. Text.*, lib. III, p. I, n. 282.

49 Cf. also reg. 68 (in VIto): "Potest quis per alium quod potest facere per se ipsum."

50 Cf. Genicot-Salsmans, *Inst. Th. M.*, I, 217; &c.

51 Cf. Noldin, *De Sac.*, n. 35; Genicot-Salsmans, *op. cit.*, II, 120; &c.

those who can assist themselves only with great difficulty, and accordingly are in probable danger of missing salvation unless externally assisted.

To constitute the obligation a grave one it must be certain that the *auxilium* be absolutely essential, that the peril of the neighbor be positively certain and that the hope of saving him be at least morally assured.[52] As a result, since "hoc sacramentum per se non sit de necessitate medii ad salutem,[53] a man can never be said to be in extreme need of Unction except in the case considered in Canon 943, where a man, desirous of receiving the sacrament, has become destitute of his senses before being able to confess. For him Extreme Unction is the "*medium unicum*" of salvation. In such a contingency a priest would be bound "*ex caritate sub gravi cum periculo vitae*" to administer it. The eternal life of his neighbor is to be preferred to his own temporal existence.[54] Of course the conditions must be verified strictly which impose a strict duty upon the priest to risk his life for his neighbor. Hence, if there is a probability that the patient has made an act of perfect contrition; or if it is probably that he will die before the priest could reach him; or if more serious evils will follow from the loss of priest's life, there cannot be said to be an obligation to subject one's self to serious peril.[55] Vermeersch-Creusen holds that the obligation to administer Extreme Unction binds in no instance that entails grave risking of life, because the internal dispositions of the man are always uncertain.[56] It seems, however, that, sometimes at least, as noted before, a fair indication of the internal dispositions of the man can be got, especially when the case of Canon 943 is verified. If it is seen that such a man has only attrition for his sins, the obligation to administer the sacrament even at the risk of health and life binds a priest, though he has not the care of the sick man's soul *ex officio*.

In grave necessity the obligation from charity is grave

---

52 Cf. Ferreres, *Comp. Th. M.*, I, 304; Noldin, *De Praecep.*, n. 78; &c.
53 Can. 944.
54 Ferreres, l.c.; Noldin, l.c.
55 Noldin, l.c.
56 *Epit.*, II, 224.

per se. However, a proportionately grave inconvenience excuses.[57] Consequently, it would be a mortal sin to refuse Extreme Unction in the case where the sacrament can be easily given to a man in sin unable to confess.[58] Outside of this instance, Extreme Unction will hardly be necessary to relieve the grave spiritual necessity of the patient; and hence there will be no serious obligation on the priest to impart it.

All these cases suppose, of course, that there is no priest at hand who is bound *ex justitia* to do this work. If he is present and willing to administer the sacrament, there is no obligation on the priest who has not the care of souls.

---

57 Genicot-Salsmans, *Inst. Th. M.*, II, 120; Ferreres, *Comp. Th. M.*, II, 304; Noldin, *De Sac.*, n. 78.

58 Genicot-Salsmans, *op. cit.*, n. 421.

CHAPTER V.

REQUISITES IN THE SUBJECT FOR ADMINISTRATION AND REPETITION

CANON 940.

1. Extrema Unctio praeberi non potest nisi fideli, qui post adeptum usum rationis ob infirmitatem vel senium in periculo mortis versetur.

2. In eadem infirmitate hoc sacramentum iterari non potest, nisi infirmus post susceptam unctionem convaluerit et in aliud vitae discrimen inciderit.

CHAPTER V.

I. Requisites for Administration.

Extrema Unctio praeberi non potest nisi fideli, qui post adeptum usum rationis ob infirmitatem vel senium in periculo mortis versetur.

The first paragraph of this canon announces in a remarkably succinct fashion the conditions essential for the valid reception of Extreme Unction. Its negative form excludes all in whom each condition is not found. The subject must present three qualifications:

1. He must be a "*fidelis.*"
2. He must have acquired the use of reason
3. He must be in danger of death from sickness or old age.

All three must be verified before administration can be validly made. Each is worthy of distinct consideration.

1.

"*Extreme Unctio praeberi non potest nisi fideli*"

In the first place, the recipient of Extreme Unction must be one of the *faithful.* The Code uses the term employed in the days of the catechumenate to distinguish those who had been baptized from catechumens. Nowadays it has come to mean those who have attached themselves to the Church, who have accepted her doctrines and who have been initiated into her rites. Hence those who are members of the true Church are meant, at least principally and primarily, by the term "fidelis" in this canon.

The problem of just how much can be done for dying Protestants has been agitating the theological world in recent years. The result seems to be a gradual increase in leniency and generosity in extending the conditional administration of the sacraments, whenever possible, to almost every dying man. Thus if a man is a baptized non-Catholic, some tell us that he is to get conditional absolution and Extreme Unction. If he is not baptized he is to receive conditional baptism and conditional Extreme Unction. If dubiously baptized, he is to have conditional baptism, conditional absolution and conditional Extreme Unction. Consequently when the Code declares that the first requisite of the recipient of Extreme Unction is that he be a "fidelis," the question of anointing non-Catholics can hardly be side-tracked.

Many hold that heretics and others not in the Church are in no way entitled to the sacraments of the Church and that it is unlawful for priests to administer such to them. They have splendid intrinsic reasons for their contention.

The Jacobean text should first be noted. The apostle used the words, "infirmatur quis in vobis," and all exegetes say that "vos" signifies the Catholic portion of the dispersed twelve tribes to whom the epistle was addressed.[1] Innocent I, in his famous letter to Decentius, gives this very interpretation of St. James' text: "Sane quoniam de hoc sunt, etc. Quod non est dubium de fidelibus aegrotantibus accipi vel intelligi debere, qui sancto oleo chrismatis perungi possunt."[2]

Moreover the term "fidelis" was used by the Fathers to denote only those who had completed the catechumenate and had been initiated into the Christian mysteries by the reception of Baptism. Tertullian[3] complained that some heretics were losing sight of the distinction that must be made between the "faithful" and catechumens. This was a very important discrimination in the early Church. The "faithful" were entitled to assist at the holy Sacrifice, to join with the priest in the "oratio fidelium," to receive the Body and Blood of Christ and the other sacraments. The catechumens had to leave the Holy Sacrifice after the sermon at the command of the deacon. The terms "faithful" and "Christian" were by no means co-extensive, as a text from St. Augustine clearly shows. "Ask a man," he writes,[4] " 'Are you a Christian?' If he be a pagan or a Jew, he will reply: 'I am not a Christian.' But if he say: 'I am a Christian,' ask him again: 'Are you a catechumen or one of the faithful?' "

---

1 Launoi, *Op. Omnia*, t. I, p. 560; Bord, *L'Extrême Onction*, p. 57.
2 Ep. "*Si instituta ecclesiastica*," 19 Mar. 416, cap. 8—M. P. L., 20, 559; C. I. C. Fontes, n. 19.
3 *De Praescr.*, cap. XLI—M. P. L., 2, 56.
4 *Tract. in Joan.*, XLIV, 2—M. P. L., 35, 1714.

The juridical argument is very convincing. On five different occasions the Holy See has declared that Penance (of which, be it remembered, Extreme Unction is the complement) was not to be given to schismatics or heretics. On February 4, 1664, the Congregation of the Propaganda[5] demanded an explicit belief in the supremacy of the Pope from Greek schismatics wishing to be absolved. In two decrees, dated August 28, 1669, and May 15, 1709, the Holy Office[6] forbade the administration to Nestorians. On September 22, 1763, the same Congregation[7] allowed the approach of Greek schismatics to Catholic churches, provided they were given no sacraments, that they did not communicate "in sacris" and that they had not been invited thereto. Practically the same answer was given in 1806 for soldiers who were doubtful Catholics.[8]

The new Code seems to support this view thoroughly. Canon 731, 2, apparently teems with finality: "Vetitum est Sacramenta Ecclesiae ministrare haereticis et schismaticis, etiam bona fide errantibus eaque petentibus, nisi prius, erroribus rejectis, Ecclesiae reconciliati fuerint." The fact that this Canon, although not found in the *Schema* of 1913, was later inserted in the Code is not without significance.

The change of wording in the Rituale is also noteworthy. Older editions of the rubrics used the word "non-baptizatis."[9] The present edition "ad normam Codicis" uses "fideli." Certainly there is furnished by this revision an added foundation for the opinion which forbids to non-Catholics a participation in our sacraments.

The force of the word "fidelis" is of paramount importance in the question at issue. Even today the word means ordinarily more than a heretic; and in fact, is often employed in contradiction to a non-Catholic. Launoi[10] defines it thus: "Fidelis autem est qui Baptismum suscepit et se in Christi familiam aggregavit." Similarly Blat[11] interprets it to signify "baptizatus

5 (C. G.) *Constantinop.*, Collectanea, n. 156 ad 2.
6 S. C. S. Off., *Mesopotamiae*—Collectanea, n. 185 ad 1; *ibid.*, n. 276.
7 Collectanea, n. 450.
8 Collectanea, n. 688.
9 *Rit. Rom.*, tit. V, cap. 1, n. 8—edit. 1913.
10 *Op. Omnia*, t. I, p. 560.
11 *Comm. Text.*, lib. III, p. I, n. 284.

habens fidem." They have evident good reason for this, because nowhere in the Code can "fidelis" be construed to include those outside the fold of faith. For example, in Canons 1161, 1162 /3, and 1169 "fideles" certainly does not comprehend within its scope either heretics or schismatics.[12] In Canon 1188 the *right* is given to all the faithful to enter public oratories at the time of divine services. Yet heretics, who are excommunicated by Canon 2314/1, have no such right, according to Canon 2259 /1. Consequently they are not "fideles."

Furthermore, in Canon 906, which commands that "*omnis utriusque sexus fidelis*" shall approach the tribunal of Penance at least once a year, there can be no doubt that only Catholics are meant. In Canon 925, which enumerates the capabilities of the recipients of indulgences, uses "baptizatus, non-excommunicatus" &c. According to Vermeersch-Creusen,[13] non-Catholics who have escaped the censure on account of good faith can gain indulgences. Yet this extension to non-Catholics seems to rest solely upon the fact that the Code does not use the term "fidelis."

Perhaps the clearest example of the meaning of "fidelis" is Canon 1152. By that canon exorcisms can be performed "non solum in fideles et catechumenos, sed etiam in acatholicos vel excommunicatos." Here the specific mention of non-Catholics as lawful subjects would indicate very strongly that where such mention is not made, those outside the Church are not suitable recipients.

From a juridical standpoint there seems to be no other solution. The wording of the law is too explicit. Yet it cannot be denied that the more merciful opinion, permitting conditional administration of the necessary sacraments to dying non-Catholics, has at least extrinsic probability; to establish this a rather copious examination of the various pronouncements of the Roman Congregations and the writings of theologians must be made.

---

[12] Cf. also canons 119; 465, 6; 467, 1 & 2; 483, 2; 684; 687; 707; &c.

[13] *Epit.*, II, 214.

The most important, of course, are

A) *The decisions of the Roman Congregations.*

Long before Quebec became the flourishing centre of Catholicity that it is today, the missionaries there spreading the gospel of Christ asked of the Holy Office: "Utrum conferendum sit Viaticum aut Extrema Unctio moribundis adultis, quos aliquando Baptismi capaces credimus, non autem Communionis aliorumque Sacramentorum?" The answer returned by the Congregation was this: "Non esse administrandum Viaticum neophyto moribundo nisi, &c. . . . Non esse pariter conferendum Sacramentum Extremae Unctionis neophyto moribundo quem missionarius capacem Baptismi credidit, nisi saltem idem habeat aliquam intentionem recipiendi Sacram Unctionem in beneficium animae pro mortis tempore ordinatam."[14] In the following century the Propaganda[15] affirmed this decree; and the very words were repeated in a later answer of the Inquisition [16] to a similar question from the Orient.

When questioned about the practice existing in Jerusalem of absolving dying heretics and schismatics conditionally without insisting on a sign of reconciliation to the Church, the Holy See replied:

> "Usum de quo quaeritur, prout exponitur, esse improbandum; et ad mentem: La mente e de accennare a Mons. Patriarca de Gerusalemme che, qualora il moribondo eretico o scismatico avesse dato un qualche signo su cui fondare un ragionevole dubbio che quegli aderisca alla santa Chiesa cattolica, in tal caso i preti di quella delegazione dovranno seguire le norme dettate da accreditati autori."[17]

To the question "An aliquando absolvi possint schismatici materiales, qui in bona fide versantur?" the same Congregation replied: "Cum scandalum nequeat vitari, Negative: praeterquam in mortis articulo, et tunc efficaciter, remoto scandalo."[18]

14 S. C. S. Off., 10 Maii, 1703—Collectanea, n. 256, ad 8.

15 S. C. P. F., (C. P. pro Sin.), 26 Sept., 1821—Collectanea, n. 768.

16 S. C. S. Off., *Tchely Meridio-Orientalis*, 10 Apr. 1861—Collectanea, n. 1213.

17 S. C. S. Off., 13 Jan. 1864—Collectanea, n. 1246.

18 S. C. S. Off., 20 Jul. 1898—Collectanea, n. 2012; A.S.S., XXXI, 254.

On May 26, 1916, the Holy Office gave a most important decision, which was never published officially. The question was asked about the lawfulness of conferring absolution and Extreme Unction upon schismatics deprived of their senses and in danger of death. The answer rendered was:

> "Sub conditione, affirmative, praesertim si ex adjunctis conjicere liceat eos implicite saltem errores suos rejicere, remoto tamen scandalo, manifestando scilicet astantibus Ecclesiam supponere eos in ultimo momento ad unitatem rediisse."[19]

This enumeration of decisions constitutes a very serious alignment of authority in defense of the proposition. The Quebec decision demanding an intention of receiving the Unction does not militate against this view. Some intention is always required in adults; but the fact that it need not be very explicit is insinuated in the employment of the term "aliquam intentionem." Hence a general intention of doing all that is necessary for salvation would include implicitly a desire to receive the Unction.[20] And in every Protestant it can actually be taken for granted that his principal and primary intention is that of doing all that Christ commanded for salvation. Even the slightest conjecture about the presence of such an intention is sufficient to act upon, for theologians of great weight hold this to be permissible. Gury, for instance, says: "In casu extremae necessitatis etiam in Sacramentorum administratione licet uti opinione etiam parum fundata."[21] Furthermore it is to be remembered that theologians admit the permissibility of construing even the vaguest sign as indicative of the intention. Neither is to be lost sight of that when a general absolution is given to an army on the battlefield, the validity of the absolution is sustained on the ground that the sign is *knowable,* but in many cases actually unperceived by the minister.[22] The inference is that the minister is justified in administering Extreme

---

19 Cited by Prummer, *Manuale Th. M.*, III, p. 223, from Lintzer Theol. Quartalschr., 1916, 693; and by Reuter, *Neo-Confessarius*, n. 203, from Kolner Pastoralblatt, 50, (1916), 504 sq.

20 Cf. Lehmkuhl, *Th. M.*, II, 66: "Voluntas christiano more moriendi includit in se voluntatem recipiendorum in articulo mortis sacramentorum Eccl."

21 *Comp. Th. M.*, II, n. 505 ad II.

22 Cf. King, *The Administration of the Sacraments to Dying Non-Catholics*, p. 24.

Unction on such grounds, because of the very tenuous probability that the sign has been given, though unperceived by himself.

In regard to the decisions of 1864 and 1898 it is to be noted that they have to do only with Penance. Yet since Extreme Unction is the complement of Penance, an *a pari* argument can be made. Of course it cannot be denied that scandal is more easily given in administering Extreme Unction to a heretic than Penance. Absolution can be made secretly even in the presence of bystanders, while unction in such a case is far more difficult. But scandal is something extrinsic, and does not avail against the intrinsic parity existing between Penance and its complement. No sacrament, not even Penance, can be imparted if scandal will follow. Hence, granted the removal of scandal, there is not valid reason why the administration of Extreme Unction cannot be extended to every case where the imparting of Penance is permissible.[23] Thus Gury, in settling a case in his *Casus Conscientiae,* wrote: "Si vero cum aliqua probabilitate nunc ad se redierit aliquis haereticus moribundus et videatur aliquod doloris signum edere, etsi dubium, tamen tentanda sunt omnia. Sed etiam in hoc casu parochus 1) condicionate tantum sacramenta administrare potest; 2) unctionem etiam clam tantum, ne alius sit scandalo." [24]

The proximity of the 1916 decision to the issuance of the Code presents a curious question, if canon 731, 2 is to be applied to all cases. One year before the encyclical of Benedict XV, "Providentissima," at a time when the schemata of the Code had been broadcast to all parts of the world for the final inspection of the bishops, the Sacred Congregation issued an instruction giving a norm of action in regard to the administration of the sacraments which they knew could be of value at most for but a few years—if the Canon is to be absolutely interpreted. It is true, as Augustine[25] says of a similar argument in another case, that this has very little juridical value; but on the other

23 This does not exclude the possibility that the imparting of Extreme Unction may be forbidden by positive and specific legislation, whereas Penance may not be. This phase will be later considered.

24 Gury, *Casus Conscientiae,* (edit. 1902), n. 625-626.

25 *A Commentary,* IV, p. 353, footnote.

hand it must be insisted that the Congregation of the Inquisition would hardly be guilty of such action as this. Roman Congregations do not move so hastily.

Reuter-Lehmkuhl-Umberg attempt to explain the question away in this fashion:

> "Petes, quid agendum sacerdoti si intelligat haereticum esse ad extrema deductum? Resp. Inprimis prae oculis habendus est can. 731, 2: 'Vetitum est sacramenta Ecclesiae,' &c. Quo canone vetatur Sacramentorum collatio haereticis et schismaticis a) mala fide errantibus, erroribus non rejectis; b) etiam bona fide errantibus, si simul, sui compotes, sacramenta petunt, erroribus non rejectis. Et sic Ecclesia hoc canone enuntiat, quid quasi officialiter concedat hac in re, quid non concedat. Ut vero sciamus, quid Ecclesia, pia mater, non-officialiter permittat, consulenda est decisio S. Officii d. 26 Maii, 1916, eo vid. tempore facta, quo canon ille sine dubio jam erat elucubratus."[26]

B) *The writings of theologians and canonists*

To the decisions of the Congregations can be added a host of eminent theologians and canonists, who, feeling that the sanctity of the sacrament is sufficiently safeguarded by a conditional administration, are mercifully impelled to extend its administration to every possible case. They believe with Tamburini: "Negotia in quibus nihil amittendum timetur, sed potius lucrum speratur, audacter sunt tentanda."[27]

In his Commentary upon Canon 731, 2, Vermeersch-Creusen writes:

> "Regula haec nulli exceptioni locum dat cum agitur de personis benevalentibus. Necessitas tamen consulendi, in periculo mortis, saluti animae, permittit ut moribundis acatholicis sacramenta necessitatis stricte vel late dictae (paenitentia et extrema unctio) administrentur, saltem condicionate, si sensibus destituti sunt, vel si, sensibus praesentes, in bona fide prudenter linquendi videantur. Ac sensibus destitutus, certius quam absolutione sacramentali, juvabitur extrema unctione, quae non exigit actus subjecti tanquam quasi-materiam sacramenti. Cavendum tamen est a scandalo vel miratione populi, si extrema unctio non possit satis secreto ministrari."[28]

Vermeersch might have some trouble proving that Canon 731, 2 applies only to the administration of the sacraments to

---

26 *Neo-Confessarius*, n. 203.
27 *Moral. Explicatio*, l. VI, cap. II, paragr. 3, n. 3.
28 *Epit.*, II, 16.

subjects who are well. Extreme Unction, it must be remembered, can be given only to the sick in danger of death. It must then be held that Canon 731, 2 does not apply to Extreme Unction at all. Yet the canon simply uses "sacramenta" without any modifying phrase that might insinuate the exception of Extreme Unction. Recalling the rule, "Legislator quod voluit expressit," it is rather hard to see the strength of Vermeersch's reasoning.

Now if Extreme Unction is included among the sacraments spoken of in Canon 731, 2, and if the recipient of Extreme Unction must be a "fidelis" in the common acceptation of the term, it seems that the Church has exempted by positive legislation the sacrament of Extreme Unction from the alignment of aids that may be offered to non-Catholics when they are dying. Perhaps this is why Pruemmer [29] allows the administration of Penance to a dying Protestant, yet does not permit the bestowal of Extreme Unction.

With varying degrees of liberality other authors allow administration to Protestants in danger of death. A writer in the *Casuist,* does not extend the lawfulness of administration to cases where the man is still conscious.[30] The reasons he proffers are that it is not a necessary means of salvation and that it can scarcely be given without grave scandal. Kern[31] limits the bestowal of the sacrament further. He holds that it is lawful to anoint such heretics only who in good faith adhere to a sect which confesses the sacramental dignity of Extreme Unction. This would reduce the lawful subjects to the Oriental Orthodox Greeks, the Nestorians and the Monophysites. Other Protestants, the author thinks, have not sufficient intention.

Murray,[32] a Redemptorist, writing in the *Homiletic and Pastoral Review,* admits the allowability of anointing all dying heretics, who are in good faith and who can be considered to have even the most tenuous probability of receiving the sacrament. Both this writer and Vermeersch make note of a reply

---

29 *Manuale J. C.,* l. III, p. I, de Sac., proem.; this was also the view of Kenrick, *Th. M.,* III, p. 223 & p. 265.
30 Vol. III, p. 43.
31 *Tract. de Ext. Unct.,* p. 317.
32 Vol. XXVI, (1926), p. 412 sqq.

of the Holy Office, dated March 17-20, 1916, which demands of the heretic formal reconciliation with the Church. Vermeersch explains the decree as follows:

> "Neque obstat particulare et tantum in ephemeride dioecesana vulgatum responsum S. Officii, 17-20 Maii 1916, quo negatum est schismaticis materialibus in mortis articulo constitutis, bona fide absolutionem sive Extremam Unctionem petentibus, sacramenta ista conferri posse, sed requiri ut 'meliori quo fieri possit modo, errores reiciant et professionem fidei faciant.' Responsum enim istud dat regulam generalem do solis schismaticis quibuscum facilius peccari potest quodam indifferentismo, et qui, ob ipsam petitionem, videntur satis commode adduci posse ad errorum abjurationem; nec casum contemplatur quo periculose, pro animae aeterna salute, bona fides turbaretur."[33]

Similarly Pruemmer[34] lays little weight on this decision of the Holy See.

Hanley is also very liberal. "It is given," he writes,[35] "to all baptized persons who are in good faith, if the priest prudently judges that it may be done." Lehmkuhl allows an administration only to unconscious heretics:

> "Immo in iis haereticis baptizatis quod in bona fide versari sumi potest, fortasse remedium reconciliationis erit, applicabile utique tantum si sensibus destituti fuerint, atque si externae sint conditiones ejusmodi, ut sine majoris mali periculo haec adjumenta valeant; quamquam etiam quoad hoc remedium satis dubium est, num in piis illorum hominum actibus, qui praecesserint, sufficiens intentio contineatur. *Kern* id admittit quoad eos haereticos tantum, quorum sectae profitentur extremae unctionis sacramentum. Iis igitur, si in bona fide existunt, sacramentum dari posse, certum est; ceteris, etsi in bona fide sint, dari non posse, ita certum non est."[36]

If we except the argument from positive and specific legislation, there is no reason why Extreme Unction cannot be given when Penance can. And indeed the explanation given by Reuter can be used in order to escape the force of this argument from

---

33 *Th. M.*, III, 195. *The Hom. and Past. Review* (l.c.) gives the text of this decision in English: "May a material schismatic in danger of death and in good faith who asks for absolution and Extreme Unction be given these sacraments? Response: Not before he rejects his errors as best he can, and makes a profession of faith."

34 *Brevis Conspectus Mutat. Th. M.*, p. 5.

35 *Treatise on the Sacrament of Extreme Unction*, p. 31.

36 *Th. M.*, II, 716.

specific legislation. Consequently the arguments of many authors in regard to the administration of Penance to dying heretics can also be extended to Extreme Unction. The alignment of authority is very impressive.

Thus D'Annibale:

> "Quod si nullum prorsus signum ediderit, morbo in instanti correptus, ut puta irruente apoplexi? Ergo ut opinor, si probabile sit non abhorrere, puta si rudis et b. f. homo sit, vel animum a catholica religione non alienum ostendit, et huic dari potest, si quid opinor: 'multo satius est nolenti dare, quam volenti negare, ubi velit an nolit sic non apparet.' "[37]

Kendrick is somewhat stricter than D'Annibale, for he allows absolution only to those who evidence a friendly mind toward the Church:

> "Qui catholicam fidem nunquam professi sunt, sed voluntatem in eam proclivem ostenderunt, possunt eo in discrimine sub condicione absolvi censuris et peccatis, si in suis sectis fuerint jam baptizati; quod si ejus voluntatis nullum datum sit indicium, non sunt absolvendi, etiamsi dent signa doloris."[38]

Telch[39] commemorates among the probable opinions the view which permits secret conditional absolution to heretics presumably attrite and in good faith.

Sabetti-Barrett[40] allows schismatic dying in good faith to absolved, and admits the probability of the opinion permitting Penance to be given to material heretics who have passed into unconsciousness. Noldin[41] and Genicot[42] admit the liceity of absolving secretly and conditionally a heretic, still conscious but

37 *Summ. Th. M.*, III, 317. The quotation used by D'Annibale as the reason for his opinion is taken from St. Augustine (cf. *infra, hoc capite,* footnote 47). An examination of this quotation reveals that St. Augustine was speaking of a case somewhat different than the one contemplated by D'Annibale. St. Augustine considered the situation where a catechumen was unable to manifest by words his desire for Baptism. And it can be seen that very great probability of the man's desire to be baptized can be gleaned from the very fact of his entrance into the catechumenate. In the case treated by D'Annibale, no such presumption of the presence of intention is deducible from the circumstances.

38 *Th. M.*, III, De Paenitent., n. 212.

39 *Epit. Th. M.*, p. 413, n. 50.

40 *Comp. Th. M.*, p. 713.

41 *De Sac.*, n. 295.

42 *Inst. Th. M.*, II, 298.

dying, who cannot be conveniently advised about conversion to the Catholic faith—provided, of course, that he can prudently be considered only a material heretic living in good faith outside the Church. Those destitute of their senses can likewise be absolved. In the former case Noldin tells the confessor to see that the man be moved to make acts of faith explicitly in the mysteries absolutely necessary and implicitly in the other articles of dogmatic truth. To these should be joined acts of trust and hope in the Divine benignity, and acts of charity and contrition whereby the subject admits that he is a sinner and asserts his willingness to do what Christ would command for salvation.[43]

Tanquerey[44] thinks that it is not forbidden to absolve dying heretics who cannot be instructed in regard to the necessity of embracing the Catholic faith. Arregui[45] agrees with this heartily and goes still further. He admits the lawfulness of absolving conditionally a *formal and public* heretic destitute of his senses, even though he did not retract his heresy when he was able to do so. Schieler-Heuser[46] believes that "one might give absolution to a baptized non-Catholic of whom it might be presumed upon any probable grounds that he is bona fide and would gladly accept the help of a priest if he knew it was necessary for him."

Thus it is seen that many authoritative minds have held the licitness of giving Penance to dying heretics. And if Penance, why not the complement of Penance? It is true that when a heretic is in possession of his senses it is far more difficult to anoint him than to absolve him "*clam et condicionate.*" Yet it would not be unreasonable or outlandish to suppose that the priest could anoint the forehead or one of the senses with a

43 The advice given by LaCroix (*Th. M.*, l. 6, p. II, n. 1866) and adopted by Reuter (*Neo-Confessarius*, n. 203) is quite impractical and very conducive to scandal in these days. They suggest that the priest change his garb and approach the sick man incognito. They hint that he may alter his dress to such an extent that the sick man may be left under the impression that he is a Protestant minister.

44 *Brev. Syn. Th. M.*, n. 1194.

45 *Summ. Th. M.*, n. 589. The probability of this teaching is admitted also by Ferreres (*Th. M.*, II, 608) and Gennari (*Il Monitore Ecclesiastico*, VI, p. 2, pag. 113); cf. also Murphy, *Delinquencies and Penalties*, pp. 5-8.

46 *The Theory and Practice of the Confessional*, p. 652.

single unction, while the bystanders would be left under the impression that it was a touch of sympathetic kindness.

At any rate a priest who gives Extreme Unction to dying heretics has enough of extrinsic probability on his side to save him from any scruples of conscience or criticism of his superiors. Again, a priest who does not anoint in these cases cannot be impugned for a lack of love towards souls. He has in support of his refusal arguments whose intrinsic worth are much greater than those which prompt the contrary mode of procedure. Such a priest may be firmly impressed by the arguments which make it absolutely wrong to administer the sacraments to these dying persons.

The words of St. Augustine may be a help to the individual priest on this matter, enabling him to fashion his mode of reasoning in concordance with one of the brightest lights in the intellectual history of the world:

> "Catechumenis ergo in hujus vitae ultimo constitutis, si morbo seu casu aliquo sic oppressi sint, ut quamvis adhuc vivant, petere sibi tamen Baptismum vel ad interrogata respondere non possint; prosit eis quod eorum in fide christiana jam nota voluntas est, ut eo modo baptizentur, quo modo baptizantur infantes, quorum voluntas nulla adhuc patuit. Non tamen propterea damnare eos debemus qui timidius agunt, quam nobis videretur agi oportere. . . . Sed non solum incredibile est, nec in fine vitae hujus baptizari catechumenum velle: verum etiam si voluntas ejus incerta est, multo satius est nolenti dare quam volenti negare, ubi velit an nolit sic non apparet, ut tamen credibilius sit eum, si posset, velle se potius dicturum ea Sacramenta percipere, sine quibus jam credidit non se oportere de corpore exire."[47]

2.

Qui post adeptum usum rationis

The second requirement for the valid reception of Extreme Unction is that the subject have attained the use of reason. This is clear from the Jacobean text: "Inducat presbyteros." A man who never had the use of reason would be incapable of such an action. "Faire venir les prêtes de l'église," writes Bord,[48] "eux et non d'autres hommes, est l'action d'un adulte."

---

47 *"De Conjug. Adult.,"* lib. 1, c. 26, n. 33—M. P. L., 40, 469.
48 *L'Extrême Onction,* p. 57.

Theologians have advanced many intrinsic reasons why children under the age of reason cannot receive Extreme Unction yet can be participants of the sacramental graces of Confirmation. Yet practically all of them can be attacked in very vital points.

For example, Suarez [49] asserts that the sacrament was instituted because of the grief and the violent temptations of the hour of death, with the purpose of overcoming the weakness that springs from sin and of remitting such sin, if necessary. Of these an infant is wholly incapable, for it can neither be tempted nor resist temptation. Accordingly an infant is an invalid subject for Extreme Unction.

However, it must be remembered that incapability of enjoying the consolation afforded by the sacrament is just as true in the case of those destitute of their senses as it is of infants. Yet the sacrament is never denied to the unconscious simply because of that reason.

The argument advanced by Albertus Magnus [50] is quite as unsatisfactory. He claims that it would stultify the sacrament to pronounce the form "quidquid deliquisti" over those who had nothing to delete. At most this would prove nothing else but the impropriety of the Western form for children. Suppose the Eastern form were employed—or one of the ancient forms which said nothing of the forgiveness of sins? Furthermore the use of such a form should be just as futile in the case of those who have no sins to wipe out, such as adults just baptized, etc.

St. Thomas advances a double argument against the capability of children to receive Extreme Unction. In the first argument, he says that children are excluded because this sacrament, like the Eucharist, demands actual devotion in the recipient.[51] The basis of this demand for actual devotion is found in the article preceding: "Quod ad effectum hujus sacramenti percipiendum plurimum valet devotio suscipientis, et personale meritum conferentium et generale totius Ecclesiae: quod patet ex hoc quod per modum deprecationis forma hujus sacramenti

---

49 D. 42, s. 1, n. 3.

50 *Comm. in lib. IV Sent.*, dist. 23, n. 10.

51 *Suppl.*, q. 32, a. 4.

confertur. Et ideo illis qui non possunt recognoscere et cum devotione suscipere hoc sacramentum, dari non debet."[52] The vulnerability of this reasoning becomes apparent when it is remembered that the Church does not exclude from participation in the sacrament those who are destitute of their senses and consequently incapable of actual devotion. Moreover the use of reason is by no means necessary for the valid reception of the Eucharist. In the early Church even infants were admitted to the Divine Banquet. Hence the parity made with the sacrament of the Eucharist is void.

The second argument of the Angelic Doctor is quite as fallacious as his first. The principal effect of Extreme Unction is, he says, the comforting and strengthening of the sick man against the debilities of fallen nature in so far as these debilities have been increased by personal sins.[53] Since an infant has committed no actual sins, he is not laboring under that weakness of nature against which the sacrament is directed. Consequently he is not capable of the actual or habitual strengthening afforded by the sacrament; in other words, he cannot receive the principal effect of the sacrament. *Qui est incapax principalis effectus, incapax est sacramenti.* Therefore children are invalid subjects for Extreme Unction.

Suarez ably answers this argument of St. Thomas:

> "Neque ex verbis Jacobi, neque ex aliquo Concilio, nec ex forma vel materia hujus sacramenti neque ex fine ejus colligi potest necessitas hujus sacramenti [i. e., debilitas naturae lapsae sit aucta per propria subjecti peccata]; et alioqui effectus primarius hujus sacramenti optime locum habet in eo qui nunquam actualiter peccavit; ergo et ipsum sacramentum."[54]

The retort that the form would be rendered *simpliciter* false in a subject who had neither sin nor sin's effects to expiate is of little worth. Infants are not excluded from admission to the sacrament because the form is not apt for them. On the contrary the Church has provided a form which does not apply to them because they are excluded. Moreover it would be nec-

---

52 *Suppl.*, q. 32, a. 3.

53 *Suppl.*, q. 32, a. 4 ad 2—This argument is also advanced by Barbosa, *De Off. et Pot. Par.*, P. II, cap. xxii, n. 12.

54 D. 42, s. 2, n. 8.

essary to extend such a contention to the case of saints who by special privilege or extraordinary penance had nothing to expiate—neither sin nor its effects—at the time they fall into danger of death. Yet such people are valid subjects, even though the Latin form be employed. It retains its verity because it expresses the power and efficacy which Unction has *ex se,* and therefore it determines the matter sufficiently to accomplish the valid confection of the sacrament.[55]

Another reason advanced against the capability of infants to be anointed is that Extreme Unction is the complement of Penance, and consequently, those unable to receive Penance are excluded from its complement, Extreme Unction. Yet altho every one capable of Penance is *per se* capable of Unction (given the necessary conditions, as danger of death, etc.), the *vice versa* is not true. The argument is based on a wrong conception of what is required in order that one sacrament be the complement of another. What is necessary here is that Extreme Unction's principal effect be of such a nature as to cause the deletion of the remains of sin, if such *reliquiae* have not been removed by Penance. It is certainly not required that the principal effect be essentially ordained against the effects of actual sin; it is quite sufficient that the removal of these effects follow from the state of soul that the primary effect produces. The principal effect of the sacrament is, of course, "roborare infirmum in eo articulo contra insidias diaboli," [56] &c.

Moreover an actual instance where a man is capable of Unction and not of Penance is that of a man just baptized. The common opinion holds that sins committed before Baptism are not matter for absolution. This *instantia contraria* destroys totally the validity of St. Thomas' argumentation.

Yet there must be some internal reason why this sacrament is not given to infants. Kern[57] seems to advance the best argument in the matter. Each sacrament, he tells us, is instituted principally for one effect, although others may follow therefrom secondarily. In Extreme Unction this effect is the *confortatio habitualis,* the right to every help or aid which pro-

55 Cf. Laymann, *Th. M.*, l. V, tr. 6, c. 3, in fine, where he teaches that in such cases "quidquid peccasti" is equivalent to "si quid peccasti."
56 D. 42, s. 2, n. 8.
57 *Tract. de Ext. Unct.*, p. 311-2.

motes alleviation of the soul. Now it needs no proof that an infant is altogether incapable of enjoying actual comforting of soul (confortatio actualis) against the debilities caused therein by sin. However, it remains to be shown that he is also incompetent to receive the habitual comfort given by the sacrament.

There is a repugnance in the very concept of giving a right which can never be used because of the want of sufficient time to come into such a position where it may be used. Kern gives an example of a prince who conceded to a pauper the right to enjoy for the following day the comforts of a palace three days' journey away. Such a right is misnamed. Similarly it would be the lot of an infant to attain to benefits which would be of value only for the time of sickness. While sick, he could make no use of it, for he is incapable of actual spiritual alleviation. He is neither tempted nor depressed. If he recovers and reaches reason's age, his title to the supernatural aids will have vanished, for the duration of these rights is co-extensive only with the period of danger of death. As a consequence, infants become, by their utter incompetency, either active or passive, of receiving alleviation, absolutely invalid subjects of Unction.

This also sheds illumination why those not having reason can validly participate in Confirmation and yet cannot receive Extreme Unction. The former gives a right, sealed by a character upon the soul, to aids against the dangers of faith. At the time of reception the infant has no actual need of such graces, but he does receive a passive potency, which will be translated into act as he "advances in age and wisdom and grace before God and men." As he matures, he becomes more and more capable of actual reception of the aids flowing from a right once held only passively. Thus an infant can validly receive Confirmation, for normally the right to graces bestowed by the sacrament realizes its object in later life. Should death call him while still an infant, such an event would be thoroughly accidental. And quite as accidental would be the phenomenon of an infant reaching the age of reason during the time of sickness. The sacraments were not instituted for such rare and absolutely extraordinary cases. Accordingly for one and the same reason a child is an apt subject for Confirmation, even though he may die before the age of reason, and is completely incapable of Extreme Unction, even though it is foreseen that his sickness will perdure until he attains the use of reason.

The exact age required for the subject of Extreme Unction has been the matter of much local legislation in the past. Most authorities placed the age for valid reception at a much higher one than the age of reason. Perhaps it was the age of puberty that first influenced earlier theologians to set this later date for valid reception. Some went further than this.

Odo, the bishop of Paris in the twelfth century, inserted in his Synodal Constitutions the following enactment:

> "Ad sacramentum Extremae Unctionis moneant populum sacerdotes, non tantum divites et senes, sed pauperes et juvenes omnes, a tempore discretionis, maxime a quattuordecim annis et supra ut se paratos exhibeant cum necesse fuerit."[58]

The same advanced age was decreed by Galon and Simon,[59] the papal legates to France under Popes Innocent III and Honorius III; by the Constitutions of Richard Poore, bishop of Sarum in England;[60] by the *Constitutiones Synodales Episcopi Anonymi,*[61] edited in 1237; by the Statutes of Peter di Collomedio,[62] archbishop of Rouen; and by an ancient Ritual of the Canons Regular of the Monastery of Aqua-Viva in the diocese of Tours.[63]

Durandus states in his *Rationale Divinorum Officiorum*[64] that the subject must have attained the age of eighteen years. This was mentioned also in a verse of an anonymous poem contained in the Codex of St. Martin of Tours: "Octo decemque tantum annos ungendus habebit."[65] This age was also prescribed by Frederick Nausea in his famous Catechism.[66] The Synod of Bayeux,[67] held at the beginning of the fourteenth

58 Cap. 8, n. 2—Harduin VI, pars 2, 1941.
59 Apud Martene, *De Antiq. Ecc. Rit.*, lib. 1, c. 7, a. 1, n. 3; Catalano, *Rit. Rom.*, t. I, p. 310, ad paragr. V, n. III.
60 Harduin, VII, 107.
61 Harduin, VII, 303.
62 Martene, *l.c.;* Catalano, *l.c.*
63 Martene, *l.c.;* Catalano, *l.c.*
64 Lib. I, c. 8, n. 25.
65 Martene, *l.c.*
66 Lib. 3, cap. 107—quoted by Martene, l.c.; Catalano, l.c. and Benedict XIV, *De Syn. Dioc.*, l. 8, c. 6, n. 2.
67 Cap. 74—Harduin VII, 1237.

century, reduced the age to fourteen, thus agreeing with the legislation of Odo.

Local rituals of the sixteenth century evidence the deferment of the Unction until the subject was fourteen years old. A rubric to this effect can be found in the Manuals of Chartres (1489 & 1544 & 1604), Rheims (1504 & 1530), Périgueux (1509), Clermont (1518 & 1525), St. Flour (1525), Châlons sur Marne (1529 & 1569), Nivernum (1533), Beauvais (1544), Meaux (1546), Verdun (1554), Limoges (1555), Arras (1563), Vienne (1577) and Maguelone (1583).[68]

Yet such a practice of delaying the unction until puberty was not universal. The Statutes of Cahors, Rodez and Tulle demanded only the age of reason.[69] Similar synodal decrees were made for Paris[70] in 1557 and for the province of Cambrai[71] in 1586. Valens Guellius, the bishop of Orleans, declared in the diocesan Statutes the ineligibility of those who had not yet communicated to participate in the reception of Extreme Unction.[72] With far more reasonableness the Pastoral of Mechlin[73] admitted to reception all those capable of committing mortal sin. Cardinal de Rohan, in the Ritual of Strasburg, prescribed: "Non denegetur etiam pueris si septimum attigerint annum, nec iis in quibus malitia supplet aetatem, etiamsi septenarii non sunt."[74]

Although the tendency of the age was to postpone the administration of Unction, nevertheless two authors claimed that it used to be imparted even to those who had not the use of reason, viz., Cardinal Nicholas of Cusa[75] and Juan Maldo-

68 Launoi, *Op. Omnia,* t. I, pp. 562-3.

69 Martene-Durand, *Anecdoctor.,* tom. IV, cap. 17—cf. Benedict XIV, *De Syn. Dioc.,* l. 8, c. 6, n. 2.

70 Cf. Martene, *De Antiq. Ecc. Rit.,* l. I, c. 7, a. 1, n. 3.

71 Harduin IX, 2164.

72 Cf. Martene, *l.c.*; Benedict XIV, *l.c.* This view was also embraced by Dominic Soto (*Comm. in IV Sent.,* dist., 23, q. 2, a. 2). Cf. also Conc. Mexicanum (anno 1589), lib. I, tit. VI, paragr. 6—Harduin X, 1610.

73 Van Espen, *Jus Eccl. Univ.,* P. II, sec. I, tit. 8, c. 2, n. 9.

74 *Rituale Argentinense,* "Tit. de Ext. Unct.," paragr. 2, p. 174—quoted by Benedict XIV, *l.c.*

75 *Epistola Tertia ad Bohemos.*

nado.[76] Cornelius a Lapide[77] denounces this statement as groundless.

Since the Council of Trent, most theologians have held it is eminently sufficient for validity if the child has attained the age of reason.[78] Later Councils have similarly been very liberal, and insist that the child is capable of Extreme Unction, even though he has not received the Eucharist—provided that he be capable of sin.[79] The deferring of Extreme Unction to any later age was denounced in no uncertain terms by Pius X: "Detestabilis omnino est abusus non ministrandi Extremam Unctionem pueris post usum rationis.[80]"

The new Code demands only the use of reason. The subject must be at least "culpae capax,[81]" even though he has never actually transgressed the law. He is, if he have reason, subject to temptations, and is in need of the comfort and solace that such a sacrament brings. Boys who have developed enough to be capable of the least venial sin are to be anointed. No appointed age can be given, for in each case special investigation is to be made into the development of the moral sense in the subject. Vicar Lebherz, writing in the *Casuist*[82] holds that children may receive Extreme Unction even before the sixth year. Benedict XIV[83] said it was to be given to boys "qui censentur capaces Sacramenti Poenitentiae, quamvis nondum tanta polleant judicii maturitate ut videantur apti ad rite participandam Eucharistiam, de cujus ineffabili excellentia et sanctitate non ita facile edoceri queunt."

If it is certain that the child has not yet reached the use of reason, the sacrament cannot be administered.[84] With children

---

76 *Disp. &c., Circa Sept. Sacramenta,* t. II, de Extr. Unct., col. 389.

77 *Comm. in Ep. S. Jacobi,* ad V, 14.

78 Cf. e.g., Suarez, d. 42, s. 2, n. 8; S. Alph., *Th. M.*, VI, 720.

79 Cf. Conc. V Mediolanen. apud *Acta Ecc. Mediolanen.*, t. I, p. I, p. 230; Prov. Councils of Cassel (1853—Coll. Lac., III, 838); Quebec (1854—ibid., p. 645); Rheims (1849—ibid., IV, 122); Bordeaux (1850—ibid., IV, 574); Kansas City, Mo. (1912—c. 13, n. 126); Rochester (1914—tit. X, c. 6, n. 341); Oklahoma (1913—n. 136); &c.

80 S. C. de Sac., "*Quam Singulari,*" 8 Aug. 1910—A. A. S., II, 583.

81 Matharan et Castillon, *Asserta Moralia,* paragr. 521, p. 237; Aureli, *De Extr. Unct.*, n. 15, p. 90.

82 Vol. II, p. 173-6.

83 *De Syn. Dioc.*, l. 8, c. 6, n. 2.

84 Cat. Conc. Trid., *De Extr. Unct.*, n. 9.

are classed those afflicted with permanent insanity. In such people there has been no evolution of the spiritual or moral life—and accordingly they experience none of the spiritual prostration which occurs in the hour of death to those who have knowledge of good and of evil. They are consequently incapable of the principal effect of the sacrament.[85]

It is by no means necessary that a man be "sui compos" at the time of the conferring of the sacrament. Those who have been rendered unconscious by the ravages of the disease[86] or those who have lapsed into insanity after the attainment of the use of reason[87] are capable of receiving this anointing. They have the potency of habitual *confortatio* at least, and this is quite sufficient to make a man a valid subject of the Unction.

Any one who has ever had a lucid interval during his life can validly be anointed. This was declared as anciently as the Council of Orange[88] and was clearly expounded by Navarrhus:

> "Cuilibet tamen hujusmodi infirmo est ministrandum, etiamsi sit amens et phreneticus, si absque irreverentia sacramenti, id fieri possit, et potuerit ante peccare, et antequam insaniret, expresse aut tacite petierit illud, aut si meminisset, petiturus fuisset, nec in peccato mortali notorio insaniret."[89]

---

85 It might be objected that the insane, though incapable of some effects, have at least the capacity to receive corporal sanation, and therefore are capable of receiving the sacrament. However "qui incapax est principalis effectus, incapax est sacramenti." Sacraments were instituted for supernatural ends, and not for natural purposes. If an effect does occur in the order of nature, it must be considered as an appendage, never as the principal effect. Cf. Trombellio, *Tract. de Sac. Ext. Unct.*, Vol. III, diss. X, n. X; Coninck, *De Sac. et Censur.*, disp. 19, dub. VII.

86 Cf. can. 943.

87 Cf. Trombellio, *Tract. de Sac. Ext. Unct.*, Vol. III, diss. X, paragr. VI, p. 26; Mastrio, *Th. M.*, disp. XXII, qu. 5, a. 1, nn. 70-71; Diana, *Op. Coord.*, tom. II, tr. IV, res. 50; Barbosa, *De Off. et Pot. Par.*, c. 22, n. 13; Tamburini, *Moral. Explic.*, "de Ext. Unct.," c. 2, paragr. 3, n. 4; Benedict XIV, *De Syn. Dioc.*, l. 8, c. 6, n. 4; Suarez, d. 42, s. 1, nn. 5-6.

88 Harduin I, 1785—can. 13.

89 *Manuale*, c. 22, n. 13. Cf. *infra*, chap. vii, p. 240, where the lawfulness of anointing a man who fell into insanity in the act of sin is treated. Cf. S. Thom., *Comm. in IV Sent.*, d. 23, q. 2, a. 2, quaestiunc. 3.

Similarly those who are delirious, or unconscious, or in convulsions, or otherwise deprived of their senses may be validly and licitly anointed.[90] Lehmkuhl sums this up briefly:

> "Deneganda non est 1) amentibus et delirantibus qui unquam antea rationis usum habuerint; 2) pueris modo rationis usum attigerint, quamquam antea neque confessi sunt neque S. Eucharistia donati."[91]

As stated before, the subject must be at least capable of sin. Whether it is necessary that he actually have committed sin is very much disputed. St. Thomas[92] holds that the principal effect presupposes the existence of a spiritual infirmity resulting from actual sin committed before or after baptism. Suarez,[93] on the contrary, maintains that it is quite sufficient to have the capability of actual sin and to possess the spiritual infirmity resulting from original sin. He is supported in his contention by Dionysius the Carthusian,[94] and St. Bonaventure.[95]

Suarez goes even further and holds that one by nature liable to contract original sin, yet by a special privilege exempt from it, can still receive the primary effect of the sacrament; and consequently is a valid subject of the Unction.[96] His opinion is subscribed to by St. Antoninus,[97] by Canisius[98] and by Henriquez,[99] at least in regard to the case of the Blessed Virgin. They base their contention upon the argument that she had the antecedent potency of sinning, even though this potency had never been deduced into act, because of her singular privileges.

The opposite opinion is taught by Victoria,[100] Vasqueth[101] and Tanner[102]—because, as Tanner remarks, the privilege bestowed on Mary was not capriciously done, but arose from a certain congruity and special excellence connected with the

90 Tanquerey, *Th. D.*, III, 782.
91 *Th. M.*, II, 723.
92 *Suppl.* q. 32, a. 4 ad 2.
93 D. 42, s. 1, n. 5.
94 *Summa Fidei*, lib. 5, c. 149 in fine.
95 *Comm. in IV Sent.*, d. 23, p. 2, a. 1, q. 2.
96 D. 42, sect. 1, n. 5.
97 *In III p. d. Thom.*, tit. XIV, c. 8 et 13.
98 *Lib. de Beata Virg.*, c. 9.
99 *De Sac.*, lib. III, c. 11, n. 7.
100 *Summa Sac.*, De Ext. Unct., n. 222.
101 *In III p. d. Thom.*, disp. 119, c. 8.
102 tom. IV, disp. 7, a. 1, dub. 3.

prerogative of the Divine Maternity. Accordingly, they say, she was in no way capable of the spiritual comfort produced by the sacrament.

A practical case will occur when a priest is confronted with the case of a child who has reached the age of reason and whom he knows from confession never to have sinned. In this situation St. Alphonsus[103] and Diana[104] decide that the sacrament should be bestowed. Two reasons would prompt this course of action: (1) the very great likelihood that the commission of actual sin is not essential for valid reception; and (2) the seal of confession, which comes into consideration at least remotely and indirectly in such circumstances.

It is certainly permitted to anoint an adult immediately after the bestowal of Baptism. This is abundantly clear from the decisions of the Roman Congregations[105] and from the teaching of theologians.[106] Laymann calls attention to the fact that the form in such cases has a conditional sense "si quid peccasti."

3. *"Ob infirmitatem vel senium in periculo mortis versetur."*

It has been shown in the first chapter that the Scriptural text speaks of those only who are seriously sick. The force of the Greek words **ασθενεῖ** and **κάμνοντα**, especially when considered in their setting in that text, refer explicitly to a subject in a dangerous state of illness.

In the course of centuries abuses and malpractices in this regard have crept into the Greek and the Latin rites. Both (and also the Greek schismatic or Orthodox Church) profess the sacramental dignity of the Unction; both concur in the question of its matter and form, its effects and its minister. But

---

103 *Th. M.*, VI, 717.

104 *Opera Coord.*, t. II, tr. IV, res. 42.

105 S. C. S. Off., 10 Maii, 1703, ad 8—Collectanea, n. 256; 10 Apr. 1861, ad. 1—Collectanea, n. 1213; S. C. P. F., 26 Sept. 1821—Collectanea, n. 768.

106 Diana, *Op. Coord.*, t. II, tr. IV, res. 47; Laymann, *Th. M.*, lib. V, tr. 8, c. III in fine; S. Alph., *Th. M.*, VI, 721; Kenrick, *Th. M.*, III, De Ext. Unct., cap. unic., n. 18; Lehmkunl, *Th. M.*, II, 722; Sabetti-Barrett, *Th. M.*, p. 805; Genicot, *Casus Consc.*, cas. 884.

in regard to the subject of the sacrament, theological history resounds with the vituperations of the West against the East and re-echoes with the arraignment of the Orient by the Occident.

Latin writers clamor that the Greeks confer, in direct contradiction to the Apostolic mandate, the *Euchelaion* on those but slightly ill or even perfectly well. Thus Arcudius wrote:

> "Ego praesentem morem Graecorum qui poenitentes, quamvis bene valentes, in omnibus iis corporis partibus adhibita quoque forma sacramenti non aliter atque infirmos inungunt, nulla ratione probare possum; et si sordidi quaestus gratia id faciunt . . . eo magis detestandus est. Cum enim subjectum non sit aptum ad recipiendum sacramentum—quando neque graviter quis infirmatur, et ad mortem, ut requirit Apostolus et exponunt sacri doctores—frustra temereque illud Graeci administrant."[107]

And again:

> "Adeo ut modo non pudeat passim Graecorum presbyteros hoc oleum instar sacramenti ex imperitia benevalentibus administrare."[108]

Similar denunciations of the practice are found in the writings of Theophilus Raynaudus[109] and Tournely.[110]

Other writers, such as Hieremias,[111] Allatius[112] and Fortescue,[113] testify to the existence of this custom. It was by no means local; as Arcudius puts it, "viget non in aliquo angulo Graeciae sed ubique passim, quam eandem retinet hac nostra aetate tota Russia universaque Moscovia."[114]

Goar admits this usage but contends vigorously that it is regarded as a sacramental. "Contingit tamen, fateor, aliquando ex officio peracto, ex astantibus plerique, vel benedictionis spiritualis obtinendae, vel levis alicujus doloris eos afflictantis leniendi gratia, Unctionis medela se curari exoptent; quod praestant sacerdotes eadem ratione ac super aegros recitata."[115] This admission is followed by arguments in proof of his con-

107 *De Concord. Eccl. Occid.*, l. V, c. 4.
108 *De Concord. Eccl. Occid.*, l. V, cap. ult.
109 *Heteroclita Spiritualia*, t. XVI, p. 164.
110 *Praelectiones Theol. de Sept. Sac.*, "De Ext. Unct.," q. 3.
111 *Censura adv. Augustanam Lutheranorum Confessionem*, l. 1, cap. 7.
112 *De Consens. Eccl. Occid. et Orient.*, l. III, cap. 16, n. 3.
113 *The Orthodox Eastern Church*, p. 425.
114 L. c., cap. 4.
115 *Euchologium*, p. 349-50. Pignatelli (*Consult. Canon.*, t. VIII, consult. 84, n. 29) thinks this is a sacramental.

tention. There is no intention of confecting the sacrament; the ceremonial which accompanies the bestowal of the Euchelaion is absent; and the form or prayer used in the Greek rite is so comprehensive that it can be used on this occasion without doing violence to the meaning. The arguments of Goar are supported by the fact that the Greeks used the oil of the sick for many other purposes than to confer Extreme Unction.[116]

Yet Kern[117] is not impressed by this reasoning, although he admits the great authority of Goar. Drouven[118] protests that we are too harsh in our judgment of the Greeks. Perhaps he is right, for today the oriental theologians confess that the administration of Unction to healthy people was certainly an abuse.[119]

In the schismatic Church this practice of anointing those not sick exists even today. It enjoys wide diffusion in the patriarchate of Constantinople, and indeed in the whole Hellenic kingdom.[120] In the Russian Church, on the contrary, there is found a firm persuasion that the Euchelaion must be reserved for those alone who are seriously sick.[121]

It was also not uncommon in days past that the reception of Extreme Unction be enjoined upon a penitent as sacramental satisfaction for his sins. Evidently this was due to a mistaken idea of the sense in which Extreme Unction is the complement of Penance. Thus Arcudius[122] tells of a reply of John Nathaniel, the great Oeconomus of Crete, to Vivian, bishop of Anagni, wherein it is stated that such was made the source of a great revenue for priests thru the charging of a fee for such unc-

---

116 Mabillonius, *Praef. ad Saec. Primum, Act. SS. Ord. S. Benedicti*, paragr. 9, n. 101.

117 *Tract. de Ext. Unct.*, p. 279.

118 *De Re Sacr.*, l. VII, q. 5, c. 1, paragr. 1.

119 Cf. Arcangelský, Mihail, "Izsledovanije ob istoriceskom razvitii cinosoversenija Jeleosvjascenija ot ustanovlenija sego tainstva do izdanija nynesnjago jego "Posledovanija," s podrobnym izjasnenijem sego poslednjago," p. 133 sqq.

120 Cf. Ralli, *Περὶ τῶν μυστηρίων*, p. 115; Mesaloras, *Ἐγχειρίδιον*, p. 218; Catechism of Constantinople and Athens—"Echos de l'Orient," avril-mai, 1899.

121 Ignatius, "O tainstvah jedinoj, svjatoj, sobornoj i apostolskoj cerkvi. Opyt arheologiceskij," p. 265; Maltzew, *Die Sakramente*, p. 451 Makarij, "Pravoslavno-dogmaticeskoje bogoslovije," t. V p. 470.

122 *De Concord. Eccl. Orient.*, l. V, c. 4.

tions. This abominable business Innocent IV[123] and Benedict XIV[124] endeavored to extirpate by determined legislation.

Even in the Latin Church, which is generally accused of delaying the administration too long, there are found isolated examples of the bestowal of this sacrament to subjects in good health. For example, Hugh of Flaviade, in the Chronicles of Verdun,[125] tells of one Odilia who received a divine forewarning that she was to die the following day. Immediately she went to the monastery of St. Vito, where she was anointed by the abbot, Richard. There is also the story of the monk who after Matins on St. Martin's day was supernally advised of his approaching dissolution. He revealed his vision to the abbot, and by his permission was anointed with holy oil. "Et Dominicis munitus mysteriis, *sanus et incolumis*, cum caeteris in conventu versatus, sequento die obiit."[126]

Similar examples are found in the Life of St. Gildasius,[127] where the anointment of a lay-brother, while well, is mentioned: and in the Life of St. Hedwig, who was anointed before she became sick.[128]

These isolated examples, Benedict XIV[129] contends, are not contrary to the practice and teaching of the Church. They are extraordinary doings, the dealings of God with His saints. As the author of St. Hedwig's life says: "Hoc tamen, quod heic diximus, admirandum potius est quam imitandum, cui Spiritui Domini per revelationem tribuit efficaciam, et in quo, ut pie creditur, sancta devotio dispensavit." Thiers[130] asserts that such people, when divinely forewarned of death, are valid recipients because they have already been stricken internally by a mortal disease.

---

123 Ep. "*Sub catholicae,*" 6 Maii, 1254—paragraph 3, n. 6—C. I. C. Fontes, n. 34.

124 Const. "*Etsi patoralis,*" 26 Maii, 1742, paragr. V, n. 1—C. I. C. Fontes, n. 328; ep. encyl. "*Ex quo,*" 1 Mar., 1756, paragr. 48—C. I. C. Fontes, n. 438.

125 p. 167—quoted by Martene, *De Antiq. Ecc. Rit.*, l. I, c. 7, a. 1, n. 1 and by Benedict XIV, *De Syn. Dioc.*, l. 8, c. 5, n. 2.

126 Mabillonius, *Acta SS. Ord. Benedicti*, saec. VI, p. 2.

127 Mabillonius, *l.c.*, saec. 1, p. 151.

128 Cap. 8—*Acta SS.*, Oct. 17, vol. 8, p. 219.

129 *L.c.*

130 *De Superstitione circa Sac. Ext. Unct.*, l. 8, c. 6, p. 377; cf. Benedict XIV, *De Syn. Dioc.*, l. 8, c. 5, n. 2.

While Goar and other Greek writers endeavor to explain the Greek practice of anointing those not seriously ill as an abuse or as a sacramental, in the Latin Church two theologians, De Sainte-Beuve [131] and Juenin [132] stoutly defend the validity of anointing those but slightly ill. They have three principal arguments for their view.

In the first place, they say, Scripture orders the unction of the sick, but it does not exclude the healthy. Much less does it proscribe an unction for those but slightly ill. These latter people can be said in truth to be sick. Moreover, Eugene IV, in his decree to the Armenians,[133] used the phrase "dari non *debet* nisi infirmo, de cujus morte timetur." He did not say "dari non potest." Moreover "*de cujus mortis timetur*" can be extended to include such sicknesses which may be only very slightly dangerous and thus cause a cursory fear of the ultimate outcome. Again the Council of Trent[134] directed that the sacrament was to be given to the sick, especially to those who were so seriously ill as to be near the end of their earthly journey. The insertion of "praesertim" evidences the Council's unwillingness to exclude those not so sick as to be in danger of death.[135]

Secondly, theologians all maintain that necessary elements for the valid administration of a sacrament are matter, form and intention. Yet these are present even when the subject is well, or but slightly ill.

Finally, although the Greeks were compelled to render a strict account of all their doings which varied from the Latin Rite, in the Ecumenical Council of Florence, yet no objection was raised to the Greek practice of anointing those not seriously ill. The Council did take note of the practice of ordering

---

131 *De Ext. Unct.*, disp. 7, a. 1-2; apud Migne, *Curs. Theol. Comp.*, vol. XXIV, 116-122.

132 *Comm. Hist. et Dog. de Sac.*, diss. 7, q. 7, c. 3.

133 Const. "*Exultate Deo*" (in Conc. Florentin.), 22 Nov. 1439, paragr. 14 —C. I. C. Fontes, n. 52.

134 Sess. XIV, *De Ext. Unct.*, cap. 3.

135 Coninck (*De Sac. et Censur.*, d. 19, dub. 8 in fine) is impressed by the phraseology of the Council, but uses it to prove only the validity of the sacrament in a putative danger of death. He seems consequently to be of the opinion that "*debere*" signifies only a necessity of precept.

unction as sacramental satisfaction, and it condemned the practice. This is a fair indication that the custom of anointing those not in danger of death did not escape the vigilance of the Council; and a lack of condemnation signifies approval.

Benedict XIV[136] calls this reasoning frivolous. In regard to the first argument, the real force of the Apostolic text has already been discussed. The strength of "dari non debet" could be *per se* preceptive, it must be admitted. Yet it can similarly be taken to signify an absolute necessity, as Barbosa[137] notes, and in dogmatic decrees it means a necessity not only of precept but of sacrament, as Suarez observes.[138] Pope Eugene and the Council of Trent intended to proclaim the whole dogma in regard to Extreme Unction, as the latter protested in the end of the third chapter on Extreme Unction. When, therefore, they said it was to be given to the sick, they meant the sick *taxative.*

In answer to the second argument, it is only necessary to remark that it is quite as essential to have a *subjectum capax* as to have the other necessary constituents of the sacrament. If this were not so, Order could be validly received by women. As Suarez [139] puts it, the subject is the "*materia in qua*" or "*circa quam*" of the sacrament—which "*ad totum sacramentum comparatur et ab illo sacramentum in suo esse pendet, ideoque merito inter ejus causas computatur.*" Hence unless they assume what they intend to prove, viz., that people slightly ill are valid subjects, their argument has no force whatsoever. And if they do assume this, they fall into a "petitio principii."

The final argument from the action of the Council of Florence would be valid if its proponents would show that the Council looked upon the Greek ceremony as a sacrament. It is just as logical to conclude that the Fathers of the Council regarded it as a sacramental.

While the Eastern theologians debated about the customs of the Greeks, Oriental writers denounced in no uncertain terms the practice of the Latins of postponing the administration of

---

136 *De Syn. Dioc.*, l. 8, c. 5, n. 5.
137 Barbosa, *De Usu Frequent.*, dist. 77, n. 1.
138 D. 42, s. 2, n. 2.
139 D. 42, *in principio.*

this sacrament until all hope of recovery had passed away.[140] In very many cases this vehemence was deserved, for it is beyond doubt that such a lamentable practice gripped the Latin Church for several centuries.

Three principal causes must be mentioned to account for the existence of this abuse in the Latin Church. They are 1) the impious avarice of many priests of the Middle Ages; 2) the insane superstitions of the people; and 3) the errors of theologians.

1. It must be admitted that the sacrilegious greed of some priests of the Middle Ages forced many to forego the advantages of this glorious sacrament. Extreme Unction was not given "sine pretio," and was available therefore only to the rich. For this reason the Waldensians were led to spurn the sacrament. Reynerius, a Dominican of the thirteenth century, states:

> "Sacramentum Unctionis reprobant quia tantum divitibus datur, et propter plures sacerdotes ibi necessarios. . . . Sacramentum Extremae Unctionis dicunt esse ultimam superbiam. Contra Jacobi ultimo: *'Infirmatur quis in vobis.'* Occasio quia hoc sacramentum nulli datur sine pretio. Et hoc facit pluralitas sacerdotum. . . . Item praedicant quidam nulli sacramentum hoc debere dari, nisi qui possit habere saltem duas vaccas. Unde pauperes graviter scandalizantur. Item dicunt quod duodecim lumina sunt necessaria in unctione, cum tamen sufficiat unicum ubi corpus Christi ministratur, quia est dignissimum sacramentum; ita et hic."[141]

The enormity of the stipend demanded was decried very bitterly by Anonymus Passaviensis[142] and by William Major, the Bishop of Angers in the last part of the thirteenth century.

---

140 Symeon Thessalonicen., *De Sacro Ritu Sancti Olei*,—M. P. L., 155, 518-9; Ignatij, O tainstvah jedinoj, svjatoj, sobornoj i apostolskoj cerkvi," p. 279; Beljaev, "Jeleosvjascenije" v "Pravoslavnoj Bogoslovskoj enciklopediji," t. V, p. 406; Makarij, "Pravoslavnodogmaticeskoje bogoslovije," t. V, n. 231, etc., among schismatic writers. See Mesaloras, Ἐγχειρίδιον p. 219, for disapproval by a Greek writer.

141 *Lib. de Waldensibus*, edited in 1254, quoted by De Sainte-Beuve, *De Ext. Unct.*, disp. 1, a. 2, apud Migne, *Curs. Theol. Comp.*, t. XXIV, col. 11.

142 *De Occasionibus Errorum Haereticorum*, edited in 1260. Cf. Preger, *Beitrage zur Geschichte der Waldenser im Mittelalter*, p. 66.

In his synod of 1294, the latter legislated:

> "Nosque accepimus referentibus fide dignis, quod dictum sacramentum, sine quo, ut dicunt sancti, periculosum est ex hac vita migrare, ex quadam negligentia omittitur, *immo ut verius loquamur, ex sacerdotum rapacitate et avaritia,* qui in collatione hujus sacramenti novas et insolitas exactiones inducunt aliunde, petendo linteamina, quibus jacens inungitur aegrotans."[143]

Synodal legislation of these centuries reveals a determined attempt on the part of the hierarchy to extirpate this abominable abuse. Thus for instance, Richard Poore, the bishop of Sarum, inserted in his Constitutions the following enactment:

> "Praecipimus quod ad Sacramentum Extremae Unctionis moneant frequenter populum sacerdotes, in necessitate videlicet: et non tantum divites, sed *pauperes,* senes et juvenes omnes, maxime a quattuor decim annis et supra. Et *omnibus* petentibus et poenitentibus *gratis* exhibeant hoc sacramentum in necessitate, cum fuerint humiliter requisiti."[144]

Similar decrees are found in the prescriptions of the synods of Paris,[145] Bayeux,[146] Exeter[147] and Valencia,[148] all of which were celebrated in the twelfth and thirteenth centuries. The Council of Angers[149] ordered the conferring of the sacrament to be postponed until shortly before death because of this avarice. The synodal statutes of Rheims and Troyes, enacted in the beginning of the fifteenth century, forbade a priest to demand a fee prior to the unction, but allowed him to take a subsequent offering.[150] The Synod of Sens in 1524 warned priests to anoint the rich and the poor alike; while the Council of Mainz denounced in burning words the execrable greed of some priests of that day.[151] Benedict XIV[152] assigns this clerical cupidity as the reason for the reduction of the ministers in the Latin Church from seven to one.

From the above sorrowful experience, it can be seen what irreparable harm the greed for gold can cause in the Church

143 Cf. Martene, *De Antiq. Rit. Eccl.*, l. 1, c. 7, a. 2, n. 10.
144 Harduin VII, 107.
145 Harduin VI, p. 2, 1941.
146 Harduin VII, 1237 (anno 1300).
147 anno 1287—Harduin VII, 1081.
148 anno 1255, Harduin VII, 1979.
149 anno 1293—Cf. De Sainte-Beuve, *De Ext. Unct.*, d. VI, a. 3 apud Migne, *Curs. Theol. Comp.*, vol. XXIV, col. 115.
150 Cf. De Sainte-Beuve, l.c.
151 Harduin IX, 2136.
152 *De Syn. Dioc.*, l. 8, c. 4, n. 6.

of God. The Divine Master carried not a copper with him, but had to resort to a miracle to procure a coin for the offering in the temple. Silver and gold Peter had not, but he was able to cure the beggar at the gate called Speciosa. Priests should take a salutary lesson from this. They should be spurred to a firm resolution never to seek a remuneration upon the occasion of the administration of the last sacraments. They should even be chary of taking voluntary offerings. Such acceptance often becomes an obstacle to the poor who feel that the priest will expect something for his visit to the sick. Customs already existing should be eradicated without compunction. Moreover, priests should not be deceived by the specious excuses of the people, who make these offerings under the guise of stipends for Masses, etc.

It is also to be noted that it is absolutely unlawful for a priest to set any fixed stipend for the administration of Extreme Unction. This has been taken entirely out of his hands by Canons 736 and 1507, 1; and reserved to a provincial council or a convention of the bishops of the province, whose decision must be approved by the Holy See.

2. The second cause responsible for the deferment of the reception of the sacrament had its origin in the superstitions of the people. The lower classes of the Continental countries had very little opportunity for education in the Middle Ages—and the percentage of illiteracy was very high. Superstition thrives upon ignorance, and thus we find every sort of despicable credulity among the people of that day. It became a matter of common belief that the recipient of Extreme Unction, if he recovered, had to mortify himself to a very great extent. He was forbidden to dance, to eat flesh meat, to touch the floor with his bare feet, to indulge in marital relations, etc.[153] Shrinking from the rigor of these, the poor misguided people postponed the summoning of the priest until every hope of recovery was gone. Lingard, in his *Antiquities of the Anglo-*

---

153 Cf. Chardon, *Histoire du Sacr. de l'Extreme Onction,* c. 3 apud Migne, *Curs. Theol. Comp.,* Vol. XX, 760 sqq.; see also the sermon by the monk Berthold of Ratisbon, apud Harduin VII, 1801.

Saxon Church, refers to these customs:

> "It appears to have been sometimes received with reluctance by the illiterate, from an idea that it was a kind of ordination which induced the obligation of continency and abstinence from flesh on those who afterwards recovered. The clergy were ordered to preach against this erroneous notion."[154]

The synodal enactment of the thirteenth century evidence not only the existence of such silly beliefs but also the strenuous steps taken to correct them. Thus Richard Poore placed among his *Constitutiones* this prescription: "Moneant sacerdotes frequenter populum hoc sacramentum licite iterari posse; scilicet in qualibet gravi infirmitate de qua metus imminet mortis. Dicant et denuncient confidenter quod post susceptum hoc sacramentum licitum est reverti ad opus conjugale.[155]" Much stronger language was used by the Synod of Wigorniensis:

> "Sunt autem quidam, ut audivimus, qui post perceptionem hujusmodi sacramenti sanitati pristinae restitui nefas reputant, vel uxores suas cognoscere, vel carnes comedere, vel etiam aliqua ratione nudis pedibus ambulare. Horum autem errorum, utpote *doctrinae sanae contrariam, execramur,* et eos excommunicationibus et monitionibus duximus corrigendos, quia ferro abscindenda sunt vulnera quae fomenta non capiunt."[156]

Similar efforts were made by the Synod of Exeter[157] in 1287; by the Councils of Normandy,[158] held under Peter di Collomedio, the Archbishop of Rouen in the middle of the thirteenth century; by the Synod of Wintoniensis[159] at the beginning of the fourteenth century; and by the Synod of Bayeux in 1300.[160]

In later years another superstition arose to the effect that wills made after Unction had no juridic value. This belief spread very widely in Belgium and in Germany. At the beginning of the seventeenth century the Council of Mechlin made

---

154 p. 156, footnote 23.

155 cap. 68 (anno 1217)—Harduin VII, 107; also apud Van Espen, *Jus Eccl. Univ.,* P. II, s. 1, tit. 8, c. 2, n. 16.

156 Harduin VII, 337—anno 1240—n. 19; also apud Van Espen, l.c., n. 17.

157 Harduin VII, 1081.

158 Cf. Martene, *De Antiq. Eccl. Rit.,* l. 1, c. 7, a. 2, n. 9.

159 Cf. Van Espen, l.c., Catalano, *Rit. Rom.,* t. 1, p. 305.

160 Harduin VII, 1237.

a determined attempt to eradicate it:

> "Falluntur qui existimant, suscepto hoc sacramento, vel testamentum condi non posse vel spem convalescendi ob id imminui. Ideoque pastores contrarium subinde populum doceant. Et si forte alicubi usu introductum sit, ut testamentum a susceptione hujus sacramenti conditum non subsistat, declarat haec synodus, ejusmodi consuetudinem pro corruptela habendam esse, utpote causam, cur differatur, iique interim effectus sacramenti non percipiant et saepe etiam sine eo moriantur."[161]

Scarcely had the faithful been liberated from such vile beliefs by the constant propaganda of the Church than the tempter of the human race injected into the minds of the people a fear worse than all the other superstitions above-mentioned. The people began to believe that the ministration of the Unction presaged the final outcome of the illness, that the reception of the oils upon the senses was an unfailing harbinger of death. The consequence was that people shrank from Extreme Unction with the same horror as they recoiled from death itself.

Naturally the Church used all her power to expugn this erroneous conception from the minds of the faithful. The Synod of Bordeaux declared:

> "Curent etiam crebris monitionibus imperitum vulgus ab illa inani et impia opinione abducere, qua plerique sinistre de hujus sacramenti virtute sentiunt, perinde ac si mortem aegris acceleret; quum certum sit ex apostoli doctrina, Deum non animae tantum, verum etiam corpori, si expedierit, virtute hujus sacramenti, salutem conferre."[162]

Especial mention of this error is also found in the decree of the Council of Mechlin just quoted. Laconically, but none the less forcefully, a rubric of the Ritual of Strasburg reads: "*Solantur* sacramenta, *non occidunt*; hoc saepe saepius Pastor mentibus fidelium inculcet."[163]

Even today this problem still confronts the Church. The minds of the people reveal at times vestiges of this old error, despite the continued efforts of the clergy to exterminate it. In the second synod of the diocese of Kansas City, Mo., held in 1912, the following enactment was made:

---

161 anno 1607—Harduin X, 1946.
162 anno 1583—tit. 13, apud Harduin X, 1347.
163 Cf. Benedict XIV, *De Syn. Dioc.*, l. 8, c. 7, n. 2.

> "Studeant igitur animarum curatores repellere insulsissimam opinionem, ne superstitionem dicamus, inter non paucos vigentem, quod receptio illius sacramenti sit mortis impendentis judicium."[164]

In a similar vein a decree of the third synod of Rochester reads:

> "Cum saepe contingat apud fideles nostrorum temporum, quod Extremam Unctionem considerent quasi nuntium mortis instanter impendentis et nullo modo velut medium illius praecavendae, studeant parochi, in suis ad populum sermonibus, hujusmodi terrorem mitigare, et ad maturam hujus sacramenti receptionem fideles adhortari, eos docendi non solum de ejusdem spirituali utilitate, sed etiam, licet secundo loco, de auxilio, quod praestat, ad sanitatem corporis recuperandam."[165]

In a letter to the Sodalists of the *Bona Mors Society,* Pius XI took advantage of the opportunity to insert a mention of the correct view:

> "In hoc autem potissimum, cum sodalium tum praecipue zelatorum studiosam voluntatem desideramus advocatam, ut exitialem quoquo pacto profligent errorem, ex quo fit, ut, cum animae detrimento, sancto oleo non ante liniantur infirmi quam, morte imminente, sensus paene vel omnino amiserunt."[166]

3. While the people floundered about in the darkness of superstition, erroneous theological opinions befogged the intellects of the priests and produced the same effects. Scotus[167] and his followers held that the principal effect of Extreme Unction was the final remission of venial sins. The consequence was the postponement of the administration of the sacrament until the subject was no longer capable of sinning, i. e., when he was very close to death.

Many priests, awed by the weight of the authority supporting this opinion[168] and conscientiously solicitous of their flock's best interests, waited in good faith until the last breath was almost drawn before they imparted Extreme Unction. It was doubtless under the influence of this doctrine that two synods

---

164 *Decreta Syn. Dioces. Kansanop. Secund.*, n. 124.
165 anno 1914—*Acta Synodi Roffensis Tertiae,* n. 340.
166 Litt. ap., "*Explorata res est,*" Feb. 2, 1923—A.A.S., XV, 105.
167 *Reportata Parisiensia,* d. xiii, q. unic.
168 Dicastillo, Sambovius, De Sainte-Beuve, Tournely, St. Bonaventure, Frassen and Mastrio—cf. *supra,* chap. 1, p.

of the sixteenth century described the subject as "the dangerously sick and almost dying."[169]

The Council of Trent succeeded in correcting this erroneous notion of practical procedure;[170] and since that time Scotists have been compelled to modify their ideas on the admissibility of sick people to the sacrament before all capability of committing sin had passed.

The cumulation of these three causes, coupled with the religious disturbances of the sixteenth century, had the unfortunate effect of producing practically a total abandonment of the sacrament in parts of Germany and Bavaria.[171] With great distress the Holy Father addressed a letter to the papal legate in that land: "Non absque gravi gemitu comperit Sua Sanctitas, in infinitis propemodum partibus Germaniae ob negligentiam parochorum ac fortasse etiam episcoporum sacramentum Extremae Unctionis pene abolitum esse.[172]"

In places where the sacrament had not fallen into desuetude, the postponement of its administration until the last moments of the dying man was found to be almost universal. It was this usage that prompted Calvin to remark with scorching scorn:

> "Quamquam etiamsi obtinuerint huic aetati convenire, quod de Unctione a Jacobo praecipitur (a qua longissime absunt), nec sic quidem adhuc multum promoverint in approbanda sua Unctione, qua hactenus illiverunt. Jacobus omnes infirmos vult inungi; isti non infirmos, sed semi-mortua cadavera sua pinguedine inficiunt."[173]

The true Catholic doctrine is found midway between the abuses of the East and of the West. It is, therefore, not to be sought in either procedure, but rather in the Conciliar statements, the dogmatic definitions and the officially approved catechisms of the Church. Thru all ages of the existence of the Bride of Christ, her official pronouncements assert con-

---

169 Conc. Aquense (Harduin X, 1535); Avenionense (*ibid.*, 1848).
170 Sess. XIV, *De Ext. Unct.*, cap. 3.
171 Knopfler, *Die Kelchbewegung in Bayern unter Herzog Albrecht V*, p. 61 sq.
172 Knopfler, l. c.
173 *Institutiones*, lib. IV, c. 19, paragr. 21.

stantly and consistently that the subject of Extreme Unction is a person *"graviter aegrotans"* in danger of death.

There is no other rational deduction from the Scriptural text, as has already been shown.[174] Tradition is even clearer, revealing a series of official and private documents gloriously in accord with the Jacobean dictum.

Thus against the Eastern abuses there is a multitude of testimony. Innocent I, in his letter to Decentius,[175] gives an official interpretation to the words of St. James. After quoting the text, the Pope remarks: "Non est dubium de fidelibus aegrotantibus accipi vel intelligi debere, qui sancto oleo perungi possunt."

Local statutes furnish abundant evidence as to the requirements of the subject in this regard. Thus the *Statuta S. Sonatii,* who was archbishop of Rheims from the year 600 to the year 631, prescribe that "Extrema Unctio deferatur laboranti et petenti."[176] Similar testimony is furnished by the enactments of Egbert of York[177] (732-766); Theodulphus,[178] the bishop of Orleans in the last quarter of the eighth century; St. Chrodegang,[179] the bishop of Metz (742-766); Halitgarius,[180] the bishop of Cambrai (817-831); Isaac,[181] the bishop of Langres (859-880), who collected decrees of the synods which had been approved by Pope Zachary in 742; and by Heardus,[182] the archbishop of Tours in the middle of the ninth century.

Later conciliar legislation carried on the tradition and corroborated the true contention that no slight illness sufficed to make the subject capable of Unction. This can be found in the canons of the Councils of Châlons-sur-Saone,[183] Aachen,[184]

---

174 Cf. supra, chap. I, sec. II, p.

175 Ep. *"Si instituta ecclesiastica,"* 19 Mart. 416, c. 8—C. I. C. Fontes, n. 19.

176 n. 15—M. P. L., 80, 445—Cf. Hefele, *Conciliengeschichte,* III, p. 77.

177 *"Exceptiones e Jure Sacerdotali Egberti, archiepiscopi Eboracensis,"* n. XXI—M. P. L., 89, 382.

178 *"Capitulare ad Prebyteros Paroeciae Suae"*—M. P. L., 126, 246.

179 *Lib. Poenitent.,* M. P. L., 105, 680.

180 *"Regula Canonicorum"*—M. P. L., 89, 1088.

181 cap. 23—M. P. L., 124, 1075 sqq.

182 *Synodus Turonensis* (anno 858), cap. 21 et 56—M. P. L. 121, 764.

183 can. 48, Harduin IV, 1040.

184 c. II, can. 5 et 8—Harduin IV, 1395, 1397.

Mainz[185] and Pavia,[186] all of which were celebrated in the ninth century.

The Greeks, too, even after the schism, professed that unction should be given only to the seriously sick. Michael Paleologus in his profession of faith at the second Council of Lyons avowed: "Aliud [sacramentum est] Extrema Unctio, quae secundom doctrinam beati Jacobi *infirmatibus* adhibeatur."[187] The perdurance of this belief is evidenced by the Metrophanes Critopolus long afterward in his definition of Extreme Unction: "Euchelaion est ritus mysticus, per oleum et preces ab ecclesia pro fidelibus *aegrotantibus* celebratus."[188]

Additional proof may be gathered from an investigation into the ancient liturgies. Generally they supposed that the man was too sick to come to the priests. The priests had to approach the sick man, and provision was made for ceremonies in a private house. The Ritual of Châlons-sur-Marne[189] explicitly states that the oils are only to be applied to those dangerously ill: "Sciendum igitur est quod non ministratur excommunicatis, &c., sed solum *graviter infirmis.*" Moreover, the elaborate ceremonial used in bestowing the sacrament was altogether too solemn to be employed in the case of those but slightly ill.[190]

The practice of the Greeks will not bear the searching scrutiny of theological reason. St. Thomas argues thus: "This sacrament is a spiritual healing . . . and is signified by way of a healing of the body. Hence this sacrament should not be conferred on those who are not subjects for bodily healing, those, namely who are in good health."[191] In answer to the objection that a more principal effect is the cure of the soul, the Angelic

---

185 c. 26—Harduin V, 13.
186 cap. 8—Harduin V, 27.
187 anno 1274—C. I. C. Fontes, n. 35.
188 Cf. Kimmel, *Libri Symbolici Ecclesiae Orientalis,* appendix, p. 151.
189 Martene, *De Antiq. Ecc. Rit.,* lib. I, c. 7, a. 4, Ordo XXVII.
190 Cf. Kern, *Tract. de Ext. Unct.,* p. 294.
191 *Suppl.,* q. 32, a. 1. This argument of St. Thomas does not impress Soto (*Comm. in lib. IV Sent.,* dist. xxiii, q. 2, a. 2) or Durandus, whom Soto quotes as stating: "Sequeretur quod baptismus non deberet applicari nisi ei qui sordidus est ut per externam lotionem designaretur interior. Imo et paenitentia non deberet impendi nisi mortuis corporaliter, quia est suscitatio spiritualis."

Doctor writes: "Although spiritual health is the principal effect of this sacrament, yet this same spiritual healing needs to be signified by a healing of the body, although bodily health may not actually ensue. Consequently spiritual health can be conferred by this sacrament on those alone who are competent to receive bodily healing, viz., the sick; even as he alone can receive Baptism who is capable of a bodily washing."[192]

After excluding those entirely well, St. Thomas proceeds to remove those but slightly ill from the number of valid recipients. "This sacrament," he writes,[193] "is the last remedy that the Church can give, since it is an immediate preparation for glory. Therefore it ought to be given to those only, who are so sick as to be in a state of departure from this life, thru their sickness being of such a nature as to cause death, the danger of which is to be feared." Truly if the end of Unction is to procure an immediate entrance into glory (provided a longer life is not more expedient), it must be given to those only who are afflicted with a disease which makes it probable that they will die. Suarez proposes this argument in these words:

> "Est hoc sacramentum institutum tanquam extremum remedium hominum infirmorum et morientium, quo et in gravissimo mortis periculo juventur et ad gloriae introitum, quoad fieri possit, disponantur; ergo ut minimum requirit hominem ita decumbentem, *ut ex tali infirmitate mors possit moraliter timeri saltem remote et quantum est ex natura talis aegritudinis in tali subjecto.* Item cum sanitas etiam corporis per hoc sacramentum procuretur, certe supponi debet infirmitas ex se gravis, nam verisimile non est, tale sacramentum esse institutum propter quamlibet levem aegritudinem curandum. Et sane, si sacramentum hoc valide dari posset cuilibet aegrotanti communi et ordinario morbo, ex quo nullum periculum timeretur, non esset, cur omnibus hujusmodi infirmis tale sacramentum denegaretur, ita ut licite illis dari non posset. Cur enim privarentur hoc sacramento, cum alias nulla tali sacramento irreverentia fieret. Requiritur ergo gravis seu lethalis morbus etiam ad valorem sacramenti."[194]

Soto (cf. *supra,* chap. I, sect. 5, n. 4) teaches that corporal cure followed in some degree from every administration of the sacrament. Hence it is but logical for him to argue as follows,

---

192 Suppl., 9. 32, a. 1 (translated by the Fathers of the Eng. Dom. province).
193 *Suppl.*, q. 32, a. 2 (translated by the Fathers of Eng. Dom. province).
194 D. 42, s. 2, n. 4.

whereby he reaches the selfsame conclusion as Aquinas and Suarez:

> 'Ratio vero potissima est quod effectus hujus sacramenti, ut dictum est, non solum est gratiam conferre, sed etiam ab infirmitate corporea liberare. Et quia ex effectu sacramenti debet judicium sumi materiae et subjecti, inde colligitur quod subjectum de essentia hujus sacramenti est homo infirmus. Itaque nullum esset sacramentum poenitentiae si absolveretur puer qui nullum haberet peccatum actuale, eo quod illud sacramentum ad remissionem illorum delictorum institutum est: ita si ungeretur ille qui non est infirmus, nullum esset sacramentum quia deesset materia effectus ejus. Et simile exemplum est in ordinibus: si mulier sacerdotio initaretur, nullum esset sacramentum, quia non est subjectum capax.''[195]

On the other hand it is certainly very alien to the mind of the Church to defer the administration of Extreme Unction until the illness has attained to such an intensity that the man is actually dying. As Martene[196] notes: "Nihil ab Ecclesiae mente et proposito ita alienum unquam extitit."

There is abundant proof to substantiate this. Once again exploring the text of Innocent's letter, we find that he speaks of "fidelibus aegrotantibus," not of "aegrotantibus ad extremam vitae spatium deductis." Then he subjoins immediately: "Poenitentibus istud infundi non potest, quia genus est sacramenti. Nam quibus reliqua sacramenta negantur, quomodo unum genus putatur posse concedi?" Yet in another letter [197] the same Pope noted that this prohibition of administering the sacraments to those doing canonical penance did not apply when such persons were "in extremo fine vitae suae." Accordingly the cessation of the cause which forbade the reception of Extreme Unction prior to that time opened the way to its legitimate reception during the last moments. If anything can be deduced at all, it is this—the Pontiff wished to indicate that the Unction could be given to the rest of the faithful even before they were actually dying, provided that they were truly *aegroti*. This is corroborated by a statute of the Council of

195 *Comm. in quart. lib. Sent.*, dist. xxiii, q. 2, a. 2.
196 *De Antiq. Ecc. Rit.*, l. 1, c. 7, a. 2, n. 1.
197 *Ep.* 6, *ad Exuperium*, n. 6—M. P. L. 20, 498-99.

Pavia, held in 850:

> "Hoc tamen sciendum, quod si is qui infirmatur publicae poenitentiae mancipatus est, non potest hujus mysterii consequi medicinam, nisi prius reconciliatione percepta communionem Corporis et Sanguinis Christi meruerit. Cui enim reliqua sacramenta interdicta sunt, hoc uno nulla ratione uti conceditur."[198]

The fact that the administration of Unction was made immediately after Penance and before Viaticum in ancient days further substantiates the proposition that Extreme Unction is not only for those actually dying. People able to receive Holy Communion are as a general rule not *"in extremis."* Martene[199] gives more than a score of examples, taken from historical sources, which evidence this order of administering the last sacraments. Similarly, Launoi [200] enumerates many Rituals which prescribe the administration of Unction prior to Viaticum. Local legislation prescribed the immediate application of the oil after the sick man's confession and deferred Holy Viaticum to a time of greater danger. Thus the famous Council of Aachen enacted: "Si subditus infirmitate depressus fuerit, ne confessione atque orationi sacerdotali necnon unctione sacrati olei per ejus [presbyteri] negligentiam careat. Denique si finem urgentem perspexerit, commendet animam christianam Domino Deo suo more sacerdotali cum acceptione S. Communionis."[201] The Capitulare of Charlemagne and of Louis the Pious contained this regulation: "Si infirmitate depressus quis fuerit, vitam suam sine communione non finiat, nec unctione sacrati olei careat, et si finem perspiciat, sacrosancto corpore Deo anima ejus a sacerdote precibus commendetur.[202]" Eucharist is ordered to be given twice, once prior to and once after the Unction. It proves clearly that two stages of the illness were recognized, viz., one when a man is seriously ill and in danger of death, and the other when a man is already "in extremis."

The proposition is further supported by the fact that Extreme Unction and Viaticum used to take place for seven suc-

---

198 cap. VIII, Harduin V, 27.

199 *De Antiq. Eccl. Rit.*, l. 1, c. 7, a. 2, n. 3. Cf. also Ordines III, IV, V, VIII, X, XI, XII, XIII, XVI, XIX, XX, XXII, XXIII, XXVI (l. c., a. 4).

200 *Op. Omnia*, t. I, p. 596 sqq. Cf. Binterim, *Denwürdigkeiten*, 6 B., 3 T., p. 306 sqq.

201 Cap. 2, can. 5—Harduin IV, 1397.

202 Launoi, *op. cit.*, p. 595.

cessive days. Old Rituals, like that of Tours,[203] etc., prescribed the imparting of Viaticum and Unction every day for a week—a certain sign that such a subject was not *in extremis*.

Other rubrics of the ancient Ordines also conspire to prove this contention. Thus the custom existed in some places to anoint in the Church;[204] while the liturgical laws of other localities directed the unction of the subject in a kneeling or a sitting posture.[205] Some rubrics ordered the sick man to chant, others to make a long and very complete confession of faith.[206] In the Greek Ritual we find the following rubric: "Tum vero in medium sacerdotum ingreditur qui Extremam Unctionem suscipit, et acceptum sanctum Evangelium ponit super caput ejus sacerdotum praecipuus."[207]

Reason itself decries the postponement of this sacrament. In the first place, a man *in extremis* can co-operate with the sacramental graces only in a very imperfect manner, and thus he may be deprived of an immediate entrance into heaven. The principal effect is frustrated to a great extent. The spiritual consolation, the comfort of the soul against torpor and temptation, against depression and despair, is reduced to almost nothing by such a tardy reception. Moreover, the possibility of recovering health is totally nullified. Such an effect follows from the redundancy of the soul's exhilaration upon the body. If the effect is obstructed in regard to the soul, there will be corresponding loss in regard to the body.

Since the Council of Florence, the matter has been settled in theory, although in practice a priest will often find that he is summoned in the last stages of sickness. Pope Eugene, in his decree to the Armenians,[208] noted that the subject was a sick man whose death was feared. The Council of Trent reiterated this statement, and made incidentally the same distinction be-

---

203 Martene, *De Antiq. Eccl. Rit.*, l. 1, c. 7, a. 4 (ordo III). Cf. also Ordines IV, VIII and XIX.

204 Cf. Martene, *l.c.*, a. 2, n. 7.

205 Cf. Martene, *l.c.*, a. 4 (Ordines IV, XII and XXV). Cf. also vita S. Ottonis, *Acta SS.* July 2, l. 4, c. 4.

206 Cf. Warren, *The Liturgy and Ritual of the Celtic Church;* Martene, *De Antiq. Eccl. Rit.*, l. 1, c. 7, a. 4 (Ordines IV, XXII, XXIII).

207 Translated into Latin by Martene, *l.c.*, Ordo XXX.

208 Const. "*Exultate Deo*" (in Conc. Florentin.) 22 Nov., 1439, n. 14—C. I. C. Fontes, n. 52.

tween the stages of illness as did the old Council of Aachen: "Declaratur etiam esse hanc Unctionem infirmis adhibendam, illis vero praesertim, qui tam periculose decumbunt, ut in exitu vitae constituti videantur." [209] In consonance with this decree the Catechism of the Council reads:

> "Quum igitur illi tantum qui morbo laborant curatione indigent; idcirco iis etiam, qui adeo periculose aegrotare videntur, ut, ne supremus illis vitae dies instet, metuendum sit, hoc sacramentum praeberi debet. In quo tamen gravissime peccant qui illud tempus aegroti ungendi observare solent, quum jam, omni salutis spe amissa, vota et sensibus carere incipiat."[210]

Since the Council of Trent local synods have exhorted the faithful to receive the sacrament at a more opportune time, to put away the foolish notion that it is a messenger of death, and to look upon it as a divine gift with far-reaching powers over the soul and the body.[211] The Roman Ritual states plainly the desirable time to confer Unction:

> "Extremae Unctionis Sacramentum . . . omni studio ac diligentia periculose aegrotantibus adhibendum est, et eo quidem tempore, si fieri possit, cum illis adhuc integra mens et ratio viget, ut ad uberiorem Sacramenti gratiam percipiendam, ipsi etiam suam fidem ac piam animi voluntatem conferre possint, dum sacro liniuntur Oleo."[212]

It is certain now that a person in order to be a valid subject for Extreme Unction must 1) be afflicted with a serious disease which is putting him in danger of death, but 2) not necessarily to such an extent that he is outside the pale of recovery. The present Canon of the Code confirms this. The subject is one "qui . . . . ob infirmitatem . . . . in periculo mortis versetur."

Hence the subject must be sick, and in danger of death from the sickness. Neither without the other is sufficient. Canon 523 shows that the Code recognizes a state of serious sickness

---

209 Sess. XIV, *de Ext. Unct.*, cap. 3.

210 *De Sac. Ext. Unct.*, n. 9.

211 Cf. Synods of Milan (1565), Bordeaux (1584) and Rheims (1584) apud Natalis Alexander, *Theol. Dog. et Mor.*, lib. II, c. 5, reg. 14; Bourges (1584)—Harduin X, 1489; Toulouse (1590)—Harduin X, 1804; Beneventano (1693)—Coll. Lac., I, p. 30; Westminster (1852), n. 20—Coll. Lac., III, 395; Aix-la-Chapelle (1850)—Coll. Lac. IV, 992; etc.

212 Tit. V, c. 1, n. 1.

that does not place the patient in danger of death. Nor is danger of death without sickness enough. It is absolutely required that the danger shall come *ex intrinseco,* from the patient himself. As Genicot-Salsmans puts it: "Necesse est ut istud periculum oriatur ex dispositione intrinseca seu infirmitate corporis, viz., ex morbo vel ex causa quae morbo aequiperari soleat."[213]

Consequently those about to be executed,[214] those entering battle, those about to start upon a perilous journey are in no wise capable of a valid reception of the sacrament from such cause alone. These dangers are extrinsic, they do not emanate "ex defectu naturae, sed ex eventu fortunae."[215] Similarly, those on a sinking ship, those in a burning building, those in danger of suffocation,[216] are not valid subjects. Martyrs, too, may not be anointed before martyrdom. However, if death is induced gradually (as in the martyrdom of St. Lawrence or of St. Sebastian), the sacrament can be efficaciously bestowed when the subject becomes in danger of death from his wounds.[217]

On the other hand, all those in danger of death from an intrinsic cause can validly and licitly receive the Unction. Hence, not only the seriously sick, but also those dangerously wounded, those who have swallowed poison[218] and those who have been taken out of the water when almost drowned[219] are able to be anointed. In each of these instances the life of the subject is threatened from an internal cause.

---

213 *Inst. Th. M.*, II, 422.

214 Baruffaldo (*Ad Rit. Rom. Comm.*, t. I, tit. xxvii, n. 85-86) makes mention of some very peculiar reasons why this sacrament cannot be administered to condemned criminals. Thus it was said that it was denied these men because of the irreverence that would be shown if the anointed feet of the criminal should touch the ground on the way to the scaffold. Another reason advanced was that the sacrament could not be given to them because one of its effects, viz., corporal cure, had no chance to be verified on account of the impending death sentence. If this were so, adults after baptism could not be anointed because the remission of sins could not be verified in them.

215 VI Conc. Beneventanum, tit. 8, cap. 1—Cf. Catalano, *Rit. Rom.*, tom. 1, p. 313.

216 Barbosa, *De Off. et Pot. Parochi*, c. 22, n. 11.

217 Cf. Gobat, *Moralium*, Tr. VIII, nn. 848-50.

218 Manual of Cambrai, apud Catalano, *l.c.;* Noldin, *De Sac.*, n. 443.

219 Dens, *Tract. De Sac. Ext. Unct.*, N. 8, p. 53.

The first question naturally is: When is a disease considered to put the patient in a danger of death? Is it sufficient that it be fatal by its very nature? Or must it have developed sufficient intensity in the case of the individual patient as to threaten his life? And finally, how serious must the danger be before administration may be made?

D'Annibale[220] states that "periculum mortis" signifies "illud rerum discrimen in quo, cum quis constitutus est, ipsum et superesse et occumbere posse, utrumque est vere graviterque probabile." The Council of Limoges, celebrated in 1519, was much stricter: "Datur infirmis graviter aegrotantibus quando magis speratur de morte quam de vita."[221] The Synod of Angers at the end of the thirteenth century had demanded even a more serious condition of the patient: "Hoc Sacramentum tantum est in extremo vitae articulo conferendum, quando infirmus in brevi ex hac vita credatur migraturus."[222]

Later authors are not nearly so strict in their demands. They state that solid probability of subsequent death resulting from the disease is quite sufficient. As soon as this probable danger of death exists, the subject becomes capable of receiving the Unction. A distinction is drawn between the time when the sacrament *may* be given and when it *must* be given. Thus St. Alphonsus:

> "Advertendum quod distinguere oporteat quando extrema unctio dari debeat, et quando dari possit. Adest quidem obligatio . . . eam ministrandi cum urget periculum proximae mortis. Caeterum communiter docent DD. valide et licite posse dari extremam unctionem statim ac prudenter judicatur infirmus laborare periculo mortis, etsi adhuc non proximae."[223]

This distinction has been accepted by many others, including Scavini,[224] Genicot[225] and Noldin.[226] A papal document of

---

220 *Summ. Th. M.*, I, 38.
221 Cf. Launoi, *Op. Omnia*, t. 1, p. 557.
222 Cf. De Sainte-Beuve, *De Ext. Unct.*, disp. VII, a. 2—apud Migne, *Curs. Theol. Comp.*, vol. XXIV, col. 119-120.
223 *Th. M.*, VI, 714.
224 *Th. M.*, III, 442.
225 *Th. M.*, II, 422.
226 *De Sac.*, 443.

extremely recent issue confirms this distinction:

> "In hoc autem potissimum, cum sodalium, tum praecipue zelatorum studiosam voluntatem desideramus advocatam, ut exitialem quoquo pacto profligent errorem, ex quo fit ut cum animae detrimento sancto oleo ante liniantur infirmi quam, morte imminente, sensus paene vel omnino amiserunt. Neque enim, ut sacramentum *valide liciteque detur,* necesse est ut mors proxime secutura timeatur, sed satis est ut *prudens seu probabile adsit de periculo judicium;* quodsi in ea rerum condicione conferri *debet,* in hac conferri utique *potest,* et illud curet ministrandum, is Ecclesiae Matris non modo doctrinam sequitur, sed optata pie ac salubriter perficit."[227]

Thus all that is required for valid and licit administration is a probable danger of death. The probability must rest on truly solid grounds, else the sacrament cannot be given, at least absolutely. "Tale judicium," writes Genicot,[228] "elicitum sive a medico sive ab alio experientia edocto, requiritur et sufficit ut extrema unctio conferri possit; ac sane optandum et conandum est ut, nisi specialis ratio differendi obstet, majus et certius periculum non expectetur."

Probability of death must be understood reasonably, in accordance with the mind of the Church. Hence, as Genicot[229] notes, a man can be in probable danger of death, even though the likelihood of his recovery is more probable. A "*dubium positivum de morte secutura*" will furnish sufficient probability for action.[230]

Sometimes there is a doubt about the solidity of the probability. In such an instance the older authors[231] forbade administration. The next canon however permits a conditional administration in this case. Hence, we must distinguish: (1) when there is a positive doubt "*de morte secutura,*" the sacrament may be bestowed absolutely; (2) when there is a positive

227 Pius XI, Litt. Ap., "*Explorata res est,*" Feb. 2, 1923—A. A. S., XV, 105. Cf. also Benedict XV, Litt. Ap., "*Sodalitatem,*" May 31, 1921—A. A. S., XIII, 342: "Qui in discrimine ultimo versantur, sacri viatici et extremae Unctionis susceptionem ne eo usque remorentur cum sensum amissuri jam sunt, sed, contra, quemadmodum Ecclesia docet et praecipit, iis roborentur Sacramentis vixdum, ingravescente morbo, prudens fiat de periculo mortis judicium."

228 *Inst. Th. M.*, II, 422.

229 *L.c.*

230 Vermeersch-Creusen, *Epit.*, II, 225.

231 St. Alph., *Th. M.*, VI, 714; Scavini, *Th. M.*, III, 442, etc.

doubt "*num infirmitas sit periculosa,*" the sacrament must be given conditionally.

It must be noted, too, that although administration is allowable to a patient when there is a probable and prudent doubt that his life is threatened by the disease, yet if *de facto* there is no danger present in him, the sacrament is not valid. Kern does not agree with this at all. "Si objectivum periculum exigeretur," he argues,[232] "non raro accidit ut aegrotus a medicis depositus, cujus mors in horas expectatur, invalide inungeretur vi morbi jam fracta, quamvis ad extra id nondum appareat. Unde si Dominus objectivum vitae discrimen fecisset conditionem essentialem, ipse sacramentum crebro periculo nullitatis et optimos quosque sacerdotes anxiis scrupulis simulque infirmos periculo exposuisset, ne supernaturale auxilium eis denegaretur tempore quo maxime apti existerent ad plenum ejus fructum accedente perfecta cooperatione propria percipienda." Vermeersch is inclined to agree with Kern: "Valide et licite confertur. . . in morbo gravi et natura sua periculoso, quamvis nullum objective sit vitae discrimen; in morbo qui natura sua est periculosus et qui simul affligit graviter infirmum, quamvis nondum videatur (subjective) discrimen vitae secum ferre."[233]

Noldin[234] and Sebastiani[235] take issue with Kern and Vermeersch and hold that Extreme Unction in a purely putative danger of death is absolutely invalid. By Christ's institution, the subject of this sacrament is a sick man in danger of death truly and actually. This is explicitly required by the present canon: "*in periculo mortis* ob infirmitatem vel senium versetur." The law does not say "versari videtur," but speaks in an objective sense. This is confirmed by the insertion of "reipsa" into the phraseology of the next canon: "Quando dubitatur num . . . infirmus . . . in periculo mortis *reipsa* versetur, hos sacramentum ministretur sub condicione." This implies that the objectivity of the danger is the determining factor whether the conditional unction will be valid or not.

---

232 *Tract. de Ext. Unct.*, p. 298.
233 *Th. M.*, III, 661.
234 *De Sac.*, 443.
235 *Summ. Th. M.*, n. 510; cf. Barry, *Irish Eccl. Record*, Fifth Series, Vol. XXVI (1925), p. 65.

Noldin's view is more probable, for there seems to be lacking on the part of the subject an essential condition for valid reception. In no other sacrament does subjective certitude on the part of the minister validate the administration to a man otherwise objectively incapable of reception.

Suppose a man in a drunken stupor was mistakenly pronounced by a physician to be in danger of death. Suppose, too, that a priest, relying on the judgment of such a one, administered Extreme Unction. Who will say that this administration is valid? How is such a subject in need of a spiritual exhilaration which presupposes a depression of soul from sickness?[236] Yet if subjective certainty on the part of the minister supplies for the lack of an essential condition in the subject, this administration must have been validly received.

How then are we to explain the various pronouncements, private and official, which permit administration of the sacrament when there is a prudent fear that death is threatening the patient? For example, Pius XI used this mode of expression: "Neque enim, ut sacramentum *valide liciteque* detur, necesse est ut mors proxime secutura timeatur, sed satis est ut prudens seu probabile adsit de periculo judicium." What can be said in answer to such phraseology?

A sharp distinction must be drawn between a valid and licit administration and a valid reception. The permissibility of administration does not automatically effect a validity of reception. The lack of an essential condition in the subject successfully obstructs such a valid and licit administration. In the confessional a priest may validly and licitly absolve a man whom he feels is well-disposed; but if *de facto* such a man has defective dispositions, the absolution is null. Hence it will be noticed that these official pronouncements and private writings speak of the legitimacy of the procedure on the part of the minister, but leave undiscussed the validity of the reception by the subject.

Since this is true, since it is required that a person be in objective danger of death for valid reception, it can be seen how erroneous the opinion of St. Alphonsus is when he asserts

236 Cf. W. McDonald, *Irish Theol. Quarterly,* Vol. II (1907), p. 54.

the validity of Extreme Unction administered in a grave sickness even where it is *known* that there is no danger of death.[237] The saint held that the danger of death was a condition required only for the licit administration and reception of the sacrament. Pius XI declared that, "ut *valide liciteque* detur," a prudent or probable judgment of the danger of death *sufficed*. If it suffices, there is also an implication that it is also required.

With these principles in mind, the various contingencies that may arise in the matter of anointing must be discussed:

1. If the disease is a slight one, even though there is a fear that it will subsequently become dangerous, Extreme Unction cannot be administered. Such a subject has not the depression of soul which the primary effect of the sacrament is ordained to remove. It is absolutely necessary that the subject be *hic et nunc* capable of receiving this spiritual exhilaration; and thus any anticipated administrations are inadmissible.

2. If a man is but lightly affected by a disease itself, but is nevertheless placed thereby in peril of sudden death, he is a valid and licit subject of the sacrament. Though severe bodily pains and depressions are to a great extent absent, nevertheless there are present all the needs for sacramental alleviation. The condition of the patient, not his symptoms, is to be considered. Cases of this kind happen frequently when persons are afflicted with cardiac conditions. It is in this way, also, that the unction of old people is justified.[238]

3. If a man is seriously affected by a disease, which is of its nature dangerous, but which has not as yet placed the life of the patient in danger, (because in the judgment of a skilled physician it is pursuing its normal course), Kern [239] thinks that the Unction can be validly and licitly bestowed. Vermeersch [240] heartily agrees with him in this belief.

Similarly, Suarez seems to incline to this view:

> "Addo in usu servandum esse, ut non solum morbus ex se gravis sit, sed etiam ut status talis sit qui infirmum in gravi periculo mortis

---

237 *Homo Apostolicus*, tr. XVII, n. 7.
238 Gobat, *Moralium*, Tr. VIII, n. 875; Gury-Ferreres, *Casus Conc.*, II, 440.
239 *Tract. de Ext. Unct.*, p. 298.
240 *Th. M.*, III, 661.

constituat. Ita docent omnes DD. &c. . . . Quia vero hic status non potest habere tantam certitudinem, multumque ex arbitrio pendet, ideo non videtur haec condicio ita substantialis, ut si forte aliquantulum praemature ungatur infirmus, sacramentum propterea sit nullum existimandum; quin potius quoties morbus ex se fuerit periculosus et gravis, existimo sacramentum esse validum, etiamsi ad statum morbi vel non satis, vel etiam nihil, attendatur.''[241]

Yet with the principles heretofore stated clearly in mind, it is hard to admit the permissibility of an unction in any case where there is not a prudent and probable danger of death. In this instance this danger will develop perhaps, but *hic et nunc* it is not present. The Code, however, seems to speak of the actual danger present at the time of reception: "Non potest praeberi nisi fideli qui . . . ob infirmitatem in periculo mortis versetur.'' Genicot takes issue with Kern and Vermeersch when he writes:

''Recipere possunt valide et licite extremam unctionem ii tantum in quibus habentur *simul* sequentes condiciones: 1) Ut sint baptizati . . . ; 2) Ut actualia peccata committere potuerint . . . . 3) ut sint *infirmi;* 4) ut *de eorum morte timeatur.*''[242]

Noldin,[243] too, requires for *validity* ''ut [infirmus] ex morbo de vita periclitetur.''

In practice even Kern[244] advises the minister to await the development of a certain danger of death, unless he foresees that by such a time the reason of the man will be so seriously impaired that he will not be able to co-operate in any desirable degree with the sacramental graces. Since the opinion of Kern and Vermeersch is only probable, a pastor who anoints according to their view, should do so only conditionally; and should repeat the unction conditionally when certain danger of death does develop.

4. If a sick man is gravely afflicted by a disease whose nature and gravity is not yet apparent, he can be validly and licitly anointed, according to Kern. ''Tantum enim abest,'' he

241 D. 42, s. 2, n. 5.
242 Genicot-Salsmans, *Inst. Th. M.*, II, 422.
243 *De Sac.* n. 443.
244 *Tract. de Ext. Unct.*, pp. 298-99.

writes, "ut illa incertitudo de natura morbi, quae ex supposito cum vehementia hominem incessit, minuat depressionem animae, ut angores soleat augere. Pariter fundat timorem, ne periculum mortis immineat." [245]

In this opinion he is not joined wholly by Vermeersch. The latter holds the permissibility of a conditional administration at least—and by his use of the term "saltem" betrays a hesitancy to condemn even an absolute administration in this case. "Sin infirmus graviter affligitur per morbum cujus natura nondum constat, poterit saltem condicionate ungi." [246]

Canon 941 seems to cover the case. It orders a conditional bestowal of the sacrament whenever the danger of death is doubtful. If there is a doubt that the subject is in danger of death *"reipsa"*—and this seems to be the case here— an absolute administration is altogether out of place. In such a sickness as this, the minister has two doubts: one as to the dangerousness of the disease *ex se,* and another as to the actual presence of danger in the patient. It is hard to see the rectitude of Kern's contention in this instance.

5. If the disease brings with it a remote yet certain danger of death, the sacrament can be validly given. The subject in such a case is actually in danger of death. Whether it is advisable in individual instances to administer the sacrament to those who have still a long time to live depends much on local circumstances. Thus the Propaganda,[247] on February 20, 1801, permitted missionaries to anoint consumptives who had several months to live, but who would die within a year, because of the likelihood that the missionary might not be able to return to them. Such extraordinary circumstances make licit the administration of the sacrament.

---

245 *L.c.*

246 *Th. M.*, III, 661.

247 S. C. P. F., (C. P. pro Sin.)—Collectanea, n. 651: "Talora i missionari visitando i loro distretti s'incontrano in qualche malato etico o d'altro morbo, che a certa sperienza durera molti mesi, ma dentro l'anno persisce: si cerca se in tale caso il missionario possa somministrargli il viatico e Estrema Unzione per la ragione che, quando sarebbe veramente nel grado suo di ricerla, allora il missionario non si potra trovare presente nel luogo per la grande distanza, e per altre circonstanze impeditive. R. Affirmative."

In other cases, such as the usual instances of consumption, cancer, etc., whose outcome will certainly be fatal yet whose danger is but remote, very many factors will have to be considered by the priest in regard to the time most opportune to anoint. The present state of the disease will first claim attention. How far it has progressed and is afflicting the subject must be considered. The hope of restoring health in virtue of the sanative powers of the sacrament and the question whether greater good will result from an administration now or later will be weighed by the prudent priest. The danger of scandal must not be overlooked. It may arise easily enough from the anointing of a subject who is still able to walk about, and even perform his everyday duties. Pastoral prudence will dictate what is to be done in individual cases.[248]

There remain for particular consideration the imparting of this sacrament in two particular cases, viz., to women in parturition and to people before surgical operations.

With regard to women in parturition, the following contingencies may arise:

1. It may be foreseen that a woman, now in pregnancy, will have a difficult parturition which will endanger her life. Can such a woman be anointed?

2. A woman, actually in parturition, may be in danger of death from the usual pains and sorrows of that time. Can such a one be given the sacrament of Extreme Unction?

3. A woman in parturition may be in danger of death from extraordinary and abnormal pains and sufferings accompanying the puerperium. Is she a valid subject for this sacrament?

I. In regard to the first case, there is hardly any dispute. As has been noted often hitherto, the administration of Extreme Unction cannot be anticipated. As the woman stands now, carrying the child in her womb, she is not in danger of death.

248 Cf. Kern, *Tract. de Ext. Unct.*, p. 299.

It will be only when she attempts to give birth to the child that the danger will arise. Hence administration is inadmissible because of the lack of an essential condition in the subject.

Petrus Dens writes: "Ob eandem rationem [i. e., quod periculum non provenit ex infirmitate] dari non potest puerperis ante partum, quamvis hic timeatur futurus periculus."[249] It is true that pregnancy was intended to be only a physiological, and not a pathological, condition. But whether it ordinarily is only physiological is quite another question. However, even though it be pathological, a woman is not in danger of death therefrom, and for this reason at least she is not capable of Extreme Unction.

Genicot mentions in his *Casus Conscientiae* the case of a priest called to anoint a pregnant woman who had been told by her physician that her every parturition would be dangerous. This is his solution:

> "Immerito [sacerdos inunxit eam], si partus et periculum tantum praevidentur. Extrema enim Unctio, saltem regulariter, in praesentibus tantum periculis posito danda est. Saepe etiam medici, talia pericula in singulis partubus praecinentes, id tantum intendunt: ob anatomicam mulieris conformationem aliasve internas causas, facile eas insurgere posse circumstantias quae verum periculum creent. Hoc igitur immerito semper tanquam praesens haberetur."[250]

II. The second case is somewhat more difficult to settle. When a woman in child-birth is suffering only from the common pains and dolors of that solemn time when a man is brought into the world, she may not, in the opinion of many theologians, be either validly or licitly anointed. They declare that such a danger of death is not a danger from sickness. The woman is in a normal, not an abnormal state, and consequently she cannot be said to be "*sick*" in the sense in which St. James used the term. St. Charles Borromeo inserted an enactment of this sort in the legislation of the Fourth Council of Milan: "Parochus Extremae Unctionis sacramentum . . . ne ministret . . . mulieribus in partu

249 *De Sac. Ext. Unct.*, N. 8, p. 52.

250 *Casus Conc.*, casus 885, II; cf. also Benedict XIV, *De Syn. Dioc.*, l. 8, c. 5, n. 1; Noldin, *De Sac.*, 443 b; Sebastiani, *Summ. Th. M.*, n. 510; Arregui, *Summ. Th. M.*, n. 666.

laborantibus." [251] Similarly Concina,[252] Bonacina,[253] Naldus,[254] St. Alphonsus,[255] Baruffaldo,[256] Scavini,[257] Aertnys,[258] Konings,[259] Gury-Ferreres,[260] Tanquerey [261] and Augustine [262] hold that women in danger of death from the common puerperal pains are not valid subjects of this sacrament.

Other authors hold that if a woman is actually dying in parturition, even though she is suffering only the normal pains, she may receive Extreme Unction. Thus, de Lugo,[263] Perin,[264] Petrus Dens,[265] Falise,[266] Kenrick,[267] Genicot [268] and Berardi [269] are among those who admit the legality of this procedure. These men contend that a true sickness has arisen from the difficulty of parturition, and that the danger of death arises principally from this sickness and not from the parturition. Parturition, then, is not a sickness, but it induces a sickness which, in turn, brings with it a danger of death.[270] Thus the Manual of the Church of Cambrai[271] directed the administration of Extreme Unction to women *"in partu deficientibus."*

All these theologians take for granted that parturition is a thing physiological and not pathological. Yet when we look into the medical world, we discover a host of authorities protesting against this view of pregnancy and parturition. De Lee, professor of Obstetrics at Northwestern University, sums

251 Pars II Constitutionum, cap. *"Quae pertinent ad Extremam Unctionem,"* apud *Acta Ecclesiae Mediol.*, t. I, p. 147.
252 *Theologia Christiana*, t. X, lib. I, *de Sac. Ext. Unct.*, c. 4, n. 6.
253 *De Sacramentis*, disp. 7, q. unic., punct. 4-5, n. 6.
254 *Summa*, verb. *"Extrema Unctio,"* n. 5.
255 *Th. M.*, VI, 713, dub. 3.
256 *Ad Rit. Rom. Comm.*, t. I, tit. 27, n. 77.
257 *Th. M.*, III, 440.
258 *Th. M.*, II, 336.
259 *Th. M.*, n. 1508, q. 3.
260 *Casus Consc.*, t. II, n. 805.
261 *Th. D.*, III, 783 (a).
262 *A Commentary*, IV, p. 402.
263 *De Sac. in Gen.*, c. 21, n. 5.
264 *Tract. de Ext. Unct.*, art. II, quaeres 3.
265 *De Sac. Ext. Unct.*, N. 8, p. 52.
266 *Lit. Pract. Comp.*, sec. V, c. 5, n. 2.
267 *Th. M.*, III, *de Ext. Unct.*, n. 19.
268 *Casus Consc.*, casus 885, II.
269 *Prax. Conf.*, n. 5000.
270 Cf. Diana, *Op. Coord.*, t. II, tr. IV, res. 49.
271 Cf. Catalano, *Rit. Rom.*, t. I, p. 313.

these up very succinctly:

> "Mariceau epigrammatically called pregnancy a disease of nine months duration. Sir James Y. Simpson said that parturition is always physiologic in its object, but not in some of the phenomena and peculiarities which attend upon it in civilized life. Engleman, after comparing the labors of primitive and civilized peoples, says that a simple natural labor is no longer possible, and, further, 'the parturient suffers under the continuance of the old prejudice that labor is a physiologic act.' Kehrer said that there was a sharp line between physiologic and pathologic pregnancy. J. O. Polak in 1910 said that parturition is rapidly becoming a pathologic phenomenon. F. S. Newell says that we must realize that 'something has gone wrong with this normal physiologic process' or that present methods are not efficacious. E. P. Davis calls the statement that labor is a physiologic process a half-truth. Schwarz, of St. Louis, says, 'tradition and ignorance are alike combined in spreading the fable that child-bearing is a physiologic process.' Moran, of Washington, asks for a 'nation-wide propaganda to teach the laity that the long-cherished fallacy that pregnancy and labor are physiologic conditions should be abandoned.' "[272]

It can be seen very easily that this array of authority is at least sufficient to constitute the legitimacy of anointing in every case when a woman in child-birth is placed, even from the ordinary pains and common sorrows, in a prudent and probable danger of death. If her condition is pathological—and there is great likelihood that it is—the unction should be given without scruple. If there is a doubt, conditional administration should be made.

Vermeersch [273] evidently is of this opinion for he says very simply "Morbo autem assimilatur . . . partus."

III. The third case to be considered, namely, that of a woman in danger of death from extraordinary circumstances of parturition can be dismissed very simply. Such a one has surely a pathologic condition, for the extraordinary dolors constitute a true sickness and induce a danger of death "ex morbo." Thus Capellman writes: "Parturientibus igitur extrema unctio tum solum conferri licite potest, si in proximo vitae periculo,

---

272 *The Principles and Practice of Obstetrics,* introduction, p. xv. Cf. also Ballantyne, "*The Nature of Pregnancy*"—Brit. Med. Jour., Feb. 1914, p. 354; Davis, in Jour. Amer. Med. Ass'n, July 6, 1912; Engleman, *Amer. System of Obstetrics,* vol. I, pp. 24 and 64; J. F. Moran, in Jour. Amer. Med. Ass'n, Jan. 9, 1915, p. 126; Simpson, *Collected Essays,* vol. II, p. 123.

273 *Th. M.,* III, 660.

in articulo mortis articulo mortis versantur, v. g., si vehementi sanguinis profluvio, interna laceratione, spasmis eclampticis, ect., status vitae periculosus adducatur." [274]

Such extraordinary circumstances may result from the difficulty of parturition,[275] from the fact that the woman "laborat extraordinariis et lethalibus doloribus" [276] or from the fact that it is necessary to extricate the fetus.[277] It is clear in every case that the extraordinary circumstances are causing the danger, and thus making the patients valid and licit recipients of the anointments.

With regard to the extraction of the fetus, it is to be noted that unction is permitted only when the fetus is actually endangering the life of the mother at the time of the bestowal of the sacrament. In such a contingency the mother should be anointed before the operation. If, however, it is simply foreseen that the mother's life will be imperilled by a parturition, and the operation is done to extract the fetus after viability in order to forestall this dangerous condition, Extreme Unction is not allowable before the operation; for the fetus has not yet endangered the woman's life. As will be seen in the discussion of anointings before operations, the administration of Extreme Unction cannot be made to one in danger of death only from the surgeon's knife.

The question of anointing before surgical operations has four different phases:

1. When a man, in danger of death from sickness, consents to undergo an operation whose outcome is uncertain.

2. When a man, in danger of death from sickness, consents to undergo an operation which will, with moral certainty, accomplish his recovery.

3. When a man, somewhat sick but not in danger of death as yet, consents to undergo an operation which is of itself serious and will put him in danger of death.

---

274 *Med. Pastor.*, p. 127; Cf. also St. Alphonsus, *Th. M.*, VI, 713, dub. 3; Genicot-Salsmans, *Inst. Th. M.*, II, 422; Scavini, *Th. M.*, III, 440; Gobat, *Moralium*, Tr. VIII, n. 845; Baruffaldo, *Ad Rit. Rom. Comm.*, t. I, tit. 27, n. 79; Tanquerey, *Th. D.*, III, 783 (a).

275 Genicot-Salsmans, *l.c.;* Bucceroni, *Inst. Th. M.*, P. II, vol. III, n. 871.

276 *Th. M.*, n. 1508, q. 3.

277 Elbel-Bierbaum, *Th. M.*, Conf. X, n. 230; LaCroix, *Th. M.*, VI, 2108.

4. When a man is not sick at all, yet who undergoes a severe and serious operation.

I. The first case is very easily solved. The patient is in danger of death from an intrinsic cause, viz., his sickness, and is a valid and lawful recipient of Extreme Unction for that reason alone. The fact that he may probably be relieved by the operation does not constitute a sufficient reason for denying him this sacrament. The means toward recovery that he is adopting does not remove the element of danger from his disease.

II. The second case considers a man in actual danger of death from sickness, yet consenting to use a means which will restore (in the opinion of trustworthy and skilled physicians) his health with moral certainty. An instance of this kind would be that of a man suffocating from an obstruction of the windpipe, the removal of which would relieve the condition and immediately restore health.

In the first place, it must be noted that if he does not consent to undergo such an operation, he is certainly a valid subject of the sacrament. Moreover, nobody is obliged to submit himself to such extraordinary procedure in order to regain health.[278] Hence if such a patient refuses to resort to the knife of the surgeon, he is not to be denied Extreme Unction.

If, however, the subject consents to undergo the operation, theologians dispute about his capability to receive the holy oils. Kern thinks such an administration absolutely invalid:

> "Simulac autem consentit consilio medicorum, mea quidem sententia se constituit inhabilem, qui sacri mysterii particeps fiat. Eo ipso enim, quod voluntate acceptat medium, cum quo certa restitutio sanitatis conjungitur, morbo suo rationem periculi adimit, omnem fundatum timorem mortis excutit et incapax fit illius confortationis, quae est sacramenti effectus principalis."[279]

Vermeersch-Creusen thinks such procedure at least illicit:

> "Illicita saltem fuerit ministratio facta infirmo consentienti in *securum* scalpelli usum, quo omne periculum ex morbo quem nunc habet removebitur."[280]

---

278 Genicot-Salsmans, *Inst. Th. M.*, I, 364.
279 *Tract. de Extr. Unct.*, p. 299.
280 *Epit.*, II, 225.

The author of the article on "*Extreme Unction*" in the Catholic Encyclopedia mentions this question and states that the arguments of Kern are "by no means convincing." Quinn [281] takes direct issue with Kern's contention. "We must confess," he writes, "our inability to see how the danger of death which is present *ex hypothesi* is fundamentally changed when one makes up his mind to undergo an operation which will (almost certainly, it is assumed) cure him. If we suppose the operation to be dangerous, Fr. Kern would have no difficulty in allowing the sacrament to be administered. It would seem more correct to hold that the proximity of danger which is about to come from an outside source does not affect the situation; if the sick person is a proper subject at all, it is because of his actual sickness."

Truly it is hard to see how a man can be refused unction because of a return to health through extrinsic means, if he cannot be anointed when the presence of an extrinsic danger imperils his life. The question of anointing considers the intrinsic conditions of the patient. They determine his receptibility of this sacrament. Hence, when he seeks a return to health thru an extrinsic way, it shauld have no influence upon his status as a valid recipient. *De facto* he is in danger of death from his sickness; he experiences that depression of soul and spiritual torpor as other people in the same condition. He is capable, therefore, of that spiritual alleviation and comfort which other sick people need in such a state. Consequently, he is capable of the primary effect of the unction; and there are no good grounds for refusing it.

This is confirmed by other theologians who make no distinction in their instructions as to administration of the sacrament prior to operations. All are found to allow a bestowal of the oil in every case where the subject labors under a serious disease and is put thereby in danger of death.

Practically, at least a conditional administration should be made in these circumstances. If, however, by any mischance the patient begins to die subsequent to the operation (as might occur when, contrary to expectation, a serious peril

281 *Some Aspects of the Dogma of Extreme Unction*, p. 120.

arises from the effect of the operation), a second conditional administration should be made. This is evidently the safer procedure, for it safeguards the welfare of the sick man as well as the sanctity of the sacrament.

III. The third and fourth cases can be answered together. The former considers the case of a man somewhat sick, even seriously, but not as yet in danger of death, who is about to undergo a serious surgical operation. This occurs when, e. g., a man is afflicted with a growth which has not yet developed sufficiently to place him in danger of death, yet, if left undisturbed, will eventually attain such a proportion. To forestall this would be the purpose of the operation. Another case is that of *chronic* appendicitis. *Per se* the condition is not dangerous, but if not removed, its *sequelae* are very perilous. Complications can result from the presence of fœcal matter or of a foreign body (such as a grape seed) in the appendix. Eventually this would cause an ulceration which would terminate in a rupture. Peritonitis often follows this breaking of the appendix, and the life of the patient is then imminently imperilled. To prevent all these *sequelae,* medical men advise an opportune operation—and this falls under the case that is being considered.

The fourth case occurs when a healthy man submits to a blood transfusion which may endanger his life—at least, probably. Attempts by surgery to correct deformities of the body are likewise good examples, for such operations (e. g., the attempt to reset a dislocated hip) are, at times, extremely dangerous to the patient.

From the principles we have applied hitherto, it can be seen that in neither case are the essential conditions in the subject verified. To receive Extreme Unction validly, a man must be seriously sick, and in danger of death from the sickness. Yet the surgeon's scalpel is as much extrinsic as the hangman's rope or the electrocutioner's switch. Until the knife has actually cut the man, there is no internal danger. Hence the Unction of such a man prior to the operation is in no way justifiable.

This is one of the instances when a man cannot receive Extreme Unction while in possession of his senses (unless, of course, a local anæsthetic has been employed). The canon demanding such an opportune administration presupposes in the subject the existence of all other conditions requisite for valid reception. Otherwise the time must be awaited until all such conditions are verified, however unfortunate the administration to an unconscious man may be. Better is it to have the sacrament when unconscious than not at all—and an administration of such a kind before operation would be positively null. At the moment of the unction the subject is not in danger of death *ab intrinseco* and may not even be grievously sick. Hence he has not the depression of soul against which the principal effect is aimed. Being incapable of receiving the principal effect, he is incapable of receiving the sacrament.

No author allows the administration of Extreme Unction to a man, about to undergo a surgical operation who will be put into danger of death from the operation alone, no matter whether the operation itself constitutes the whole danger of death or whether an intrinsic condition, not of itself dangerous, but coupled with the operation will embody the peril. Hear a few. Thus Capellman:

> "Ante mortiferam aliquam operationem tum solum licet sacram unctionem administrare, si morbus ille, qui operationem exigit, ipse per se vitae periculum secum fert, v. g., in sectione caesarea, quum partus alia ratione fieri nullatenus possit. Quodsi infirmitas *per se non est mortifera,* Sanctam Unctionem administrare non licet ante *operationem quamvis mortiferam,* quae ad curandum morbum instituenda est. Exempli causa, si propter malignum tumorem, qui in posterum quidem, sed non statim vitae periculosus sit, gravis et mortifera operatio facienda esset, illud vitae periculum, quod in ipsa operatione oriretur, non directe ex morbo proveniret, sed operatione demum productum vel proprium effectum esset, quare tum S. Unctionem conferre non liceret."[282]

Hanley:

> "Some authorities claim that a person who is slightly indisposed can be validly anointed, provided he will die during the operation. This is not, I believe, in accordance with the principles of theology."[283]

282 *Med. Past.,* p. 127.
283 *Treatise on Sac. Ext. Unct.,* p. 34.

Genicot-Salsmans:

> "Sequitur perperam conferri iis qui periculosam operationem chirurgicam subituri sunt, nisi jam antea ex infirmitate periclitentur."[284]

Similar quotations can be made from Arregui,[285] Scavini,[286] Lehmkuhl,[287] D'Annibale,[288] Berardi,[289] Reuter,[290] Noldin[291] and Sebastiani.[292] Finally Vermeersch-Creusen notes:

> "Qui manus chirurgi passuri plerumque, jam actu, interno mortis periculo sunt obnoxii, ita ut jam ante scalpelli usum ungi possunt. Si tamen quis corpore sanus periculosum scalpelli usum subiturus sit, v. g., ad deformitatem corrigendam, non possit ungi antequam ipse usus scalpelli periculum internae rationis induxerit."[293]

Hence a priest is to prepare a man in these cases by Penance, if necessary, and by Viaticum, which may be given in extrinsic dangers of death. The oils, however, should not be applied until such notice that the patient is in danger of death from the actual cutting.[294] This, indeed, may be very inconvenient—and in many hospitals the authorities may not acquiesce to the incursions of the priest into the operating room. Such visits will not be so very frequent as may be imagined, however. Rarely will emergencies of so great urgency arise. At any rate, it is worse than useless to apply, either out of mistaken zeal for souls or for a mistaken leaning towards one's own comfort, the holy oils to the sick man before such an intrinsic danger is induced. The administration is nullified, the sacrament profaned and its effects frustrated.

It follows *a fortiori* from this that a man cannot be given Extreme Unction merely because he is about to receive an

---

284 *Inst. Th. M.*, II, 422.
285 *Summ. Th. M.*, n. 666.
286 *Th. M.*, III, 440.
287 *Th. M.*, II, 722.
288 *Summ. Th. M.*, III, 417, footnote 18.
289 *Prax. Conf.*, n. 5000; *De Parocho*, n. 294.
290 Reuter-Lehmkuhl-Umberg, *Neo-Conf.*, n. 225.
291 *De Sac.*, 443 b.
292 *Summ. Th. M.*, n. 510.
293 *Epit.*, II, 225.
294 Cf. Konings, *Th. M.*, n. 1508, quaeres 3 ad b, cum notula 51.

anæsthetic before his operation. If in individual instances there is a danger to the patient from the reception of ether, the priest must wait until the ether has actually been administered. Not only does this apply to patients who are well, but to those who are afflicted with a physical condition which might be aggravated by the administration of the anaesthetic. Hence a man with a heavy cold or with a cardiac condition who is not *per se* in danger of death therefrom, can only be anointed after the application of the anæsthetic.

It is to be remembered that physicians will not administer, as a rule, ether or chloroform if there will be any danger to the patient. Consequently the mere inhalation of ether, given by order of a skilled physician, will not of itself justify the administration of Unction, even after the anæsthetic has been applied. In this regard Hanley says simply: "A person cannot be validly anointed merely because he is under the influence of ether.[295] Lehmkuhl discusses the action of a certain priest (Fridericus who anointed every patient immediately after the administration of the anæsthetic prior to the operation, "cum aliquoties accidsset ut ejusmodi homines e narcosi non evigilarent." In his decision he writes:

> "Narcosis chloriformica inducta, nisi alia afflicta valetudo accedat, morale periculum mortis non censetur constituere. Quare nisi medicus judicaverit subesse periculum in casu singulari, Fridericus debuit non jam dare unctionem, utpote quae invalida vel dubie valida esset ac proin postea, cum de periculo constaret iteranda. Quam primum vero per ipsam operationem periculum inductum est, sane tempus est ministrandae unctionis, ne forte in operatione homo decedat sacramento non munitus; de qua re ante narcosin aegrotus moendus est."[296]

Hence in these cases the sick man should be told before the operation that Extreme Unction cannot be given to him then, but that it will be conferred if any danger does arise. He should be also spurred to make a firm intention of co-operating with its sacramental graces, an action which reveals to the priest explicitly that the subject has the correct intentions in this matter.

---

295 *Treatise on the Sacrament of Extreme Unction,* p. 49.
296 *Casus Consc.,* II, cas. 195, p. 384.

Ob senium.

Cicero has said succinctly: "Senectus ipsa morbus est." And thus it has been regarded down all the ages of the Christian era in connection with the administration of Extreme Unction. It is, of course, intrinsic in its origin; and when it has advanced so much as to induce a danger of death, it verifies the conditions required for valid bestowal.[297]

The Sixth Council of Beneventano, held in 1375, prescribed: "Senibus autem datur qui moriuntur etiam sine aliqua infirmitate, quia defectus naturae reputatur in eis pro actuali infirmitate."[298] In similar fashion Benedict XIV wrote: "Conceditur senibus, qui prae decrepita aetate, licet nulla alia speciali afficiantur aegritudine, in dies morituri creduntur; ipsa enim gravis et annosa senectus infirmitas est quae interiora vitae organa labefactat, et mox ducit ad interitum."[299] Trombellio gives as the reason why unction of old men is allowed: "Nam his imminet periculum improvisae mortis et subitae suffocationis."[300]

Old age commences with the sixtieth year. This is the opinion of Augustine[301] and is confirmed by Canon 1254, 2, which exempts from the obligation of fasting all who have attained that age. Yet years alone do not make old age a "sickness." All authors demand that there be a marked decline in the physical forces of an old person before he becomes a fit subject of the sacrament. Thus the Roman Ritual, before its latest revision, denoted an advance to such a degree of weakness that the old men seem "in diem morituri,"[302] before Unction was to be given. Augustine[303] insists on the presence of some signs of the approaching dissolution, such as fainting or sinking-spells.

There is, however, no need to wait until death is actually imminent. The sacrament is validly and licitly given when

---

297 Cf. Dens. *Tract de Ext. Unct.*, N. 8, p. 52.
298 Tit. 8, cap. 1; cf. Catalano, *Rit. Rom.*, t. I, p. 311.
299 *De Syn. Dioc.*, lib. 8, c. 5, n. 2.
300 *De Ext. Unct.*, disp. X, c. I, q. 2, n. III.
301 *A Commentary*, IV, 402.
302 Tit. V, c. 1, n. 5 (edit. 1913). Cf. St. Charles—IV Prov. Conc. Mediolanen., cap. "*Quae pertinent ad Extremam Unctionem,*" apud *Acta Eccl. Mediolanen.*, t. I, pars I, p. 147.
303 L.c.

a man is in a prudently probable danger of death arising from the weaknesses which now afflict him. As Lehmkuhl says, "sufficit et requiritur probabile periculum ne brevi vita finiatur: nullatenus requiritur ut mors jam immineat, aut ut instantis mortis periculum adsit . . . Sufficit . . . morbi ex natura sua diuturni status in quo juste timeri ne brevi vita finiatur. Senectutis talis condicio ut vires in dies videantur." [304]

II. Requisites for Repetition.

2. "*In eadem infirmitate hoc sacramentum iterari non potest, nisi infirmus, post susceptam unctionem convaluerit et in aliud discrimen inciderit.*"

The question of the valid repetition of Extreme Unction in the same danger of death has already been treated in the first chapter.[305] Here only the legality of the procedure need be considered.

Until the year 1000 little is known about the repetition of the sacrament.[306] In 1093, Godfried, the abbot of Vindocensis, sought the opinion of his learned contemporary, St. Yves, bishop of Chartres, in regard to the custom of reanointing then in vogue in Benedictine monasteries. He felt that to reanoint under any circumstances, even in distinct sicknesses, was altogether inadmissible. "In hoc," he wrote,[307] "non mediocriter errant, quod Unctionem Infirmorum, cum a Sancta Catholica et Apostolica Sede sacramentum vocetur, et cum nullum sacramentum iterari debeat, iterandum putant." The reply of St. Yves evidences a hearty concurrence in the reasoning of his friend: "Unctionem infirmorum non aestimo esse repetendam, quia sicut ipse asseruisti . . . genus est sacramenti, qui autem sacramenta Christi et Ecclesiae repetit, injuriam ipsis sacramentis ingerit." [308]

About the same time the abbot, Theobald, of the Monastery of St. Columba in the city of Sens questioned Peter the Venerable (also known as Peter of Montbossier), the abbot of Cluny,

304 *Th. M.*, II, 722.
305 Cf. *supra*, chap. I, sec. VI, n. 3, p. 51, sqq.
306 Cf. Launoi, *Op. Omnia*, t. I, p. 555.
307 M. P. L., 157, 87-88.
308 M. P. L., 157, 88.

"cur unctio infirmorum sola, hoc apud Cluniacum solummodo, reiteretur." Peter's reply is magnificent vindication of the Benedictine practice. After overturning the arguments of the adversaries of the practice, he gives in very convincing fashion the reasons in its favor. Thus in part he writes:

> "Nam si aeger post semel redditam sanitatem nunquam in morbum incideret; si nunquam post primam unctionem in peccata corrueret, fateor quod nunquam deinceps unctionem jam dictam iterari fas esset. Quod si rursum infirmatus fuerit, si rursum peccaverit, quae ratio, ut rursum ei allevietur, ut ei peccata dimittantur, denuo eum inungi prohibebit? Nonne et apostolus hoc se indicat velle, ut quoties quis infirmatus fuerit, toties inungatur? Nam quid aliud sonant verba illa illius: 'Infirmatur quis in vobis? Inducat presbyteros Ecclesiae?' Non enim ait: 'Infirmatur quis in vobis, inducat presbyteros semel,' sed nulla mentione unius, binae vel ternae unctionis facta jubet nullo praefixo numero induci ad aegrum presbyteros eccelesiae, fidei orationem fieri, ad alleviationem et peccatorum remissionem eum oleo sacro inungi. Non igitur mihi videtur dicendum esse, quod apostolus non dixit addendum esse, quod ipse non scripsit, sentiendum quod ipse, ut verba ejus indicant, non sensit."[309]

Peter's letter had the happy effect of destroying the belief which allowed Unction to be given only once in a person's lifetime. The statements made by Ciacconius[310] and Ughellius,[311] biographers of Pius II, to the effect that there were vehement disputes in Rome whether the sick Pontiff was capable of Unction as he approached death, since he had already been anointed when he was stricken with a plague a few years previous, are regarded as fabulous and untrue by Benedict XIV [312] and Catalano.[313] Other biographies of the Pope make no mention of such dispute, although they contain minute accounts of the

309 *Epp.*, l. 5, ep. 7—M. P. L., 189, 392-93. It must be noted that such a custom was not confined to Cluny. Peter Cantor of Paris and Cardinal Robert de Corceon testify to the existence of a similar practice among the Cistercians of Clairvaux (Cf. Launoi, *Op. Omnia*, t. I, p. 549 sqq.). Similarly, the monks of Hirksau allowed repetition of the anointing provided that at least three years had elapsed since the previous Unction (Cf. Catalano, *Rit. Rom.*, t. I, p. 316.)

310 *Vita S. Pii*, tom. II, p. 1005.

311 *Italia Sacra*, tom. II, p. 553.

312 *De Syn. Dioc.*, l. 8, c. 8, n. 3.

313 *Rit. Rom.*, t. I, p. 316.

314 Cf. Biographies written by Campano, apud Muratori, *Rev. Ital. Script.*, III, ii, 967-92; and Commentaries of Cardinal Papiensis—quoted by Catalano, *l.c.*

days immediately preceding his death.[314] Moreover by the middle of the fifteenth century, when Pius reigned, theologians and synods had generally allowed a re-administration of the unction.

From the year 1130 to the year 1350 it was generally held that the sacrament might be repeated under certain circumstances. The old opinion had not altogether been eradicated, as Alanus Porretanus notes: "Sunt qui dicunt de hoc sacramento quod iterari non possit, siceut nec Baptismus; sed quia sacramentum paenitentiae est, et paenitentia iterari potest, probabile est hoc sacramentum iterari posse." [315]

The great writers, however—Peter Lombard,[316] William of Auxerre,[317] Thomas Aquinas,[318] Hugh of St. Victor [319] and St. Bonaventure [320]—all maintained the reiterability of Extreme Unction in different and distinct danger of death, even though occurring in one and the same sickness. Albertus Magnus[321] demanded an interval of a year between unctions in protracted illnesses, regardless of whether the man lapsed more than once into a dangerous state. Though scoffed at, after a fashion, by St. Bonaventure,[322] who remarked the absurdity of regulating the sacraments by the stars, he nevertheless obtained considerable adherence to his opinion, not alone among his contemporaries, but also and especially in later writers.[323]

Local legislation asserted the liceity of repetition. Richard Poore stated in his Constitutions: "Moneant sacerdotes frequenter populum licite iterari posse: scilicet in qualibet gravi infirmitate de qua metus imminet mortis." [324] The Synod of Bayeux,[325] celebrated in 1300, insisted likewise that the reiterability of the sacrament be inculcated in the minds of the people.

---

315 *Maxima Theologiae,* n. xciii—cf. Launoi, *Op. cit.,* p. 550.
316 *Lib. IV Sent.,* dist. xxiii— M. P. L., 192, 899.
317 *Summa Aurea,* lib. 4, tr. 7, c. 2.
318 *Suppl.* q. 33, a. 1 et 2.
319 *De Sacramentis,* p. XV, c. 3.
320 *Comm. in IV lib. Sent.,* d. xxiii, a. 2, q. 4.
321 *Comm. in lib. quart. Sent.,* d. xxiii, a. 21.
322 L.c.
323 Cf. Hugo of Salisburg, inter *Opera B. Alberti,* t. 34, p. 232.
324 Harduin VII, 107.
325 Harduin, VII, 1237.

William, the bishop of Paris, in his book on the Sacraments,[326] taught the lawfulness of repeated Unction not only in different sicknesses but also in each danger of death in the same sickness.

Between 1350 and the Council of Trent the permissibility of repetition was held by all. The great influence of Albert and Thomas made itself plain in two widely divergent schools of thought in the matter of procedure in repeating the sacrament. Those who followed Thomas held that it was to be repeated in every danger of death in lingering diseases. Albert's followers contended that in these cases once a year was the extent of the frequency of repetition. Some extremists[327] taught that the sacrament could not be given within a year from its previous bestowal, even in a different sickness.

Synodal legislation reveals traces of this division of thought. Thus the allowability of reanointing was declared by the Sixth Provincial Council of Beneventano with these words:

> "Et quia de iteratione fuerunt dubitationes, ideo dicimus secundum communem opinionem, quod quaedam sunt infirmitates non diuturnae: unde si eis datur hoc sacramentum tunc cum homo ad statum illum pervenerit, quo est in periculo mortis, non recedit a statu illo, nisi infirmitate curata, et ita iterum non debet inungi. Sed si recidivum patiatur, erit alia infirmitas, et ita iterum poterit inungi. Quaedam vere sunt aegritudines diurnae, ut ethica et hydropisis, etc., in talibus non debet fieri inunctio nisi quando videntur inducere mortis periculum. Si homo illud evadat, eadem infirmitate durante, et iterum ad simile periculum per infirmitatem reducatur, potest iterum inungi, quia quasi erit alius status infirmitatis."[328]

In concordance with this enactment are the decrees of the Synods of Langres (1404), Chartres (1526) and Sens (1524),[329] as well as the diocesan statutes of Daniel, bishop of Nantes, Robert, bishop of Cambrai (1550), Maximilian, bishop of Cambrai (1567), Stephen Poncherius, bishop of Paris (1550) and

---

326 *De Septem Sacramentis*, c. 23—Cf. Trombellio, *De Sac. Ext. Unct.*, vol. III, diss. XIII, n. ix, p. 91.

327 Peter Cantor (*Summa*, c. 132—quoted by Catalano, *Rit. Rom.*, t. I, p. 310) forbade repetition during that time; as also an ancient song: "Nonnisi semel in mense tantum communicet aeger. Hic idem solo non bis ungatur in anno" (Martene, *De Antiq. Rit. Eccl.*, l. I, c. 7, a. 1, n. 3).

328 Tit. 8, c. 1—Cf. Trombellio, *De Ext. Unct.*, vol. III, diss. XIII, n. 8.

329 Natalis Alexander, *Th. D. et M.*, lib. II, c. 5, reg. 19.

later archbishop of Sens (1574), and Louis, bishop of Chartres (1576).[330] Similarly the manuals of many individual churches contained a rubric permitting renewal of the sacrament in a diverse danger of death.[331]

The Synod of Ypres, held in the beginning of the sixteenth century, explicitly condemned the opinion holding the inadmissibility of repeated Unction for a year after a bestowal of the sacrament:

> "Proinde consuetudinem, secundum quam non consuevit hoc sacramentum intra annum secundo suscipi, etiamsi altera gravis obveniat infirmitas, tanquam noxiam abrogemus."[332]

On the other hand the power of Albertus' teaching made itself apparent in the rubrics of many diocesan rituals which were edited shortly before the convening of the Council of Trent or even while it was in session. Examples of such are the *Manualia* of the Church of Chartres (1489), Périgueux (1509), Rheims (1504 and 1530), Clermont (1518), Autun (1523), Châlons-sur-Marne (1529), Mende (1530), Beauvais (1544), Meaux (1546), Verdun (1554), Limoges (1555) and Arras (1563).[333]

The question was settled by the Council of Trent: "Quod si infirmus post susceptam hanc unctionem convaluerint, iterum hujus sacramenti, subsidio juvari poterunt, cum in aliud simile vitae discrimen inciderint."[334]

Since that time there has been no question of the permissibility of reanointing. The Catechism of the Council[335] specifically allows a second unction in the same sickness, but in a distinct danger of death from that in which the former anointing was made. The Roman Ritual, before its latest revision, contained the rubric: "In eadem infirmitate hoc sacramentum iterari non debet, nisi diuturna sit, ut si, cum infirmus

---

330 Cf. Launoi, *Op. Omnia*, t. I, p. 552.

331 Cf. Launoi, *l.c.*—Manuals of the Churches of Cambrai (1552), Vienne (1577) Rheims (1585), Auxerre (1586), Lyons (1592), Malines (1598).

332 Van Espen, *Jus Eccl. Univ.*, P. II, sect. I, tit. 7, n. 37.

333 Cf. Launoi, *Op. Omnia*, t. I, p. 553.

334 Sess. XIV, *de Ext. Unct.*, c. 3.

335 *De Ext. Unct.*, n. 11.

convaluerit, iterum in periculum mortis incidat." [336] Other Rituals, edited since the Council of Trent, also direct a second anointing in the same sickness after the partial recovery and subsequent relapse of the patient.[337]

Some synods have made very strict demands in regard to the verification of change of status in the disease. Thus unless certainty that a new danger of death was actually present they would not allow the repetition of the sacrament. The Manual of Rheims, for instance, decreed:

> "Denique potest hoc sacramentum iterari, et quidem in eadem infirmitate, quandoquidem quis est in articulo mortis, modo casus sit diversus, ut, qui in hydropisi, aut longa febri, postquam evasit periculum, rursus post aliquot menses de vita periclitatur."[338]

In similar fashion the Synod of Namur[339] did not wish a second administration in the same sickness "nisi *peritorum judicio* status morbi mutatus fuerit."

Other synods caught the spirit of Trent in the matter and legislated in a milder mode. The Council of Salerno (1579) enunciates the practice followed even today: "In eadem infirmitate nonnisi semel Sacra Unctio adhibeatur; nisi illa longe existente, pluries vitae periculum, pluriesque salutis spes insurgeret." [340] Thus, too, St. Charles wrote in his "*Instructiones*:"

> "Intelliget parochus infirmum, quamdiu in eadem aegrotatione et in eodem mortis periculo versatur, semel tantum esse Extrema Unctione liniendum. Quod si unctione suscepta convaluerit, quoties postea vitae discrimen inciderit, toties hoc sacramentum et adhibebitur. Item in morbis quibusdam diuturnis, puta in hydropisi, si ob mortem impendentem quis unctus fuerit et evaserit, deinde ex eodem morbo in alium similem casum et periculum mortis inciderit, rursus etiam ungi debebit."[341]

---

336 Tit. V, c. 1, n. 14—edit. 1913.

337 Cf. e. g., *Manuale Salisburgense* (p. 324—Cf. Trombellio, *De Ext. Unctione*, dis. XIII, n. 8): "Hoc vero sacramentum in eodem homine iterari potest, non in variis solum, sed in eodem etiam morbo, cum diversa vitae pericula post dierum aliquot intervalla impendent, ut si nunc remittente, nunc rursus ingravescente, morbo mors imminere videatur;" Cf. also *Rituale Cardinalis Sanctorii*—apud Benedict XIV, *De Syn. Dioc.*, l. 8, c. 8, n. 4.

338 Cf. Van Espen, *Jus Canon. Univ.*, P. II, sect. I, tit. 7, n. 36.

339 Tit. IV, c. 8—Cf. Van Espen, l.c.—anno 1639.

340 Tit. 32, c. 3—Cf. Catalano, *Rit. Rom.*, t. I, p. 317.

341 Pars IV, *Acta Eccl. Mediolan.*, t. I, tit. "*Quoties hoc sacramento utendum est,*" p. 604.

Hence all theologians of today admit the permissibility of conferring Extreme Unction in each danger of death, whether it be that of entirely new sickness, or a second danger of the same sickness. Extreme Unction is a remedy against the evils which sick men in danger of death suffer. Consequently, as long as the danger and depression continue, only so long does the right to the supernatural graces of the sacrament remain. A sick man whose infirmity is no longer conjoined with a danger of death has no more right to the aids than a sick man whose sickness is not yet coupled with a danger of death. Hence, if a man falls again into danger of death, he needs the right to the spiritual aids which evanesced when he passed out of the *periculum mortis* the first time. The only way to recapture this right is by a second administration of the sacrament.[342] Consequently the subject is to be anointed a second time.

Repetition can be made as often as the dangers of death occur. If it is without doubt that the first peril has been removed and the patient has recovered only to fall subsequently into another new danger, the repetition of the sacrament must be made, even though the interval of time between the unctions be very short. This, too, whether the second danger occur from the same sickness as the previous peril or from an entirely distinct cause.

The cases of lingering illnesses (and, *a pari*, old age) can give some difficulties to a priest, and therefore require a lengthier consideration. Three contingencies may occur:

1. When the danger of death has certainly passed away from such a patient, and he subsequently falls into a second danger of death.

2. When a man, suffering from a protracted illness, has but doubtfully passed from one danger of death into another.

3. When it is certain that the same danger of death is perduring.

I. In the first instance it is clear that the man must be reanointed. Noldin distinguishes between an obligation and a

---

342 *Tract. de Ext. Unct.*, pp. 335-6.

permissibility to reanoint. When it is a second danger of the same sickness the sacrament may be repeated, whereas when the sickness itself is an entirely distinct infirmity, the Unction must be conferred the second time.[343] The distinction between the cases is entirely unwarranted. The sick person has lost his title to the spiritual comfort and alleviation furnished by the previous Unction. This evanesced when he passed from out the pale of danger. When he falls again into danger of death, he is as much in need of these aids as if a new sickness fell upon him.[344]

Some theologians teach that repetition of the sacrament can be made when a man, already anointed in imminent danger of death, has been somewhat relieved and subsequently fallen again into imminent danger, even though his temporary relief did not put him beyond danger even for an instant. The proponents of this opinion are St. Bonaventure[345] and Laymann[346] among the older writers, and De Augustinis,[347] Prummer[348] and O'Kane [349] among recent authors. Indeed other authors seem to be speaking of the same thing when they talk of the recovery of a patient from danger of death. Rarely does it seem that they understand a convalescence to such an extent that the disease has temporarily lost its fatal character. This can be seen from the fact that the examples of such authors are consumption, tuberculosis, and dropsy, which seldom allow a recovery to such an extent that a man cannot be said to be in at least a remote danger of death.[350]

With regard to this opinion Kern[351] takes sharp issue. He claims rightly that the sacrament of the Unction was instituted for those who are seriously sick and in danger of death, at least, remotely. Hence when once anointed, the efficacy of the Unction extends thruout the entire time that the man is in danger, no

343 *De Sac.*, n. 447.
344 *Op. cit.*, p. 338.
345 *Comm. in lib. quart. Sent.*, d. xxiii, a. 2, q. 4 ad 2.
346 *Th. M.*, l. V, tr. 8, c. 4, n. 5.
347 *De Re Sacramentaria*, II, p. 408.
348 *Manuale Th. M.*, III, 582.
349 *The Rubrics*, n. 877.
350 Elbel-Bierbaum, *Th. M.*, P. VIII, Conf., X, n. 219; Lehmkuhl, *Casus Consc.*, II, 679; O'Kane, *The Rubrics*, n. 876; Kenrick, *Th. M.*, III, "*De Ext. Unct.*" cap. unic., n. 21.
351 *Tract. de Ext. Unct.*, pp. 337-8.

matter how much his condition changes therein, provided, of course, that never does he pass beyond a remote danger. If, therefore, a consumptive is anointed when he is first declared in danger of death by the physicians, he receives the benefits of that unction thruout the entire duration of such a danger. How then can Extreme Unction be given in this case? If not invalid, it seems quite illicit. It is no escape to say that Extreme Unction may, but need not, be repeated within this time. Either the man is again in need of the efficacy of the sacrament, or the effects of the first unction are still perduring. If he is in need of the Unction, the sacrament not only *may* be repeated, but *must* be again conferred—and that, too, by the same obligation in justice or charity which bound for the original administration. If the efficacy of the first unction still perdures, then a repeated unction is altogether unlawful.

Authors, however, advance some reasons in defense of this practice. They claim that morally a new danger is present, and is actually considered to be present in the common estimation of men. Those who have been in imminent danger and have recovered gradually for a notable space of time, are usually considered out of danger, although *de facto* they may not be. The recuperation is popularly considered to be evidence of the successful negotiation of the crisis. If one of these patients should fall again into imminent danger of death, a new danger is thought to have risen. Genicot goes so far as to say that this popular belief on the subject should be preferred to a medical opinion to the contrary: "Cui vulgari existimationi inhaerendum est potius quam scientificae medicorum existimationi, in regula vulgo applicanda." [352]

There is enough probability here to justify an administration in such cases. The intrinsic and extrinsic bases supply a sufficient defense for the legality of their action. Priests who have convinced themselves that re-administration in the same danger of death is positively invalid, can take sufficient care of the patient's soul by making a conditional administration. Even this seems hardly of obligation, for the sacrament has surely the efficacy it was designed to have, and this efficacy

352 *Casus Consc.*, cas. 889, p. 576.

continues. Moreover, who is to say when popular belief looks upon the old danger as passed and the new one as arrived? And again, it might be difficult to show by what power the common estimation of men changes an essential condition in a subject. Suppose common estimation thought some substance was bread, while chemists declared scientifically that it was not. Could the fact that in the popular mind such a substance was bread make it valid, not to say even lawful, matter for the Eucharist?

The obligation of a pastor in this case is not strict. He is certainly not bound to anoint in such cases. His procedure will depend on the appeal which the arguments of one or the other opinion have for him.

With regard to a partial recovery, whereby the patient is placed probably out of the danger of death, followed by a relapse, it may be said that Extreme Unction may be repeated in such a case—just as it can be given originally when there is a prudent fear that danger is present. In the present case all that is necessary would be a probable judgment that a new danger of death has arisen. With regard to the obligation of conferring the sacrament, it can hardly be said to be very urgent, for it is by no means certain that the man has lost the efficacy of the former unction.[353]

II. The second case, wherein it is doubtful whether a man has recovered and lapsed again into a second danger of death, provides several problems which are not easy to solve. Suppose a patient is anointed because he is remotely in danger of death. He lives on for a notable period of time without much change of condition apparently. Or his condition may be quite variable. One day he is quite sick, the following day much relieved —and in this spasmodic fashion he continues for some months. Can Extreme Unction be repeated upon such persons? And if so, how frequently?

To verify the word "convaluerit," used by this canon, there must be some improvement. A mere continuance of life does not of itself justify a second administration.[354] Some kind of a recovery is required, and that recovery must continue for an

---

353 Cf. Bucceroni, *Inst. Th. M.*, vol. III, P. II, n. 871.
354 O'Kane, *The Rubrics*, n. 877.

appreciable length of time. Thus Noldin says: "Idem periculum perdurare censetur, si infirmus per breve solum tempus, per aliquot scilicet dies, se melius habuit, nisi ex natura morbi aliud constet."[355] Genicot[356] thinks an improvement lasting over four or five days is not sufficient. This, too, is the opinion of St. Alphonsus[357] and of D'Annibale.[358]

O'Kane[359] is of the opinion that a man who lives a month after the conferring of Extreme Unction furnishes thereby a positive doubt as to his recovery. All things considered, it is quite hard to tell as a general rule whether or not the danger has actually continued during the whole time or whether it has ceased to exist at any time.

In this case theologians allow a repeated administration of the sacrament, and they urge priests to incline towards repetition. Thus Van Espen:

> "Discat parochus ab iteratione hujus sacramenti se non debere scrupulose abstinere ob periculum nullitatis sacramenti; sed duntaxat, ne in disciplinam jam stabilitam impingat: adeoque si dubium sit, num forsan morbi status ita fuerit mutatus, ut etiam juxta modernam disciplinam reiterari queat, magis pro reiteratione inclinandum; eo quod haec reiteratio conformior fit veteri Ecclesiae consuetudini, tum quod per eam novum ipsi infirmo subsidium spirituale sperari possit."[360]

This admonition to pastors was repeated by Benedict XIV,[361] St. Alphonsus,[362] Kenrick,[363] Scavini,[364] Gury,[365] O'Kane[366] and Genicot.[367]

355 *De Sac.* n. 447. Cf. Dens, *Tract. de Ext. Unct.*, N. 11, pp. 59-60: "Satis non est quod morbi status parumper mutetur, v. g., aeger mane melius se habeat et vespere iterum pejus; quod febris una die remittat aut etiam cessat, altera die redeat aut augeatur; sed talis mutatio intercessisse debet, ut dici possit infirmum convaluisse et in aliud periculum incidisse." Cf. also Kenrick, *Th. M.*, III, "*De Ext. Unct.*," n. 21.

356 *Inst. Th. M.*, II, 423.

357 *Th. M.*, VI, 715.

358 *Summ. Th. M.*, III, 417, footnote 20.

359 *The Rubrics*, n. 878.

360 *Jus Eccl. Univ.*, Pars II, sec. I, tit. 7, n. 40.

361 *De Syn. Dioc.*, l. 8, c. 8, n. 4.

362 *L.c.*

363 *L.c.*

364 *Th. M.*, III, 442.

365 *Th. M.*, II, 691.

366 *The Rubrics*, n. 878.

367 *Th. M.*, II, 423.

Repetition is thus allowed on the ground that a man who can live for a month without showing much change of condition has really recovered to some extent and in the estimation of men a new moral danger of death has arisen. This is the reason commonly assigned by theologians for this practice. However, a curious explanation was suggested by Dr. Walter McDonald, Dean of the Dunboyne Establishment at Maynooth, to justify the present practice:

> "There are but two courses open—either to give up repeating the sacrament in those cases of lengthened illness, or to maintain that the repetition is not a true repetition, as the sacrament was not validly administered in the first instance. The only conceivable reason for this latter course would be that it is only those who are in proximate danger of death that are capable of receiving the sacrament. It would remain to determine some measure of proximity; and as to this I should be prepared to accept as a working measure the month rule now acted on by most priests, understanding it in this sense, that if it is a month since the sacrament was administered, and there has been no amelioration, amounting to convalescence, in the patient's condition, that fact is to be regarded as proof sufficient that he was not in proximate danger, nor therefore capable of receiving the sacrament, when it was previously administered."[368]

Quinn[369] commemorates this opinion but does not agree with it. Toner [370] notes that it involves a serious breach with the tradition of the first twelve centuries; and this for him is a strong, if not a fatal, objection. Indeed McDonald's opinion demands a stage of disease as acute as that demanded by the Scotists. It has already been shown how untenable such a view is.[371] The Propaganda[372] did not consider such a contingency when it allowed the administration of the sacrament to one afflicted with lung trouble who would live for several months.

Quinn [373] proffers a different explanation. The theologians who sanction this practice had in mind the ordinary case—wherein recovery occurs within a month. They did not enter into the question of the fluctuations of the disease; they used

368 Irish Theological Quarterly, vol. II (1907), p. 343.
369 *Some Aspects of the Dogma of Extreme Unction,* p. 133.
370 Irish Theological Quarterly, l.c., p. 250.
371 Cf. *supra,* p. 156-7; 161-5.
372 S. C. P. F. (C. P. pro Sin.), Feb. 20, 1801—Collectanea, n. 651.
373 *Op. cit.* pp. 133-34; Cf. Irish Eccl. Record, Fifth Series, vol. XIV (1919), p. 485.

the normal case as the basis of their instruction. Their teaching saves the minister from the difficulty of deciding whether a real recovery and relapse had intervened since the bestowal of the previous administration. Though this occasionally results in invalid receptions, nevertheless the principle "sacramenta propter homines" should govern, especially "when there is a question of the sacrament that is the culmination of the whole Christian life."

Those who hold the validity of repeated Unction in the same danger of death would look upon the matter in a different light. For them there would be no invalid administrations. Since persons who live a month after unction furnish a prudent and probable doubt that they have recovered and relapsed again into a new danger, repetition of the sacrament can be validly and licitly made. Validly, since according to their conviction, the sacrament can be given more than once even in the same danger of death; licitly, because it is quite probable that it is not the same danger, and therefore, the law forbidding repetition ceases to bind (*Lex dubia non obligat*).

The amount of time that must pass to give origin to such a doubt as to the change of status of the sick person must, as has been said, be a notable one. Noldin,[374] Konings,[375] Genicot[376] and O'Kane[377] hold that such an interval is the space of one month. Barbosa[378] demands a few weeks. Other theologians do not demand such a long time; and it must be remembered that Bonaventure's remark as to the absurdity of regulating sacraments by the stars applies with all its force in these instances. Thus Telch[379] says that one week is a sufficient interval between the anointings of a consumptive, although for other cases he demands a month. Elbel-Bierbaum [380] is inclined to a similarly generous opinion of one week. Suarez gives some

374 *De Sac.*, 447.
375 *Th. M.*, 1508, quaeres 6.
376 *Inst. Th. M.*, II, 423.
377 *De Off. et Pot. Par.*, c. 22, n. 38.
378 *The Rubrics*, n. 878.
379 *Epit. Th. M.*, p. 304.
380 *Th. M.*, Conf. X, n. 231.

very sane advice on the matter:

"Constat necessarium esse status illos aegritudinis per aliquam diuturnam moram interrumpi, ita ut secundum communem existimationem diversi censeantur. Frivolum autem est unius anni interruptionem postulare, quia intra illud tempus coelestium corporum, praesertim solis, revolutio perficitur, ut Albertus philosophari videtur; quid enim hoc refert ad sacramenti necessitatem vel dignam administrationem? Alii unius mensis tempus assignant, voluntario magis arbitrio, quam certa ratione. Paludanus pro regula assignat, quoties probabile est in nova peccata venialia incidisse; juxta quam regulam nihil aliud expectandum videtur, nisi quod homo simpliciter dici possit evasisse prius periculum, ita ut medicorum et prudentum judicio censeatur esse liber ab illo aegritudinis statu; nam si postea iterum recidat, etiamsi illo medio statu brevi tempore duraverit, poterit iterum inungi; nam in quolibet brevi tempore timeri possunt nova peccata, praesertim venialia. . . . Etiam haec regula non est admodum certa, ideoque prudenti arbitrio hoc relinquendum est ut nimirum considerata diurnitate aegritudinis et statuum ejus, et interruptionis eorum inter se, practica et communi existimatione illa censeantur diversa pericula et status ita diversi, ut perinde se habeant ac si essent morbi omnino distincti."[381]

Administration is to be made in these cases, as in other cases of doubt, *sub conditione*.[382] This would follow from the wording of the canon, and from the likelihood that any other procedure would be construed as illegal.

Practically it will be lawful for the pastor to repeat Extreme Unction whenever he doubts prudently that the status of the disease has changed. Should he be unable to determine this from observing the patient, he may act upon the opinion that permits the Unction to be given in all such cases at least once a month.

His obligation of repeating it is a different question. It is hard to say that he has any duty in this regard from justice. Theologians, as will be remembered, persuade him to this mode of action, not because of his office, but because the procedure itself seems in closer conformity with the ancient practices of the Church, and because of the spiritual benefit which accrues to the sick man.[383]

III. The third case takes up the question of repeating the sacrament when a man, already anointed in danger of death,

---

381 D. 40, s. 4, n. 7.
382 Cf. Sebastiani, *Summ. Th. M.*, n. 510; Rohling, *Medulla*, p. 380.
383 Cf. Grosam, *Linz. Quartal.*, anno 1926, II, pp. 352-358.

has never passed beyond the border-line of peril. In him there has been no recovery, but simply a gradual decline towards death. Can such a one be anointed a second time?

The words of the Council of Trent show clearly that a recovery of some kind is required. It is not merely a question of length of time in the danger, but a question of recovery and relapse. Hence when the danger of death is certainly the same, no theologian will permit a reanointment. Thus St. Alphonsus says: "Unde adverte quod in morbo diuturno, si infirmus post unctionem certe manserit in eodem periculo mortis, non poterit rursus ungi."[384] Bishop MacDonald notes that it is not a question of time at all, it is "a question of growing better and then again getting worse—of being pronounced out of danger and then falling back into a like danger again."[385] Hence, he says, a person once anointed, who lingers on for two or three months, sinking slowly but perceptibly all the time, cannot be refreshed a second time with the sacrament of the Unction. In similar fashion Noldin writes: "In eadem autem infirmitate sacramentum iterandum non est, quamdiu certo idem mortis periculum perdurat."[386]

Moreover, the prescriptions of the canon are in no way verified if no new danger has arrived. The canon asks for a convalescence and another *discrimen vitae.*

It is to be noted, however, that if the danger of death is of extremely long duration, e. g., for over a year, Genicot allows repetition of the unction. Such a danger, he says,[387] "quamvis verius physice jugiter permansisse dicendum sit, moraliter tamen ex aestimatione communi aliud censetur." Accordingly in his *Casus Conscientiae,* he permits the anointment of a lady in the same physical danger of death for over two years, adding as a reason that in the popular estimation a new danger had arisen, "cui vulgari aestimatione inhaerendum est potius quam scientificae medicorum existimationi, in regula vulgo applicanda."[388]

---

384 *Th. M.*, VI, 715.
385 The American Ecclesiastical Review, vol. XLII, p. 20; cf. vol. XIX, p. 429.
386 *De Sac.*, 447, 3.
387 *Inst. Th. M.*, II, 423.
388 *Casus Consc.*, cas. 889, p. 576.

Another question in regard to repetition is this: "Must the sacrament be given a second time in the same danger of death, if it has been received sacrilegiously the first time?

The answer can be simply given. The law against repetition is absolute. No allowance is made for the case where the patient was not in good dispositions at the time he first received the sacrament. Moreover the powers of reviviscence possessed by the sacrament regain the graces for the subject after the obstacle has been removed.[389] Babenstuber expresses this well:

> "Quaeritur an istud sacramentum possit esse validum et informe ita ut recedente fictione conferat suum effectum? Respondeo affirmative cum communi Doctorum. Ratio est: quia est sacramentum initerabile, saltem pro certo tempore, nempe durante eodem morbo seu statu morbi . . . ; adeoque, si sine aliquo defectu substantiali et cum solo obice sive defectu dispositionis ex parte subjecti requisitae fuit receptum, postea vero obex removeatur, ponaturque sufficiens dispositio, effectum suum producit, ne infirmus fructu illius totaliter privetur."[390]

The final question in this regard has to do with the admissibility of repeating unction in the case where a man, already anointed because he is in danger of death from one source, falls into a second danger of death from another source independent from the first. Such a contingency would occur when a sick man would be mortally wounded or should drink poison, etc.

Diana distinguishes as to the mode of procedure. If the second danger is one closely connected with the first, so that by its very nature it is ordinarily concomitant with or consequent to the first danger, it should be considered as the perdurance of one and the same state of sickness. If, on the other hand, the second danger is absolutely independent from the first, and is in itself sufficiently vehement to put the man in danger of death, even if the first danger of death were not at all present, Diana thinks it not improbable that the sacrament can be validly and licitly repeated. Such a man has a new sickness and a new danger of death. Consequently he comes again from a new reason under the scope of the Jacobean prescription. The first

389 Cf. *supra*, chap. I, sec. VI, n. 2, p. 50, sq.
390 *Ethica Supernat.*, De Ext. Unct., art. 5, n. 5.

sacrament spends its effects against the first danger; its possibilities of corporal cure do not extend to this second and subsequent sickness. To obtain these effects a new administration of the sacrament has to be made. Accordingly, Diana concludes: "Probabile omnino puto posse iterum licite et valide Extremam Unctionem recipere.[391]

Dicastillo,[392] Gobat [393] and Elbel-Bierbaum [394] concur in this view of Diana. On the other hand permissibility of reanointing is denied by Petrus Dens.[395] Such a patient, he says, does not fall into a different danger of death. Rather the existing danger is increased and intensified by a new cause. "Hic non attenditur ad diversitatem causarum ex quibus periculum oritur, sed ad ipsum moriendi periculum, quavis ex causa ortum: hoc autem supponitur non fuisse sublatum, sed potius ex nova causa adauctum." In similar fashion Noldin writes: "In eadem autem infirmitate sacramentum iterandum non est, quamdiu certo idem mortis periculum perdurat. Quodsi mortis periculum accedente novo morbo augetur, idem, non novum, periculum censetur." [396]

The canon does not forbid a second administration in such a case. It uses the phrase "in eadem infirmitate;" but this is not the case here. Even conceding Noldin's point (which should be better proven by him) that it is but an increased danger of death, it can rightfully be claimed that there is a new illness. Indeed it seems truer to say that the man is in danger of death from a double source, and not from an intensified cause. Suppose that the first sickness receded, while the second danger still threatened the life of the man. If with Dens and Noldin we hold that no attention is to be given to the sources of danger, but simply to the status of the recipient, in this latter case no repetition can be made. If, however, we realize that the passing of the patient out of danger from that score means the passing of the *radix periculi* which created the condition in him nec-

---

391 *Op. Coord.*, t. II, tr. IV. res. 40.
392 *De Sacramentis*, t. I, tr. 7, disp. 1, dub. 10, n. 164.
393 *Moral.*, tr. VIII, n. 899.
394 *Th. M.*, III, Conf. X, n. 231.
395 *Theol. Mech.*, "De Ext. Unct.," N. 11, p. 60.
396 *De Sac.*, 447, 3.

essary for the first unction, it would seem that a reiteration of the sacrament is wholly permissible.[397]

In practice, in regard to the original question, either opinion can be safely followed. Both seem to be endowed with probability, both intrinsic and extrinsic. No obligation can be placed on the pastor, however, to make him perform the second administration. The right of the patient to such a bestowal is not in any way clear.

---

397 *Th. M.*, III, Conf. X, n. 231.

CHAPTER VI.

CONDITIONAL ADMINISTRATION

CANON 941.

Quando dubitatur num infirmus usum rationis attigerit, num in periculo mortis reipsa versetur, vel num mortuus sit, hoc sacramentum ministretur sub conditione.

CHAPTER VI.

Our sacraments are holy treasures, bequeathed by a merciful God to be dealt to sinners in order that they may become like to Him. They are not rewards of holiness, but are given to make men holy. Yet their intrinsic sanctity is so paramount, that they may not be scattered indiscriminately to all comers. The wedding garment must be donned before admission can be had to the viands of the king.

Gifts as hallowed as these will not permit profanement by a distribution which may be frustrated by the lack of necessary qualifications in the recipient.

On the other hand it would be too cruel to admit an administration only to those who could furnish certain and unimpeachable evidence of their right to receive this sacred legacy. The benefits derived therefrom are too enormous to any one who has the least title to them. At the close of life, a deprivation of them would entail unspeakable consequences. The dying man needs every assistance against the perils of that period.

In her provident wisdom the Church has found a way to safeguard the sanctity of her treasures and the rights of her children at such a time. She decrees that in the face of a doubtful right to the sacrament arising from the dubious presence of a necessary qualification a conditional administration of the sacraments necessary to salvation is to be made.

Accordingly in this canon such an administration is permitted when the doubt revolves about the presence of a necessary corporal disposition in the subject. In the Canon 940 administration was forbidden except to a faithful, who after the attainment of reason has fallen into a danger of death from sickness or senility. This canon provides for situations where any of these conditions is lacking. Thus if there is a doubt that the subject has attained the use of reason, or whether he is actually in danger of death (from sickness or senility), or whether he is still living, the sacrament is imparted conditionally. Each of these conditions is required for the validity of the administration. The lack of any one of them makes the subject totally unfit for reception; and administration to one who is certainly lacking in one of these qualities is not only null but sacrilegious. Shrinking from even the possibility of a frustrated administration in this regard, yet eager to attempt all for the salvation of the subject, the Church instructs her ministers that in such instances both the sanctity of the sacraments and the salvation of their subjects must be equally protected by a conditional application. *"In extremis extrema tentanda sunt."*

A) *"Num infirmus usum rationis attigerit."*

The use of reason is attained when the person is capable of distinguishing between right and wrong, of realizing a sense of moral responsibility, although imperfectly, for the actions which he performs. Such a development appears at no definite age. Some children of four and five years of age have a finer appreciation of moral values than others at ten or twelve. Accordingly no respect is to be paid to the age in this question.[1] Simply and solely the moral development in the mind of the child must be noted. Pius X[2] declared it to be a detestable abuse not to confer Extreme Unction on children who had reached the use of reason.

The very little that is required of the child in order to furnish a positive doubt that he has passed out of the realm of irresponsibility can be better appreciated when compared with what is necessary for an unconditional administration of the Sacrament. Extreme Unction can be given absolutely when the child is *capable of committing* the least venial sin, i. e., at the very beginning of his use of reason.[3] Consequently all that is required to permit a conditional administration is a positive doubt that the child realizes at least in a confused way that there is a difference between right and wrong. Any well-founded suspicion on the part of the priest that the child has crossed the border-line into reason's realm is enough to allow this conditional administration.

---

1 Cf. Blat, *Comm. Text.*, vol. III, p. I, n. 285.

2 S. C. de Sac., *"Quam Singulari,"* 8 Aug. 1910, n. VIII—A. A. S., II, 583.

3 Cf. *supra*, chap. IV, p. 141.

Prior to the Code it was much disputed as to the "modus agendi" in such a case, although the more common opinion held that a conditional administration was to be made. St. Alphonsus[4] recounts three different opinions. The first advanced according to the Saint[5] by Soto, Aureoli and Zambranus, denied the administration altogether because it exposed the sacrament to the peril of frustration. The second, championed by Sporer[6] and LaCroix[7] permitted an unction absolutely. St. Alphonsus asserts the more probable opinion to be that which directs a conditional administration, and he aligns himself with the proponents of this view.[8] The canon has confirmed this opinion by raising it from probability to the positive norm of action in such cases.

Accordingly all children are to be anointed if they have at any time revealed any signs of moral consciousness. For children seven years of age and over such use of reason can be presumed, and administration should be made without scruple, unless it is positively certain that they have not yet any moral sensibilities.[9] For children under that age an investigation of some kind should be made into their mental status. Pastors are bound to such an investigation, for otherwise they do not provide for the welfare of the child sufficiently and securely. As soon as it is evident that the child has or had even a vestige of reason, the priest should proceed to the unction without delay. Lehmkuhl[10] thinks that even though penance has been conditionally imparted, it is a most grave sin to refuse to administer Extreme Unction to a child whose doubtful use of reason makes his salvation uncertain. Lebherz[11] holds that children even four and five years old may receive Extreme Unction. Genicot[12] imposes a corresponding obligation on the pastor to impart the sacrament.

4 *Th. M.*, VI, 719.
5 L.c.
6 n. 94.
7 *Th. M.*, lib. 6, pars 2, n. 2111.
8 Lugo, Renzi, Dicastillo and Diana. Cf. S. Alph., *Th. M.*, VI, 719; Diana, *Op. Coord.*, t. II, tr. 4, res. 43.
9 Cf. Can. 88, 3—Tanquerey, *Th. D.*, III, n. 781; "Certo ungi possunt qui septennium attigerunt."
10 *Th. M.*, II, 723.
11 *The Casuist*, II, p. 176.
12 *Casus Consc.*, cas. 888, p. 575; cf. Berardi, *Prax. Conf.* II, 5000.

What has been said of the evolution of moral life in children, can be said also of insane people. If at any time during their lives they placed an action which gave an intimation that it was the act of a being who realized in at least a confused way any moral responsibility, they are to be anointed *sub conditione.*[13] Indeed there will rarely be a case where a man is so totally insane that it can be said that at no time in his life was he at least doubtfully capable of moral imputability. Hence, in practically every case of an insane subject, the sacrament is to be conferred at least conditionally.[14]

The condition to be used in the administration to children should be *"Si unquam usum rationis habueris,"* or more simply, *"si capax es."* In the conditional administration to insane people, Clericatus[15] states that the condition should be "Si aliquam culpam in vitae tuae decursu commisisti." Such a condition is not strictly correct. As has been seen in the treatment of Canon 940, the actual commission of sin is not required, but simply the capability to commit sin. The condition should then read *"Si aliquam culpam in vitae tuae decursu committere potuisti,"* or, as in the case of infants, *"Si capax es."* The briefer clause includes within its comprehension all the elements which are necessary for valid receptibility.

B) *"Num in periculo mortis reispa versetur."*

The second corporal disposition enumerated by the canon which may be a matter of doubt is the presence of a real danger of death in the sick man. It has been seen in the treatment of the preceding canon that Extreme Unction can be given only to him whose sickness has advanced to such a state as to imperil his life. The progress of the disease to this period is generally noted by a physician, a nurse or some other skilled person. There are times, however, when such professional advice is lacking, and the priest is left without any efficient means of diagnosing the gravity of the case.

---

13 St. Alphonsus, *Th. M.*, VI, 732; La Croix, *Th.* M., lib. VI, pars 2, n. 2111; *Aertnys, Th. M.*, II, n. 366.

14 Trombellio, *De Ext. Unct.*, III, diss. X, p. III, n. xi, p. 28; Gobat, *Moral.*, tract. VIII, n. 828-30; Tamburini, *Th. M.*, *"de Ext. Unct.,"* c. 2, paragr. 3, sub. n. 3, *"Si dubitetur;"* Clericatus *Decis. Sac.*, *"de Ext. Unct.,"* dec. 80, n. 440.

15 *L.c.*

Such instances are not infrequent. They may occur, e. g., when a priest finds in a state of unconsciousness a person who is addicted to fainting spells. It is present also when a disease refuses to reveal its seriousness or non-seriousness, even to a physician.[16] Prior to operations a doubt may occur whether the patient, suffering from an internal disease, is placed by such disease in danger of death. Lastly, in lingering diseases, such as consumption and cancer, there may be often real doubt as to whether the life of the patient is as yet threatened.

In all such instances Extreme Unction is to be given conditionally. The doubt, it is to be noted, should rest on good reasons. Reasons grave enough to constitute probable danger of death are not necessary, for then the sacrament may be given unconditionally; but some caution must be used against a hasty conclusion regarding the serious state of the man.

Genicot in his "*Casus Conscientiae*"[17] severely rebukes a priest who interrupted Mass to anoint a man presumably stricken down with apoplexy but who only a few minutes later was found simply to be intoxicated. Such hasty administrations expose the sacrament to the derision and ridicule of the bystanders. It is advisable consequently to await a physician's decision, if at all feasible. If this cannot be done, Extreme Unction should be given conditionally in every case where the priest fears that the patient's affliction may be endangering his life. A few judicious words of explanation will effectually remove scandal and will preserve the reverence due to the sacrament.

In such cases of conditional unction—when the doubt revolves about the presence of the danger of death in the subject—it is to be noted that a second conditional administration should always be made when the presence of this danger becomes a certainty. For instance, a man anointed before an operation because of a probable danger resulting from his disease should be again anointed (of course *sub conditione*) after the operation, if he has become certainly in danger of death thru the use of the surgeon's scalpel[18] or the increased violence of the disease he originally had.

---

16 Cf. Vermeersch, *Th. M.*, III, 661.
17 Cas. 886, p. 575.
18 Cf. *supra*, chap. V, p. 177 sqq.

C) *"Num mortuus sit."*

It is not an unusual experience in a priest's career to find that he has arrived "just a few moments too late" to administer the last sacraments to one of the souls in his care. The last breath has been drawn, the heart no longer gives forth a pulse, and the physician with stethoscope in hand announces that the man is "dead." It is a source of true grief to the priest as he stands there, armed with tremendous powers to save souls, yet unable to apply them because the man is no longer a "homo viator."

Certainly the immensity of the benefits accruing to the recipient of the last sacraments require that only the most absolute certainty of death shall totally preclude every attempt to administer them. With this in view, scientific men have applied their efforts, especially in the present century, to an investigation of the exact degree of certitude that can be accredited to the popular notion that a man is dead when circulation ceases and respiration ends.

Back in the eighteenth century a Spanish Benedictine, Fr. Feijoo, challenged the truth of these conclusions of the common opinion in two works, a letter entitled *"Contra el Abuso de Acelerar mas que conviene los Entierros"* (edit. Rivadeneyra) and a book called *"Señales de la Muerte Actual."* He attacks the infallibility of the signs ordinarily believed to be beyond question. "No one knows," he writes, "what is the soul's last influence on the body, nor in what precise condition the body must be in order to preserve its union with the soul. Hence it is impossible to know just when a man dies. Let us take a body that has so wasted away as to seem utterly lifeless; let it be without respiration, without color, without feeling, without motion. We can be certain of only one thing about this body. There is in it no perceptible soul-influence. But what is to make us sure that in some one or other of the internal organs the soul does not perform some function or other? You tell me that life comes to an end when the blood ceases to flow and the heart ceases to beat. I ask you how you know this. You can be sure of no such thing unless by divine or angelic revelation. All we can be certain of is the absence of any vital action that may be perceived by the senses."[19]

In the last part of the nineteenth century, Dr. Icard claimed that dissolution actually took place when the heart stopped beating; but he denied the possibility of ascertaining with certainty whether the heart-beat had really ceased unless the eye confirmed the judgment of the ear either by baring the heart to view or by the insertion of a long delicate needle thru the body into the heart.[20]

At the beginning of the present century Father Ferreres, S. J., invited the Catholic Medical Society (Academia de los Santos Cosme y Damián) of Barcelona, to make a study of the difference between real and apparent death and to determine the symptoms which reveal without peradventure of doubt the fact that a man is truly dead. In 1904 he published in the periodical, Razon y Fé, the answer of the Society and his own personal conclusions.[21] Since that time practically all theologians have treated the question in some fashion, while all pastoral theologies give generous space to this important proposition.[22]

All authorities are inclined to agree with Feijoo that the patient usually is not dead immediately upon the cessation of circulation and respiration. O'Malley claims that even in cases of decapitation it is very probable that the patient does not die at once.[23] Somatic death is a gradual thing; all organs do not die at once definitively, i. e., lose their proper operations. First the senses of taste and smell leave the dying man; and then the sense of vision weakens—as is evidenced by the patient's complaints about the fading light. The sense of touch is often lacking, especially in the extremities, which become cold before the rest of the body. Hearing perdures practically to the end, even

19 *Señales de la Muerte Actual,* 252, sect. IV.

20 *La Mort Réelle et la Mort Apparente,* pp. 89-90.

21 *Razon y Fé,* vol. VIII, pp. 100-07, 236-38, 371-75, vol. IX, pp. 99-115. This appeared in English in the *American Ecclesiastical Review,* vol. XXXIII, pp. 168-73, 273-85, 347-61, 484-95, 587-95, vol. XXXIV, pp. 70-78; and in book-form in 1906 (B. Herder, St. Louis).

22 Cf., e. g., Antonelli, *Med. Past.,* vol. II, pp. 563-613; Sanford, *Pastoral Medicine,* Appendix— *"The Moment of Death"*—by Walter M. Drum, S. J., pp. 223-35; O'Malley, *"Ethics of Med. Homicide,"* cap. iv, pp. 83-91; &c.

23 O'Malley, *"Ethics of Med. Homicide,"* p. 83.

though the sick man seem without movement and apparently dead.[24] Even the lack of activity in the greater vital organs, the brain, the heart and the lungs, are no longer considered infallible signs of the separation of the soul from the body.

Drs. Coutenot, Laborde and Blanc, together with the members of the Barcelona Academy, unite in their opinions that the soul may adhere to the body without exerting the great vital functions.[25] Since that time, more recent experiments show that cardiac activity may continue even after it becomes imperceptible by a stethoscope, and even after respiration has ceased. Dr. Robinson of the Rockefeller Institute for Medical Research in New York found that the heart may beat for half an hour after all vascular and circulatory sounds have ceased to be heard.[26] Icard discovered exactly the same in his professional experience. He tells of a case where the physician, tried unsuccessfully for an hour to listen to heart-beats, and then upon opening the thoracic cavity the heart was found to be still beating and the subject still living.[27] If such scientific methods fail to note the presence of life, it can easily be seen how positively obsolete the old-fashioned candle-test and mirror-test are in connection with this question.

Other uncertain signs of death are 1) the absence, even for a long time, of sensibility of the skin and of intelligence; 2) the gathering of a viscous covering over the cornea of the eye; 3) the unusual amplitude of the pupil of the eye; 4) the relaxation of the sphincters; 5) the failure of the blood flowing from the canals of circulation to coagulate; 6) the loss of tissue-elasticity, due largely to solidification of subcutaneous fat, so that the position assumed by the surface tissue at the moment of

---

24 Antonelli, *Med. Past.*, II, p. 565. A practical caution can be deduced from the fact that the patient can hear until almost the last moment. The priest and attendants should be careful to say nothing which will hasten the death of the sick man by depressing his spirits with remarks about the hopelessness of the case, &c. On the other hand, they should make many pious ejaculations into the ear of the patient, speaking slowly and distinctly—but not shouting.

25 Countenot, in "*Etudes Franciscaines,*" Jan. 1901, p. 44; Laborde, *Bulletin de l'Académie de Médicine,* seance du 4 janvier, 1900, p. 64; Blanc, *El Criterio Catolico en las Ciencias Medicas,* 1903, p. 171.

26 "*A Study with the Electrocardigraph of the Mode of Death of the Human Heart,*" in the *Journal of Experimental Medicine,* 1912, xvi, p. 291.

27 *La Mort Réelle et la Mort Apparente,* pp. 89-90.

solidification tends to become fixed.[28] None of these is a sufficient indication to the physician to enable him to pronounce with any finality the death of the patient.

There are, however, several signs of death that are regarded by physicians to be clear evidence of the dissolution of the soul and the body. The first of these is the absolute absence of motions of the heart. We have already cited Drs. Coutenot, LaBorde and Blanc against this contention. Furthermore Dr. Crile, of Cleveland, whom O'Malley terms "one of best medical authorities on this matter of somatic death," says that the human respiratory centre may survive anemia from thirty to fifty minutes, and in the meantime cardiac resuscitation may be attempted.[29] Dr. Wayne Babcock, of Philadelphia, reported to the American Therapeutic Society some very interesting cases of his own, which were recorded in the "Proceedings" of that Society for the year 1912. All this conspires, of course, against the certainty of this sign of death, with the consequence that there is still at least a tenuous probability of the presence of life, even in those whose heart-beats have surely ceased.

A second sign is the "frigus cadavericum," the constantly growing coldness that overtakes the body after the departure of the soul. Yet it must be remembered that some diseases increase the heat of the body at the time of agony and even after death. The age of the person and the nature of the disease also determine to a great extent the amount of heat in the body. Those afflicted with chronic illnesses, as hemorrhages, or those asphyxiated by drowning evidence much less heat of body than those stricken down by an acute disease like apoplexy. As a result the presence or non-presence of heat is far from infallible in determining the existence of somatic death in the subject.[30]

Another sign is the rigidity of the body (rigor cadavericus), whereby the muscles become so stiff and taut that they can no longer be extended or distended. If this is certainly present, it must be conceded that death has really occurred. There is a great liability, however, that physicians may mistake a catalep-

---

28 Antonelli, *Med. Past.*, II, pp. 571-72; Adami, *The Principles of Pathology*, p. 915.

29 Cf. O'Malley, *Ethics of Med. Homicide*, p. 84.

30 Antonelli, *Med. Past.*, II, p. 580.

tic or tetanic stiffness for the *rigor mortis*.[81] However, as Icard notes,[82] expert examination of the corpse can deduce positive indications of dissolution from the rigidity. Accordingly the presence of this sign determines death with certitude only for the skilled examiner.

A third indication of death is cadaveric lividity. Due to the gravitation of the blood to dependent capillaries, the lower parts of the body show within a few hours after death a livid reddening, or, where the blood is more venous, a bluish purple color. If there has been a cyanosis with a great distention of the superficial capillaries before death (as occasionally occurs in the vessels of the neck and face when death is due to asphyxia), a similar and even more intense lividity may be present over surfaces not dependent. In places where there is pressure, as over the shoulder-blades, the mere weight of the body effectually prevents the coloring of the capillaries, and consequently these regions remain pale.[83] Lividity is not by any means an infallible sign of death. It is quite possible even for physicians to confuse it with *purpura hemorrhagica,* a disease in which blood is extravasated within the tissues.

Various other signs of death have been advanced but none have proved very satisfactory, with the exception of those which will be immediately noted. The Paris Academy offered a prize to the one who would find any certain sign of death other than rigidity and putrefaction. One hundred and two papers were submitted; but all of them failed to prove that the lesser functions were no longer carried on when the greater vital actions ceased.

---

81 A very recent incident of this appeared in the Philadelphia Public Ledger, Jan. 3, 1923. It reads as follows: "*Public Ledger Foreign Service*: Madrid, Jan. 2, 1923 (By Cable)—The most sensational event that ever occurred in the town of Zamora was the discovery on New Year's Day at a graveside that a supposed corpse was alive. Virtually all the town attended the funeral of Dona Laura Rodriquez, widow of a commander in the army and well known in Madrid society. At the last moment before the coffin was lowered into the grave, it was uncovered to permit her eight children to have a last look at their mother. When a physician approached the coffin he was dumbfounded to notice signs of life in its occupant. Other doctors were hurriedly sent for and they verified that her heart was still beating. The 'corpse' was in a state of catalepsy."

82 *La Mort Réelle et la Mort Apparente*, p. 25.

83 Adami, *The Principles of Pathology*, p. 915.

The sign regarded by all as certain is putrefaction or decomposition. This sets in when rigidity ceases, and consists in a general mortification of the body. It generally commences over the abdomen as a greenish discoloration. Its onset is indeed variable, and is delayed considerably by a great cold and hastened materially by heat and warmth. The organs which are normally moist and which contain abundant bacteria exhibit signs of putrefaction first. The intestinal canal is most markedly affected. Many factors, however, may enter into the putrefactive process. For instance, cases of acute infection and of bacteremia are especially susceptible to early decomposition. This is ascribable not only to the action of the specific pathogenic organisms but also to the fact that the protective substances of the organism have been exhausted in the course of the infection with the consequence that the growth of putrefactive bacteria is in no way inhibited. Snake poisoning, in which there is a rapid decomposition of the antibodies, induces a speedy decomposition. On the other hand arsenical and certain other intoxications may very appreciably delay the onset of putrefaction.[34] Only one caution must be noted. Decomposition of the whole body in advanced state should be demanded. A decomposition that has just commenced may be the result of a gangrene that precedes death, and not that which follows it.

Two other tests were used during the recent World War upon many soldiers brought into dressing stations apparently dead from shell-shock, from head or spinal wounds or from asphyxiation. The first test was to inject a little alkaline solution of fluorescine beneath the skin. If there is any circulation at all, the dye will be carried to the eye and will color the conjunctiva green. The second test was to puncture the spleen or liver with a needle and draw therefrom a tiny bit of pulp. When the blood was withdrawn this pulp was applied to blue litmus paper. The reaction of living pulp is alkaline, blue; of dead pulp, red or acid.[35] Although, it is true, these tests may produce some degree of certainty, it is needless to say that they

---

34 Adami, *The Principles of Pathology,* p. 915.

35 Sasse, *Presse Medicale,* xxiv, 66—O'Malley, *Ethics of Med. Homicide,* pp. 90-1.

can be applied only in very unusual circumstances, due to lack of necessary equipment.

For the priest ordinarily the only sign which he can regard as indicating certain death is putrefaction. What he must be most careful of is not to mistake "apparent" death for real somatic death. The more frequent cases of apparent death are those resulting from asphyxia, swooning, lethargy, catalepsy, epileptic coma, electric shock, paralysis and narcotic poisonings. Asphyxia consists in an apparent lack of respiration and blood circulation. It occurs when the air supply to the lungs has been cut off by drowning, strangulation or the inhaling of poisonous gas.[36] Such a condition can perdure several hours. Swooning or fainting fits manifest a more or less perfect suspension of respiration and circulation, and not rarely induce a diminution of the heat of the body. Catalepsy is a nervous disease which occurs intermittently without fever. Sensibility becomes altogether lacking, the muscles become inert and rigid, consciousness often departs and the body keeps in the same position as if petrified. Its duration may extend over many hours and even days. Lethargy consists in a profound stupor, with the eyes almost closed, the members taut and all sensibility lacking. It may last thruout several days. Epileptic coma is a state of unconsciousness which follows grave convulsions in epileptics. It is characterized by a tranquil respiration and is rarely remembered by the patient upon his return to normalcy. Electric shock occurs when a man is struck by lightning or comes into contact with an electric current. These men do not always die immediately, for artificial respiration has revived many. Usually a paralysis of the centre of respiration is induced, which will have a fatal termination unless immediately overcome. Hence the result of this shock can be said to be a form of asphyxia. Paralysis consists in the loss of the power of voluntary motion, with or without sensation. It often results in the abolition, either complete or partial, of some of the functions of the body. Narcotic stupors are profound sleeps caused by narcotic drugs such as laudanum, morphine, cocaine, hasheesh, etc. The physical effects of heavy indulgence in these are, chiefly, a diminution of pulse, a deep pallor, dilation of pupils,

36 Capellman, *Med. Past.*, p. 179 sqq.

coldness of the extremities and almost imperceptible or spasmodic respiration. It may affect the body in this fashion for several days.

Various authors go to great lengths to cite examples of apparent death resulting from each of the causes enumerated.[37] Occasionally, also, the daily press carries the news of incidents of this kind,[38] thus adding example to example in proof of the contention that no sign of death is unfailing except putrefaction. The Barcelona Academy was convinced of this, for among the resolutions it adopted, the following is found with no dissenting voice: "Resolved: Facts have demonstrated that a man can be revived after remaining hours in a state in which all signs of life have disappeared, such as consciousness, speech,

---

37 Antonelli, *Med. Past.*, II, pp. 595-602; Ferreres, *Real and Apparent Death*, pp. 72-101; Sanford, *Pastoral Medicine*, 233-5; O'Malley, *Ethics of Med. Homicide*, pp. 84-7.

38 E. g. The following article appeared in the daily press recently: "Madisonville, Ky., March 9—Roscoe Qualls, nine-year-old son of Lonnie Qualls, yesterday had literally come back from the valley of death. For hours his parents and other relatives believed him dead. Their grief was piteous. The certain arrangements to be made for burial were discussed. The boy heard every word of the arrangements being made, but he could not move a muscle of his body, wink an eye or twitch a lip, nor do anything to show that he still lived.

"Roscoe Qualls, while skating on a pond at his father's farm, fell, striking his head. Paralysis soon set in and it was found that he had concussion of the brain and had lost power of speech. Liquid food kept him alive, but finally this failed to improve him, and while the physician was absent, his parents believed death had come. Roscoe says his greatest dread while he lay helpless listening to the discussion of his own death was that he would be buried alive. He realized that he could not lift a finger to show that he still lived. When all hope seemed lost to the boy, an examination was made, and he was found to be still breathing. Doctors ministered to him and soon afterwards the lad was sitting up."

Another case appeared in the Washington Post on March 10, 1926, and evidences how apt physicians may be to error in accident cases: "An ambulance ride was enough to revive Thomas Barnes . . . . last evening after he had been declared 'dead.' Barnes was riding a motorcycle, which collided at Florida Avenue near Seventh Street, N. W., with a street car . . . . Barnes was thrown to the street, unconscious, with blood streaming from cuts on his face. Traffic Policeman Tompkins called Casualty Hospital, and Dr. Krouse, of the hospital staff, responded with an ambulance. Dr. Krouse, upon his arrival, pronounced Barnes dead, and the colored man's body was lifted into the ambulance. Employes of the hospital were about to lift the body from the ambulance and place it in the hospital morgue, when Barnes sat up. His cuts were treated and he went home."

sensibility, muscular movement, respirations and beatings of the heart. This state may logically be called apparent death."[39]

Between the moment ordinarily held to be that of death and the moment at which death actually occurs there is then a period of latent life. "Death never comes at a leap," writes Dr. Icard,[40] "life is extinguished slowly, gradually, even then when death is sudden, as we sometimes call it. That intermediate state between life and death exists always; it is a normal physiological state, thru which we all pass departing from life."

The length of this period of latent life is of paramount importance. It is generally conceded that it is of far greater duration in cases of sudden deaths than demises following long illnesses. The vitality of the man stricken down in his health furnishes much more resistance to the grip of death than the cells of one who has been ravaged by disease. To determine exactly the interval between the appearance of death and death itself is very difficult to do. Authors vary as to the extent of time because of this very reason.

Dr. Bassols in the discussions of the Barcelona Academy of January 22, 1903, stated that in his opinion the period of latent life in sudden deaths lasted until the instant when the *rigor cadavericus* appears.[41] Ferreres extends it up to the time when mortification commences.[42] In prolonged sicknesses there is more harmony of opinion. Practically all later writers have put one-half hour as a reasonable limit for the latent period after long sicknesses.[43] There are some who are even more generous than this, such as O'Malley, who allows one hour at least in every case of apparent death.[44]

The practical advantage of all this for the priest lies in the fact that he can with safe conscience absolve and anoint conditionally at any time during this period of latent life. In cases of sudden deaths, where the period of time is long, the sacra-

---

39 Concl. 3, *El Criter. Catol.*, Augusti 1903, pag. 227.
40 *La Presse Medicale*, quoted by Ferreres, *Real and Apparent Death*, p. 61.
41 Gury-Ferreres, *Casus Consc.*, II, 1208.
42 *Real and Apparent Death*, p. 81 sqq. It is to be noted that the "putredo mortis" must be somewhat advanced in order to distinguish it from the putrefaction resulting before death from gangrene.
43 Ferreres, *Real and Apparent Death*, p. 87 sqq.; Noldin, *De Sac.*, 294; Genicot-Salsmans, *Inst. Th. M.*, II, 422.
44 *Ethics of Med. Homicide*, p. 87.

ments may be administered as long as there is a tenuous probability that the man is latently alive. Noldin[45] thinks that the sacraments should be administered within two hours after the declaration of death. Genicot[46] is no more generous in sudden deaths than in cases of slow, drawn-out diseases. Drum[47] allows a conditional administration until the presence of an advanced stage of decomposition is evident. O'Malley[48] thinks three hours a not unreasonable extension of time after the "pronouncement of death."

Recent Synodal legislation also allows and instructs Unction to be administered during the period of latent life. Thus the Synod of Madrid (1909) permits an unction in cases of sudden death after several hours and even after an entire day has passed since death became "apparent." [49]

It will be easily seen that sufficient authority can be educed from the various opinions to allow a very wide latitude of action. In practice a priest is amply justified in anointing a man supposedly dead (from a sudden and unexpected cause) up until the time when advanced decomposition has set in.[50] This period may last for many hours and even thru several entire days, depending of course, upon the rapidity with which the putrefaction occurs. In the cases of those who have been vexed with lingering diseases, the unction may be given conditionally within at least a half an hour. As noted before, O'Malley is more liberal than this. "For a whole hour after apparent death," he writes, "the probability that the soul has not departed is so strong that, in my opinion, a priest who does not give the necessary sacraments is virtually as guilty as if he neglected to administer them to a person evidently alive. Crile, one of the best medical authorities on the matter of somatic death, holds that the human respiratory system may survive

---

45 *L.c.*

46 *L.c.*

47 Sanford, *Pastoral Medicine*, p. 235.

48 *Ethics of Med. Homicide*, p. 87.

49 Lib. 2, tit. 3, const. 6, p. 194. Cf. also *Syn. Auriensis*, const. 78, page 48 (Orense, 1908); *Syn. Cordub. in America*, n. 180; *Malacitan*, lib. 3, tit. 7, c. 2 n. 9 (Malaga, 1909); *Ancudien.*, part 2, c. 6, pag. 74 (S. Carlos de Ancud, 1907); *Manilanen.*, n. 73 (Manila, 1911); *Cebuen.*, n. 87 (Manila, 1911); *Calbayogan.*, tit. 2, const. 2, p. 76 (Manila, 1911), &c.

50 Gury-Ferreres, *Casus Consc.*, II, 1218.

anemia for from thirty to fifty minutes. How long after the hour a priest may administer the sacraments is not known, but a second hour, or even a third, are not unreasonable periods of time during which the sacraments may be administered conditionally."[51] Ferreres[52] allows an extension of time if death in the lingering disease is brought on prematurely by an accident, or by sudden and unforeseen complications. Hence if cessation of breath and motion, coupled with apparent insensibility, occurs at the time when the patient is in high fever or during an acute colic, the change must be ascribed, not to the disease, but to a morbid condition of the system. This results in a state not unlike asphyxia or syncope; and puts this mode of dying midway between sudden deaths and lingering dissolutions. Hence conditional administration of the sacraments can take place two and even three hours after apparent death. In fact, it will be very often uncertain that such an accident or complication did not occur; with the result that practically always, even according to Ferreres' notion, it will be permissible to anoint for two or three hours after pronouncement of death in lingering illnesses. It must be noted, too, that when Ferreres speaks of "one-half hour after apparent death," he means one-half hour after a competent physician with the help of the most accurate medical instruments declares the man dead. Very often a physician will not be present at this time, and if he is, he may not have employed such careful means to determine the presence of death. Accordingly for a very appreciable time after the man is popularly thought to have yielded up his soul, the conditional administration of the necessary sacraments is allowed.

Priests will find a practical application of these opinions not only in the many accidental deaths which occur daily, but in the executions of criminals by hanging, electrocution or shooting. In every instance the priest should endeavor to administer as quickly as possible the sacraments of Penance and Extreme Unction to the unfortunate man.

It is quite probable that Extreme Unction will be of more

[51] *Ethics of Med. Homicide,* pp. 87-88.

[52] Gury-Ferreres, *Casus Consc.*, II, n. 1221; *Real and Apparent Death,* pp. 102 sqq.

avail to the patient than absolution in these instances. Penance requires the acts of the penitent as at least quasi-matter; and their presence is at most a very dubious thing in such men, apparently dead. On the other hand, Extreme Unction demands only an habitual intention on the part of the recipient, and has, besides its own proper efficacy, all the efficacy of Penance—secondarily, it is true, but none the less *per se.*[53]

When administering the sacraments in these contingencies, the priest must take precautions not to give scandal to the bystanders. Often he will be able to make the single unction (and Extreme Unction should always be given in apparent death by the short form) without attracting attention. By grasping the patient's hand, he may anoint the palm, unnoticed.[54] If this cannot be done, an admonition or explanation of the procedure to the bystanders will effectually remove all wonderment.[55]

It is to be noted that it follows as a logical consequence that the body should be handled very carefully during the period of latent life. It should not be washed or dressed; the eyes and mouth should not be closed; the hands should not be joined nor the face covered—at least until the appearance of the "rigor cadavericus." Otherwise there is serious danger of causing the real death of the patient by asphyxiation.[56]

Another deduction can be made in regard to the observance of the rubric of the Ritual which instructs the priest to leave off and proceed no further if the man dies during the rite.[57] Of course the Ritual means the true demise of the subject. Under the recent investigations it would be very difficult to see how a priest can know with any degree of certainty that the man is truly dead. Consequently, if the man seems to die after the rite of the unctions has commenced, the priest may go ahead

53 Villada, *Casus*, vol. 3, sect. 7, n. 76; Pesch, *Prael. Dogm.*, VII, 86; Tanquerey, *Th. D.*, III, 784.

54 Gury-Ferreres, *Casus Consc.*, II, 1216. Gury-Ferreres notes that it can be done on the forehead in such a way that others will not note it. To anoint the hand seems easier still, and, as shall be seen in the treatment of Can. 947, the unction is just as valid.

55 O'Malley, *Ethics of Med. Homicide*, p. 88; Antonelli, *Med. Past.*, II, 1029.

56 Antonelli, *op. cit.*, vol. II, n. 1030.

57 *Rit. Rom.*, tit. V, cap. 1, n. 13: "Si vero dum inungitur infirmus decedat, Presbyter ultra non procedat, et praedictas Orationes omittat."

and finish the other unctions conditionally.[58] Even the strictest theologians hold the perdurance of life for a few minutes after the appearance of death, and as a consequence the continuance of the rite is justified by another rubric of the same chapter (n. 14): "Quod si dubitet an vivat adhuc, unctionem prosequatur, sub conditione pronuntiando formam, dicens: 'Si vivis, per istam,' &c." Doubt—very positive doubt—will always be present during the very few moments required to complete the anointings; and consequently a priest shall never be justified in cutting the rite short for the reason that the patient has passed away.

The condition to be attached to the form in all cases like this is *"Si vivis."* It should be expressed as the rubrics command, although its verbal omission will not affect the validity of the mental condition. The Ritual seems to follow the suggestion of St. Charles in regard to this express mention of the condition. In his Instructions "De Extrema Unctione" the great Saint wrote: "Ministrabit autem dum aeger integris sensibus est. Quodsi aliqua morbi vi infirmus oppressus, dubitatur vivusne sit an mortuus, tunc diligenter de hoc sacerdos videbit, consulto etiam medico, si tanta temporis brevitate potest; si non potest, et in dubio est, ea conditione utetur: *'Si es vivus, per istam,'* &c."[59]

---

58 Ferreres, *Comp. Th. M.*, II, 856; Homiletic and Pastoral Review, XXVI (1926), pp. 851-2; Genicot, *Casus Consc.*, cas. 887, p. 575.

59 *Acta Eccl. Mediol.*, pars IV, tom. I, p. 603.

CHAPTER VII.

DENIAL TO IMPENITENTS

CANON 942.

Hoc sacramentum non est conferendum illis qui impoenitentes in manifesto peccato mortali contumaciter perseverant; quod si hoc dubium fuerit, conferatur sub conditione.

CHAPTER VII.

The subject of Extreme Unction must have not only physical but also spiritual requirements. In this double demand—*ex parte corporis et ex parte animae*—Uniction shares its distinction with Matrimony and with Orders.

The two preceding canons revealed the physical conditions necessary for valid reception, viz., serious illness and a danger of death ensuing therefrom. They likewise disclosed two requisites of the soul, quite as indispensable in the recipient, namely, the presence of the baptismal character and the attainment of the use of reason. The present canon continues the consideration of the spiritual fitness of the subject with a view *at least* to the lawfulness of conferring the sacrament.

The canon forbids bestowal of Extreme Unction to an impenitent person who is contumaciously persevering in manifest mortal sin. Authorities are divided in their opinions as to whether this law was intended to deal primarily and principally with the dispositions or with the intention of such a recipient. Thus Alb. Scmitt, writing in the Lintzer-Quartalschrift,[1] contends that the point at issue is the presence of the intention in the subject. Dispositions of soul, such as found in the contumaciously impenitent, are so evil in their nature that an intention of receiving the sacrament cannot coexist with them, prescinding of course from the physical possibility (which because of its horror is not taken into account here) that a man out of perverseness of heart might have the deliberate intention of receiving the sacrament sacrilegiously. Though *prima facie* deal-

1 Vol. LXXI (1918), S. 419, footnote: "Dieser Kanon handelt vom Zweifel an der intention, nicht vom Zweifel an der Disposition (wie irrtuemlicherweise behauptet wurde, so dass in manchen Kreisen ein Abweichen des neuen Rechtes von der bisherigen Praxis angenommen wurde). Erst der folgende Kanon handelt von zweifelhafter Disposition. Es ist das nich das gleiche; zweifelhafte Intention macht die Gueltigkeit zweifelhaft; bei zweifelhafter Disposition aber ist das Sakrament gueltig, nur ist der fruchbringende Empfang Frage gestellt. In diesem Falle darf es gar nicht bedingungsweise gespendet werden, damit es nach Sicherstellung der Disposition wieder aufleben kann."

ing with disposition, yet this canon radically and essentially is concerned with the intention of the recipient; and denial of the sacrament is consequently ascribable to the lack of the essential element of intention and not of the non-essential requisite of disposition.

This view is accepted wholeheartedly by Noldin,[2] Koudelka,[3] and Woywod.[4] It is implicitly adopted by at least some of the theologians [5] who teach that in case of doubt the condition appended should never be "Si dispositus es"—lest reviviscence be entirely precluded. Kern,[6] though writing before the Code, asserted the lack of intention to be the reason of the denial of this sacrament in the case contemplated in this canon.

Another group of theologians contend that this law considers primarily and principally the dispositions of the sick man. Unction is forbidden to such a person because there is little likelihood that he will come into a better disposition; and an administration to him in such a condition of soul would be inexcusably irreverent. The refusal of the sacrament is thus a punishment, "a well-deserved—yea, necessary—punishment. The punishment is well-deserved, since such an impenitent, obstinate sinner despises the sacraments and the Church's means of grace or otherwise he would amend his ways. The punishment is necessary, because under such conditions the sacrament would be frustrated and dishonored. The sacraments cannot give grace nor increase it in the case of one who will not absolutely renounce sin. In such cases the words of our Savior are pertinent: 'Nolite dare sanctum canibus' (Matt. vii, 6)."[7]

---

2 *De Sac.*, 445.

3 *Pastors, Their Rights and Duties*, p. 153.

4 *A Practical Commentary*, I, n. 865: "Some commentators explain those words of the Code as a lack of will and intention to receive the Sacrament, and, when interpreted in that sense the Code agrees with the common teaching of theologians that, if there is a doubt about the intention to receive the Sacrament, it can, at most, be administered conditionally. This acceptation of the words of Canon 942 seems reasonable. No adult who has or has had the use of reason, can receive any gift of God unless he is *willing* to receive it. Obstinate perseverance in open mortal sin excludes all will and intention to receive a Sacrament."

5 Cf. e. g., Telch, *Epit. Th. M.*, p. 300; Genicot-Salsmans, *Inst. Th. M.*, II, 423, footnote.

6 *Tract. de Ext. Unct.*, p. 320.

7 Pruemmer, in *The Homiletic and Pastoral Review*, XXVI (1926), pp. 740-41.

Those who maintain this latter view of the question, besides Pruemmer, are Blat,[8] Tanquerey,[9] Vermeersch[10] and O'Donnell.[11] Mothon[12] also seems to espouse this opinion when he speaks of the "state of soul of the sick man" (*l'état d'âme du malade*) in his treatment of this canon. For them it is not a question of validity of administration, but rather of the liceity of the action.

This latter seems the better view. In the first place, it is not alien to the policy of the Church to forbid the anointment of a subject whose dispositions are so evil as to be incompatible with the intrinsic sanctity of the sacrament. This is evident from a decision of the Holy Office[13] in 1892, whereby Catholics who had ordered their bodies to be cremated were to be denied the sacrament, unless upon advisement they retracted their perverse wills. The denial of the sacrament is due to the refusal on the part of these men to do what they are bound under pain of mortal sin to do. They might have every intention of receiving the sacrament, they might even have asked that it be bestowed, and they may evidence contrition for all sins except the one mentioned in the decree. Nevertheless, the sacrament must be withheld, despite the fact that it can be received validly by such subjects.

This is likewise revealed by an inspection of the rubric of the *Rituale* before its latest revision. According to its prescriptions Extreme Unction was not to be conferred upon impenitents and *those dying in manifest mortal sin.*[14] It is indeed difficult to see why an intention of receiving Extreme Unction could not co-exist with the state of soul of one dying in manifest mortal sin. This clearly shows that the Holy See believes that, at least under certain circumstances, the reverence due the sacrament is not to be sacrificed to the possible benefit that may accrue to an improperly disposed subject.

And if at times the Holy See prohibits the administration

8 *Comm. Text.*, lib. III, p. I, n. 286.
9 *Th. D.*, III, 784.
10 *Th. M.*, III, 662 & 184.
11 I. E. Record, vol. XII, Fifth Series (1918), p. 287.
12 *Institutions Canoniques*, II, p. 233, art. 2030; cf. Bargilliat, *Droits et Devoirs des Curés*, 245 (c).
13 S. C. S. Off., 27 Jul. 1892, ad I—Coll. S. C. P. F., n. 1808.
14 Tit. V, c. I, n. 8.

of this sacrament to those who lack certain dispositions of soul, it is quite probable that this canon is an example of such a policy. For contumacy, which the canon speaks of, is certainly a state of the soul. Primarily and directly it refers to the lack of disposition; only remotely and indirectly does it have any relation with the intention of the sick man. True, the disposition influences, in many cases, the intention to receive, or not to receive, this sacrament. And it also seems to be possible that a man can have the will and intention to receive the sacrament and also not have a detestation of and aversion to mortal sin.[15] Yet in every case of contumacious perseverance in manifest mortal sin the sacrament is to be withheld. As a consequence the refusal must be ascribed to the presence of the unworthy dispositions of the sick man.

As yet, there has been no official solution of the question. Many authors accordingly content themselves with a simple mention of the canon and do not wish to enter into the matter until further decision.[16] In practice there will be no difficulty; for whether the man's incapacity arises from the lack of an essential element, or from the lack of even the minimum soul-disposition necessary for licit bestowal, the result is the same —such a man is not to receive the sacrament.

What are these conditions of soul which are so frightful that conferring of the sacrament is altogether forbidden? Though ever shrinking from sacrilege, the Church is not unmindful of the weaknesses of her children—and when they are in extreme necessity, she will go far before forbidding the treasures of grace to them. She realizes full well the import of the phrase "Quantum humana fragilitas nosse sinit." She knows the maze of contending motives and principles within men—and she realizes, too, that in many cases only God can tell what is in us and what is of us. So in her mercy, the Church denies this sacrament to those only whom she is strictly bound to exclude. And the unworthiness of even these men must be strictly verified before administration can be totally

[15] Cf. Woywod, "*The Sacrament of Extreme Unction,*" in the Homiletic and Pastoral Review, XXII, p. 768, where he practically admits this.

[16] Cf. Ferreres, *Comp. Th. M.*, II, 848, Quaer. 8; Sabetti-Barrett, *Th. M.*, p. 808; Augustine, *A Commentary*, IV, p. 404; Mathaian-Castillon, *Asserta Moralia*, n. 521; Arregui, *Summ. Th. M.*, n. 665, &c.

refused. If there is the slightest doubt, conditional administration not only may, but must be made—"*conferatur* sub conditione."

As before stated, this canon forbids the bestowal of Unction upon an *impenitent man who is persevering contumaciously in manifest mortal sin.* Primarily the law obligates the minister, but *ratione subjecti.* Holy things are to be treated in holy fashion, and not wasted indiscriminately upon subjects either totally unworthy or positively unwilling to receive them.

In order to justify the absolute denial of the sacrament, the minister must be morally certain that the patient is impenitently and contumaciously persevering in manifest mortal sin. Five things then are required: the subject must be 1) obstinate and contumacious in 2) his impenitence with regard to a 3) manifest 4) mortal sin; while the minister must 5) have certainty with regard to the existence of this soul-condition of the subject.

It is necessary that a man be not only impenitent in the eyes of the minister, but that he contumaciously persevere in such impenitence. Certainty of his continued and prolonged refusal is required. Impenitence signifies the lack of sorrow necessary for the remission of sins either *per se* or with the help of the sacraments. Blat[17] states simply that "*impaenitentes*" are "*poenitentiam cordis qua indigent non habentes.*" Baruffaldo[18] declares that they are those "*qui, cum publice peccaverint, nullum paenitentiae signum dederunt, adeo ut a peccato suo non recessisse nemini notum sit.*" O'Kane[19] agrees with this definition of Baruffaldo. And practically this should be accepted as the more merciful opinion. Hence nothing short of a total dearth of signs of repentance for a notable length of time is sufficient to constitute the contumacious impenitence of the patient.

The impenitence must have to do with a sin that is manifestly mortal. The rubric of the Ritual,[20] before its latest re-

---

17 *Comm. in Text.*, l. III, p. I. n. 286.

18 *Ad Rom. Rit. Comm.*, t. I, tit. 27, n. 72; cf. Gobat., *Moral.*, tr. VII, 602-3.

19 *The Rubrics*, n. 864.

20 Tit. V, c. 1, n. 8 (edit. 1913): "Impoenitentibus vero, et qui in manifesto peccato mortali moriuntur . . . penitus denegetur."

vision, distinguished the "impenitent" from "those dying in mortal sin," but withheld the sacrament from both groups. The present canon (and similarly the rubric of the new Ritual —Tit. V, c. 1, n. 10) differs from the former rubric in an important respect. Now there is required a prolonged, a contumacious impenitence in a manifest mortal sin. The old rubric seemed to forbid the administration also to those who were "*actu*" in mortal sin, thus depriving of the sacraments persons rendered unconscious in the act of sin.[21] Now it is not altogether unlikely that a man in mortal sin *actu* should have an intention of afterward repenting and receiving the sacraments. Such a man the present canon does not seem to exclude, because it demands a *contumacious* impenitence which presupposes absolute unworthiness of the sacrament, for it precludes the possibility of the intention of subsequent repentance.

The sin of the subject must be mortal—and manifestly so. There must be no room for doubt that the man is laboring under ignorance or a false conscience. Hence the gravity of the sin must be subjective on the part of the patient. If the minister knows of certain theological quirks which the patient possesses on certain matters, inclining the patient to view sins objectively serious as only venial, he may not deny at least a conditional administration of the sacrament. Such action would be positively unjustifiable.

Finally, at least moral certainty as to the evil state of the subject's soul is required of the minister. Probability in such a matter is under no circumstances enough to deprive a soul wholly of its right to this source of grace. The slightest doubt not only warrants, but makes of *obligation,* a conditional administration.

When all these requirements are verified, the priest may not proceed to anoint. According to one opinion, recounted above, such an unction would not only be illicit, but positively invalid; while all theologians agree that it would be certainly sacrilegious.

---

21 Thus commentators of the old rubric looked at the matter. E. g., Baruffaldo (*Ad Rom. Rit. Comm.,* t. I, tit. 27, n. 72) defined manifest sinners as those "qui in *actu* mortaliter peccaminoso morte correpti sunt, aut actualiter peccando, sensibus destituti sunt." O'Kane (*The Rubrics,* n. 864) gives as an example a murderer wounded mortally in the act of killing his victim."

To whom, then, must be denied even a conditional administration of this sacrament? In the case of a patient still conscious the priest will have an opportunity to explore the dispositions and to arrive at a prudent judgment as to his procedure in the matter. Surely the sacrament cannot be given to those who obstinately refuse to do what they are bound under pain of mortal sin to perform. "Moraliter enim certum est," says Kern,[22] eos *habitualiter* permanere in sua obstinatione ideoque positive esse indignos."

Thus Catholics, though not Masons nor even influenced by Masonic principles (and hence not excommunicated), who order the cremation of their bodies and persist in their will even after an admonition, cannot be granted the sacraments of the dying.[23] Whether, however, they should be admonished, or simply left in good faith, is left to the prudence of the priest, who should act in accordance with the direction of the approved authors, with an especial regard toward the avoidance of scandal.

In like manner, Catholics who have become notorious members of the Odd Fellows must show signs of reconciliation, if possible, before any sacraments can be bestowed. If they are prevented by weakness or other cause, and if they exhibit marks of penance and devotion, they may receive the sacraments and have ecclesiastical burial.[24]

Other examples of a man refusing to do what he is obliged *sub gravi* to perform would be the unwillingness of a man to leave his concubine, the refusal of a woman to renounce a life of harlotry, &c. In this class, too, can be placed, manifest sinners who reject the sacraments repeatedly, though aware of their value, by the deliberate will of dying without them. As long as consciousness perdures, these people cannot be anointed without their consent.[25]

Not to be confused with such a perverse will is the refusal of one to receive the sacrament, not from the intention of dying without it, but simply because of a belief that he is not in danger of death or of a fear that reception betokens the certainty

---

22 *Tract. de Ext. Unct.*, p. 321.
23 S. C. S. Off., 27 Jul. 1892 ad 1—Coll. S. C. P. F., n. 1808.
24 S. C. P. F., 10 Maii, 1898—A. S. S., XXXI, 320; Cf. Amer. Eccl. Review, XX, p. 506.
25 Tanquerey, *Th. D.*, III, 784.

of death.[26] In such cases it should be investigated what intention would prevail if the truth were known. This can generally be deduced from the willingness or refusal of the patient to cooperate in the other aids of religion. It will be discovered that the intention of receiving the sacrament regularly predominates.[27]

The question may arise of the procedure to be taken in the case where a man, known to be in mortal sin, declares that he is contrite yet refuses to go to confession before receiving Extreme Unction. Can the refusal of a man to confess himself be regarded as a sign of contumacious perseverance in sin?

There is, of course, a divine precept, whereby all in mortal sin are bound to receive the sacrament of Penance if in danger of death.[28] Yet it is easily seen, especially in lingering illnesses and where death is not extremely close, that such confession can be made subsequently to the unction and not necessarily prior thereto.[29]

But what of the rubric of the Ritual, found even in the new edition: "In quo illud in primis ex generali Ecclesiae consuetudine observandum est ut, si tempus et infirmi condicio permittat, ante Extremam Unctionem, Poenitentiae et Eucharistiae Sacramentae infirmis praebeantur?"[30] Similarly, the Catechism of the Council of Trent instructs us: "Servanda est Catholicae Ecclesiae perpetua consuetudo, ut ante extremam

---

26 Cf. Berardi, *Prax. Conf.*, II, n. 5003; Cf. Amer. Eccl. Review, LX, pp. 572-3.

27 Cf. Noldin, *De Sac.*, 41.

28 Genicot-Salmans, *Inst. Th. M.*, II, 231.

29 Indeed, some authors hold that if there is only time to receive one or the other sacrament, it is permissible to choose Extreme Unction, despite the divine command to confess one's sins (cf. Telch, *Epitome Th. M.*, p. 301; Noldin, *De Sac.*, n. 444—for the opposite opinion, see Suarez, d. 44, s. 1, nn. 9-10). In such a case, Extreme Unction effects all that Penance accomplishes plus many mighty results peculiar to itself. The case in practice hardly seems likely. If it is a question of receiving one sacrament or the other before lapsing into unconsciousness, it seems wiser to select Penance first, for Extreme Unction can be given absolutely to those in unconsciousness, according to the prescriptions of the next canon.

30 Rit. V., cap. 1, n. 2.

unctionem, poenitentiae et eucharistiae sacramentum administretur."[31]

Furthermore, some theologians like Gury[32] and Billuart[33] prescribe confession previous to Unction for those in mortal sin because the latter is the complement of the former.

In the face of all these reasons can and must a man physically able to confess his sins be compelled, under threat of refusal of Extreme Unction, to receive the sacrament of Penance first, even though he asserts he has contrition for his sins? Clericatus[34] insists that it is certainly not permissible to anoint without prior confession, "*praesertim si in illa infirmitate ipsemet infirmus non fuerit confessus peccata sua; . . . . nam si effectus sacramenti est, inter alios, augere gratiam, quomodo augebitur ista gratia in eo qui nullam gratiam habet, imo obicem habet ad illam recipiendam?*"

Extreme Unction, it is true, is primarily a sacrament of the living, and consequently requires the state of grace. But the state of grace can be gained as well by perfect contrition *cum voto Poenitentiae* as by the sacrament of Penance with simple attrition. In this lies the falsity of Clericatus' reasoning, for he evidently presupposes that the state of grace can only be attained thru the reception of Penance. Sacraments of the living *per se* do not require previous confession by those who are in mortal sin. *Per accidens* confession may be required by specific legislation.

The Council of Trent[35] demanded that confession be made prior to Communion alone. Now, it is to be noted that the Ritual requires not only the reception of Penance, but also

---

31 *De Ext. Unct.*, n. 12. Cf. the law promulgated by the Synod of Chartres held in 1526: "Cum hoc sacramentum fit ultimum sacramentorum, inhibemus illud dari infirmo, nisi post Confessionem peccatorum suorum et post Corporis Christi Communionem, si possibile est infirmum communicare." (apud Nat. Alex., *Th. D. et M.*, lib. II, "*De Extr. Unct.*," cap. II, reg. 21).

St. Charles Borromeo similarly prescribed confession prior to the administration of Extreme Unction. (*Instructiones de Ext. Unct.*, capite inscripto, "*Quae praeparatio ad Extremae Unctionis sacramentum adhibenda*"—apud *Acta Eccl. Mediol.*, pars IV, tom. I, p. 604).

32 *Comp. Th. M.*, II, 693.

33 *Summa S. Thomae*, "*De Ext. Unct.*," disp. unic, a. 7 in fine.

34 *Decis. Sac.*, *De Ext. Unct.*, dec. 80, nn. 1, 2, 3.

35 Sess. XIII, *De Euch.*, can. 11.

that of the Eucharist. Hence it might be argued—and not unreasonably—that Penance is required before Extreme Unction by strict precept, not by reason of the Unction but rather by reason of the Eucharist.

But even prescinding from the force of this argument, theologians do not demand that Penance be received necessarily before Extreme Unction may be administered. O'Kane says simply: "In strictness, no doubt, it suffices that he (the subject) elicit an act of contrition before Extreme Unction."[36] In like manner St. Alphonsus writes: "Licet autem, per se loquendo, confessio non necessario praemittatur, cum per contritionem se disponere possit" &c.[37] Vermeersch-Creusen[38] declares: "Ut sacramentum hoc cum fructu recipiat, debet infirmus qui conscius sit peccati mortalis vel confiteri ante quam ungatur vel *perfecte conteri* si possit. Existimata igitur contritio sufficit, immo serius conatus contritionis, si copia confessionis non datur, dummodo habeatur attritio."

Suarez[39] treats the question at some length—and, although admitting the possibility of an obligation from some other source, concludes that *per se* it is not necessary to confess before being anointed. He cites an example of one who fell into mortal sin after he had received Penance and Viaticum but before the reception of Extreme Unction. Although recommending a confession whether the sin be occult or public, he, nevertheless, asserts the sinlessness of receiving unction without previous confession—provided always, of course, that the subject has contrition *cum voto Poenitentiae* and that there is no danger of his dying without a later opportunity to confess.

Examples may be cited when a man would refuse to go to confession before the bestowal of Extreme Unction. By some caprice or even from good reason he may dislike the pastor (who has, be it remembered, the sole right to give Extreme Unction). As a consequence, the man insists that another priest be summoned from some distance, in order that he may make his confession to him. While the confessor is on his way to the sick man, the pastor may deem it advisable to administer

36 *The Rubrics*, n. 850.
37 *Th. M.*, VI, 716. Cf. also Lehmkuhl, *Casus Consc.*, II, 664.
38 *Epit.*, II, 226.
39 D. 44, s. 1, nn. 9-10; cf. also Diana, *Op. Coord.*, t. II, tr. 4, res. 23.

Extreme Unction. The lawfulness of this administration seems hardly questionable. Another case would be had when the priest who administers Unction is a relative to whom the patient would feel much embarrassment in confessing. Then, too, it would be reasonable to accept the sacrament by preparing one's soul with contrition, coupled with the intention of receiving Penance later.

There are some theologians who assert that such an inversion of the sacraments is not a *mortal* sin, thus probably implying that it cannot be done without some blame. E. g., Barbosa [40] says: "Credo non esse peccatum mortale conferre Sacramentum Extremae Unctionis infirmo antequam susceperit Sacramentum Poenitentiae et Eucharistiae, quia infirmus potest per contritionem se disponere ad suscipiendum hoc sacramentum, tum quia aliquando fieri potest, ut quis recipere possit Extremam Unctionem, non vero Poenitentiam, vel Eucharistiam, ut quando aliquis patitur vomitum, aut ita repente morbor praevenitur, ut non dederit signa Sacramenti Poenitentiae."

Yet if there is present a reasonable cause, as in the examples cited above, it is hard to see how such an inversion is any sin at all. Venial obligations do not bind under serious inconvenience; any just cause suffices to release the binding force of the law.

It should be noted that it cannot be argued from the letter of Innocent I to Decentius:[41] that previous confession is necessary. "Nam poenitentibus istud infundi non potest, quia genus est sacramenti. Nam quibus reliqua sacramenta negantur, quomodo unum genus putatur posse concedi?" Innocent was speaking of public penitents, who, while doing penance for their sins, were forbidden participation in the sacraments until their period of penance was completed.

The conclusion is that *per se* a penitent does not have to preface the reception of Extreme Unction with sacramental confession. It is sufficient that he be contrite for his sins and that there be no danger that he will die before fulfilling the divine precept of confessing in danger of death. As Lehmkuhl puts it:

---

40 *De Off. et Pot. Par.*, p. II, c. XXII, n. 37.
41 cap. 8, 19 Mar. 416—C. I. C. Fontes, n. 19.

Ante Extremam Unctionem *aut* confessio *aut* perfecta contritio per se fiat a quolibet qui gravis peccati reus sit.''[42]

Hence a priest cannot demand prior confession under penalty of withholding the sacraments—nor is he obliged to do this by the rubric. ''Si enim,'' Suarez[43] writes, ''poenitens ad id non tenetur, unde obligabitur sacerdos, si videat signa contritionis et propositum confessionis, absque morali periculo moriendi sine illa, et praesertim si aliqua rationabilis causa occurrat differendi confessionem, ne videlicet detur hic et nunc aliqua occasio manifestandi peccatum vel quid simile? Prudentiae igitur sacerdotis hoc relinquendum est, ut et confessionem praemitti procuret, si commode potest, et non nimium molestus sit, sed *credat infirmo* suam contritionem ostendenti.''

Since, therefore, the refusal to confess prior to the reception of Extreme Unction cannot be construed as a sign of impenitence, in such cases where signs of contrition are exhibited, a priest wrongly deprives a man of this sacrament by declining to administer it in such a case.

The question may arise, however, with regard to a man bound by an excommunication or personal interdict. Is prior confession demanded of him? Such persons are prohibited by law from a reception of the sacraments.[44] In such an extreme time as the danger of death, however, the absolution from these censures can be given in both *fora* by any priest, if the contumacy has been broken.[45] Accordingly, even in this case, the priest cannot insist upon confession as a means to absolution from the censure; nor can he take a refusal to confess as a *certain* sign of impenitence. He can impart absolution in the external forum, and pave the way by this to an administration of Extreme Unction.[46]

From this discussion, it can be seen that obstinate impenitence in manifest grievous sin is not an easy thing of which to convict a man. Yet it alone will justify a complete denial of Extreme Unction. Every condition must be rigidly fulfilled;

---

42 *Th. M.*, II, 712.
43 D. 44, s. 1, n. 11.
44 Can. 2260, 1; 2275, 2.
45 Can. 2252.
46 Cf. Can. 2251.

and the slightest probability warrants a conditional administration.

When all the requisites for denial are surely present, however, it is a grave sin to confer the sacrament. "Constat fore peccatum grave," Suarez states, "dare sacramentum homini habenti obicem et nullo modo, i. e., nec expresse nec implicite nec interpretative petenti sacramentum et salutis suae remedium, saltem per signa attritionis aut bonae vitae."[47]

When men are conscious, little trouble will be experienced practically in determining the dispositions of their souls. Generally, it will be easily discernible whether they are shrinking from the sacraments because of a natural fear of death or from hardness of heart.

In the case of a man destitute of his senses, a priest is liable to be troubled with many scruples about the state of soul of the patient. If the man is discovered unconscious and the priest has no knowledge whatsoever of his condition of soul, there should be at least a conditional administration of the sacrament. In such an instance nothing certain is known—and consequently the conditions required by the canon for absolute denial of the sacrament are not fulfilled.

Two other cases may give some trouble to a priest zealous for souls, yet equally desirous of protecting the sanctity of the sacraments. The first is that of the man stricken down to unconsciousness in the very act of grievous sin. The second is that of the man who obstinately refuses the sacraments up to the very moment of unconsciousness.

In regard to the former case, it may be said that theologians since the time of La Croix and Alphonsus have allowed the conditional administration of Extreme Unction to such a subject. A few dissenting voices have been heard, especially those of the commentators on the rubrics. These men, it must be confessed, were faced with a rubric far different in phraseology than the one found in the latest edition of the Ritual. Baruffaldo,[48] was so impressed by the express wording of the rubric that he discarded in its favor the opinions of very weighty theologians. "Hoc non obstante," he writes, "textus noster clare loquitur,

47 D. 42, s. 1, n. 8.

48 *Ad Rit. Rom. Comm.*, t. I, tit. xxvii, n. 76.

prohibens talem administrationem, qui textus cum per consensum Ecclesiae Universalis sancitus sit est magis attendendus quam opinio doctorum licet classicorum." O'Kane,[49] too, though admitting the external probability of the opposite opinion, states that the wording of the rubric would seem to deny a man in this situation the aids of the unction. Berardi,[50] likewise, queries: If these cases are not meant by the rubric of the Ritual, "de quibusnam Rituale loqueretur?"

Since the revision of the Ritual's rubrics, such an argument from the text of the Ritual is altogether inadmissible. The present rubric uses the identical terminology of the Code, thus destroying all the value of the reasoning from such a source. The former rubric divided into distinct classes impenitents and those dying in manifest mortal sin. The Code speaks of only one class, viz., those who are contumaciously impenitent in manifest mortal sin.

Moreover, theologians of the past and the present admit a conditional administration in these cases. A host of authorities can be adduced. Hear Lehmkuhl, for instance:

> "Ii quos sumi licet catholice voluisse mori excludi non debent ab Extrema Unctione: 1) si sensibus destituti reperiuntur, etsi parum christiane vixerint; 2) neque si in ipso actu peccati, signo poenitentiae non manifestato, sensibus destituuntur: quibus quamquam S. Eucharistia danda non est, tamen cum condicionata absolutione Extrema Unctio omnino concedenda est. Nam si forte internum actum miser peccator habuit, longe tutius, immo certo ejus salus procurabitur per unctionem, per absolutionem valde dubie. Atque etiam quando sine justa dispositione, dummodo valide, Extremam Unctionem homo sensibus destitutus suscepit, postea per actum attritionis fortasse sacramenti effectum atque aeternam salutem consequetur."[51]

And Tamburini:

> "Huc pertinent peccatores . . . si post peccatum commissum, v. g., post duellum, tempus superfuit, quo vulneratus poenitere potuit, praesumendum esse, saltem per attritionem poenituisse, nisi contrarium clare constet, quod certe clare constare difficile est. Quare si sit a sensibus alienatus, unde non possit nec conteri nec sacramentalem

---

49 *The Rubrics*, n. 864.

50 *Prax. Conf.*, II, n. 5004. Other theologians who would deny the sacrament in these cases are Concina (*Theol. Christ.*, vol. X, "*De Ext. Unct.*," dis. I, c. IV, n. 5), and Scavini (*Th. M.*, III, 440 ad 4).

51 *Th. M.*, II, 724.

absolutionem cum attritione suscipere, erit regulariter per Extremam Unctionem reficiendus, quia regulariter praesumitur attritus, et non potest de statu actuali peccati constare.''[52]

To these names can be added the great authority of La Croix,[53] St. Alphonsus,[54] Clericatus,[55] Diana,[56] Konings,[57] Ballerini-Palmieri,[58] Rohling,[59] Aertnys,[60] Kern,[61] Vermeersch-Creusen[62] and Genicot-Salsmans.[63] Consequently without the slightest scruple the priest should proceed to anoint those who have been rendered unconscious in the very act of sin. Hence 1) those shot in adultery, burglary, &c.; 2) those wounded in a duel, a brawl, a riot; 3) those found unconscious after an attempt to commit suicide [64]—and all other similar cases—will permit of a conditional ministration of the sacrament to the subject. Such people may at least have made an act of attrition in the fraction of time which they had of consciousness before their wound robbed them of their senses.

Telch [65] makes an exception to the above rule. He denies the permissibility of anointing those dying in complete drunkenness which is gravely sinful. Those perfectly drunk commit mortal sin by drinking until they have lost the use of their reason—and having lost it, they are incapable, for the time being at least, of any act of sorrow.

St. Alphonsus [66] and La Croix [67] say that a conditional administration can be made when it is not certain that such a man is in mortal sin. And, in truth, it is difficult to say with finality that any case of perfect drunkenness is seriously sinful, as Konings [68] indicates. *''Id vero,''* he writes, *''tunc tantum*

52 *Th. M.*, lib. VI, c. 2, paragr. 4, n. 2.
53 *Th. M.*, lib. VI, p. 11, n. 2110.
54 *Th. M.*, VI, 732.
55 *Decis. Sacramentales*, dec. 80, *''De Extr. Unct.,''* nn. 5-6.
56 *Op. Coord.*, tom. I; tr. IV, res. 65.
57 *Th. M.*, n. 1508, q. 8.
58 *Op. Th. M.*, vol. V, tr. X, sec. VI, n. 32.
59 *Medulla*, p. 380.
60 *Th. M.*, II, 367, 2.
61 *Tract. de Ext. Unct.*, p. 322.
62 *Epit.*, II, 226.
63 *Inst. Th. M.*, II, 423.
64 Cf. Amer. Eccl. Review, LVII, p. 433; LVIII, p. 80.
65 *Epit. Th. M.*, pp. 294-5.
66 *Th. M.*, VI, 732.
67 *Th. M.*, lib. VI, p. II, n. 2110.
68 *Th. M.*, page 421, note 30.

constare videtur quando evidens est ipsum sese ex proposito perfecte inebriasse: id vero, in casu solitariae inebriationis vix evidens esse poterit: poterit vero, si agitur de illis ebriosis, qui usque ad finem vitae in consuetudine hujus vitii notorie perseverarunt." Usually it can be said that it is far from clear whether a man has deliberately made himself totally intoxicated. There is generally the probability that he misjudged his powers in regard to the quantity of liquor he could consume without losing totally his use of reason.

Some theologians are even more lenient. They go as far as to allow anointing even when the drunkenness was certainly gravely sinful. Thus Lehmkuhl[69] directs an administration—conditional, of course—"licet culpabiliter se inebriasset [subjectum]," adding that it must be given "*a fortiori*" when it is not clear whether the intoxication is culpable or not. Rohling[70] concords in this very merciful view. This practice may be followed, for it can be truly said that it is never known whether the drunken stupor has subsided sufficiently to allow some little use of the reason, thus making the possibility of at least some kind of attrition quite tenable.

Arguing *a pari* it can be said that Extreme Unction can be administered to those who fall into insanity while in the act of sin or (as shall be seen presently) while refusing the sacraments. With some truth it can be presumed that they have elicited an internal act of attrition. Insanity differs from unconsciousness, it is true. It takes away the use of reason, while the latter takes away only the use of the senses. However, it can be presumed that the insanity did not overtake the man in such a speedy fashion that he did not have at least a moment in which to repent.

It might, indeed, be asked how a priest can conscientiously give a sacrament of the living to a man whose attrition (and even his intention) is very little more than a possibility. The answer lies in the old axiom: "*In extremis extrema tentanda sunt.*" The sanctity of the sacrament is safeguarded by the conditional administration; and the eternal welfare of the subject similarly protected. There is no new sin on the part of

69 *Casus Consc.*, II, n. 665.
70 *Medulla*, p. 380.

the subject in thus receiving it, because his unconscious state makes him incapable of sin as long as it lasts. On the other hand, the huge advantage gained by the patient is worth the inconvenience caused by administration to those who are so very dubiously disposed for its reception.[71]

The second case that must be considered is that of a man who has up until the very moment of unconsciousness refused the sacraments explicitly or equivalently, i. e., by a positive refusal to do something demanded of him under pain of mortal sin. Thus a man may refuse to give up a wife married to him only civilly, while his first wife is still living, or a woman in harlotry may refuse to promise a relinquishment of her trade upon recovery, &c. In such cases, while the patient is still conscious, the priest can surely do nothing in the way of administering sacraments.

When the use of the senses is gone, however, the question is somewhat different. Testimonies of medical men and of experience have proven the capability of the reason to function, even though externally there seems to be no rational activity. In such a case it is not improbable that a change of dispositions might take place. Theologians are very much divided on this question. Many would deny all administration until some doubtful signs, at least, of penitence have been shown.

The ancient statutes of the Church of Troyes, together with the Ritual, forbade Extreme Unction to those who were excommunicated or of a notoriously bad life, giving as the reason: "*Si semel malus, semper praesumitur malus, nisi probetur contrarium.*"[72] Kern, too, will not allow this bestowal of the sacrament:—

> "Sane excesserunt theologi qui docebant, Extremam Unctionem ob reverentiam sacramenti denegandam esse omnibus qui actu non fruuntur usu rationis. Sed pejus excedunt qui, nulla habita ratione sanctitatis sacramenti, attentant illud conferre omnibus qui mentis non sunt compotes. . . . Quod spectat adagia commemorata, sacramenta certe sunt pro hominibus, sed danda tantum iis quos non esse indignos prudenter existimatur. In extrema necessitate omnia sunt tentanda, quae sanctitas mysteriorum et praecepta Ecclesiae per-

71 Cf. Suarez, d. 42, s. 1, n. 10; Tamburini, *Th. M.*, lib. VI, c. 2, paragr. 4, n. 4.

72 Launoi, *Op. Omnia*, t. I, p. 559.

mittunt. Si moriturus, qualem descripsimus (i. e., Catholicus qui Ecclesiam non deseruit at fidem abjecit et hostilem contra religionem animum gessit, vel saltem qui omnibus exercitiis religionis abjectis, curam salutis penitus neglexit), ante exitum eliciat actum attritionis tantum, manifesto non salvabitur, etiamsi sit inunctus. Sacramentum enim invalidum ob defectum intentionis in subjecto per nullum ejus actum subsequentem evadit validum. Igitur conetur sacerdos tales infirmos juvare unico medio quod superest; implorando pro illis infinitam misericordiam Dei, qui eos, si vult, etiam sine ritu sacramentali ab interitu vindicare valet.''[73]

When confronted with the objection that such a one may have by chance made a merely internal act of attrition before he had been completely bereft of consciousness, and would, thru the administration of Extreme Unction be assured of his salvation, Kern replies:—

''Peribit propria culpa, sacerdos autem suae obligationi satisfecit, quia mera possibilitas sufficientis dispositionis non fundat prudens judicium, de facto adesse, quae ex parte subjecti requiruntur. Si illa mera possibilitas existentiae necessariae dispositionis sufficeret, omnes Judaei morituri et sui non amplius conscii recte baptizarentur; forte enim, antequam mente penitus exciderunt, internum actum attritionis et desiderii Baptismi habuerunt.''[74]

In like manner Tanquerey,[75] Baruffaldo,[76] Lehmkuhl,[77] Noldin,[78] Berardi[79] and a writer in the American Ecclesiastical Review[80] would forbid such an administration. Telch[81] adds his authority to these, with the remark that occult miracles of grace cannot be a norm for the administration of the sacraments.

Despite this array of authority, there can be found as many, if not more, theologians who advocate the more merciful side. Too often unconsciousness is considered to be present, when a man is unable to manifest any sign by physical motion. The soul can be active, despite the inability to express such activity externally. Very frequently, too, though persons are apparently

73 *Tract. de Ext. Unct.*, pp. 319-20.
74 *Tract. de Ext. Unct.*, p. 320.
75 *Th. D.*, III, 784 (e).
76 *Ad. Rom. Rit. Comm.*, tom. I, tit. 27, n. 76.
77 *Th. M.*, II, 724.
78 *De Sac.*, 444.
79 *Praxis Conf.* II n. 5004.
80 Vol. LX, pp. 572-73.
81 *Epit. Th. M.*, pp. 294-5.

destitute of their senses, it is simply extreme weakness which has prostrated them, and their rational life is still vigorous. Frequently, in these people the sense of hearing remains. Experience itself taught Diana the truth of this and made him reverse his opinion on the permissibility of conferring unction on dying persons apparently unconscious. He had been seriously sick and had been bereft of all sensibility except hearing. Nevertheless he remained possessed of the use of reason and had the ability to make a true and firm judgment. Learning from the talk of the doctors and from his extreme weakness that he was near the end, he found himself able to commend his soul to the mercy of God. He attempted to externalize his pious emotions, by signs, by breathing, &c., but the bystanders considered them only signs of suffering nature.

"Ab illo tempore," Diana wrote,[82] "in animum induxi, quod si quovis modo aliquem Catholicum sic oppressum reciperem nec signum aliquod mihi intelligibile poenitentiae dare posset; nihilominus sub conditione absolverem, eo quod forte aliquod signum poenitentiae edat, etsi mihi incognitum; cum (ut dixi) hoc fit charitatis, et conditio omnem defectum auferat, qui administratione sacramenti contingere posset."

If absolution can be given, it is to be noted that Extreme Unction can also be imparted. Thus Tanquerey declares: "Quando aegrotus usu rationis gaudet, non potest licite ungi sine suo consensu; sed quando est sensibus destitutus, potest ungi in omnibus casibus in quibus absolvi potest; immo tutius est in hoc casu unctionem dare quam absolutionem, quia ad hanc sufficit attritio interna, cum ad Paenitentiam requiritur valde probabiliter attritio signis sensibilibus manifestata."[83]

Conditional anointing in these cases appeals to Ballerini-Palmieri,[84] Clericatus,[85] Genicot,[86] Rohling,[87] Murphy[88] and Piat.[89] Vermeersch-Creusen[90] denies the possibility of ascer-

---

82 *Op. Coord.*, tom. I, tract. IV, res. 65.
83 *Th. D.*, III, 784 Cf. also Bouvier, *De Ext. Unct.*, c. 7, a. 3, 7; O'Kane, *The Rubrics*, n. 864, etc.
84 *Op. Th. M.*, vol. V, tr. X, sec. VI, n. 32.
85 *Decis. Sac.*, "*De Ext. Unct.*," decis. 80, nn. 5 & 6.
86 *Inst. Th. M.*, II, 423.
87 *Medulla*, p. 380.
88 *Delinquencies and Penalties*, pp. 21-22.
89 *Nouvelle Revue Theologique*, XXXI, p. 482.
90 *Epit.*, II, 226.

taining with certainty the fact of contumacy in a person destitute of his senses. Sabetti-Barrett,[91] though evidently inclined to the opposite opinion, would not condemn a priest who anointed a man that had spurned the sacraments *ex contemptu* up to the very moment of unconsciousness.

Surely, then, there is sufficient external probability that even when a person perseveres in the state of sin and refuses the sacraments up until the moment of unconsciousness, he may be conditionally anointed. In practice, too, this should be done—although it is hard to say that there is an obligation on the priest to administer it. True, many authorities think it altogether unlawful, but surely, a man should not be deprived of the sacrament who may have made an act of imperfect contrition and whose salvation rests upon the reception or nonreception of the sacrament.[92] When Kern says that he perishes thru his own fault, he does not breathe the mercy of the Master. If the miserable sinner finds it hard while conscious to give up the ways of sin, and yet, at the very last moment, though physically prostrated, he summons enough courage to become attrite, it cannot be held that his failure to do so before merits for him eternal damnation. Everybody who perishes, perishes thru his own fault. Yet God gave the sacraments to save the attrite. Why should they not be imparted at a moment when, if ever they could do good, it will be just then?

Telch's argument that occult miracles of grace are not the norms of conferring the sacraments has not much face value. It can easily be retorted that such final co-operation with grace smacks little of the miraculous. Sinners, finding themselves really going to die, often begin to fear hell and become attrite, yet they may not be able sensibly to express themselves. But even granting this, it can be said that even if only a miracle of grace could save the man, nevertheless, there is no profanation done to the sacrament because of the conditional administration.

---

91 *Th. M.*, p. 808.

92 Cf. *The Casuist*, V, 232: "Where the worthy reception is in doubt the sacrament should be administered absolutely. This should be done unless it is positively certain that a person wills to die in his unbelief and unrepentance, and unreconciled with his God, which we may never assume with certainty of a person bereft of his senses, '*cum homines etiam pessimi et perditissimi in mortis confinia deducti serio salvari cupiant.*' "

It must be remembered that in anointing in cases where a man is stricken down in the act of sin or when he has refused to have the sacraments up until the time of unconsciousness, great caution and prudence will be at all times necessary to protect the faithful from scandal and from a loss of respect for the sacraments. In fact, this very reason is given as one of the arguments which opponents of this practice assert for the denial of the sacrament in such cases.[93]

In the latter case where the sacraments have been spurned, Genicot [94] advises that it will be wiser to abstain from unction until signs of penance appear, especially if many are aware of the circumstances of the case. However, if the priest, by a word or two of explanation, can effectually remove the scandal, he should make the admonition and proceed with a clear conscience.

In no case can Unction be given if scandal will result. The short form may be utilized if necessary to conceal the proceedings from the bystanders. A deft anointing of the sick man's hand can very easily be accomplished without attracting any attention; and this is permissible by Canon 947.

The condition to be attached to the administration of the sacrament in these cases wherein it is doubtful whether or not the subject is contumaciously persevering in manifest mortal sin will depend to a great extent upon the convictions of the priest. In the first place, however, the condition "si dispositus es" should never be appended. Such a condition would make the validity depend upon the dispositions of the subject at the time of reception. Consequently, if *de facto* he is not well-disposed, he is not anointed. *"Dispositus"* includes within its scope more elements than the law contemplates. A man *actu* in mortal sin is certainly not disposed; yet he is not excluded by the terminology of this canon. Only the contumaciously impenitent are to be denied the sacrament; yet there is a great chasm between those rightly disposed for reception and those who are obstinately impenitent. The inadequacy of the condi-

---

93 Cf. Telch. *Epit. Th. M.*, pp. 294-5 and Berardi, *Prax. Conf.*, II, n. 5004.
94 *Inst. Th. M.*, II, 423.

tion "si dispositus es" becomes apparent. Thus Kern writes:

> "Hinc illa regula pro praxi magni momenti, nunquam Extremam Unctionem esse ministrandam sub conditione: 'si dispositus es.' Si enim ista conditio adicitur et subjectum reipsa est fictum etsi materialiter tantum, nullum fit sacramentum, proinde quantumvis aegrotus postea, forte in momento tandem mortis, defectum corrigat, nullum amplius fructum salutaris mysterii nanciscitur. Caeterum haec regula non est propria Extremae Unctionis, sed valet etiam de aliis sacramentis quae possunt reviviscere."[95]

Neither can a condition be attached which might allow a future reviviscence, as, for example, "Si es nunc dispositus vel eris dispositus." Future conditions are inadmissible except in the matrimonial contract.

Those who hold that this canon regards primarily the intention of the recipient teach that the administration must be made absolutely *quoad dispositionem.* If any condition is to be appended, it must be concerned with an essential for validity, i. e., the intention. At first blush it may seem a great irreverence to make an absolute administration (*quoad dispositionem*) to those evidently in mortal sin. Yet it must also be remembered that persons bereft of their senses cannot commit an actual sacrilege; while the probability—or as a writer in the Casuist[96] says, even the mere possibility—of a reviviscence is sufficient to warrant an unconditional administration without scruple. Noldin[97] notes that it is lawful to administer a sacrament to a man whose dispositions are very dubious, not only when such a sacrament is the only means (*medium unicum*) of salvation, but also when its reception is highly advantageous to the subject. Accordingly, then, these theologians suggest the use of "*si capax es,*" for thereby the elements for validity are generally understood.

Those who teach that this canon is concerned with the dispositions of the patient are not agreed as to the exact formula to be employed in the condition. Pruemmer[98] and Mothon[99] suggest "*si capax es*"—probably understanding thereby "Si

---

95 *Tract. de Ext. Unct.*, pp. 375-6; cf. also Lehmkuhl, *Th. M.*, II, 724 and *Casus Consc.*, II, 665; Telch, *Epit. Th. M.*, p. 300; Noldin, *De Sac.*, 445.

96 vol. V, p. 231.

97 *De Sac.*, 445.

98 "*The Recipient of Extreme Unction*" in the Homiletic and Pastoral Review, XXVI (1926), p. 742.

99 *Institutions Canoniques*, II, p. 233, art. 2030.

capax es—ad normam juris." Blat[100] recommends "*Si non es impoenitens in mortali.*" A more correct formula would be "*Si non es contumaciter impoenitens in mortali*"—for by it only those whom the canon wishes to be excluded would be denied the sacrament. In practice it may often be rather difficult to keep the various elements of this condition in mind. Since the condition need not be expressed, it may be advisable for a priest simply to intend the bestowal of the sacrament "*ad mentem Ecclesiae*" or "*ad normam juris.*"

Suppose that a person thus anointed when unconscious in the cases discussed above should regain consciousness and evidence a change of dispositions. Such a man may have been validly anointed—and yet there is room for much doubt. Repetition of the unction in the same danger of death is very probably valid, yet certainly illicit. A second administration under the condition "*Si capax es*" would still allow the possibility of a second valid unction in the same danger of death—against the prescriptions of Canon 940, 2. In order to keep within the law, it will be necessary to apply the oil in such a case under the condition "*Si nondum es unctus.*"[101]

It can easily be seen that if Extreme Unction may be imparted in extreme cases such as the ones dealt with hitherto, it can surely be permitted in the not infrequent instances of persons who have lived in little accord with Christian principles, yet without showing themselves hostile to religion. These men may be presumed to desire to die in a Catholic fashion; and rarely can they be suspected of contumacious impenitence. Similarly, there can be little doubt about their intention of receiving the sacrament, and thus their valid capacity is unquestioned. To such men Extreme Unction should be given unconditionally, so that every opportunity can be afforded for reviviscence.[102]

All the cases hitherto considered in this canon supposed that the dispositions of the sick man were known at least to the immediate family and attendants of the patient. The question may be asked about the procedure to be followed when the priest

---

100 *Comm. Text.*, lib. III, p. I, n. 286.

101 Vermeersch-Creusen, *Epit.*, II, 226.

102 Cf. Kern, *Tract. de Ext. Unct.*, pp. 321-3; Casuist, vol. V, p. 228 sq.; Noldin, *De Sac.*, 445; Lehmkuhl, *Th. M.*, II, 724; cf. also S. C. S. Off. 9 Maii, 1821—Collectanea, n. 757; *infra*, chap. viii, p.

alone knows of the absolute unworthiness of the sick man, and grave scandal will arise if the sacrament is refused. An incident of this sort would occur if the priest were asked to confer Extreme Unction upon one who he knew through a consultation with the physician was about to undergo an illicit operation occultly. A similar case would result if the priest on a visit privately to the sick man, without the knowledge of the family (as could be done easily enough in a hospital), finds the patient unwilling to make restitution in a serious matter. Later he is summoned while the family is present. The sick man asks for the Unction. What is the priest to do?

He has hardly any alternative. Here is an occult sinner seeking a sacrament publicly. He cannot be denied it, even at the expense of the sanctity of the sacrament. Should the priest desert the sick man in this case, he would bring defamation upon the patient, accusations against himself and fears to the faithful that they might be repulsed from the sacraments. All these considerations compel the priest to proceed in the anointment of this unworthy subject.[103]

A final instance is that of the unworthiness of the sick man known only from the seal of confession. A priest is summoned to attend a sick man. The attendants escort the priest to the sick room and retire so that the patient's confession can be heard. The sick man refuses to do something which requires a denial of absolution by the priest. The confession over, the attendants come in—and await the anointing. The sick man himself says nothing. Again there is no escape for the priest. What he knows *sub sigillo* is not his knowledge. The sick man is seeking the sacrament, even by his very silence. The identical considerations, danger of scandal, loss of reputation to the sick man, fears of the faithful, etc., apply also in this case as well as in the above circumstances. Consequently, the priest should bestow the Unction without hesitation.

Even if the sacrament were sought occultly by such a man, a priest should administer it. Unworthiness known only from the seal of confession is not enough to refuse the sacraments to an occult sinner, even when occultly seeking them.[104]

---

103 Cf. Noldin, *De Sac.*, 36-7; Genicot-Salsmans, *Th. M.*, II, 122-3.
104 Cf. Genicot-Salsmans, *Th. M.*, II, 122 & 392; Cappello, *De Sac.*, I, 70, iv.

CHAPTER VIII.

ADMINISTRATION TO THE UNCONSCIOUS

CANON 943.

Infirmis autem, qui, cum suae mentis compotes essent, illud saltem implicite petierunt, aut verisimiliter petiissent, etiamsi deinde sensus vel usum rationis amiserint, nihilominus absolute praebeatur.

CHAPTER VIII.

All the sacraments, with the very probable exception of the Eucharist, demand from those who have attained the age of reason an habitual intention, at least, of receiving them. The absence of such an intention completely frustrates the administration of the sacrament and nullifies its effects. It is an essential element to its valid confection.

Neither an actual nor even a virtual intention is required in the recipient. An habitual intention is eminently sufficient.[1] Such an intention consists in an act of the will once made and never since retracted, yet not adverted to at the time of reception and in no way flowing into or determining the act of the recipient.[2]

Nor is it required for Extreme Unction that this habitual intention be *explicit,* that is, an express act of the will to receive this particular sacrament. It is quite enough if it be *implicit,* or in other words, contained in some action with which the will of not receiving it cannot accord.

Intention is, of course, an internal thing; and its presence is known only by some external revelation or manifestation. This need not be by direct statement of the subject; other actions accomplish this equally as well. Thus a Catholic who, by frequent reception of the sacraments and by compliance with the Church's laws, exemplifies his faith has certainly the intention of receiving the last sacraments and of dying as a Catholic should. In this instance the intention of the man is habitual and is *internally explicit,* although its external manifestation can be called only implicit. On the other hand a man may habitually have the intention and even openly declare his willingness, of performing everything required for salvation, yet at the same time

---

1 Some authors contest this in regard to Penance and Matrimony; but other authors of great weight teach the absolute sufficiency of an habitual intention—cf. Genicot-Salsmans, *Th. M.,* II, 125; Noldin, *De Sac.,* 41. However, such a dispute is beside the question here, as it does not regard Extreme Unction.

2 Genicot-Salsmans, *l.c.*; Noldin, *l.c.*

know little or nothing about Extreme Unction and from ignorance may even reject it. Such a man has the *implicit* intention of receiving the Unction and has *explicitly* manifested his internal intention. Finally, one may have internally an implicit intention of doing all required for salvation without, however, making a specific act of the will in regard to Extreme Unction. Suppose that this man has revealed his implicit intention only equivalently, and not explicitly, e. g., by living up to the best lights of his conscience. Thereby he shows that he has an *implicit habitual* intention of receiving the unction. It is wrong to call such an intention *interpretative,* if by that we mean an intention which would be present if certain other conditions existed or other facts were known. An intention of such kind does not really exist at all nor did it ever exist. Here the intention of receiving Extreme Unction is actually resident implicitly in the general intention of doing all that is necessary or extremely useful or beneficial in the time of death. It is thus seen that, although there is a close connection between an intention and its manifestation, nevertheless they are two quite different things. This will be of great benefit in understanding the phraseology of this canon.

It is not enough, consequently, to have no intention at all, to hold one's self passive to an administration. Neither is a histrionic reception valid. There is required some positive act of the will in regard to reception, either in a particular or in a general sense.[3]

The words of this canon refer strictly, not to the presence of the intention, but to its externalization in the form of a petition or request for the sacrament. When this is made, the minister is certain about the existence of intention.

In the older rituals it was very often required that the sick man specifically ask for the Unction before it could be conferred. This was demanded, not only that a sufficient intention of receiving the sacrament might be revealed, but to comply in the most literal sense with the Jacobean prescription: "Inducat

---

[3] Cf. Noldin, *De Sac.*, 41: De Lugo, *De Sac. in Gen.*, disp. 9, s. 7, n. 116; Cf. also S. C. S. Off, 10 Maii, 1703—*Quebec.*—ad VIII, Collectanea, n. 256; 10 Apr. 1861—*Tchely Meridio-Orientalis*—ad I, Collectanea, n. 1213.

presbyteros Ecclesiae." Thus the *Codex Ratholdus* contained the following ceremony:

> "Incipit Ordo Unctionis Infirmi. Hic dicat sacerdos ad infirmum: 'Quid me avocasti frater?' Ille ait: 'Ut mihi unctionem tradas.' Dicit sacerdos ad eum: 'Donet tibi Dominus noster J. C. veram facilemque unctionem,' " &c.[4]

Ancient legislation to this effect is also found Ælfricus, the Bishop of the Angles, inserted in his canons: "Nemo praesumat eum ungere nisi exoratus."[5]

Daniel, bishop of Nantes, made a similar rule. Moved to drastic action because of the doleful negligence of the sick in regard to the sacraments, he drew up and promulgated the following enactment:

> "Nos tantis animarum periculis, quantum possumus, occurrere cupientes in virtute sanctae obedientiae, omnibus Capellanis et Curatis nostrarum civitatis et dioecesis, eorumque subcapellanis praecipimus et mandamus ut singulis diebus Dominicis parochianos suos sollicite moneant et hortentur, ut statim atque in lecto jacuerint, Sacramenta Ecclesiastica *petant.*"[6]

In the sixteenth century local rituals abound, which contain the prescription that the priest be summoned at least by those in charge of the sick. Thus the Ritual of Toul, edited in 1559, reads as follows:

> "Ordo ad visitandum infirmum. Imprimis interrogetur si *petat* sacramentum ultimae Unctionis, et si in fide velit illud recipere. Respondeat: 'volo.' "[7]

Similarly, the Church of Mende placed in its ritual the rubric: "Est notandum quod non datur nisi *petentibus verbo* vel *signo.*"[8] Directions of this kind were found in very many other

---

4 Daniel, *Codex Litugicus*, tom. I, p. 310; Cf. also the "interrogatio" of the Codex Remigio-Remensis, which is not quite as explicit as this (apud De Sainte-Beuve, *De Ext. Unct.*, disp. VIII, a. 1—apud Migne, *Curs. Theol. Comp.*, vol. XXIV, col. 127).

5 N. 32—M. P. L., 139, 1475.

6 Launoi, *op. cit.*, p. 557.

7 Launoi, *l.c.*

8 Launoi, *Op. Omnia*, t. I, p. 557. This ritual was published in 1530.

places where local rituals were in use.[9] Thus, it will be noted that a widespread custom insisting upon the external expression of an implicit intention by the patient was in vogue.

It was permitted, nevertheless, to confer the sacrament on those who had requested it in signs or in words, but who lost the use of reason or of their senses before the arrival of the priest. The Sixth Provincial Council of Beneventum in 1374 directed this manner of procedure: "Unde nullus ungendus est, nisi qui primo compos mentis existens, verbis aut signis id postulaverit . . . Si vero infirmus, qui *petit* hoc sacramentum, amiserit notitiam vel loquelam, nihilominus dum tamen vitam habeat concedatur eidem." [10]

In the newer discipline, especially since the seventeenth century, no such legislation is found. The rubric of the Ritual before the latest revision did not demand the explicit petition of the sacrament. Signs of sorrow were quite sufficient.[11]

Neither does the present canon demand the formal and explicit seeking of the former days. Rightly so, for the "*petitio*" is simply the external manifestation of the sick man's intention. The intention can be present in all its vigor, even though there is no revelation of its existence made through outward sign or word.

"Infirmis autem qui cum suae mentis compotes essent."

The phraseology of the canon does not signify that the petition for the sacrament must be made only after the inception of the sickness. "*Infirmis,*" it is true, refers to the present status of the subject—but the preterite tense of "*petierunt*" evidences the validity of the act when done in past time. It is sufficient, therefore, that a man have shown at some time during his con-

---

9 Launoi (*l.c.*) includes in his collection the following Rituals with this rubric: AEduensis (1523), Chartres (1489, 1544 & 1604), Périgueux (1505), St. Flour (1525), Rheims (1504 & 1530), Clermont (1518), Nîmes (1533), Maguelone (1533), Troyes (1541 & 1573), Meaux (1542), Beauvais (1544), Verdun (1554), Limoges (1555), Uzès (1550), Langres (1573), Vienne (1577), Auscuensis (1602).

10 Tit. 8, cap. 1—apud Catalano, *Rom. Rit.*, t. I, p. 311.

11 Tit. V, cap. 1, n. 6 (edit. 1913): "Infirmis autem qui, dum sana mente et integris sensibus essent, illud petierit, seu verisimiliter periisent seu dederint signa contritionis, etiamsi deinde loquelam amiserint, vel amentes effecti sint, vel delirent, aut non sentiant, nihilominus praebeatur."

scious life his desire to receive Extreme Unction when in danger of death.

"Illud saltem implicite petierunt."

It is easily deducible from this terminology that an habitual intention is sufficient for the recipient of Extreme Unction. Again "petierunt" presupposes the existence of an intention in the past—else how could there be a *"petitio?"* If a petition made in past time suffices, the intention which prompted it is similarly adequate.

As noted before, the words of this canon speak of the manifestation of the intention in the form of a petition for the sacrament. The phrase "saltem implicite" implies the preferability of an explicit petition. This would be had in the request of a man to receive Extreme Unction specifically, if he should fall into danger of death from sickness.

Yet this express and explicit petition is not necessary. Any implicit seeking of the sacrament suffices. Blat [12] gives as an example the command of one to summon a priest when he is attacked by serious sickness. Any other externalized manifestation of intention, if not explicit, will fall in this category.

"Aut verisimiliter petiissent."

There are some theologians who say that the phrasing here denotes the sufficiency of an interpretative intention.[13] Yet this is altogether an erroneous deduction. What the canon considers is an interpretative *"petitio,"* i. e., the externalization by the subject of his habitual intention, had he adverted to it. An interpretative intention is one which does not actually exist, but would exist if certain other facts or conditions had been known. On the other hand, an habitual intention *de facto* has existed, even though never revealed externally in a "petitio."

The sacraments may be given to all who have at least an implicit habitual intention of receiving them. These people would petition the sacraments if they adverted to the usefulness of such a thing. Consequently, they are said to make an interpretative request for their administration.

---

12 *Comm. Text.*, lib. III, p. I, n. 287.

13 Cf. O'Kane, *The Rubrics*, 862; Ferreres, *Comp. Th. M.*, II, 296.

Such an interpretative "petitio" is always realized in the case of those who have lived Catholic lives. "Qui enim Christianus est," says De Lugo,[14] "et vult in Ecclesia Catholica vivere et mori, vult etiam Ejus sacramenta debito tempore juvari: quam voluntatem Ecclesiam praesumit de omnibus qui signa poenitentiae suo tempore exhibuerunt." And again:[15] "Homo Christianus ex vi illius voluntatis generalis vult quidem sumere sacramenta more Christiano, quando scilicet debito tempore Christianis dari solent, atque ideo habuit jam voluntatem accipiendi Extremam Unctionem et Eucharistiam in mortis periculo."

Theologians are very generous in their allowance of what is required of the subject in order to furnish a basis for the presumption of this interpretative petition. Thus Suarez says:

> "Ut autem susceptioni talis sacramenti consentire censeantur, satis est quod signa aliqua contritionis ediderint, vel quod quacumque ratione probabili praesumantur esse dispositi ad sacramentum recipiendum, quoties contrarium non constat, quia qui malus non probatur, bonus esse praesumitur. Qui autem praesumitur contritus vel bene dispositus ad justificationem etiam credere habere, et revera habet virtute voluntatem suscipiendi illa media, quae hic et nunc ad suam salutem vel necessaria sunt vel valde utilia, et haec voluntas sufficit ad valorem hujus sacramenti. . . [Sufficit ut] antequam aliquis amittat usum rationis, hoc sacramentum petierit, aut si meminisset, petiturus fuisset. Et in hoc sensu dicunt fere Doctores omnes, quod licet ad recipiendum hoc sacramentum necessaria sit intentio seu petitio recipientis, juxta illius Jacobi, 5: 'Inducat presbyteros Ecclesiae,' non tamen semper sit formalis necessaria, sed virtualis seu interpretativa sufficiat."[16]

Any one who has the intention of dying a Catholic makes at least an interpretative petition for the sacrament. It is not required that he have lived in exemplary fashion. Those who have not been always loyal in their obedience to the commands of God and His Church may still receive the sacrament, provided that it cannot be shown that they have done anything which would contradict their desire to die "in osculo Domini ac intra

---

14 *De Sac. in Genere*, disp. 9, s. 7, n. 122.
15 *L.c.*, n. 127.
16 D. 42, s. 1, n. 6.

Ecclesiam." Indeed, as Benedict XIV [17] says, it must be presumed that the faithful will desire this sacrament in the hour of death, unless there are clear and certain arguments to the contrary. Accordingly, all who would declare (although *de facto* they did not do so) that they would wish to die as Catholics, must be considered to have an habitual intention of receiving the sacrament, which, if possible, they would reveal by a petition for its administration.

Missionaries in this country were concerned by many cases of men who were utterly careless of salvation. Though baptized with Catholic rites, some of them never had attended church since childhood. What could be done for these when they fell into a dangerous illness? The missionaries were very dubious as to the correct procedure, and hence the Holy See was asked:

> "Qui consuetudinarii sunt, recidivi, salutis incurii, sacramenta per annos relinquentes, etc., morbo correpti sacerdotem advocant, datis signis quibusdam infirmis quidem et valide suspectis, quae sacramenta ipsis ministrari absolute debent, supposito mortis periculo? quae negari? Quid si talis infirmus necdum primam Communionem fecerit?"

The following answer was given:

> "Consulat missionarius probatos auctores. Meminerit tamen in mortis periculo quemlibet fidelium, qui dat signa resipiscentiae, a quolibet sacerdote absolvi de quibusvis peccatis et censuris posse, et neminem tunc repelli a participatione sacramentorum, nempe Extremae Unctionis, si aegrotent, et SSmi Viatici, nisi quoad Viaticum objiciatur consuetudo, qua iis qui extremo supplicio mox punientur denegatur, de qua quidem consuetudine nihil hic pronunciatur."[18]

As has been shown, approved authors state that, when signs of sorrow have been given, Extreme Unction may be conferred. The reply of the Holy Office allows anointing after absolution has been imparted. A priest thus called has evidence of an ex-

---

17 *De Syn. Dioc.*, l. 8, c. 6, n. 5: "De quolibet fideli de quo contrarium non constat, praesumendum est fuisse hoc sacramentum petiturum, si potuisset: passim siquidem videmus, Extremam Unctionem muniri, qui subita vi morbi oppressi, sensibus destituuntur, nec ullum Sacramenti desiderium significare valent: eorum quippe perspecta pietas et fides, non obscurum praebet argumentum desiderii, quod, si posset, demonstrarent."

18 S. C. S. Off., 9 Maii 1821 (*Kentucky*)—Collectanea, n. 757.

plicit petition for the sacraments and at least an implicit request for Extreme Unction. There is no contumacy in manifest mortal sin; and hence, there is no obstacle from that quarter. It is true that the absolution of such a man, if he be unable to make a confession, is very dubious. But the fact of its possible inefficacy should not prevent the bestowal of the Unction. The very fact that Unction is secondarily a sacrament of the dead shows that Christ Himself intended it as an escape from sin for those incapable of making a confession at the time of anointing.

The conclusion logically drawn from this is that every one, regardless of the evil life he has led, should be given the sacrament, if there is a prudent judgment that he would have asked for and accepted the consolations of the Church in the hour of danger. Since even the most dissolute and abandoned sinners seriously desire salvation when they discover themselves near death, the priest must not judge too harshly in regard to the presence of an interpretative petition. The Casuist[19] allows the anointment of a man who was a notorious drunkard, who lived a very irreligious life, who was a libertine, even though he fell into unconsciousness in the act of sin. Extreme Unction is probably the only refuge of such a man, especially since it may often be difficult for him to conceive an act of perfect contrition.[20]

Moreover, the sacrament should not be denied its ability to revive in these cases by a bestowal under the condition "*si dispositus es,*" as shall be noted later in the treatment of this canon.

"*Etiamsi deinde sensus vel usum rationis amiserint.*"

Since the petition is an act of the will, it must be done in conscious life. In the case of an interpretative petition, the rational actions of the subject are to be considered. Even when bestowed on those who fall into unconsciousness after persistent refusal of the sacraments, the action is based on the possibility of sorrow occurring in the fraction of time prior to absolute unconsciousness, or because oftentimes such a complete state of insensibility has not possessed the patient.

---

19 Vol. V, pp. 230-2.

20 Cf. *supra*, chap. vii, p. 237 sqq.; also Kern, *Tract. de Ext. Unct.*, p. 321.

When this petition, explicit, implicit or interpretative, has been made, the sacrament can be given even though in the meanwhile the subject has lost his senses by becoming unconscious or his reason by becoming insane or delirious.

In administrations to insane people as well as to those who are delirious there is great danger that irreverences may be committed. Because of this, and also because of the mistaken view that actual devotion was required in the recipient, some theologians forbade an administration to these people, no matter how sincere their wills before such lapses from reason. For example, St. Thomas wrote:

> "Ad effectum hujus sacramenti suscipiendum, plurimum valet devotio suscipientis et personale meritum conferentium, et generale totius Ecclesiae. Quod patet ex hoc, quod per modum deprecationis forma hujus sacramenti confertur; et ideo illis qui non possunt cognoscere et cum devotione suscipere, hoc sacramentum dari non debet: et praecipue furiosis et amentibus, qui possunt irreverentiam sacramento facere, nisi haberent lucida intervalla in quibus Sacramenta recognoscerent, et sic eis conferri in statu ipso posset."[21]

In similar fashion the Sixth Provincial Council of Beneventum (anno 1374) excluded these unfortunates from participation in the sacrament:

> "Phreneticis et amentibus illis praecipue dari non debet qui possunt sacramento irreverentiam per aliquam immunditiam facere, nisi haberent dilucida intervalla in quibus sacramentum recognoscerent, quia tunc eis in aliquo statu conferri potest, maxime ubi in sana mente constituti petivissent, quia ad hoc, quod prosit hoc sacramentum requiritur devotio quaedam interior, quam furiosi et similes habere non possunt. Unde nullus ungendus est, nisi qui primo compos mentis existens, verbis aut signis id postulaverit."[22]

Later legislation and theological opinion[23] did not coincide with such an absolute exclusion of those who were in delirium or insanity. Actual devotion was not demanded of the recipient, and unction was allowed if the danger of irreverence was removed and there was evidence of a "petitio" before the subject lost the use of reason. Thus the Ritual of the Church of Meaux,

---

21 *Comm. in IV lib. Sent.*, dist. xxiii, q. 2, a. 2, quaestiunc. 3.

22 Tit. 8, cap. 1; cf. Catalano, *Rit. Rom.*, t. I, p. 311.

23 Cf. e. g. Estius, *Comm. in IV Sent.*, dist. xxiii, paragr. 13.

published in 1547, contained this rubric: "Sciendum est quod ministrari non debet excommunicatis, &c . . . nec furiosis, nec phreneticis (nisi ante phenesim aut maniam petierunt)."[24] Thus, too, the Ritual of Vienne, edited thirty years later (1577): "Hoc sacramentum datur solum infirmis, adultis et poenitentibus, et qui sunt in periculo mortis, quique illud petunt, vel ante petierunt, quam per infirmitatem intellectu et bono sensu privarentur."[25]

The Synod of Paris in 1557 also legislated in this merciful vein: "Si qui vero ex morbi gravitate in amentiam inciderint, consideranda est eorum vita praecedens; qui si laudabiliter, vitam duxerint ante actam et Christiane, ab hujus perceptione arceri non debent."[26]

St. Charles Borromeo[27] is equally as generous, but he also stresses the necessity of avoiding all possible irreverence. The Roman Ritual before its latest revision made a similar provision against irreverence: "Sed si infirmus, dum phrenesi aut amentia laborat, verisimiliter posset quidquam facere contra reverentiam Sacramenti, non inungatur nisi periculum tollatur omnino."[28] This rubric is not found in the latest edition of the *Rituale.*

However, the intrinsic sanctity of the sacraments demands that every precaution be taken against any possible irreverence or indecency on the part of the subject. Suarez[29] notes that the reverence due to the sacrament is to be preferred to the benefit accruing to the individual. Consequently it is of paramount importance for the minister to see that the sanctity of the sacraments do not suffer. What means are to be taken to accomplish this is left to the prudent judgment of the attendant priest.

24 Launoi, *Op. Omnia,* t. I, p. 562.
25 Launoi, *Op. Omnia,* t. I, p. 563.
26 Natal. Alex., *Th. D. et M.,* lib. II, *tr. de Ext. Unct.,* c. 5, reg. 16.
27 "*Instructiones de Sac. Ext. Unct.,*" apud *Acta Eccl. Mediol.,* t. I, pars IV, p. 604: "Infirmis autem qui, sana mente dum erant, illud petierunt, aut verisimile est quod petiissent, etiamsi postea in amentiam inciderint, vel ratione sermoneve uti desierint, ministrabitur item. Si vero dum infirmus amentia phrenesive laborat, verisimile sit, ut indecore aut spurce, impureve aliquid agat, quo irreverentia Sacramento huic fiat, non ungetur, nisi alicujus complexu ita teneatur ut firmus stabilisque haereat."
28 Tit. V, c. 1, n. 7 (edit. 1913).
29 D. 42, s. 1, n. 9.

As a last resort, an insane or delirious patient may be strapped or held down with force while the sacrament is being conferred.[30] If the patient is very violent and can be forced into submissiveness for only a very brief period, the priest will do well to resort to the short method of conferring the sacrament.

Diana [31] and Barbosa [32] think that lay people should be excluded when a man is thus quieted by force, in order that no scandal may be given. Yet in practice, especially in our land where the priest has no clerics to assist him, it will be very difficult to procure any but laymen to subdue the insane man. Moreover, there is little danger of scandal, for all realize that such a patient is altogether irresponsible for his doings.

If a man is known to suffer spasms of violence periodically, a priest would do wrong to wait purposely until such a time to confer the Unction. Reverence for the things of God would be sadly lacking in his heart. It will be often just as well to wait until the patient subsides, unless it is clear that the spell may so weaken him as to lessen appreciably the power of the sacrament in regard to corporal sanation.

"Nihilominus absolute praebeatur."

In all the cases above mentioned the sacrament is to be given absolutely. There is to be no conditional qualification making the validity of the sacrament dependent upon the present moral status of the man's soul. The activities for reviviscence are not to be stinted in any way.

By these words the Code declares that in these instances the necessary intention is not lacking and that such men are not unworthy of the sacramental fruits.[33]

Even if they are not *de facto* worthy at the moment of reception, yet the probability that they will come into a state of worthiness is sufficient to compensate for the peril of frustration of the Sacrament through an unconditional administration.[34]

---

30 Cf. Diana, *Op. Coord.*, t. II, tr. IV, res. 50; Mastrio, *Th. M.*, D. 19, q. 5, a. 1, n. 71; Lehmkuhl, *Th. M.*, II, 723; St. Alph., *Th. M.*, VI, 732; O'Kane, *The Rubrics*, n. 863.

31 *L.c.*

32 *De Off. et Pot. Par.*, cap. 22, n. 13.

33 Blat, *Comm. Text.*, lib. III, p. I, n. 287.

34 Cf. Kern, *Tract. de Ext. Unct.*, p. 375-76; Noldin, *De Sac.*, 445.

CHAPTER IX.

OBLIGATION UPON THE SUBJECT

CANON 944.

Quamvis hoc sacramentum per se non sit de necessitate medii ad salutem, nemini tamen licet illud negligere; et omni studio et diligentia curandum ut infirmi, dum sui plene compotes sunt, illud recipiant.

CHAPTER IX.

In canon 939 the obligations on the part of the minister in regard to the administration of Extreme Unction were considered. The present canon treats of the obligations in regard to its reception, not only on the part of the subject but on the part of those who are bound to look after his welfare. Prior to a consideration of this question, however, it will be quite necessary to make a preliminary investigation into the necessity of this sacrament in the economy of our salvation.

"Quamvis hoc sacramentum per se non sit de necessitate medii ad salutem."

A thing is said to be necessary *necessitate medii* when even its inculpable omission would preclude possibility of salvation. It can possess this prerogative in two ways. It can be so ordained by its very nature that no substitution can be made for it (as e. g., faith in an adult for Baptism or Penance)—and then it is said to be intrinsecally necessary *necessitate medii.* On the other hand a thing is said to be extrinsically necessary, *necessitate medii,* when it is required for our salvation by positive ordinance of God but in such fashion that salvation is not altogether thwarted by the substitution of other means (for example, Baptism by water, or attrition with Penance). The former necessity is *absolute,* the latter *relative* or *hypothetical.*

It is easily seen that Extreme Unction is not *absolutely* necessary *necessitate medii.* If baptism by water is not so necessary, nor the reception of the sacrament of Penance for those in mortal sin, neither can this be predicated of the complement of Penance, Extreme Unction.

A thing is said to be *per se* necessary to salvation when it is required as the ordinary means to reach that blessed goal. It is necessary *per accidens* when, due to some obstacle which prevents the use of ordinary means, it becomes the only expedient by which eternal happiness can be gained.

The first problem then is whether Extreme Unction is *per*

se necessary *necessitate medii relativa.* It was evidently held to be such in some places. Thus the Synodalia of the Church of Rheims[1] and of the Church of Troyes[2] contained this enactment:

> "Saepe moneant sacerdotes populum quod priusquam quartum decimum annum compleverint, maxime Sacramentum extremae Unctionis petant, et recipiant reverentur, si timeatur verisimiliter de morte infirmorum, quia *necessarium est ad salutem* istud Sacramentum, si possit haberi."

Kern[3] concords in this view, maintaining that it is at least probable that Extreme Unction is relatively necessary for salvation, *necessitate medii.* His arguments are well worth noting. In the first place, the Council of Trent[4] declared that it was Christ's wish to furnish to His faithful the aids necessary to stave off the assaults of the enemy on every occasion of their earthly journey. These aids are found in an especial manner in the sacraments. Six sacraments supply every assistance required to battle the temptations during the ordinary course of life. When the end approaches, however, bringing with it added assaults of the devil in a last frantic effort to tear the soul from God, a special help is given to fortify the sick man in such an hour so that his salvation may be assured. This special help is the sacrament of Extreme Unction, which consequently becomes the one ordinary means of salvation for dying sick people. Hence the reception of this sacrament is *per se* necessary *ad salutem.*

Kern draws a second argument from the teaching of the Council of Trent on this point. A man in danger of death is subjected to temptations fiercer in intensity than at any other time in life. Satan explores the totality of his fiendish ingenuity in an endeavor to snare the soul near the end of its journey. Against such frightful tortures of soul the sick man lies in urgent need of an especial aid. Knowing this full well, Christ instituted Extreme Unction with this very aid as its

---

1 Natalis Alexander, *Th. D. et M.*, lib. II, c. 5, reg. 20; cf. De Sainte-Beuve, *De Extr. Unct.*, disp. 7, a. 3, prop. 5 apud Migne, *Cursus Theol. Comp.*, vol. XXIV, col. 125.

2 apud De Sainte-Beuve, *l.c.*

3 *Tract. de Extr. Unct.*, pp. 364-72.

4 Sess. XIV, *De Ext. Unct.*, proem.

primary effect. Certainly, then, it was intended as the ordinary means of bridging the gulf between the valley of death and the gates of heaven. If so intended, it is *per se* necessary, *necessitate medii,* for salvation.

Moreover, Kern attacks the statement of Suarez that a man can protect himself sufficiently in this hour by prayer and by sacrifices.[5] He demands proof of this; and urges in retort that very questionable dispositions must surely be present in one who in such an hour refuses the aid explicitly designed by a loving God to conquer the perils of that very occasion. Instead of complying with the means proposed by St. James in verse 14 of the fifth chapter, he is employing the expedients recommended by the saint in the verse immediately preceding, which are intended for the other trials of life. When serious sickness occurs, the apostle speaks of a new and entirely distinct help—and there is no implied meaning of the text that the Lord would "save" and "raise up" the sick man if this especial means was not employed by the patient. If, as the Council of Trent said, the temptations and trials of that hour are extremely vehement, and if this sacrament was instituted expressly against them, how can the validity of Suarez's statement be admitted that neglect of Extreme Unction does not expose a man to serious sin? He requires extraordinary power, extraordinary strength in that hour. Of what avail are the usual means of buffeting temptation in an unusual situation like this? As Gregory the Great exclaimed: "Quid ergo facient tabulae, si tremunt columnae? Aut quomodo virgulta immobilia stabunt, si hujus pavoris turbine etiam cedri quatiuntur?"[6]

Finally Kern notes that there can be no argument against him drawn from the words of St. Thomas:[7] "Quamvis effectus principalis alicujus sacramenti possit haberi sine actuali perceptione hujus sacramenti vel sine sacramento vel per aliud sacramentum ex consequenti nunquam tamen haberi potest sine

5 Suarez, d. 44, s. 1, n. 4: "Potest aliis modis subvenire sibi per orationem et sacrificia, quia licet hoc sacramentum multum ad hoc conferat, non est tamen necessarium medium, nec ob illius carentiam exponit se homo morali ac proximo periculo peccandi mortaliter in alio genere, seu consentiendi alicui tentationi daemonis."

6 *Moral.*, 1. XXIV, c. 11—M. P. L., 76, 306.

7 *Suppl.*, q. 30, a. 1, ad 1.

proposito illius sacramenti." Surely, says Kern, there would not even be a "propositum sacramenti" present in a man who, given the opportunity, would neglect or refuse to receive the sacrament.

Few theologians go as far as Kern in their assertions. Albertus Magnus demands at least the "*votum sacramenti.*" "Quia non est sacramentum necessitatis," he writes,[8] "sufficienter periculo infirmorum provisum est in hoc quod ministri sunt parati; et si contingat ipsum, *dummodo sit desiderium sumendi,* sufficit coram Deo ad salutem, licet non ita forte cito plenae liberationis effectum consequatur infirmus."

By far the majority of theologians[9] insist that Extreme Unction is not the *unicum medium* of salvation for the sick, and is therefore not *per se necessary, necessitate medii.* They allow its eminent utility and its extensive effects, but they emphatically deny its indispensability. As Elbel-Bierbaum puts it, "Hoc sacramentum non tam est necessarium quam utile."[10]

This opinion was corroborated, to some extent at least, by a decision of the Inquisition[11] in 1656. Missionaries were allowed to omit some sacramentals in the Baptismal rite and the entire sacrament of Extreme Unction in the case of Chinese women. The distinction between the sacramentals of Baptism and the entire sacrament of Extreme Unction is worthy of note. Even

---

8 *Comm. in quart. lib. Sent.*, dist. 23, a. 3, ad 4.

9 Cf. Babenstuber, *Ethica Supernat.*, tr. VIII, pars VI, disp. VII, a. 1, n. 4; Salmanticenses, *Cursus Theol.*, tr. VII, cap. 4, punct. 2, n. 10; Tamburini, *Th. M.*, Lib. VI, *De Ext. Unct.*, cap. 2, paragr. 5, n. 7; Suarez, d. 44, s. 1, n. 4; Elbel-Bierbaum, *Th. M.*, vol. III, Conf. X, n. 220; Estius, *Comm. in lib. quart. Sent.*, dist. 23, paragr. 15; Pesch, *Prael. Dog.*, VII, 557.

10 *Th. M.*, III, Pars VIII, conf. X, n. 220.

11 S. C. S. Off., 23 Mar. 1656, ad 2—Coll. S. C. P. F., n. 126 (vol. I, page 38); "Secundo quaeritur: Utrum omnia sacramentalia in Baptismate foeminarum adultarum adhibenda sint. Quaeritur iterum: utrum sufficiat foeminis, petentibus tantum, Extremae Unctionis Sacramentum conferre. Quaeritur iterum: num etiam petentibus negandum cum incommoda et pericula christianitatis totius prudenter futura praevidentur. Ratio dubitandi est, incredibilis apud Sinas foeminarum modestia, zelus et laudabilis earum ab omni virorum, non solum congressu, sed et aspectu fuga; qua in re, nisi magna adhibeatur a missionariis cautela, scandalum ingens Sinis datur, totaque christianitas evidentissimo periculo posset exponi.

Sacra Congregatio, juxta ea quae superius proposita sunt censuit: Ex gravi necessitate proportionata posse omitti quaedam sacramentalia in Baptismate foeminarum, ac etiam posse omitti ipsum Sacramentum Extremae **Unctionis.**"

though urgent reasons required extraordinary measures, yet if Extreme Unction were necessary for salvation, the permission to disregard the bestowal of the sacrament entirely would be given only after all other expedients had been exhausted.

The new Code agrees with the opinion denying the necessity of Unction, and for practical purposes settles the question. The canon states categorically that this sacrament is not required *per se* for salvation. Extreme Unction presupposes the state of grace—a state sufficient of itself to obtain eternal life. "*Gratia autem Dei vita aeterna.*" [12]

There are however, some contingencies in which Extreme Unction is the only, and consequently the necessary, means of salvation. Such an occasion occurs when a sick man, attrite for a mortal sin, is unable to confess it.[13]

Heaven lies open to him only by the sacrament of the Unction. Through that portal he must enter, or must die. Such a status of soul is altogether accidental, however, for the primary end of Extreme Unction is not the forgiveness of sins. Hence it must be concluded that in such cases this sacrament is only *per accidens* necessary for eternal life.

This is corroborated by the discipline of the Decretals. In times of interdict Extreme Unction could be prohibited,[14] thus indicating that it was considered a sacrament of the living, and therefore not *per se* necessary. Otherwise the Church could not forbid it. When Penance could not be given, however, moralists and canonists taught that Extreme Unction could then be lawfully administered,[15] implying that Unction became *per accidens* necessary for salvation.

"Nemini tamen licet illud negligere."

Besides the "*necessitas medii*" there is also the "*necessitas praecepti,*" in virtue of which a thing is prescribed in such a fashion that a deliberate omission of it would result in sin. Evidently this necessity is not as strict as the former. Indeed non-

12 *Ad Rom.*, VI, 23.

13 Cf. Scavini, *Th. M.*, vol. III, n. 430; Blat, *Comm. Text.*, lib. III, p. I, n. 288.

14 c. 11, X, *de Paenitentiis*, V, 38: "Licet autem per generale interdictum denegetur omnibus tam unctio quam ecclesiastica sepultura."

15 Cf. e. g., Reiffenstuel, *Jus Canon. Univ.*, V, tit. 39, n. 203; Pesch, *Prael. Dog.*, VII, 557.

fulfillment of the precept is excused by any cause which ordinarily exempts from mortal sin, such as ignorance, moral impossibility, &c.[16] Accordingly, the next question to be considered is whether Extreme Unction is of necessity by precept, either divine or ecclesiastical.

The result of the first problem, viz., whether the reception of Extreme Unction has been divinely commanded, hinges to a great extent upon the force of the Jacobean text: "Inducat presbyteros Ecclesiae." Do these words implicitly contain a command, or should they be regarded as merely admonitory or exhortatory?

Some theologians construe the words of St. James as the promulgation of a strict precept. Cornelius a Lapide [17] says that "inducat" contains "non tantum consilium sed et praeceptum." Juenin,[18] Tournely [19] and Concina [20] render the very same exegesis of the scriptural text. Weinhart, in the article on "Extreme Unction" in the *Encyclopedie de la Theologie Catholique,* expressed the same view:

> La réception de ce sacrament n'est pas absolument nécessaire necessitate medii, on a même prétendu qu'il n'y a pas commandement à ce sujet, de sorte que ce ne serait, pas l'absence, mais le mépris de l'Extrême Onction qui serait coupable. Mais les paroles de S. Jacques suffisent por établir le précepte, et par consequent, la nécessité du sacrement."[21]

Conciliar legislation revealed the same frame of theological thought. The second Council of Châlons-sur-Saone[22] seems to imply a divine precept: "*Secundum beati Apostoli Jacobi documentum,* cui etiam documenta patrum consonant, infirmi oleo quod ab episcopis benedicitur, a presbyteris ungi debent." In similar fashion the Council of Cologne [23] legislated: "Est autem Unctio impendenda, cum expositione Unctionis et *mandati Apo-*

---

16 Cf. Tanquerey, *Th. D.*, III, 420; Cappello, *De Sac.*, I, 126.
17 *Comm. in Ep. S. Jac.*, V, 14.
18 *De Sac. in Gen. et in Specie,* dis. 7, q. 9, c. 2.
19 *Praelect. Dog.*, tom. II, q. ult. a. 2.
20 *Theol. Christiana,* vol. X, l. 1, *de Ext. Unct.,* c. IV, n. 7-8.
21 Tom. 16, p. 363.
22 Anno 813—can. 48, apud Harduin IV, 1040.
23 Anno 1536,—part. VII, cap. L, apud Harduin, IX, 2011.

stolici, quod sic habet: 'Infirmatur aliquis in vobis? Inducat presbyteros Ecclesiae; &c."

Thus too spoke the second Council of Baltimore:

> "Quum igitur Christus Dominus per Apostolum loquens *praecepto* urgeat quumque tam salutares effectus ex hoc Sacramento profluant, curent omni, quo par est, studio animarum Pastores, ut ex populo sibi commisso *unusquisque, qui ad id tenetur,* salutari hoc praesidio munitus de vita decedat."[24]

The provincial Council of Colocza also made mention of this as an obligation:

> "Agant proinde pastores animarum, ut fidelium aegre discumbentium rationem habeant, quos, si expedierit, suscipiendi hujus sacramenti *obligationis* paterne admoneant."[25]

The Council of Trent would naturally furnish the most formidable argument in this connection:

> "Quare nulla ratione audiendi sunt, qui contra tam apertam et dilucidam apostoli Jacobi sententiam docent, hanc unctionem vel figmentum esse humanum, vel ritum a patribus acceptum, *nec mandatum Dei,* nec promissionem gratiae habentem."[26]

On the other hand there are many weighty theologians who hold that there is not a divine precept of reception.[27] They base their argument on the interpretation of the words of St. James and upon the statement of Innocent III in the Decretals,[28] that its administration could be forbidden to all in time of interdict. This latter argument, though advanced with great stress by Suarez, Pesch, Pierrot and others, seems to prove nothing. In the early days of the Church the Viaticum was sometimes forbidden to penitents even in danger of death, though at such a time there is a divine precept to receive it.[29] If the

---

24 Anno 1866, tit. V, cap. 7, n. 306—Coll. Lac., t. III, col. 480.

25 Anno 1863: Tit. III, cap. X—Coll. Lac., t. V, col. 655.

26 Sess. XIV, *De Ext. Unct.,* cap. 3.

27 St. Thomas, *Comm. in lib. quart. Sent.,* dist. 23, q. 1, a. 1, sol. 3 ad 1; Suarez, d. 44, s. 1, a. 2; St. Alphonsus, *Th. M.,* VI, 733; De Sainte-Beuve, disp. VII, *De Ext. Unct.,* art. 3—apud Migne, *Curs. Theol. Comp.,* XXIV, col. 124; Pesch, *Prael. Dog.,* VII, 557; Berardi, *Prax. Conf.,* II, n. 5008; Pierrot, *Theologie Morale,* col. 1073-4; &c.

28 c. 11, X, *de Paenitentiis,* V, 38.

29 Ep. 6 Innocentii I, *ad Exuperium,* n. 6—M. P. L., 20, 501 A.

Church can consider that the *bonum publicum* is so bettered and benefited at such a time as to interpret the divine precept which was made for private good of the individual, certainly the argument can be extended *a pari* to the case of Extreme Unction.

The better argument is the former, viz., that the Jacobean text contains a counsel rather than a precept. The tense employed in verse 14 of the fifth chapter is exactly the same as that employed in verse 13, which reads: "Tristatur aliquis vestrum? oret. Aequo animo est? Psallat." Without interruption the sacred text continues: "Infirmatur quis in vobis? Inducat presbyteros Ecclesiae." It is evident, then, that if it is maintained that the text imposes an obligation upon the sick to summon the priests, it must be held with equal insistence that the "joyful in mind" must sing songs. Thus Bord writes: "Mais l'écrivain inspiré n'intime certainement pas aux fidèles, qui sont dans l'allégresse, l'ordre strict d'entonner des chants pieux. Il est à croire que semblablement il ne veut pas imposer à ceux que la maladie afflige l'obligation rigoureuse de recevoir les onctions purificatrices des presbytres."[30]

The argument from the wording of the Council of Trent, which at first sight seems so formidable, loses much of its vigor when compared with the phraseology of Canon IV of the section "de Extrema Unctione" (Sess. XIV): "Si quis dixerit, presbyteros Ecclesiae, quod beatus Jacobus adducendos esse ad infirmum inungendum *hortatur,* non esse sacerdotes, &c., anathema sit." Moreover "mandatum" of the other passage is interpreted, not as inducing a strict obligation, but rather as a recommendation (*"commendatum"*).[31]

As a consequence the more common, and likewise the more probable opinion is that there is no divine precept ordering the reception of Extreme Unction in danger of death.

Is this sacrament prescribed, then, by ecclesiastical precept? There is certainly no express ecclesiastical precept now in force except that contained in this canon of the Code. But has not the constant, consistent, continual and universal custom among the faithful of receiving this sacrament come to receive the force of a law? Such an argument appealed very strongly

30 *L'Extrême Onction,* p. 59.

31 Cf. Petrus Dens, *Theol. Mech., "De Ext. Unct.,"* N. 10, p. 55.

to Concina.[32] The solicitude of the Church that the faithful should always be furnished this sacrament, together with the persuasion of the faithful that they are bound to receive it, was enough to convince Roncaglia[33] and Juenin[34] of the existence of a precept.

On the other hand these arguments do not influence many theologians of great weight. These men cannot persuade themselves that the custom of the faithful or the solicitude of the Church is enough to create a strict law in this matter.[35] Moreover, the cautious terminology always used in official documents upon this matter indicates the lack of certainty on the subject. Innocent I, writing his famous letter to Decentius, used this terminology: "Omnibus Christianis uti *licet.*"[36] The Council of Trent[37] anathematized those who declared that the sacrament could be *contemned* without sin—but said nothing about those

---

32 *Theol. Christ.*, tom. X, lib. I de E. U., diss. I, c. IV, n. 8: "Quid? Ecclesia catholica sacramenta habet otiosa, indifferentia, in cassum instituta? Utique non adest praeceptum expressum et peculiare ab Ecclesia latum, jubens hanc sacramenti susceptionem; sed consuetudo perpetua, constans et universalis fidelium suscipiendi hoc sacramentum vim legis obtinet. Quorum tot Ecclesiae studia in afferendo adversus Novatores hoc sacramento, si nulla urgeret necessitas, nullumque praeceptum ejusdem usus?"

33 *Univ. Theol. Mor.*, "*De Ext. Unct.*," p. 122, q. 7.

34 *De Sac. in Gen. et in Spec.*, dis. 7, q. 9, cap. 2.

35 Cf. e. g., Suarez (disp. 44, s. 1, n. 2): "Nec tale praeceptum sufficienti aliqua traditione aut consuetudine introductum est, cujus argumentum est, quod theologi non agnoscunt."

De Sainte-Beuve (*De Ext. Unct.*, d. 7, a. 3 apud Migne, *Curs. Theol. Comp.*, vol. XXIV, col. 125): "Nullo praecepto ecclesiastico singuli fidelès adulti tenentur suscipere in exitu Unctionem infirmorum . . . . Nulla lex eccelsiastica hujusmodi proferri potest. Neque etiam id evincitur ex praxi Ecclesiae, tum quia ostendi non potest ea semper fuisse praxis Ecclesiae; tum quia etiamsi praxis ea fuerit, posset dici praxis fuisse orta ex consideratione utilitatis atque exhortationis Apostoli, non ex obligatione; quod requiritur ut praxis inducat praeceptum." Cf. also Ballerini-Palmieri, (*Op. Theol. Mor.*, vol. V, tr. X, sect. 6, n. 59); AErtnys (*Th. M.*, II, 369); D'Annibale (*Summ. Th. M.*, III, 419); Noldin (*De Sac.*, 446); Lehmkuhl (*Th. M.*, II, 726, footnote). St. Alphonsus (*Th. M.*, VI, 733), though holding that the obligation to receive it is grave, rejects the argument that the source of this obligation lies in an ecclesiastical precept.

36 Ep. "*Si instituta ecclesiastica,*" 19 Mar. 416, cap. 8—C. I. C. Fontes, n. 19.

37 Sess. XIV, *De Ext Unct.*, can. 3.

who said it might be *omitted* without sin. Benedict XIV[38] warned bishops not to legislate in such terminology as would imply an absolute necessity of receiving the sacrament.

Rome has shown good example. In the investigation of faith proposed for those suspected of being Wicliffites and Hussites, the query asked was: "Utrum credat quod Christianus *contemnens* susceptionem sacramentorum Confirmationis vel *Extremae Unctionis* aut solemnizationis Matrimonii peccet mortaliter."[39] As noted before, there is a great difference between "contemnens" and "omittens" or "negligens." This was recognized by Martin V when he wrote: "Hoc sacramentum [i. e., Extrema Unctio] neque negligi sine *culpa,* neque contemni posse sine *peccato mortali.*"[40]

In the Ritual, too, the same official viewpoint is manifested. The pastor is urged to see to it that the sacraments be received in due time—but there is not a word of explicit obligation on the part of the recipient.[41] Similarly in drawing up the present law, the legislator seems especially unwilling to decide the question. A controversy had long been raging in regard to the duty of receiving Confirmation and Extreme Unction. In treating of this, the Code uses the identical phrase for both sacraments: "Non licet illud negligere." Consequently theologians feel that the legislator wished to make no great change in this matter.[42]

Practically, then, the only obligation arising *ex jure ecclesiastico* has its source in the words of the present canon. Though not in absolute need of Extreme Unction, the Code states, a man is not allowed to neglect it, i. e., voluntarily and without sufficient reason to omit its reception. The obligation contained

---

38 *De Syn. Dioc.,* l. 8, c. 7, n. 4: "Quum tamen celerem commendat hujus sacramenti administrationem, abstineat a verbis quae videantur significare ejusdem recipiendi absolutam necessitatem: ne secus videatur ipse quaestionem dirimere hactenus indecisam."

39 Const. "*Inter Cunctas*" (in Conc. Constantien.), 22 Feb. 1418 ("*Tenor interrog. juxta quae haeretici, aut de haeresi suspecti interrogari debet*"—n. 19)—C. I. C. Fontes, n. 43.

40 Cf. S. Alph., VI, 733.

41 Tit. V, c. 4, n. 10. In the first rubric of chapter I of this title the words of the Code are repeated. Their force will be the same as those of the canon, and consequently what will be said of the canon will equally apply to the rubric.

42 Cf. Noldin, *De Sac.,* 446; Ferreres, *Comp. Th. M.,* II, 847; Woywod, *A Practical Commentary,* I, n. 867.

therein is surely not serious, for the phraseology is too mild.[43] Genicot's observation seems especially pertinent: "Si daretur gravis obligatio, Ecclesia eam jam saepius scripta lege proposuisset."[44]

It remains then to be seen whether or not there is an obligation arising from some other source than divine or ecclesiastical law. Negligence of this sacrament always horrified and saddened pious minds. Impressed by what seemed a spiritual prodigality, they investigated how seriously the virtue of charity *erga se* was binding upon a sick man in this regard. Another controversy arose, more vehement in its intensity, and effecting a greater division in the ranks of theologians than any other dispute on this point.

St. Alphonsus,[45] though generously admitting the probability of the opposite opinion, was impressed by this argument founded upon the obligation of loving one's self. It is possible, the saint said, for a man oppressed with sickness to strengthen himself against the temptations of that time by means other than Extreme Unction. Yet it is none the less true that the weakened powers of the body make co-operation with grace very much more difficult at that time. As the physical forces are ebbing, the temptations increase in frequency and intensity, causing a ceaseless disturbance of the tranquility of soul so beneficial to a dying man. "Nullum tamen tempus est," says the Council of Trent,[46] "quo vehementius ille omnes suae versutiae nervos intendat ad perdendos nos penitus, et a fiducia etiam, si possit divinae misericordiae deturbandos, quam cum impendere nobis exitum vitae prospicit." What the sick man needs is something to give him grace "ex opere *operato;*" to obtain it "ex opere *operantis*" is becoming more difficult every minute. Now Extreme Unction has been instituted for this specific purpose; against the peculiar temptations of that hour, this sacrament is man's most potent protection. Surely the neglect of this heaven-given safeguard seems to entail a serious

---

43 Cf. Noldin, *De Sac.*, 446; Vermeersch-Creusen, *Epit.*, II, 228; Augustine, *A Commentary*, IV, p. 405; Genicot-Salsmans, *Inst. Th. M.*, II, 424; Sabetti-Barrett, *Th. M.*, p. 806.

44 *L.c.*

45 *Th. M.*, VI, 733.

46 Sess. XIV, *de Ext. Unct.*, proem.

imperilment of eternal salvation—and consequently a serious breach of charity toward one's self.

This argument of St. Alphonsus appealed very strongly to Petrus Dens [47] and to De Augustinis.[48] Perin [49] argues from a similitude. Just as a person gravely sick sins seriously in refusing medicine greatly helpful to his recovery, in similar fashion —or, as Perin puts it, *a fortiori*,—negligence to receive this sacrament, instituted by Christ *per modum medicinae spiritualis pro salute animae et corporis*, is likewise gravely sinful. Roncaglia [50] used this obligation of charity as one of the reasons for his opinion that there was a serious obligation on the sick man to obtain for himself this sacrament.

On the contrary, the gravity of the obligation from charity is rejected by many other theologians. This sacrament, they say, is an aid, not a necessity. It is the best means in the situation, but not the only means. Charity toward one's self does not obligate one *sub mortali* to take the *better* means. At most then, there is but a venial obligation on the subject from this virtue.

Suarez expresses this opinion thus:

> "Et quamvis videatur quaedam prodigalitas spiritualis, sine cogente causa perdere tantum spiritualem fructum, tamen intrinsece ac per se non est peccatum mortale, quia sine illo fructu potest diligi Deus super omnia et salus aeterna obtineri. Neque etiam ex parte periculi, cui homo se exponit, in articulo mortis omittendo tale remedium contra insidias inimici, est per se peccatum mortale, quia potest aliis modis subveniri sibi per orationem et sacrificia, quia licet hoc sacramentum multum ad hoc conferat, non est tamen necessarium medium, nec ob illius carentiam exponit se homo morali et proximo periculo peccandi mortaliter in alio genere, seu consentiendi alicui tentationi daemonis."[51]

A host of authors accept this opinion and teach that there is *per se* no grave obligation in charity to partake of this sacrament. Some deordination is present, nevertheless, when a man, against the dictates of sound reason, neglects to avail himself of

47 *Theol. Mech.*, "*De Ext. Unct.*," p. 56.
48 *De Re Sacramentaria*, II, p. 407-8.
49 *De Ext. Unct.*, art. 2, q. 5.
50 *Univ. Theol. Mor.*, "*De Ext. Unct.*," p. 122, q. 7.
51 D. 44, sec. 1, n. 4.

this super-powerful safeguard, instituted for his help in the very crisis thru which he is passing. But this obligation is not serious enough to convict those neglecting it of mortal sin.

Thus it is seen that the obligation of receiving Extreme Unction is a highly disputed question. Two camps of theological thought continue to hold their ground today with as much vehemence as ever. An idea of the solid external probability both opinions have can be gained from this enumeration of the chief proponents of each. Without any respect to the reasons which they urge, the best known champions of the view which place a grave obligation on the subjects are: Peter Lombard,[52] Scotus,[53] St. Bonaventure,[54] Juenin,[55] Cornelius à Lapide,[56] Tournely,[57] Roncaglia,[58] Antoine,[59] Drouven,[60] Petrus Dens,[61] Perin,[62] Concina,[63] St. Alphonsus,[64] Scavini,[65] De Augustinis,[66] Kern[67] and Ferreres.[68] On the opposite side the principal proponents of the teaching that the obligation is but venial, are as follows: Cabbasutius,[69] St. Thomas Aquinas,[70] Henriquez,[71] Coninck,[72] Diana,[73] Salmanticenses,[74] Estius,[75] Billuart,[76]

52 *Libri IV Sententiarum*, lib. quart., dist. 23, c. 3—M. P. L., 192, 900.
53 *Comm. in lib. quart. Sent.*, disp. 7, qu. 2.
54 *Comm. in lib. quart. Sent.*, dist. XXIII, dub. IV, in fine; cf. dist. XII, p. I, a. 2, q. 1.
55 *De Sac. in Gen. et in Spec.*, dis. 7, q. 9, c. 2.
56 *Comm. in Ep. S. Jacobi*, V, 14.
57 *Prael. Dog., De Ext. Unct., quaest. ult.*, a. 2.
58 *Univ. Theol. Mor.*, De Ext. Unct., q. 7.
59 *Th. M.*, t. V, *Tract. de Ext. Unct.*, qu. 7.
60 *De Re Sacramentaria*, lib. VII, Qu. 5, cap. 2.
61 *Theol. Mech.*, "*De Ext. Unct.*," pp. 55-6.
62 *De Ext. Unct.*, art. 2, q. 5.
63 *Theol. Christ.*, tom. X, dis. I, De E. U., c. 4, n. 7-8.
64 *Th. M.*, VI, 733.
65 *Th. M.*, t. III, n. 430.
66 *De Re Sacramentaria*, II, pp. 408-9.
67 *Tract. de Ext. Unct.*, p. 369.
68 *Comp. Th. M.*, II, 847.
69 *Jur. Can. Theor. et Prax.*, l. 3, c. 15, n. 8.
70 *Comm. in lib. quart. Sent.*, dist. 23, q. 1, a. 1, quaestiunc. 3 ad 1; *Suppl.* q. 29, a. 3, ad 1.
71 *De Sac.*, lib. 3, c. 10, n. 3.
72 *De Sac. et Censuris*, disp. de E. U., dub. 10.
73 *Opera Coordinata*, tom. 2, tr. IV, res. 25.
74 *Cursus Theol.*, Tr. VII, cap. IV, punct. 2.
75 *Comm. in quart. lib. Sent.*, d. 23, paragr. 15.
76 *Tract. De Ext. Unct.*, diss. unica, art. 7.

Sporer,[77] Babenstuber,[78] Tamburini,[79] Laymann,[80] De Sainte-Beuve,[81] Suarez,[82] Pesch,[83] Noldin,[84] Vermeersch-Creusen,[85] Kenrick,[86] Genicot-Salsmans,[87] Tanquerey,[88] Augustine,[89] D'Annibale,[90] Sabetti-Barrett,[91] Lehmkuhl,[92] Konings,[93] Ærtnys,[94] Berardi,[95] Sebastiani,[96] Matharan-Castillon[97] and Ballerini-Palmieri.[98]

From a glance at the mighty names aligned upon either side of the question, it can be seen that adherence to either side is entirely justifiable. Practically, however, the reception of Extreme Unction cannot be urged as a serious obligation. Two venial sins can rightly be laid at the feet of those who neglect it, one of disobedience against the precept of this canon and the other of a lack of charity toward one's self.

While this great divergence of opinion exists about the simple negligence of the sacrament, there is no such division of thought in regard to the gravity of the obligation when there is danger of contempt or scandal connected with the negligence. The Council of Trent has decided the gravity of such a sin: "Neque vero tanti sacramenti contemptus absque ingenti scelere, et ipsius Spiritus Sancti injuria esse posset."[99] Prior to that

---

77 *De Sac. in Genere*, n. 24.
78 *Ethica Supernat.*, tr. 8, disp. 7, art. 1, n. 4.
79 *Th. M.*, Lib. VI, *de Ext. Unct.*, cap. II, paragr. 5, n. 7.
80 *Th. M.*, *Tr. de Ext. Unct.*, cap. 7, n. 1.
81 *De Ext. Unct.*, disp. 7, a. 3 apud Migne, *Curs. Theol. Mor.*, vol. XXIV, col. 124-5.
82 D. 44, s. 1, n. 2.
83 *Prael. Dog.*, VII, 557.
84 *De Sac.*, 446.
85 *Epit.*, II, 228.
86 *Th. M.*, III, "*De Ext. Unct.*," cap. unic., n. 22.
87 *Inst. Th. M.*, II, 424.
88 *Th. D.*, III, 785-7.
89 *A Commentary*, IV, p. 405.
90 *Summ. Th. M.*, III, 419.
91 *Th. M.*, p. 806.
92 *Th. M.*, II, 726.
93 *Th. M.*, n. 1508.
94 *Th. M.*, II, 369.
95 *Prax. Conf.*, II, n. 5008.
96 *Summ. Th. M.*, n. 512.
97 *Asserta Moralia*, n. 521.
98 *Op. Theol. Mor.*, tom. V, tr. X, sect. VI, n. 59.
99 Sess. XIV, *De Ext. Unct.*, cap. 3.

time it was officially insinuated that such was the case, when the Wicliffites and Hussites were to be asked: "Utrum credat quod Christianus contemnens susceptionem Extremae Unctionis ...peccet mortaliter."[100] Local Councils forbade ecclesiastical burial to those who held Extreme Unction in contempt.[101]

It is quite necessary that real contempt be distinguished from negligence or laziness. Pesch[102] says that it consists in a refusal of the sacrament because it is considered something vile or useless. It is distinguished from negligence by the reason which motivates its non-reception. Even if the negligence proceeds from human respect or from fear, it cannot be said to be contemptuous.[103] Similarly, repugnance to reception, which is ascribable to an erroneous belief that it is an unerring harbinger of death or that recovery will entail the loss of marriage rights, etc., is not contempt of the sacrament[104] The fear that it will hasten death, it must be noted, is objectively a mortal sin against faith.[105] On the other hand, to shrink from the sacrament because of the false impression that the use of marriage and other things will be forbidden upon recovery cannot be said to be seriously wrong. Such an error is not violently pernicious, nor irreverent, nor contrary to true faith in the sacrament.

There will also be a grave obligation on the part of the subject to receive Extreme Unction when negligence or refusal would cause great scandal to others. Such an instance would be the case of a bishop or a pastor who does not receive this sacrament, although there is ample opportunity to do so.[106] Scandal would likewise be given if such a refusal would lead bystanders to think that the subject had become a heretic,[107] or

100 Martinus V (in conc. Constantien.) const. "*Inter Cunctas,*" 22 Feb. 1418, § 14, art. 19, de quo errorum Wicleff et Husz suspecti interrogandi—C. I. C. Fontes, n. 43.

101 Cf. Council of Cologne (sub Adolpho)—apud Harduin IX, 2110; and the synods of Langres, Troyes and Paris—apud Natalis Alexander, *Th. D. et M.*, lib. 2, c. 5, r. 20.

102 *Prael. Dog.*, VII, 557.

103 Suarez, d. 44, s. 1, n. 6; Genicot-Salsmans, *Inst. Th. M.*, II, 424.

104 Elbel-Bierbaum, *Th. M.*, III, pars VIII, Conf. X, n. 227; Billot, *De Eccl. Sac.*, thesis xxv, p. 239; Gury-Ferreres, *Casus Consc.*, II, 810.

105 Elbel-Bierbaum, *l.c.;* Gury-Ferreres, *l.c.*

106 Genicot, *Casus Consc.*, cas. 891; Elbel-Bierbaum, *Th. M.*, III, Pars VIII, Conf. X, n. 221.

107 St. Alph., *Th. M.*, VI, 733.

that the sacrament was of little account or altogether worthless.[108]

It may be asked why actions such as these are *grievously* scandalous. Rarely will they induce others not to receive Extreme Unction; but even granting that they did, it would revolve about a matter only of venial obligation. How can the scandal be said to be mortal which results in the transgression of a light obligation by those scandalized? The answer is given by Suarez:

> "Ex eo solo capite non esset proprium et rigorosum scandalum. Posset tamen eam rationem habere, si eo exemplo inducerentur fideles vel ad parvipendendum hoc sacramentum, vel ad negligenda generaliter remedia suae salutis, vel ad judicandum temere et cum publica detractione de salute spirituali talis personae, vel alia similia, quae respectu communitatis non sunt sine gravi periculo multorum peccatorum mortalium, vel certe non sine gravi detrimento spirituali ejusdem communitatis, quod interdum potest sufficere ut scandalum sit grave peccatum."[109]

"Et omni studio et diligentia curandum ut infirmi, dum sui plene compotes sunt, illud recipiant.

Solicitous as she has always been, the Church not only recommends, but commands, that the sacraments be given to the sick at a time sufficiently seasonable to allow the effects of the sacrament to be exercised to their fullest extent. Naturally enough, therefore, she has inserted in her code of law an injunction that diligence and zeal be used in conferring Extreme Unction at the time most beneficial to the recipient. Such a time will be, of course, when the subject is in full possession of his senses, because his will can then co-operate to the greatest extent with the actions of grace resulting from the reception of the sacrament. The capabilities of corporal cure, resident in the sacrament, can also have their fullest freedom, so that, if God wills it, the cure can be effected with ease by the overflow of the grace of the sacrament from the soul upon the body.

---

108 Petrus Dens, *Th. Mech.*, "*De Extr. Unct.*," p. 56; AErtnys, *Th. M.*, II, 369.

109 D. 44, s. 1, n. 5.

Since the time of the Council of Trent, the Church has insisted in general legislation and thru particular councils that care and diligence be taken to insure an opportune administration of Extreme Unction. The Catechism of the Council [110] states that it is a very serious sin to defer the anointing until all hope of recovery is gone and the sick person is sinking into insensibility. The very first rubric in the Ritual (Tit. "De Extrema Unctione") orders the employment of diligence in administering this sacrament to the sick and urges that the anointing be done while the patient is in the possession of his senses.

In the first Council of Milan, St. Charles Borromeo decreed that the Unction be given to the sick man "dum integris est sensibus."[111] He repeated this legislation in the fifth Council of Milan [112] and included it in his "Instructiones" upon the Sacrament of Extreme Unction.[113] Similar enactments were made by the Councils of Bourges,[114] Bordeaux,[115] and Rheims.[116] Benedict XIV [117] asked bishops to commend such a timely administration in their synodal legislation.

There have been two very recent papal pronouncements on this point. On May 31, 1921, Pope Benedict XV wrote in an apostolic letter entitled *"Sodalitatem:"*

> "Qui in discrimine ultimo versantur, sacri viatici et Extremae Unctionis susceptionem ne eo usque remorentur cum sensum amissuri jam sunt, sed contra, quemadmodum Ecclesia docet et praecipit, iis roborentur sacramentis vixdum, ingravescente morbo, prudens fiat de periculo mortis judicium."[118]

---

110 *De Ext. Unct.*, n. 9 & 14.

111 *Acta Eccl. Mediol.*, pars I, tom. I, p. 18.

112 *Op. cit.*, p. 250.

113 *Op. cit.*, pars IV, tom. I, p. 603.

114 anno 1584—apud Harduin X, 1489: "Administretur tempestive a sacerdote Extrema Unctio, ita ut Christianus mente adhuc integra Sacramenti efficaciam agnoscere possit."

115 anno 1583—apud Harduin X, 1347: "Non eo usque differendum est dum aeger omnibus paene sensibus destitutus sit."

116 anno 1583—apud Harduin X, 1288: "Parochus . . . . caveat ne vel mors Unctionem praeveniat, vel morbo invalescente semimortuus non sentiat."

117 *De Syn. Dioc.*, l. 8, c. 7, n. 4.

118 A. A. S., XIII, 342.

More recent still is the brief of Pius XI, "*Explorata res est,*" dated February 2, 1923:

> "In hoc autem potissimum, cum sodalium, tum praecipue zelatorum studiosam voluntatem desideramus advocatam, ut exitialem quoquo pacto profligent errorem, ex quo fit ut cum animae detrimento sancto oleo ante liniantur infirmi, quam morte imminente, sensus paene vel omnino amiserunt. Neque enim, ut sacramentum valide liciteque detur, necesse est ut mors proxime secutura timeatur, sed satis est ut prudens seu probabile adsit de periculo judicium; quodsi in ea rerum condicione conferri debet, in hac conferri utique potest, et qui illud curet ministrandum, is Ecclesiae Matris non modo doctrinam sequitur, sed optata pie ac salubriter perficit."[119]

This canon does not lay an obligation in this regard on any particular person by explicit mention. The general term "curandum" includes all who are bound in justice and charity. Hence the pastor, the relatives, the physician, the nurse, and any others connected with the patient by a special title fall within the scope of this obligation.

A. The duty of the pastor.

It has already been seen that the pastor is bound to the actual administration of Extreme Unction by Canon 939. The present prescription binds him to more than a mere administration. With all zeal and diligence ("*omni studio et diligentia*") he is to see that the sick shall receive this sacrament during consciousness.

The phrase "*omni studio et diligentia*" is far-reaching in its meaning. He is to leave nothing undone that will promote the timely administration of the sacraments to the sick.

For this purpose he will lay a remote as well as a proximate foundation. He will pave the way by urging his people from the pulpit and on other occasions to summon him as soon as possible, without any regard to the time of day or the amount of inconvenience it may cause him.[120] In his sermons he will try to uproot from the popular consciousness the idea that the reception of the Unction presages the fatal outcome of the illness. He will lay especial stress on the powers of corporal sana-

---

119 A. A. S., XV, 105.

120 *Rit. Rom.*, Tit. I, *De Administr. Sac. in Genere,* cap. unic., n. 5.

tion vested in the sacrament, and appeal to their self-interest to allow these capabilities an opportunity to act.[121]

He will use every expedient to find who are sick in his parish. To this end he will induce the physicians of the locality to notify him if his parishioners are among the patients who are gravely ill.[122] He will beg his parishioners to tell him of those who are afflicted with a fatal disease. He will stand on no ceremony in connection with the reception of this information, but will immediately use it by calling without delay upon the sick person.[123] He will keep a careful watch over the condition of the patient, and at the first true sign of danger of death, he will administer Extreme Unction.[124]

Very frequently it will become the pastor's duty to reveal to the sick man his perilous condition. Too often the patient is deceived by the blandishments of his kindred, the promises of his physicians and the astuteness of the devil. When the priest perceives such to be the case, he has no alternative than to break the news. The rubric of the Ritual just quoted requires this. Baruffaldo, in his Commentary on this rubric, notes: "Ut plurimum qui graviter et cum periculo mortis laborant, periculum proprium ignorant, seque dicunt bene sentire: quod ma-

---

121 Cf. III Synod of Rochester (1914), n. 340: "Cum saepe contingat, apud fideles nostrorum temporum, quod Extremam Unctionem considerant quasi nuntium mortis instanter impendentis et nullo modo velut medium illius praecavendae, studeant parochi, in suis ad populum sermonibus, hujusmodi terrorem mitigare, et ad maturam hujus sacramenti receptionem fideles adhortari, eos docendo non solum de ejusdem spirituali utilitate sed etiam, licet secundo loco, de auxilio, quod praestat, ad sanitatem corporis recuperandam." (*Acta Syn. Roffensis Tertiae,* p. 78.)

Also Synod of Kansas City, Mo., (1912), n. 124: "Studeant igitur animarum curatores repellere insulsissimam opinionem, ne superstitionem dicamus, inter non paucos vigentem, quod receptio illius sacramenti sit mortis impendentis indicium." (*Decreta Syn. Dioc. Kansanop.* II, p. 52.)

In the nineteenth century this had been prescribed by the Provincial Council of Aix, held in 1850: c. 6—"Curent etiam crebris admonitionibus imperitum vulgus ab illa inani et impia opinione abducere, qua plerique de virtute hujusce sacramenti inepta sentiunt, perinde ac si mortem aegris acceleret." (*Coll. Lac.,* t. IV, col. 992-3.)

122 Cf. Micheletti, *De Pastore Animarum,* n. 410.

123 *Rit. Rom.,* Tit. V, c. 4, n. 1. Cf. Council of Rheims (1583), apud Harduin X, 1288; Council of Bois-le-duc, apud Van Espen, *Jus Eccles. Univ.,* Pars II, sec. I, tit. VIII, cap. 3, n. 13; also II, Plenary Council of Baltimore, n. 306.

124 *Rit. Rom.,* Tit. V, c. 4, n. 10.

xima fallacia est. Hinc originem habet illa tarditas in recipiendis Sacramentis, adeo ut sint haec postea ministranda festinanter, imo praecipitanter, et quandoque dum infirmus non tota mente sanus et integer est. Quapropter parocho incumbit (si nullus adsit qui hoc officum praestare velit) veritatem infirmo revelare, et statum periculosum aperire, ut sedulo cogitet ea, quae pro salute animae necessaria sunt. Scio equidem odiosum esse hoc officium, sed praestat ut tale sit." [125]

It is needless to say that this information must be given the patient in a very prudent and diplomatic fashion. The pastor should not pattern himself after Isaias boldly telling Ezechias, the king: "Haec dicit Dominus Deus, 'Praecipe domui tuae, morieris enim tu et non vives.' " [126] gradually and gently it should be impressed upon the mind of the patient that he is in such a state of sickness as to warrant the administration of the last sacraments. Pastoral prudence will determine very often how this should be said. Petrus Dens goes to some lengths in laying down a very commendable mode of procedure:

> "Ita vero procedant necesse est, ut infirmus inde non gravetur, sed e contra solatium et fiduciam concipiat: quapropter ad eum accedentes quandoque a longe incipere debent, inquirendo de statu et causa morbi; deinde paulatim progrediendum est dicendo morbos acque ac sanitatem ex Dei providentia nobis obvenire; imo qui hodie sani sumus cras infirmos esse posse; sanos igitur aeque ac aegrotos semper ad mortem paratos esse debere; felices esse qui per morbum praemonentur, ideoque morbos merito misericordias Domini vocari; nihil porro plus conducere ad morbos patienter tolerandos, imo superandos, quam recursum ad Deum et ad Ecclesiae Sacramenta; Extremam quidem Unctionem id speciale habere quod sanitatem restituat si infirmo utile fuerit, ideoque consultum esse ut eam suscipere non differat."[127]

The pastor's duty is far from finished, if he admonishes the sick man of his danger, only to find him reluctant to receive the sacrament. The Ritual itself gives the mode of procedure: "Tunc non omnino desperanda res est, sed quamdiu ille vivit, repetendae sunt frequentes variae et efficaces Sacerdotum et alio-

---

125 *Ad. Rit. Rom. Comm.*, tom. I, tit. xxx, n. 31.

126 IV Regum, XX, 1; Cf. Benedict XIV, *Institutiones*, xxii, n. 9 sqq., for arguments of Galen and Augenius as to what should be done.

127 *Theol. Mech.*, "*De Ext. Unct.*," p. 56-7.

rum piorum hominum exhortationes; proponendaque aeternae salutis damna, et sempiternae mortis supplicia; ostendendaque immensa Dei misericordia, eum ad poenitentiam provocantis, ad ignoscendum paratissimi."[128]

Lehmkuhl[129] thinks that it is seriously incumbent upon the pastor to endeavor to induce a reluctant patient to receive the sacrament. Apostolic zeal is not easily rebuffed; and serious obligations are not relieved by a mere refusal to allow them to be discharged. Repugnance or reluctance often springs from error; and in reality there is frequently no intention of rejecting the sacraments finally and absolutely. A steady bombardment of gentle exhortation should be trained against these barriers of superstition and prejudice, not only by the priest but by others of pious character. Little by little the patient has to be disengaged of the inane notion that Extreme Unction is an augury of death. For this purpose the possibility of corporal cure from the sacrament should be greatly emphasized.[130] The Council of Pavia, held in 850, urged the pastor to invite the neighboring priests to come to his assistance in his difficulty.[131] Recourse to prayer, both public and private, is also advised by the Ritual,[132] but the reputation of the sick man must be sedulously guarded if the prayer is publicly made when his refusal is occult. Hence the petition must be couched in extremely general terms in such a case, as e. g., prayers for an urgent special intention, &c.

If the man is given scandal by his refusal, special efforts should be spent in an endeavor to win him to conversion.[133] In

128 *Rit. Rom.*, Tit. V, c. 4, n. 11.

129 *Th. M.*, II, 727—*Casus Consc.*, II, 677.

130 Cf. Council of Langres, anno 1404: "Dicendum est eis [i. e., qui differunt hujus sacramenti receptionem] quod non debent dubitare quod per receptionem hujus sacramenti veniat mors, verum potius veniet utraque sanitas mentis et corporis, si devote et digne recipiant." (apud De Sainte-Beuve, *De Extr. Unct.*, disp. VII, art. 2—Migne, *Curs. Theol. Comp.*, vol. XXIV, col. 121-2.)

131 Capitulum 8: "Sed quia frequenter contingit, ut aegrotus aliquis aut sacramenti vim nesciat, aut minus periculosam reputans infirmitatem salutem suam operari dissimulet, aut certe morbi violentia obliviscatur: debet eum loci presbyter congruenter admonere, quatenus ad hanc spiritualem curam secundum propriae possibilitatis vires vicinos quoque presbyteros invitet." (Harduin V, 27.)

132 *Rit. Rom.*, tit. V, c. 4, n. 11.

133 Lehmkuhl, *Th. M.*, II, 727—*Casus Consc.*, II, 667.

such a case he is bound *sub gravi* to receive the sacrament; and even if he be in good faith or in invincible ignorance, he should be warned of his obligation to permit the unction.

Sometimes, however, it will be necessary for the priest to admit the unsuccessfulness of his best efforts. Despite earnest warnings, the sick man will conjure himself into the frame of mind that he is not in danger of death, and consequently he will refuse to receive Extreme Unction. If such a man is in good faith and there is little hope of convincing him of his error, it is unwise to change his good faith into bad faith. Such a patient will generally show that he is not adverse to religion by his reception of Penance and the Eucharist. Moreover it is always to be remembered that he is not seriously bound (practically) to receive the sacrament of the Unction. In this case a priest should try to drive a bargain with the man to allow an administration of Extreme Unction after he has lost the use of his senses.[134] If he consents, it will be clear that his reluctance to receive the sacrament in his present condition is springing from a superstitious fear, and that there is no contempt present. When he sinks into insensibility, this subject can be anointed, even though he shows some signs of reluctance. His intention of receiving it in this proximate danger of death outweighs the seemingly opposite intention expressed by these signs of unwillingness. Generally the reluctance will have its origin in an erroneous appreciation of the gravity of the danger.[135]

Sometimes it may be prudent for a priest not to press the question of Unction too much. Refusal to receive may arise from a firm belief that it is an unfailing harbinger of death. If it is known that the patient's obstinacy springs from this source, and a priest foresees the failure of his attempts to overcome it, he need not be troubled if he omits an insistence of reception. "Circumstances may minimize or entirely remove this obligation of the pastor. He has fulfilled his duty when he has done his best to persuade the dying person to receive this sacrament, which he stands ready to administer if the one in need of it will

134 Lehmkuhl, *Casus Consc.*, II, 678—Hanley, *Treatise on the Sac. of Ext. Unct.*, p. 44.
135 Noldin, *De Sac.*, 41, 4.

consent to receive it."[136] In this case, too, the adherence of the patient to the faith will evidence itself by a reception of Penance and the Eucharist. Often patients of this kind are not to be blamed too severely. They do not really commit a mortal sin by their refusal. They do not believe that Extreme Unction will really cause their death, but, "not being properly instructed in the knowledge of its effects, they have accustomed themselves to the opinion that its reception means that all hope of recovery must be abandoned."[137] Such a state of mind, since it results from ignorance, is not grievously sinful. Accordingly Penance and the Eucharist can be given to them without scruple.[138]

A caution should be added against annoying the sick man with too many exhortations to receive this sacrament. In this way a priest can very easily become a "persona non grata" to the patient. Obstinate inmates in hospitals must be handled with an extra degree of prudence; for the hospital authorities are apt to forbid all access of the priest to them, asserting that their well-being is being interfered with and their hopes of recovery being frustrated.[139]

We have seen by Canon 939 that those who neglect to administer this sacrament altogether are guilty of mortal sin. We have seen, too, by this canon that a priest is bound to inform souls under his charge of their state of sickness, if it is not already known, so that they may be able to receive the sacraments in due season. The question now arises as to how much delay on the part of the pastor is required to constitute a serious sin, when the sacrament, though requested, is deferred for a time. In other words, how soon after its petition must the sacrament be administered? Can the pastor delay its administration as long as he pleases, provided, of course, that there is no serious dan-

---

136 *The Casuist*, V, p. 234.
137 The Casuist, V, p. 234.
138 Even the form "Corpus Domini DNJC" can be substituted for the regula formula prescribed for Viaticum, "Accipe frater viaticum," if the latter will disturb the patient (Cf. Genicot-Salsmans, *Inst. Th. M.*, II, 188).
139 *Casuist, l.c.;* cf. Berardi's fine advice, *Prax. Conf.*, II, n. 5010.

ger of the man dying without the sacrament? This point has been touched upon in the treatment of canon 939.[140] It remains to be developed a little more at present.

Before the Council of Trent, those who belonged to the school of Scotus delayed administration of the sacrament until the person was no longer capable of committing venial sin. This was simply the logical sequel to the theory of the *Doctor Subtilis* that the principal effect of Extreme Unction was the remission of venial sin.[141] Since the days of the great Council, however, the Church has urged a much earlier administration of this gift of God. Thus the Catechism of the Council [142] condemned as guilty of most serious sin those who deferred the administration of Unction until the time when, "omni salutis spe amissa, vita et sensibus carere incipiat." In the Fifth Council of Milan, St. Charles Borromeo gave the following warning: "Caveat parochus ne in eo ministrando negligentiam, ullamve morae culpam contrahat. Alioqui si ad illius administrationem accersitus ire neglexerit, cum rationem Deo reddet, tum poena ad Episcopo graviter plectatur." [143] Priests were urged by this Council [144] and that of Bois-le-duc [145] to take as their exemplar a bishop named Malachias. This holy man had the unhappiness of learning that a woman had died without the sacraments through his negligence. Overwhelmed with grief, he implored heaven with tears and sighs throughout the entire night, until a compassionate God took cognizance of the grief of His servant and rejoined the soul and body of the dead woman. After receiving the sacrament from the bishop, she recovered from her disease.

The legislation of local Councils has shown how contrary it is to the wish of the Church that Extreme Unction be in any way delayed. Thus the Synod of Benevento in 1693 stated in its constitutions that culpable negligence in administration in-

140 Cf. *supra*, Chap. IV, p.
141 *Reportata Parisiensia,* d. xiii, q. unica.
142 *De Ext. Unct.*, n. 9.
143 *Acta Eccl. Mediol.,* pars I, tom. I, p. 250.
144 *L.c.*
145 apud Van Espen, *Jus Can. Univ.*, P. II, s. I, tit. 8, cap. 3, n. 14.

volved a very serious default of duty.[146] In similar fashion the second Council of Baltimore evidenced the mind of the Church: "Neque dubium est contra morem mentemque Sanctae Matris Ecclesiae agere sacerdotem, qui expectat donec aegrotus in agone mortis jaceat ut eum Sacro Oleo inungat." [147]

The pastor's duty is to give the sacraments to those reasonably seeking them, unless a just cause excuses. Surely the reasonableness of the request cannot be called into question when the sacrament is petitioned at the very time the Church wishes it to be administered. As a consequence any serious delay, especially when it endangers the probability of reception while the patient is still conscious, is grievously wrong.[148] The amount of usefulness ordinarily obtainable by an opportune administration will determine the gravity of the sin. Hence a delay which imperils to an appreciable extent the powers of sanation or the comfort in the last agony given by the sacrament deprives the sick man of great graces, and makes the pastor recreant to his duty in a grave matter.

Serious reasons will release a pastor from immediate administration, if it is morally certain that it can be conferred before death. They need not be as serious as those which excuse him from administering the sacrament altogether, but they must be genuinely and proportionately grave. A serious reason would be e. g., if the priest's life or liberty were in peril by walking through the street during the day, and consequently when it would be wiser to take advantage of the cover of night in order to approach the sick man.

It does not follow, however, that a priest must always be convicted of *serious* delinquency of duty if he fail to confer the Sacrament at the very hour or even on the very day that he realizes that his client is in probable or remote danger of death.

---

146 Tit. 7, c. 1: "Non est sine animadversione praetereundum a Parochorum quamplurimis, extremae Unctionis Sacramentum collaturis, ex culpabili negligentia illud differri donec aegrotus, amissis sensibus, animam agere incipiat: quod (ut Catechismo Romano admonentur) jus sacramenti gratiam percipiendam plurimum valere, si aegrotus, cum in eo integra mens et ratio viget fidemque et religiosam voluntatem afferri potest, sacro oleo liniantur." (Coll. Lac., t. I, col. 30).

147 n. 306.

148 Fanfani, *De Jure Parochorum*, 239 b; Kenrick, *Th. M.*, III, "*De Ext. Unct.*," cap. unic., n. 20; Genicot-Salsmans, *Inst. Th. M.*, II, 422.

It may be morally certain, especially in lingering diseases as consumption or cancer, that no considerable change will occur before the next visit of the priest. In such cases it can hardly be maintained that the priest is gravely recreant to his trust, although if there is no good reason for the delay, it is hard to see how any neglect is altogether blameless.[149]

A check on the fulfillment of this duty of administering the sacraments to the sick by pastors is to be made by the vicar forane of the district.[150] Benedict XIV also prescribed episcopal vigilance in this regard.[151] On the occasion of the official visitation the bishop should take special pains to learn "an aegrotantibus et in extremo vitae agone laborantibus debita spiritualia subsidia praestet, et sacramenta Ecclesuae *tempestive* conferat."

The Code prescribes the mode of procedure to be employed by the Ordinary against pastors who have been gravely negligent in the administration of the sacraments and in assistance to the sick.[152] It is prescribed by the thirty-second title of the fourth book—"De modo procedendi contra parochum in adimplendis paroecialibus officiis negligentem."[153] The pastor is to be warned by the bishop first, who shall recall to the pastor's mind the strict obligations that are his and the severe penalties to which he is exposing himself. Such a monition is not a paternal, but a canonical one, made in accordance with Canon 2143. If emendation does not follow, the Ordinary shall ensure himself of the certainty of the grave omission for a notable length of time,[154] and of the lack of a sufficient cause to extenuate this

149 Cf. Barry, "*The Subjects of Extreme Unction,*" in the I. E. Record, Vol. XXVI, Fifth Series (1925), pp. 63-64.

150 Can. 447, paragr. 1, n. 1.

151 Const. "*Firmandis,*" Nov. 6, 1744, n. 9—C. I. C. Fontes, n. 349. Prior to this St. Charles had decreed in the Fourth Provincial Council of Milan that rural deans should require from the pastors of their respective districts a report of those who had died during the interval between reports, including among the information given the fact whether or not the patients had been given the sacraments opportunely and whether the pastor had been present when death occurred. Negligent pastors were to be reported by the dean to the bishop. (*Acta Eccl. Mediol.*, t. I, p. 148).

152 Can. 2382.

153 Cann. 2182-5.

154 Vermeersch-Creusen, *Epit.*, III, 371; Cf. S. C. Consist., 20 Aug., 1910, A. A. S., II, 638. One month is a notable length of time, according to Vermeersch-Creusen, *l.c.*

action on the part of the pastor. If both of these are verified, a consultation should be held with two examiners and the pastor must be given a chance to defend himself. If he is deemed guilty, the Ordinary shall mete out a punishment commensurate with the seriousness of the neglect.[155] Even suspension does not seem beyond the powers of the bishop at this stage, provided that the gravity of the crime warrants it.[156]

If these measures prove ineffectual, the bishop shall again summon the examiners to discuss the case and provide the pastor with another opportunity of self-defense. Should it be shown that this same culpable neglect of duty continues, the bishop can remove a *removable* pastor from his parish without further procedure. If the pastor is irremovable, the bishop shall deprive him of all or of part of his income, according to the grievousness of the offense, and distribute this to the poor. The continuance of this misconduct on the part of an irremovable pastor after this deprivation of salary, will, after a procedure identical with the former ones, result in the pastor's removal from his parochial benefice.[157]

B. The duties of others in charge of the sick.

Not only the pastor, but all others bound to the patient by a title other than that of common charity are obligated especially by this canon to use all care and diligence in providing the timely administration of Extreme Unction for the sick man. Parents, children, superiors, consorts, doctors, nurses, infirmarians, &c., come within the scope of our investigation. A distinction of the utmost importance must be made immediately between those who are bound by special title to the spiritual care of the sick, such as parents, children, consorts, superiors, and those who are bound *ex officio* only to the corporal welfare of the patient, such as physicians, surgeons, nurses, &c.

It must be noted too that we are not treating here of the obligation of advising the sick that he is in danger of death. We are considering simply the duty of procuring for the sick man the sacrament of Extreme Unction specifically. By the

---

155 Cf. Canon 2309.
156 Can. 1933, 4—Augustine, *A Commentary,* VIII, p. 467.
157 Can. 2185.

law of nature the physician is bound primarily and *sub gravi* to announce to the patient that he is in danger of death. This warning can be made personally or thru others, such as the pastor, the relatives, &c. When they are reluctant, this obligation becomes strictly personal.[158] He is excused from this only when he is morally certain that the sick man is in the state of grace and has made settlement of his temporal affairs; or when it is clear that, even when advised, he would persevere in his sin, spurn the sacraments, and make no further disposition of his temporalities.[159]

If the physician refuses to do his duty, the obligation becomes incumbent upon the patient's relatives or his superior, all of whom are bound *ex officio* to him. When these, too, refuse to break the news, the pastor must take upon himself this unpleasant task.

This, however, is not strictly the question. Here the force of the obligation on these persons is sought only in regard to procuring for the patient the Sacrament of Extreme Unction—a sacrament, be it remembered, that he is not bound to receive under pain of mortal sin.

Those who have the spiritual care of the sick by a special title are certainly obliged to procure for their charges the sacrament of the Unction when that sacrament is petitioned. In the opinion of Noldin,[160] Lehmkuhl,[161] Ærtnys,[162] and Gury-Ferreres[163] this obligation is grave. Lehmkuhl and Gury-Ferreres extend the obligation not only to those cases where the sacrament is sought explicitly or implicitly, but also to the instances where it would be requested, if the seriousness of the situation were known by the sick man, i. e., where it is sought interpretatively.[164] Lehmkuhl[165] and Sebastiani[166] further assert that there is even a duty upon those bound to the spiritual care of the

158 Noldin, *De Praeceptis*, 746; Genicot-Salsmans, *Inst. Th. M.*, II, 21; Gury, *Th. M.*, II, 31-3.
159 Noldin, *l.c.*, Genicot-Salsmans, *l.c.*
160 *De Sac.*, 446.
161 *Th. M.*, II, 727.
162 *Th. M.*, II, 369.
163 *Casus Consc.*, II, n. 808.
164 Cf. Lehmkuhl, *l.c.;* Gury-Ferreres, *l.c.;* Prov. Conc. Amer. Lat., n. 564; Conc. Manilanen., n. 668.
165 *L.c.*
166 *Summ. Th. M.*, n. 512.

sick to endeavor to induce the sick man not to neglect such a great spiritual good, so exceedingly useful in the last fight for salvation.

On the other hand Suarez,[167] Laymann,[168] Babenstuber,[169] Elbel-Bierbaum [170] and Ballerini-Palmieri [171] teach that the negligence of procuring the sacrament for the sick man is venial, even if it is done without reasonable cause. Moreover, contrary to the opinion of Lehmkuhl and Sebastiani, Kenrick [172] holds that neglect to urge upon a sick man, otherwise prepared, the reception of Extreme Unction is not a serious sin. The sick man, it is argued, has no serious obligation of receiving the sacrament. Those in charge of the sick cannot reasonably be said to have a greater obligation to procure it for the man than he himself has to receive it.

Both opinions are probable, with the consequence, of course, that no strict obligation can be imposed upon such people in regard to the sacrament of Extreme Unction. *Per accidens,* however, all concede that the obligation can become grave. Such an occasion occurs if there is danger of contempt or scandal, or if Extreme Unction is the only certain means of salvation for the patient.

In regard to those who have not the spiritual care of the sick man, as doctors, nurses, infirmarians, etc., little need be said, except in an historical way.

Of old it was not permitted to physicians to undertake the care of the bodily illness of the patient until the man had remedied his spiritual ills by going to confession. This law was first promulgated by the Fourth Council of Lateran, held in 1215, under Innocent III.[173] In 1311 Clement V renewed this Constitution in the Council of Ravenna.[174] Pius V in 1566 made the law still stricter by compelling all physicians to swear prior to reception of the degree of doctor of medicine that they would

167 D. 44, s. 1, n. 6.
168 *Th. M.*, l. 5, tr. 8, c. 7, n. 2.
169 *Ethica Supernat.*, tr. 8, p. 6, disp. 7, a. 1, n. 5.
170 *Th. M.*, III, (Pars VIII, Conf. X) n. 233.
171 *Op. Theol. Mor.*, tom. V, tr. X, sect. VI, n. 58, xix.
172 *Th. M.*, "*De Ext. Unct.*," III, cap. unic., n. 22.
173 c. 13, X, *de Paenitent.*, V, 38.
174 Rubrica 15, *de Paenitentiis;* Harduin, VII, 1367.

advise all patients seeking their care to request spiritual aid, and if any patient failed to do so within three days they would cease their professional attention to such a man.[175] Gregory XIII [176] forbade the employment of Jew and infidel physicians, and confirmed at the same time the foregoing decrees in all their vigor.

As a consequence of this legislation, it is not strange to find that old canonists and theologians discussed the obligation of the physician in instances of this kind.[177] In many places such decrees were never put into effect; while in other localities time mellowed the harshness of their prescriptions.[178] Today such laws are nowhere in force, but there remains the divine and natural precept binding each one to prevent a serious loss to his neighbor, if it can be conveniently done.

Petrus Dens [179] thinks a physician is bound by virtue of his office to procure the eternal salvation of his patient. Hence he condemns as grievously sinful the negligence of a physician which causes the loss of Extreme Unction to the sick person. This seems too much. A physician has not the spiritual care of the sick man. His duty concerns the well-being of the body, not of the soul. Hence he is bound only by the precept of common charity toward the spiritual welfare of his patient. Such an obligation in charity cannot be greater upon him than the obligation on the sick man of charity towards himself (*erga se*). It has already been seen that the sick man's obligation is *per se* venial. Accordingly, it must be conceded that the physician is not bound grievously in this matter.

It is needless to remark that what has been said of the physician's obligation applies equally well to that of nurses and others who have not the spiritual care of the sick. Only in the case where Extreme Unction is the sole means of salvation can

---

175 Const. "*Supra gregem,*" 8 Mar. 1566, § 3—*Bull. Taur. Edit.*, VII, 430.
176 Const., "*Alias,*" 30 Maii, 1581—*Bull. Taur. Edit.*, VIII, 371 sqq.
177 Cf., e. g., Schmalzgrueber, *Jus Ecc. Univ.*, Vol. XI, pp. 351-2, n. 101-2; Diana, *Opera Coord.*, tom. I, tr. 3, res. 198-9.
178 St. Alphonsus, *Th. M.*, VI, 664; Noldin, *De Praec.*, 746; Genicot-Salsmans, *Inst. Th. M.*, II, 21, footnote.
179 *Theol. Mech.*, "*De Ext. Unct.*," N. 10, p. 56.

a grave obligation be put upon these persons. Such a contingency arises when a man, attrite for his sins, becomes unconscious before confession has been made. Here charity requires that our neighbor be succored in his dire necessity—and consequently failure in this regard would entail serious sin.[180]

---

180 Noldin, *De Sac.*, 446.

CHAPTER X.

THE BLESSING OF THE OIL

CANON 945.

Oleum olivarum, in sacramento Extremae Unctionis adhibendum, debet esse ad hoc benedictum ab Episcopo, vel a presbytero qui facultatem illud benedicendi a Sede Apostolica obtinuerit.

CHAPTER X.

The third chapter of the Title on Extreme Unction in the Code has to do with the rites and the ceremonies of that sacrament. It contains three canons, two of which are devoted to the remote matter and the third to the proximate matter of the sacrament.

We have already learned that olive oil is the remote matter of this sacrament.[1] We have learned too, that there is a need of some kind of blessing. We can pass over these points, therefore, and address ourselves immediately to a consideration of the nature or quality of the blessing required.

No evidence can be gathered from Scripture; but Tradition constantly and consistently avers that an episcopal benediction of the oil is essential. As far back as 390 A. D., the second Council of Carthage [2] forbade a presbyter to bless the *Oleum Infirmorum.* Shortly afterwards this prescription was confirmed by the third Council of Carthage: (398) "Presbyter, inconsulto episcopo, . . . chrisma vero nunquam conficiat." [3] Evidently in Spain priests were trying to usurp this episcopal prerogative, for the First Council of Toledo,[4] held in the year 400, legislates against such an abuse. A few years later, Innocent I, in his letter in Decentius [5] wrote that the sick should be anointed "sancto oleo ab Episcopo confecto." The Council of Braga [6] in

1 Cf. *supra,* chap. I, sect. IV, p. 24; and also chap. II, p. 72.

2 can. 3—apud Harduin I, 952; Mansi II, 693; c. 1, C. XXVI, q. 6.

3 c. 2, C. XXVI, q. 6—also apud Harduin I, 964, Mansi II, 885.

4 Cap. XX (apud Mansi II, 1002)—"Quamvis pene ubique custodiatur ut absque Episcopo Chrisma nemo conficiat; tamen quia in aliquibus locis, vel Provinciis, Prebyteri dicuntur Chrisma conficere, placuit ex hac die nullum alium, nisi episcopum Chrisma facere et per dioecesim destinare."—N. B. Altho this may apply to the chrism used in Baptism, nevertheless the oil of the sick was commonly called *chrisma* in those early days, Cf. *supra,* chap. I, sect. I, p. 4; Suarez, d. 40, s. 1, n. 10.

5 Ep. "*Si instituta ecclesiastica,*" 19 Mar. 416, cap. 8—C. I. C. Fontes, n. 19.

6 can. 19 (apud Harduin III, 352): "Item placuit ut si quis presbyter, post hoc interdictum, ausus fuerit chrisma benedicere, aut ecclesiam aut altare consecrare, a suo officio deponatur: nam et antiqui hoc canones vetuerunt."

Portugal (561) ordered priests who dared to confect the chrism to be deposed. Similarly, the Council of Seville [7] in Spain (619) reserved the consecration of the sick man's oil to the Bishop.

St. Bede remarks, in his Commentary on the sixth chapter of the Gospel of St. Mark,[8] that the custom of anointing the sick with consecrated oil has descended from the Apostles themselves and is of divine institution. In the ninth century the Councils of Châlons-sur-Saone [9] (813) and Aachen [10] (836) mention only the bishop as minister of the benediction of the oils, while the Synod of Worms[11] (868) employs the very words of the letter of Innocent I in this regard. Shortly afterwards, Jonas, the Bishop of Orleans, sternly rebuked those who sought the aids of divination when sick, and urged them to comply with the Apostolic tradition "ut . . . quilibet aegroti ungantur oleo *pontificali benedictione* consecrato.[12]

Though quite unnecessary, the great authority of the Scholastics can be invoked in this matter. All of them held that the power of blessing this oil belongs properly to the bishop alone—and this in spite of the fact that the opposite opinion had been already expressed by Bonizone in the eleventh century.[13] Hear the Master of the Sentences: "Unctio illa fieri non potest nisi de oleo ab *episcopo* consecrato; ideoque illa sanctificatio ad virtutem sacramenti pertinere videtur." [14] With him agreed the great doctors of the School, Blessed Albertus Magnus,[15] Thomas of Aquin,[16] St. Bonaventure,[17] Dominic Soto,[18] Dionysius the Carthusian,[19] and Durandus.[20]

---

7 Cap. 7—Harduin III, 559-60.
8 Ad vers. 13,—M. P. L. 92, 188B.
9 Can. 48—apud Harduin IV, 1040.
10 Cap. 2, tit. 8—apud Harduin IV, 1395.
11 cap. 72—apud Harduin V, 746.
12 *De Instit. Laicali*, lib. 3, cap. 14—M. P. L., 106, 260.
13 M. P. L., 150, 864B—"Hoc [i. e. oleum infirmorum] omni tempore inter missarum solemnia a presbyteris in eo loco, ubi sic legitur: 'Per quem haec omnia bona creas,' solebat consecrari. Nunc vero a solis episcopis in eodem loco missae in Coena Domini consecratur."
14 *Lib. IV Sent.*, dist. XXIII, apud M. P. L., 192, 900.
15 *Comm. in lib. IV Sent.*, dist. 23, a. 3, ad qu. 2.
16 *Suppl.*, q. 29, a. 6.
17 *Comm. in IV Sent.*, dist. 23, a. 1. qu. 3, ad 7.
18 *Comm. in IV Sent.*, dist. 23, a. 1, a. 3.
19 *Comm. in IV Sent.*, dist. 23, q. 2.
20 *Comm. in IV Sent.*, dist. 23, q. 2, ad 2.

Innocent III prescribed that the Waldensians should make a statement of reverence towards the Unction of the sick "cum oleo *consecrato;*"[21] while Eugene IV, in the Council of Florence, proclaimed to the Armenians that the matter of Extreme Unction was "oleum olivae per *episcopum* benedictum."[22]

It is small wonder then that the Council of Trent should declare "intellexit Ecclesia materiam esse oleum *ab episcopo* benedictum;"[23] and that seventy years later Paul V should categorize as "*reckless and proximately erroneous*" the proposition that Extreme Unction might be validly administered "*oleo benedictione episcopali non consecrato.*"[24] And truly, in view of such an imposing array of evidence affirming the necessity of an episcopal blessing, it becomes apparent how "reckless and proximately erroneous" it is to assert the possibility of confecting the sacrament with oil blessed by other than a bishop. Indeed the testimony seemed so formidable to Coninck,[25] Estius,[26] and Suarez[27] that they denied even to the Pope the power to appoint a simple priest to bless the oil.

Yet when we look into the ceremonies of the Greek rite, we discover that from the earliest times priests have been blessing the *Oleum Infirmorum.* Thus the Penitential of St. Theodore, the archbishop of Canterbury, contained the following statement: "Secundum Graecos presbytero licet . . . facere oleum exorcizatum et infirmis chrisma, si necesse est. Secundum Romanos *non* licet nisi episcopo soli."[28] The antiquity of this Greek custom is also emphasized by John Nathaniel writing to the Archbishop of Anagni[29] and by Leo Allatius.[30] It can also be read in the Greek "*Euchologion*" under the title "*Officium Sancti Olei.*" Not alone among the Greeks, but also among the Armenians this practice has long obtained. Pope John XXII

---

21 Ep. "*Ejus exemplo,*" 18 Dec. 1208, Professio fidei Waldensibus, praescr.: "*Unctionem infirmorum cum oleo consecrato veneramur.*" C. I. C. Fontes n. 30.

22 Const. "*Exultate Deo,*" Nov. 22, 1439, paragr. 14, C. I. C. Fontes, 52.

23 Sess. XIV, *De Ext. Unct.*, cap. 1.

24 Denziger-Bannwart, *Enchirid.*, n. 1628: also Coll., n. 956.

25 *De Sac. et Censuris,* t. II, disp. 19, *de Ext. Unct.,* dub 2, n. 6.

26 *Comm. in IV Sent.*, dist. 23, paragr. 9.

27 D. 40, sec. 1, n. 8.

28 M. P. L., 99, 929.

29 Arcudius, De *Concordia Eccl. Occid.*, &c., lib. V, c. 2.

30 *Eccl. Occid. et Orient. Consens.*, l. III, cap. 16.

noted it in a letter to Ossinius, the King of Armenia: "Ipsi etiam Sacerdotes Oleum, quod Infirmorum dicitur, consecrant pro Sacramento Extremae Unctionis, cum tamen apud nos ad Episcopos solos spectet."[31] Nor has such a custom flourished because of an official oversight of Rome, or in spite of a disapproval of the Pope; for time after time various Pontiffs have gloriously vindicated to them the legitimacy of their actions.

Thirty years after the Council of Trent had instructed Catholics that the matter of Extreme Unction was "oleum ab Episcopo benedictum," Clement VIII[32] confirmed to Italo-Greek priests the power to bless this oil. Yet Paul V, his almost immediate successor, condemned as rash and proximate to error the proposition that Extreme Unction could be validly administered "Oleo episcopali benedictione non consecrato."[33] In the next century Benedict XIV renewed the decree of Clement VIII for the localities in which the custom was still in vogue,[34] and in an encyclical letter to the Uniat Greeks a few years later bemoaned the woeful ignorance displayed by Western theologians in regard to the customs of the Eastern rites.[35] At the time of the French Revolution, the Holy See was asked to permit priests in France to bless the *Oleum Infirmorum*. Pius VI denied this request because of want of precedent and lack of

---

31 Benedict XIV, *De Syn. Dioc.*, l. 8, c. 1, n. 4.

32 Instr. "*Sanctissimus*," Aug. 31, 1595, paragr. 3—C. I. C. Fontes, n. 179: "Non sunt cogendi Presbyteri Graeci Olea Sancta praeter Chrisma ab Episcopis Latinis Dioecesanis accipere, cum hujusmodi Olea ab eis, in ipsa Oleorum et Sacramentorum exhibitione, ex veteri Ritu conficiantur, seu benedicantur."

33 Denziger-Bannwart, *Enchiridion*, n. 1628.

34 Const. "*Etsi pastoralis*," 26 Maii, 1742, paragr. IV, n. 1—C. I. C. Fontes 328.

35 Ep. encycl. "*Ex quo*," 1 Mar. 1756 parag. 7—apud Coll. Lac. t. II, col. 538-9; also apud *Bened. XIV Bullarium*, tom. 4, vol. XI, p. 295: "Injusta quippe et fallax Ecclesiaeque paci atque unitati contraria est eorum judicandi ratio, qui Latinorum tantummodo ritualium notitiam habentes nec aliud scientes praeter ea, quae tradiderunt nonnulli ex nostris scriptoribus nostrarum quidem rerum periti sed Graecarum consuetudinum rudes ejusque rationis ignari, quam semper cum ipsis secuta est apostolica Romana Sedes, non dubitarunt damnare, in sacris Graecorum ritibus ea omnia quae cum Latino ritu conformia et consentanea non reperiebant."

necessity, without however asserting the incompetency of priests to receive such power.[36]

In 1842 Gregory XVI declared that a pastor could not, even in case of necessity, administer Extreme Unction with oil blessed by himself.[37] Gregory's decree was reaffirmed by a decision of the Holy Office in 1878, to the effect that the practice of blessing the oil by one only in priestly orders could not be approved or tolerated.[38] Yet in 1894 Leo XIII sanctioned the ancient practice of the Greeks for various bodies of the Eastern Uniats.[39] Finally the new Code announces, generally [40] in regard to all consecrations and specifically in regard to the Oil of the sick, that it is quite sufficient for the minister of the blessing to have priestly orders and an apostolic indult.

We have here truly an anomalous situation. Apparently at least, the Roman Pontiffs have been continually contradicting one another—and that, too, in a matter of gravest importance! What explanation can be given, for, even prescinding from the protection of the Paraclete, it seems unthinkable that each successive Pontifical decree should have been promulgated with the intention, implicit or explicit, of contradicting its predecessor?

Several explanations have been suggested. A possible solution, proposed by Quinn,[41] may be sketched in this way. Without attempting to solve the question whether the episcopacy and

---

36 Const. "*Sollicitudo omnium ecclesiarum,*" 28 Maii, 1793, responsum 13: "Cum deprehensum fuerit, insuetum esse in Ecclesia Latina hujusmodi potestate simplices presbyteros ab Apostolica Sede insigniri, a qua quidem regula eo minus recedi non debere judicatum est, quod impossibile non sit, triplex oleum a catholico episcopo benedictum, si non ex proximis, ex remotis saltem dioecesibus habere" (*Bull. Taur. Edit.*, X, 2623— also apud Muhlbauer, *Decr. Auth. S. C. R.*, t. II, p. 426).

Magistretti (*Pontificale in Usum Eccl. Mediolanen.*, p. 95) declares that until the eleventh century priests blessed the oil in Milan. Pius VI apparently was not aware of any such custom; nor Benedict XIV, either, for in his "*De Synodo Dioecesana*"—l. 8, c. 1, n. 4—he states the contention of many theologians "*nunquam* in Ecclesia Latina fuisse aegrotantes oleo inunctos ab Episcopo antea non consecrato."

37 S. C. S. Off., 14 Sept., 1842—Coll., n. 956; Denziger-Bannwart, *Enchirid.*, n. 1629.

38 S. C. S. Off., May 15, 1878—Coll. S. C. P. F., n. 1494.

39 Litt. ap. "*Orientalium,*" Nov. 30, 1894—A. S. S., XXVII, p. 257 sqq.

40 Can. 1147, 1.

41 *Some Aspects of the Dogma of Extreme Unction*, pp. 58-9. Quinn does not subscribe to this theory, but simply gives it as a possible one.

the presbyterate were the same grade of Orders in the times of St. Paul, as Theodulf of Orleans[42] asserts, it is beyond peradventure of doubt that later they were very distinct degrees of that sacrament. Those who have not the plenitude of Orders in these latter days may or may not have the power to bless the oil, depending, of course, on the proximity with which the order that they hold approaches the fulness of power. Now the priests of the West cannot bless the oil, whereas the priests of the East can. Accordingly, the power which the Oriental presbyterate possesses approaches closer to the plenitude of the episcopacy than the power of the presbyterate of the Occident. Since the former bless the oil by virtue of Orders and not of jurisdiction, it follows that the priesthood of the Greeks is of a higher degree than that of the Latins.

Such an explanation is entirely unsatisfactory. It is a very difficult thing to prove that the priesthood of the Orient is and always has been of a higher grade than in the Latin rite. But granting such a thing for the moment, this theory offers no solution for the case where a Western priest is empowered to bless the oil. In him an authorization of the Holy See would produce a power of Orders, which prior to authorization, he did not possess. Yet how can this act of the Holy See be construed in any other light than a delegation of jurisdiction? And again, how can the power of Orders be given by rescript, which might limit the duration of the power or restrict it to a certain number of cases.

Another solution [43] can be outlined in this fashion. Priesthood of itself confers the power required to bless the oil of the sick. In every case wherein a priest is the minister, whether in the Occident by indult or in the Orient without it, he blesses in virtue of his priestly orders. But in regard to the West the Church has enacted legislation which forbids priests to exercise this power under pain of invalidity. To bless the oil in the West then, the authorization of the Holy See must be viewed as a dispensation from this invalidating law rather than a concession of new power. Jurisdiction is required neither in the

[42] *Capitulare*—M. P. L., 105, 220C.

[43] Advanced by Cajetan, (*in III part.*, q. 72, a. 2) and Perin (*De Extr. Unct.*, art. 1, quaer. 4).

East nor in the West; there is solely a question of the valid use of the power of Orders.

This contention is also highly improbable. It would seem to presuppose that the Church has changed the matter of the sacrament. Time after time she has asserted that the matter of Extreme Unction is oil consecrated by an episcopal benediction. It would be necessary then to fall back on the theory which holds that the Church has the prerogative of introducing changes in the elements of the various sacraments by allowing in regard to Extreme Unction oil blessed with a priestly benediction to suffice for oil consecrated by a bishop. Although sacramental theology can show fairly well that the Church has probably changed the matter and form of some sacraments, yet the extension of this explanation to Extreme Unction should only be admitted upon the production of incontestable evidence to that effect. This is not the case here. Moreover, this view would imply that the exercise of priestly orders has been restricted in the Latin Church. The Council of Trent insinuates the very opposite when it says: "Intellexit Ecclesia materiam esse oleum ab episcopo benedictum."[44] Neither did Benedict XIV look on it in this fashion. On the contrary he asserted very positively that either tacit or explicit delegation from the Pope was absolutely necessary to qualify Eastern priests for the valid performance of this blessing. "Neutiquam autem," wrote he[45] "id tolerandum fuisset, si oleum, simplicis Sacerdotis benedictione sacratum, ne per potestatem quidem a Romano Pontifice sive expressa sive tacite eidem sacerdoti factam, esset materia idonea ad conficiendum Sacramentum Extremae Unctionis."

A real power is conceded therefore, and not a permission to exercise a power already possessed. This is the way the Greeks themselves look at the matter, as is evidenced by the decrees of two of their councils, viz., Zamos and Mt. Libanus. The former, held in 1720, legislated thus:

> "Extremae Unctionis materia est oleum, cujus benedicendi *potestatem* multis abhinc saeculis in orientali ecclesia sacerdotibus *concessam* praesens Synodus nequaquam adimendam existimavit."[46]

---

44 Sess. XIV, *De Extr. Unct.*, cap. 1.
45 *De Syn. Dioc.*, l. 8, c. 1, n. 4.
46 Tit. III, paragr. 6—Coll. Lac., t. II, p. 36.

The latter council enacted the following law:

> "Olei benedicendi potestas primario et principaliter penes episcopum residet et ab hoc in ecclesia occidentali una cum aliis SS. oleis benedicitur quotannis fer. V, in Coena Domini; per *delegationem* vero oleum infirmorum presbyteri simplices consecrant in ecclesia orientali . . . Sacerdotibus quidem illud oleum benedicendi potestatem confirmamus."[47]

Lehmkuhl, who made a special study of the Sacrament of Confirmation, seems to teach that the sacramental effect in Confirmation when conferred by a priest is immediately due to the delegated authority.[48] Transferring the case to Extreme Unction, the contention would be that the effect produced in the oil when blessed by a priest must be ascribed principally and immediately to the delegated authority. In Penance Lehmkuhl thinks that jurisdiction is much more than a condition *sine qua non* for the exercise of the power of order; it is there at least a coordinate, if not a superior power.[49] In Confirmation, however, he believes that the power of priestly orders gives an initial dignity which is completed by the delegation.[50] What the minister receives by this delegation is not the power of jurisdiction, "sed est dignitas, quae ad eandem speciem refertur ac potestas ordinis.[51] Yet Lehmkuhl says that it is not right to term this power or dignity as a power of orders "quia non intrinsecus per ordinationem, sed extrinsecus per delegationem confertur."[52] The effect resulting from this combination is due more immediately to this completing part of the dignity rather than to the initial dignity which the priest had through his priesthood. Thus, too, with the blessing of the oil. According to this theory, the blessing would result rather from the delegation received than from the priesthood already possessed.

---

47 Anno 1736—p. II, cap. 8, n. 2, apud Coll. Lac., t. II, p. 150.

48 *Th. M.*, II, 135-6.

49 *Op. cit.*, II, 481: "Jurisdictio autem sensu omnino proprio vera potestas est, imo sensu magis proprio quam ipsa ordinis potestas."

50 *Th. M.*, II, 135: "Potestas ordinis (quae in sola dignitate consistit), completur in sacerdote, non vero potestas ordinis cum potestate jurisdictionis conjungitur ac si in hac conjunctione evaderet completa potestas confirmandi."

51 *Th. M.*, II, 136.

52 *Th. M.*, II, 136.

This view is attacked by Dr. McDonald in the Irish Ecclesiastical Quarterly.[53] In the first place, says he, the oldest and best tradition holds that the *presbyteratus* is much more than a basis of dignity; it is a true physical power. Secondly, the tradition is deeply rooted that the sacramental effect is due rather to the power of Orders than to the superadded delegation or dignity. Furthermore, this dignity is more akin to the power of jurisdiction than to the power of orders, for the very reason that Lehmkuhl uses to support his own argument to the contrary: "quia non intrinsecus per ordinationem, sed extrinsecus per delegationem confertur." And if this is so, how can the effect of this dignity, which is akin to the power of jurisdiction, accomplish an identical effect to that of an episcopal character?

Quite a different theory is advanced by Father Kern.[54] All the Pontiffs, he claims, without exception have regarded an episcopal blessing of the oil necessary for the validity of the sacrament. But who may give an episcopal blessing? A bishop, surely, for he "per suum ordinem" possess such power. But cannot the bishop delegate his power of blessing the oil to a competent subject (*subjectum capax*) who is not of the episcopate; and thus cause the blessing of such a one to become in virtue of the delegated authority also truly episcopal. In the opinion of Father Kern, yes—a bishop can make such a delegation of power to one of his priests, for a priest, and he alone, is in virtue of his sacerdotal order a "subjectum capax" of receiving this grant of power. In other words there is resident in the *presbyteratus* an obediential potentiality of conferring this episcopal blessing; which potentiality, be it remembered, can be evoked into act only thru the delegation made to the priest by the bishop. In this way the blessing of a priest becomes truly episcopal, not *vi sui ordinis*, but *per potestatem delegatam*. *Per se* bishops have the right to delegate priests to bless this oil. The decree of Mt. Libanus,[55] just quoted, evidences this. Moreover this decree was confirmed by the Holy See a few years after it had been enacted, giving it thereby

---

53 Vol. II, (1907), p. 337-8.

54 *Tract. de Ext. Unct.*, pp. 127-8.

55 P. II, cap. 8, n. 2—Coll. Lac., t. II, p. 150.

added authority.[56] Consequently, neither by divine nor by ecclesiastical law is the faculty of delegation reserved by the Holy See in regard to the Eastern rites. In the Latin Church, however, the Supreme Pontiff reserves to himself by explicit legislation—both in this canon and in canon 210—the privilege of conferring this delegation.

There are certain objections which prevent an unreserved adoption of this view. Here the question might be asked: Is this delegation a part of the power of order or of the power of jurisdiction? If it is not a part of the power of order, why cannot it be withdrawn even from a bishop? Yet all claim that such cannot be done; that even heretical bishops can bless the oil validly. And if it is a part of the power of order, how can it be said to be delegated? The difficulty arises from the fact that priests may be delegated to bless the oil, while bishops cannot be deprived of that power because of their episcopal character. It is curious indeed if delegation—jurisdiction—can supply for the lack of episcopal character in a minister, especially to such an extent that *in hac re* the minister can be said to be acting *virtualiter* as a bishop. "It would almost be enough," writes Dr. McDonald,[57] "to decide one to adopt the Scotists' view, that the power of Order itself is nothing more than a delegation, did we not know that both powers seem to act very differently in the administration of Penance."

Kern's theory has something in its favor from Canon 210. There the possibility of delegating a power of orders is recognized, even though the Holy See reserves this right to itself. This canon differs in this from the law of the Decretals,[58] which apparently allowed no outlet or exception. Other theories try to explain the matter by taking for granted that there can be no delegation of higher power of orders and consequently they are compelled to resort to very peculiar expedients. From the Code itself we know now that at least a delegation, not only of

---

56 Benedict XIII, const. "*Apostolatus Officium*," July 19, 1724—Coll. Lac., t. II, p. 2.

57 Irish Theological Quarterly, vol. II, (1907), p. 338.

58 c. 9, X, *de consecrat. eccl.*, III, 40: "Licet episcopus committere valeat quae jurisdictionis existunt, quae ordinis tamen episcopalis sunt, non potest inferioris gradus clericis demandare."

jurisdiction, but also of orders is possible and in some cases permissible.[59]

Still another theory is sponsored by Dr. Quinn.[60] All priests, according to this explanation, have sufficient power of orders to bless the oil in the same fashion as they have the requisite power of Orders to administer Penance. In Penance they need jurisdiction to act validly; to bless the *Oleum Infirmorum* jurisdiction, or something akin to it, is likewise required. Bishops and priests, when blessing the oil, use the selfsame power of Orders; but the former differ from the latter in so far as they have the requisite power of jurisdiction permanently, while the priests have it only when and as long as it is granted to them.

This theory is not without its flaws. It must be remembered that heretical bishops consecrate the oil validly. Yet if the power is jurisdictional, why cannot the bishops be dispossessed of it just as freely as priests? We are forced to seek with Dr. Quinn a refuge in the contention that "episcopal orders carry with them at least some jurisdiction—of which bishops, as of divine institution cannot be deprived."[61] It would be very hard to prove the incompetency of the Holy See to deprive a bishop of this power, if it is really a power of jurisdiction. However, Dr. Quinn seems to think that the use of the term "facultatem" in this canon seems to favor the notion of jurisdiction.

It must be noted, too, that this theory demands jurisdiction for priests from the Holy See *per se*, and not from bishops, as Father Kern would have it. This would be in keeping with the statement of Benedict XIV that tacit or explicit delegation of the Pope was required by the Eastern priests for this bless-

59 Cf. Cocchi, *Comm. in Cod.*, lib. II, p. I, s. I, n. 135; Blat, *Comm. Text.*, lib. II, n. 159; Chelodi, *Jus de Personis*, n. 127; Wernz-Vidal, *De Personis*, II, 383, and others on this point. They declare that the Holy See can delegate the power of orders only in regard to functions attached to a specific grade of Order *jure ecclesiastico*. Consequently there could be no alternative than to accept the conclusion that the blessing of the oil of the sick is attached to the episcopate by ecclesiastical law. At any rate this would be no worse than the labored hypotheses to which the proponents of other theories are driven.

60 *Some Aspects of The Dogma of Extreme Unction*, pp. 59-63.

61 *Op. cit.*, p. 63.

ing.[62] In the light of this the decree (already quoted) of the Council of Mt. Libanus, would have to be taken—seemingly with much violence to the ordinary meaning of the words—not as an actual delegation of this power on the part of the legislators but simply as an admission by them of its presence because of papal delegation. It could be retorted, too, that even if Benedict XIV asserted that priests of the East need express or tacit papal delegation, it would not follow that bishops *per se* could not delegate such a power. At most it could be held that such a power had been taken away from the Eastern bishops in the same fashion as from the Western episcopacy, and reserved throughout the entire church to the Holy See. However, as Benedict XIV was writing at the time in a capacity far from that of the head of Christendom, there is no obligation—although, indeed, it may be safely done—of accepting his reading of history as absolutely true.

From amidst this maze of theological tangles, the juridical facts stand out, unobscured and undisputed. No matter how it is to be explained, it is none the less plain that a Latin priest can bless the Oil of the sick only with an Apostolic faculty. This ceremony is a consecration, and these are reserved to Bishops or to priests possessing a papal permission.[63] Cardinals who are not bishops, though permitted to make many consecrations, are not allowed to consecrate the *Oleum Infirmorum*. Specific exemption of this is made in Canon 239, § 1, 20°. On the other hand, benediction by any bishop suffices, whether he be titular or residential.[64] Even an heretical bishop would bless validly if he employed the correct form with the right intention, for, as has been noted before, it is a prerogative of which those having an episcopal character cannot be despoiled.

Ad hoc benedictum.

After a review of the qualities required in the blessing *ex parte ministri,* we are led to a consideration of the requirements of the blessing itself. Are there any further determina-

---

62 *De Syn. Dioc.,* l. 8, c. 1, n. 4; cf. *supra,* p.

63 Canon 1147, 1.

64 Blat, *Comm. Text.,* lib. III, p. I, n. 13; Paschang, *The Sacramentals,* pp. 52 and 59.

tions of the blessing other than that it must be episcopal—or does any blessing whatsoever performed by a bishop suffice?

It is quite evident that Christ prescribed no exact formula of blessing. The huge differences in the prayers used from the most ancient times establishes this beyond doubt. The Collection of Serapio,[65] the sacramentary of Gelasius,[66] the *Testamentum D. N. J. C.*,[67] the present formula in the Greek Euchologion[68] and the formula which was used in the Coptic rite,[69] give a fair conception of the divergence of prayer. All these were surely valid forms, for the rites which employed them were approved by the Holy See. It is likewise true that any blessing found in the various rituals today which have been approved by the Holy See is valid.

It should be noted that all the blessings given above have one common note. Sanctification of the oil is asked of Divine Goodness, so that it may become salutary and profitable to the sick in soul and in body. One might indeed be tempted to conclude that Christ commanded this note as essential to the blessing of this particular oil. In regard to validity, the presence of this one note would then seem to be all that is required. Ordinarily it would follow that bishops would be held to no particular form in regard to validity, but simply to the insertion of the essential element common to all the extant forms of blessing. Undoubtedly this is so in the Eastern rites today, and before the Code was also true in the West.[70] Suarez noted very well, however:

> "Fortasse tamen fieri potest ab Ecclesia, ut talis benedictio irrita sit, nec apud Deum habeat rationem consecrationis, sed execrationis

---

65 Wobbermin, "*Texte und Untersuchungen zur Geschichte der altchristlichen Literatur, herausg. v. Gebhardt u. Harnack,* t. 17, fasc. 3, 3 b.

66 M. P. L., 74, 1100.

67 Rahmani, p. 49.

68 N. B. The prayer of blessing has been the same both in ancient and recent times, and both in the schismatical and the Uniat Churches. Its Latin translation is given by Martene, *De Antiq. Eccl. Rit.*, lib. I, c. vii, art. 4, Ordo XXX; "Domine, qui in misericordia et miserationibus tuis animarum corporumque contritiones curas: ipse, Domine, oleum hoc sanctifica; ut in medelam omnis passionis carnalis et spiritualis inquinamenti et omnis denique mali depulsionem ex illo unctis fiat: ut in eo glorificetur sanctissimum nomen tuum, Patris et Filii et Spiritus Sancti nunc et semper et in saecula saecûlorum, Amen."

69 Denziger, *Ritus Orientalium,* t. II, p. 487.

70 Cf. Suarez, 40, s. I, n. 9; Kern, *Tract. de Ext. Unct.*, pp. 130-1.

> potius; et hoc modo fieri etiam poterit benedictio ab Ecclesia instituta necessaria sit, quia ex ea pendet, ut Christi institutio impleatur.''[71]

This has actually come to pass in regard to Latin bishops. Canon 1148, 2, contains a new enactment in regard to consecrations and blessings: ''Consecrationes et benedictiones sive contitutivae sive invocativae invalidae sunt, si adhibita non fuerit formula ab Ecclesia praescripta.'' Hence in the Occident today the only valid formula of benediction is that found in the Pontificale.[72]

In regard to the blessing performed by priests, it need only be said that both in the East and the West, both before and after the Code, it has been required that they use the formula prescribed by ritual. They act in virtue of delegated authority only, and such an authorization is surely made under the condition that they observe the rite of consecration *adamussim.*[73] In the West there is, of course, the added reason for invalidity arising from the prescriptions of the Canon.

Before an investigation of what is necessary for the licitness of blessing the oil, the value of the words ''ad hoc'' in this canon must be considered. What is their force in regard to the validity or liceity of the blessing? In other words can the Sacrament of Extreme Unction be confected validly by the employment of other oils blessed by a Bishop, viz., the *Oleum Catechumenorum* and the Sacred Chrism or is the Oil of the Sick strictly essential for this purpose?

This question differs from the one just treated. There the point revolved about whether the oil was blessed at all; here it is a question of the applicability of oil already blessed, according to the formula given for the benediction of chrism or oil of the Catechumens. Granted the validity of its blessing, can the application of such oil or chrism be extended beyond the cases for which the blessing intends it? Can oil blessed for use in Baptism or Confirmation be validly applied in Extreme Unction?

---

71 *L.c.*
72 ''*De Officio in Feria V Coenae Domini.*''
73 Cf. Kern, *Tract. de Ext. Unct.*, p. 131; The Cath. Encyc., art. ''*Extreme Unction.*''

Grave and weighty theological minds can be aligned on either side of the question, thus enhancing both opinions with probability. Those who allow the validity do so on the contention that such oil is truly "oleum ab episcopo benedictum," which the Council of Trent declared is the matter of this Sacrament. If the Sacred Synod wished to determine the matter to an oil specially blessed for the sick, it would have so specified, by saying, e. g., that the "materia" was "oleum Infirmorum ab episcopo benedictum." [74] It is true that the blessings of chrism and the oil of the Catechumens do not contain the common element of impetration begging Divine mercy and goodness to bless this oil for the easements of the soul and body of the sick. But the presence of such an element in all the formulae does not conclusively prove that Christ commanded this as essential to a valid blessing for unction. The very nature of the business of blessing the oil of the sick could bring it about that all such blessings have this common element. It is surely most appropriate to the formula—and as a consequence its insertion can be ascribed to the fine perception of the "eternal fitness of things" on the part of those who composed the various ritualistic blessings.[75] Consequently, Suarez writes: "Existimo, seclusa tamen Ecclesiae prohibitione, nullum peccatum esse uti chrismate proprio ad hoc sacramentum perficiendum, et praesertim si aliud oleum simplex et sanctificatum deesset." [76]

Some of the older authors declared the absolute invalidity of chrism, while seemingly admitting the validity of the Oleum Catechumenorum. Chrism, they claimed, lost the "esse olei" when balsam was added to the oil.[77] Suarez, however, though denying the possibility of the reverse, thinks that the chrism is equally as valid as the Oil of the Catchumens, because it was used, he alleges, in former days for unction.[78] Laymann [79] teaches that in practice it is not at all allowable to use chrism even if the oil of the sick is not at hand and there is danger in

[74] Cf. *The Casuist*, vol. II, p. 83.
[75] Cf. Kern, *Tract. de Ext. Unct.*, p. 131.
[76] D. 40, s. 1, n. 11.
[77] Soto, *Comm. in IV Sent.*, dist. 23, q. 1, a. 3; Paludanus, *Comm. in IV Sent.*, dist. 23, q. 1, a. 1.
[78] D. 40, s. 1, n. 10.
[79] *Th. M.*, tract. VIII, "*De Ext. Unct.*," c. 2, n. 3.

postponing the unction. If a priest, however, has anointed thru mistake with chrism, "probabiliter dici posse videtur nihil esse repetendum, sed rem Domino commendandum; tum quia plerumque non posset fieri iterata unctio sine scandalo, tum quia valde probabile est sacramentum Extremae Unctionis valide conferri in materia sacri chrismatis; seu quia olim consuetum erat talem materiam adhibere, ut Suarez existimat, seu quia mixtio balsami tam exigua esse solet, ut oleum nec physice nec omnino moraliter suam naturam exuisse censeatur quod vero hac vel illa benedictione oleum consecratum sit, non videtur pertinere ad sacramenti substantiam." [80] With this latter statement Diana agrees.[81] He allows nevertheless an unction with chrism in case of necessity if the oil of the sick is not handy "nam utilitas, quam hoc sacramentum affert infirmo praeferenda est." The latter reason is given by Tamburini.[82] On the other hand LaCroix [83] is displeased at the prohibition of conditional repetition made by Laymann. "Dicendum est" he writes, ". . . contra Laymann, sacramentum repeti sub conditione, quia dubium est, an cum chrismate fuerit validum."

Diametrically opposed to the opinion maintaining the valid confection of the sacrament with the oil of the Catechumens and chrism is the teaching of Babenstuber,[84] and Barbosa.[85] They maintain the absolute invalidity of the use of any oil but that of the sick. Their contention is based on the ground that each oil by its own peculiar blessing is made apt for use only for the purpose specified in such blessing. Hence they cannot be validly interchanged even in the greatest emergency.

St. Alphonsus [86] admitted the probability of both opinions, but taught that the former could not be put into practice except when the oil of the sick was not to be had. This is in accordance with the condemnation by Innocent XI of the proposition: "Non est illicitum in sacramentis conferendis sequi opinionem probabilem de valore sacramenti, relicta tutiore, nisi id vetat lex,

80 Laymann, *l.c.*
81 *Op. Coord.*, tom II, tract. IV, De Ext. Unct., res. 2 et 7.
82 *Moral. Explic.*, lib. VI, De Ext. Unct., c. 1, paragr. 1, n. 5.
83 *Th. M.*, lib. VI, p. II, n. 2090.
84 *Ethica Supernat.*, Tract. 8, p. 2, disp. 7, a. 2, n. 3.
85 *De Off. et Pot. Par.*, p. II, c. 22, n. 24.
86 *Th. M.*, VI, 709.

conventio aut periculum gravis damni incurrendi. Hinc sententia probabili tantum utendum non est in collatione baptismi, ordinis sacerdotalis aut episcopalis." [87] Since that time practically all theologians acknowledge the permissibility of anointing with the oil of the Catechumens in case of necessity.[88] A recent note in the controversy is heard from Fr. Umberg.[89] Arguing from Canon 1148, 2, he states that not only is a competent minister required, but also the corresponding formula for the blessing. "Quodsi chrisma adhibetur," he writes, "idem est ac si adhibetur oleum sine legitima forma benedictum." Most authors, on the other hand, think that this controversy is untouched by the Code.[90] Blat [91] joins with Umberg in stating that no substitution can now be made. Woywod does not agree with him: "The fact that others think that this question is not decided by canon 1148, 2 is proven by their recognition of the probability of this opinion even in editions of their books published since the promulgation of the Code. The Code does not state . . . whether any of the holy oils blessed by a bishop may be valid 'materia' in Extreme Unction. The question remains open and, therefore, if the priest has only the oleum *catechumenorum* or the *sanctum chrisma* at hand, he may anoint the sick conditionally in an urgent case, but if there is time, he must repeat, likewise conditionally, with the oleum infirmorum." [92]

---

87 S. C. S. Off., 2 Mar. 1679—Denziger, *Enchiridion*, n. 1151.

88 Cf. Dicastillo, *De Sac.*, tom. I, tr. 7, disp. I, lib. 3, n. 38; Scavini, *Th. M.*, t. III, n. 432, 3; Kenrick, *Th. M.*, III, "*De Ext. Unct.*," cap. unic., n. 3; Dens. *Tract. de Ext. Unct.*, N. 2, p. 20; Konings, *Th. M.*, n. 1502, quaer. 4; Pesch, *Prael. Dog.*, vol. VII, n. 525; Genicot-Salsmans, *Inst. Th. M.*, II, 416—*Casus Consc.*, p. 568, cas. 876; AErtnys, *Th. M.*, II, n. 357; Tanquerey, *Th. D.*, III, n. 765; Gury-Ferreres, *Comp. Th. M.*, II, nn. 833 et 254—*Casus Consc.*, II, n. 785; Sebastiani, *Summ. Th. M.*, n. 508; Gury, *Th. M.*, II, n. 877; Noldin, *De Sac.*, 432; Lehmkuhl, *Th. M.*, II, 717; Telch, *Epitome Th. M.*, Appendix III, "*Sent. Prob.*," n. 64, p. 415; *Sabetti*-Barrett *Th. M.*, p. 801; De Augustinis, *De Re Sacramentaria*, II, thesis II, "*De Ext. Unct.*," scholion I, pp. 376-7; O'Kane, *The Rubrics*, n. 853; *The Casuist*, II, p. 85; Rohling, *Medulla*, p. 378; Vermeersch-Creusen, *Epit.*, II, 230; Ballerini-Palmieri, *Op. Th. M.*, vol. V, tr. X, sec. VI, n. 11.

89 *Neo-Confessarius*, by Reuter-Lehmkuhl-Umberg, n. 226.

90 Cf. Noldin, *De Sac.*, 432; Woywod, *A Practical Commentary*, I, n. 868.

91 *Comm. Text.*, lib. III, p. I, n. 290.

92 *L.c.*

Cases of necessity may arise easily enough. By mistake, a priest could bring to the sick room the oil of Baptism or the Chrism of Confirmation. The person is dying very rapidly and will very likely have passed away, by the time the priest could retrace his steps to the rectory and back again to the sick house. If the sick call were in the rural districts, a very considerable amount of time would be required for this.

Another emergency would occur when a priest, called to baptize a child, would suddenly find the mother dying also. If there is danger in delay, the Oil of the Catechumens or the Chrism may be employed for the unction. It need hardly be said that such an unction is to be made under the condition, at least mentally expressed, "Si materia est valida."[93]

If the oil of the sick is obtained while the person is still alive, a second unction is to be made. This, too, should be conditional, "Si nondum es hoc Sacramento refectus."[94] St. Alphonsus[95] does not mention the conditional nature of the second administration, although most probably he implied it, for he refers to LaCroix[96] who directs a conditional administration. St. Charles similarly omitted mention of the fact that the second administration ought to be *sub conditione.*[97]

Practically all of the later theologians have explicitly ordered a condition to be inserted in this repetition "ad cautelam."[98] Lehmkuhl,[99] however, thinks that if a man has been absolved and received Communion, and the priest notices during the unctions that he is using the wrong oil, it is more advisable to risk a return to the rectory for the correct oils, even though there is danger that the man may die in the meantime. The completion of the other unctions is simply piling doubt upon

---

93 Cf. Scavini, *Th. M.*, III, n. 432.

94 Scavini, l.c. N. B. As noted before, the condition should not be "*Si capax es,*" for it is quite probable that a person may validly be anointed twice or more in the same danger of death—yet such a repetition is altogether illicit.

95 *Th. M.*, VI, 709.

96 *Th. M.*, l. 6, p. 2, n. 2090.

97 *Acta Eccl. Mediol.*, Pars IV, "*Instruct. De Ext. Unct.,*" t. I, p. 603.

98 Cf. Scavini, *l.c.*, Kenrick, *l.c.*, Dens, *l.c.*, Pesch., *l.c.*, Konings, *l.c.*, Genicot-Salsmans, *l.c.*, Tanquerey, *l.c.*, AErtnys, *l.c.*, Gury-Ferreres, *l.c.*, Sebastiani, *l.c.*, Gury, *l.c.*, Noldin, *l.c.*, Telch, *l.c.*, Sabetti-Barrett, *l.c.*, DeAugustinis, *l.c.*, O'Kane, *l.c.*, The Casuist, *l.c.*

99 *Casus Consc.*, II, 668.

doubt, whereas, since a single unction suffices for validity, time may be saved by interrupting the unctions and hurrying for the proper oils. Elbel-Bierbaum[100] teaches that if the pastor learns after a time that he has been using the *Oleum Catechumenorum* by mistake, he need not go back and repeat the unctions with the Oleum Infirmorum when the subject has received the other sacraments. However, if Extreme Unction was the only sacrament which the subject could have with certainty received, e. g., if he were unconscious, then in every case of this kind the sacrament is to be repeated.

The reasons he alleges for the first case are three: 1) The unction with chrism (or oil of the Catechumens) was probably valid; 2) the sacrament is not absolutely necessary; 3) the impossibility of reanointing without exciting the wonderment of the people—a phenomenon which never lacks an element of scandal. The third reason would surely not be hard to verify if many sick were at that time in the parish. It would soon be breezed far and wide that the pastor had made some great mistake, because all the sick in his parish were reanointed. On the other hand, a judicious handling of the situation would prevent such a condition of affairs. Those nearest death could be anointed first—and if necessary, by a single unction, so that the bystanders could not notice it. One by one the others could be attended so that gradually, through diplomacy, all the sick of the parish would receive what was in justice due to them from the pastor.

It may be remarked that if a choice can be made between the oil of the Catechumens and the chrism, it is safer, and, therefore, wiser, to choose the former. Never was it questioned that the oil of the Catechumens had the "*esse olei,*" but, as has been seen, some theologians contested the availibility of chrism as valid matter for this sacrament. Schmalzgrueber[101] implies the preferability of the *Oleum Catechumenorum,* when he states

---

100 *Th. M.*, III, P. VIII, Conf. IX, n. 203-4.

101 "Multo minus iterandum aliquid erit in casu quo sacerdos per errorem oleo catechumenorum ungeret infirmum; licet enim diversa sit hujus et olei infirmorum benedictio, in substantia non differunt." *Jus Ecclesiasticum Universum,* lib. I, tit. xvi, n. 5.

that the obligation of repeating the sacrament thus confected is much less than when it has been administered with chrism.

The liceity of the blessing of this oil depends upon the observance of further requirements. The blessing may not be performed at any time of the year at the pleasure of the bishop. By canon 734, 1, this consecration is restricted to Holy Thursday of each year. The rite to be observed is found in the *Pontificale* under the title *"De officio in Feria V Coenae Domini."* "Hac die" reads the first rubric of that title, "singulis annis benedicitur Oleum Catechumenorum et Infirmorum, et conficitur Chrisma." The blessing is done at the Mass on that day, immediately before the words of the canon, *"Per quem haec omnia, Domine, semper bona creas."* When he arrives at this prayer, the bishop purifies his hands and proceeds to the table prepared for him. At the command of the Archdeacon, a subdeacon and two acolytes bring the oil from the sacristy and present it to the Archdeacon. The Archdeacon, in turn, presents it to the bishop, who immediately exorcises it. Then the blessing is given straightway with the words: "Emitte, quaesumus, Domine, Spiritum Sanctum tuum Paralictum de coelis in hanc pinguedinem olivae, quam de viridi ligno producere dignatus es, ad refectionem mentis et corporis; ut tua sancta benedictione sit omni hoc unguento coelestis medicinae perunсto, tutamen mentis et corporis, ad evacuandos omnes dolores, omnes infirmitates, omnemque aegritudinem mentis et corporis, unde unxisti Sacerdotes, Reges, Prophetas et Martyres; sit Chrisma tuum perfectum, Domine, nobis a te benedictum, permanens in visceribus nostris: In nomine Domini Jesu Christi." The oil is brought back to the sacristy and the Mass proceeds.

In the Roman Breviary under date of January 20th, it is stated that the customs of blessing the oil on Holy Thursday was due to a decree of Pope Fabian.[102] Catalano[103] is inclined to believe that this decree, included by Gratian in the *Corpus*

---

102 "Idem statuit ut quotannis feria quinta in Coena Domini, vetere combusto, chrisma renovaretur."

103 *Rit. Rom.*, t. I, p. 309.

Juris,[104] is supposititious. The Council of Toledo, celebrated in the year 400, stated that it was licit for bishops to confect chrism at any time during the year.[105] Hence, Cavallieri [106] declares that the custom cannot be said with certainty to be older than the seventh century, when mention of it is made in the Gregorian Sacramentary. St. Isadore [107] mentions the performance of this ceremony on Maundy Thursday, while St. Thomas[108] and Durandus[109] vie with each other in asserting mystical reasons for the appropriateness of the day. The custom, even at that time, was co-extensive with the Latin Rite.

After this blessing has thus taken place, it becomes incumbent on the pastors of the diocese to seek a supply of the freshly blessed oil and use it thruout the year. Oils blessed in previous years become illicit for use, except in case of necessity.[110] Consequently the newly blessed oil must be sought as soon as possible.

Canon 735, makes it obligatory upon the pastor to seek it from his own Ordinary. Such legislation is extremely old, dating back as far as the fourth Council of Carthage in 398.[111] The Fifth and Sixth Provincial Councils of Beneventum, one thousand years later (1331 and 1374), hurled an excommunication

104 c. 18, d. III, *de cons.* : "Litteris vestris inter cetera insertum invenimus, quosdam religionis vestrae episcopos a vestro nostroque ordine discrepare, et non per singulos annos in coena Domini crisma conficere. Errant vero qui talia excogitant, et mente vesana potius, quam recta sentientes haec facere audent. Sicut enim ipsius diei solemnitas per singulos annos est celebranda, ita ipsius sancti crismatis confectio per singulos annos est agenda, et de anno in annum renovanda, et fidelibus tradendum, quia novum sacramentum est et per singulos annos, in jam dicta die innovandum, et vetus in sanctis ecclesiis cremandum. Ista a sanctis apostolis et successoribus eorum accepimus, vobisque tenenda mandamus."

105 can. xx—C. 124, D. III, *de cons.*: "Omni tempore Episcopus licere chrisma conficere et per suas dioecesas destinare."

106 *Opera Liturgica,* tom. IV, cap. 26, "*De Sacris Oleis,*" decretum I in Ord. 168, page 199.

107 *De Ecclesiasticis Officiis,* Lib. I, Cap. 29, "*de Coena Dom.*"—M. P. L., 83, 764.

108 III P., q. 72, a. 12 ad 3.

109 *Rationale Divin. Officiorum,* lib. 6, cap. 74.

110 Can. 734, 1. It is not required that the oil be recent but that the consecration be recent. Cf. S. R. C., 22 Mar. 1862, ad IV, Coll. 1225; D. A., ad V, n. 3114.

111 Canon 36—C. 123, D. IV, *de cons.*

latae sententiae against priests who sought the oils from a bishop other than their own.[112]

The pastor is to procure the oils from his own Ordinary whether the latter be a bishop or not. The Ordinary is bound to supply the sacred oils for the territory he governs.[113] The obtaining of the oils from him is an acknowledgment of the Ordinary's jurisdiction and is an indication of the organization of the diocese.[114] If the see is vacant (and there is no Ordinary), Genicot teaches that the oils can be gotten from a neighboring bishop.[115]

Pastors may not be dilatory in their application for the newly blessed oils. Promptness was prescribed by the Council of Vasense (442) [116] and before it, by the Fourth Council of Carthage.[117] The reason for this prescription was due to the fact that the oil of the catechumens and the chrism were necessary for the services of Easter night, which were then similar to the Holy Saturday services of today. The Sixth Provincial Council of Benevento (1374) required the pastors to seek the three oils on the very day of consecration, Holy Thursday.[118] Benedict XIV [119] urged the obligation on the pastors of procuring the Holy Oils of the Sick as diligently as that of procuring the other two oils. In 1826, the Congregation of Rites

---

112 This decree is found in Tit. 3, cap. 3 of the Sixth Council, paragr. "*Sed ante,*" and from cap. 49 of the Fifth Council; apud Catalano, *Rit. Rom.*, t. I, p. 71.

113 Blat. *Comm. Text.*, Lib. III, p. 1, n. 14, Fanfani, *De Jure Paroch.*, n. 230.

114 Cf. Augustine, *A Commentary*, IV, p. 30.

115 *Inst. Th. M.* II, 416; Cf. answer of Pius VI to priests of France—footnote 36 of this chapter.

116 Can. 3—"Per singula territoria presbyteri vel Ministri ab Episcopis, non prout libitum fuit, a vicinioribus sed a suis propriis per annos singulos chrisma petant, appropinquante solemnitate Paschae." *Summa Conciliorum*, II, 146.

117 Can. 36—C, 123, D. IV, *de cons.* See also C. 122, D. III, *de cons.* If a pastor neglects to get the oil and dares to administer the sacraments with old oil, he does such a thing validly but so illicitly that "*pro temeritatis ausu ipse in se suae damnationis protulisse sententiam manifestatur.*"

118 tit. 3, c. 3—"Praecipientes ut singulis annis in die Jovis sancta Coenae Domini presbyteri parochiales . . . Chrisma novum, et Oleum novum Catechumenorum . . . et Oleum novum Infirmorum . . . a nobis in nostra dioecesi, seu suffraganeis nostris in eorum Dioecesibus, vel Archiprebyteris nostris suscipiant, sicut est consuetum;" Cf. Catalano, *Rit. Rom.*, t. I, p. 76.

119 *Institutiones*, lxxx, n. 3.

condemned expressly the custom prevailing in some places of deferring the distribution of oils until after Low Sunday.[120] The annotator on this decision states that the "*quamprimum*" of the rubric[121] is to be interpreted in light of the obligation to use new oils on Holy Saturday.[122] Hence, according to him, nothing but grave necessity would justify any delay. It must be remembered that this decree had to do with obtaining only the oils necessary for the blessing of the font. Yet the annotator urges the obligation of procuring the oil of the sick with the same stress as that of the other oils.

The obligation of procuring the oils promptly is binding under grave sin, according to the more probable opinion.[123] The additional obligation of applying to one's own Ordinary for the renovation of the oils is similarly grave.[124] Consequently only proportionate inconvenience will excuse from the observance of these obligations. Delay in procuring the oils can be condoned by reason of great distance, difficult roads, heavy storms, &c.[125] The latter obligation can be omitted in turbulent times, or when a strike would interrupt communication between a pastor and his own bishop.[126] Pastors regular, however, are not exempt from this obligation, but must apply to the diocesan bishop for their supply of oils.[127]

Since there is an obligation on the pastor to approach his Ordinary for the holy oils, there is a corresponding obligation on the Ordinary to furnish sufficient oil for the needs of the priests in his territory. The Oil is to be kept in the Cathedral Church and to be dispensed therefrom by the Dignitaries.[128] No fee should be charged for the oil, and the bishop may not allow

---

120 16 Dec. 1826, *in una Gandav.*, ad IV,—D. A., n. 2650.
121 *Rit. Rom.*, Tit. II, c. 1, n. 48.
122 apud D. A., vol. IV, p. 284.
123 Cf. Alphonsus, *Th. M.*, VI, 708; Konings, *Th. M.*, n. 1502, quaer, 1; Sabetti-Barrett, *Th. M.* p. 800; Noldin, *De Sac.* 433, Vermeersch-Creusen, *Epit.*, II, 230; &c.
124 Cf. Canon 735; Noldin, *De Sac.*, 433; Genicot-Salsmans, *Inst. Th. M.*, II, 416.
125 Cf. O'Kane, *The Rubrics*, n. 251.
126 Cf. Augustine, *A Commentary*, IV, p. 30.
127 Clement XIII, const. "*Inter Multiplices*, Dec. 11, 1758, paragr. 5-6—C. I. C. Fontes, n. 449.
128 S. R. C., Aug. 19, 1619—D. A., n. 375.

any gratuitous offerings to be accepted.[129] The bishop must provide the oils for the exempt places of his dioceses (*terris et locis immunibus*), such as the monasteries of the orders of both sexes.[130] Clement VIII in a Constitution dated March 24, 1599, ordered bishops to give the oil to regulars "*prompte et liberaliter*," [131] In the month preceding the issuance of this constitution the Congregation for Bishops and Regulars had declared that "*regularibus sanctum oleum ab Episcopis denegari non potest.*"[132] Three later decisions decide that "immo episcopi tenentur iisdem illud dare."[133]

It is not necessary that the pastor should make petition for the oils in person. The Fourth Council of Carthage [134] and the Council of Vasense (442) [135] demanded application thru a deacon or subdeacon. The Council of Auxerre,[136] held in 578, allowed the Archdeacon or the Archsubdeacon to appear for the priest, if he were ill. The Sixth Provincial Council of Beneventum [137] prescribed that the pastors should receive the oils "per se ipsos aut clericos, saltem adultos." This decree was corrected later in the Thirteenth Provincial Council, held at the same place, by demanding that "quotannis mittatur sacerdos aliquis, aut saltem aliquis in sacris constitutus qui nova accipiat." [138] St. Charles, likewise, restricted to men in sacred orders the bearing of the oil from the Cathedral to the pastor.[139] The rubric of the Roman Ritual[140] now reads: "Parochus, quantum fieri potest, curet, ne per laicos, sed per se, vel alium sacerdotem, vel saltem per alium Ecclesiae ministrum haec Olea deferantur." The insertion of the clause "*in quan-*

---

129 S. C. EE. et RR., 6 Sept., 1604—apud Cavallieri, *Opera Liturgica*, vol. IV, cap. 26, decr. 9.

130 Cong. EE. et RR., 1 Jan. 1610—apud Cavallieri, *ibid.*, decr. 6, page 200.

131 Const. "*Exponi Nobis*"—*Bull, Taur. Edit*, vol. X, p. 484—n. 201.

132 S. C. EE. et RR., Feb. 2, 1599—apud Cavallieri, *ibid.*, decr. 7, page 200.

133 S. C. EE., 20 Nov. 1601; 4 Jun. 1602; Nov. 10, 1659—apud Cavallieri, *ibid*, decr. 8, p. 200.

134 Can. 36—C. 123, D. III, *de cons.*

135 cap. 3—*Summa Conciliorum*, II, 146.

136 can. 6—Harduin III, 444.

137 held in 1374—tit. 3, cap. 3—Catalano, *Rit. Rom.*, t. I, p. 76.

138 Tit. XI, n. 1—Catalano, *l.c.*

139 II Prov. Conc. Mediolan., Tit. I, decr. IX—apud *Acta Eccl. Mediolan.*, tom. I, p. 68.

140 Tit. II, cap. I, n. 54.

tum fieri potest" saves the prohibition from being absolutely iron-bound. Laics are not excluded entirely, and consequently may touch the vessels of oil for a sufficient reason. Hence, Catalano claims[141] that they may be employed when a pastor cannot conveniently approach the Cathedral during Holy Week. Services usually keep pastors extremely busy during the latter part of that week; and to deprive the people of the grand ritual of those days would wreak a real spiritual hardship upon pious souls.[142] Another reason might well be the advanced age or the feebleness of the pastor, thereby making a trip to the Cathedral a great hardship. In short, any just and reasonable cause permits the pastor to engage a layman to go to the Cathedral for the oils on Holy Thursday.[143]

The question was settled specifically for the United States in 1901 in an answer given to the Bishop of Leavenworth.[144] The Propaganda took care to insert, however, that the layman employed should be trustworthy—with the consequence that the pastor should make use of much discretion in selecting the person to whom he is to entrust this sacred mission.

Baruffaldo[145] thinks that laymen are guilty of grievous sin who touch the vessel of oils without necessity. O'Kane[146] rightly holds this is too severe; and declares that the offense is serious only when committed with contempt. It must be remembered that this prohibition is binding only when the vessels actually contain the holy oil, for, since they are not consecrated, but simply blessed, they may be handled by anyone when empty. Some idea of the deep reverence due them when filled can be gained from the prescriptions of the ancient synods which commanded them to be borne "*sicut reliquiae sanctorum deportari solent.*"[147]

---

141 *Rit. Rom.* t. I, p. 76.

142 "In necessitatis casu, si nempe sacerdoti non suppetat tempus ecclesiam adeundi, ut ipse oleum assumat, deficiente oleo ministro sacro, potest laicus minister illud deferre, occulte tamen et reverenter." (Pourbaix-Coppin, *S. Liturg. Comp.*, N. 687, ad 3).

143 DeHerdt, *Lit. Prax.*, III, 157; Cf. also the annotator of the *Decreta Authentica,* Vol. IV, annotation to decree 2650, p. 285.

144 S. C. P. F., 1 May, 1901—apud Amer. Eccl. Review, vol. XXV, p. 87.

145 *Ad Rit. Rom. Comm.*, t. I, tit. X, n. 25.

146 *The Rubrics*, n. 269.

147 Conc. Vormatiense (anno 868), can. 60—apud Harduin V, 745; Conc. Autissiodorensis (anno 578), can. 6—Harduin III, 444.

The oils may not be trusted to the national mail nor to a reliable express company for transportation. A writer in the Ecclesiastical Review[148] was inclined to believe that this was lawful, asserting that the carrying services of our express companies and the efficiency of the mail transportation is as perfect here as in any country. A parcel sent thru either medium is guarded, especially if registered, as safely as if it were in the personal possession of any person, cleric or lay. Shortly after this was written, however, the Bishop of Leavenworth queried of the Holy See: "Licetne sacra Olea ab Episcopo consecrata per societatem mercatoriam 'The Express' ad sacerdotes transmittere?" The Propaganda answered to this: "Non licere." [149]

Two years later a bishop of one of the vast dioceses of Brazil reported the difficulties of some of the pastors in reaching the episcopal city to get the oil, and begged that the urgency be relieved by the permission to use the national mail as the means of transmission of the holy oils to these distant parishes. Again the Holy See refused, and published with its refusal the decree given by the Propaganda to the Bishop of Leavenworth.[150] The consequence of these decisions is the utter unlawfulness of employing either express or mail service in the distribution of the oils thruout the diocese.

The old oils, or at least part of them, must be kept until the new oils arrive. This is evident, for otherwise, the dying could not be provided for in the meantime.[151]

As long as the necessity prevents the replenishing of the supply, the old oils may be lawfully used. This is clear from

---

148 vol. XXII, pp. 311-2.

149 This decision was forwarded to the editor of the Ecclesiastical Review by the Bishop of Leavenworth, and was published in that journal soon afterwards—vol. XXV, pp. 61-2.

150 S. C. S. Off., 14 Jan. 1903—A. S. S., XXXVI, 14.

151 O'Kane, *The Rubrics*, n. 857; Gavant, *Manuale Episcoporum*, V, E. U., n. 10. It is very advisable to have two ampullae for each oil, so that one may be kept while the other has been sent to the Cathedral for replenishing—cf. St. Charles Borromeo in the Fourth Provincial Council of Milan, *Pars Secunda Constitutionum*, cap. inscripto "Quae ad sacramentalia vel ad Sacramenta pertinent," apud *Acta Eccl. Mediolanensis*, t. I, pars 1, p. 140.

decisions of the Roman Congregations,[152] and from Canon 734, 1. Occasionally in the past the Holy See has granted various localities the permission to use old oil, because of missionary conditions there existing.[153] By the Constitution "*Trans Oceanum,*"[154] for example, all Latin America and the Philippine Islands were allowed to use the old oils for four years, if, after due diligence, they could not obtain newly-blessed or more recently blessed oil. Now, however, no such indult is necessary, if the necessity is truly present.[155]

After the arrival of the new oil, it becomes altogether unlawful to use the old oil. It is the common opinion of theologians that such a procedure is mortally sinful.[156]

The old oil is to be burned, as the Pontifical prescribes.[157] If there is any oil in bottles or vases, it should be poured into the lamp which hangs before the Blessed Sacrament. What is contained in the cotton in the oil-stocks for ordinary use should be burned together with the cotton.[158] Before the cotton is placed in the fire, however, it may be squeezed over the sanctuary lamp so that the loose oil will be deposited therein. After the cotton is burned, the ashes are to be thrown into the sacrarium.[159]

The custom of burning the oil is extremely ancient. There is mention of it in the pseudo-Fabian letter.[160] A similar prescription is found in the Pontifical of Emesa in Syria, edited in 1214, and in the Pontifical of Arles, which also dates back

---

152 S. C. EE. et RR., March 20, 1590—apud Cavallieri, *Opera Liturgica,* tom. IV, Cap. 26, *De Sacris Oleis,* n. VII, p. 199; S. R. C., Jan. 19, 1608—D. A., n. 244.

153 Cf. S. C. P. F., 13 Aug. 1669 (C. P. pro Sin.)—Coll. 183; 18 Feb. 1783 (C. G.) *Sophiae*—Coll. 561; 27 Sept. 1835 Gregory XVI granted Bishops and Vicars Apostolic in China and adjacent lands the faculty *in perpetuum* of using old oils—Coll. 840.

154 Cf. Ferreres, *Comp. Th. M.*, II, 255.

155 Augustine, *A Commentary,* IV, p. 30.

156 Barbosa, *De Off. et Pot. Parochi,* p. II, cap. 22, n. 25; Baruffaldo, *Ad Rit. Rom. Comm.*, t. 1, tit. 27, n. 3; De Herdt, *Lit. Prax.* III, 155; Genicot-Salsmans, *Inst. Th. M.*, II, 416; cf. C. 122, D. III, *de cons.*

157 Pars. III, "*De Off. in Fer. V Coena Dom.,*" in fine.

158 Pontificale, *loc. cit.*

159 Cavallieri, *Opera Liturgica,* t. IV, cap. 26, *De Sacris Oleis,* n. VIII; O'Kane, *The Rubrics,* n. 254; De Herdt, *Lit. Prax.*, III, 155.

160 c. 18, D. III, de *cons.*

to the thirteenth century.[161] In the Fourth Provincial Council of Milan,[162] this regulation was likewise decreed. In 1579, the Provincial Council of Salernitano[163] commanded this disposition of the old oil.

This practice was not universal, however. Other Pontificals instructed the old oil to be mixed with the new oil. Thus the Pontifical of Beauvais, edited about 800, plainly states: "Tunc Chrisma novum misceatur cum veteri, si quid residuum sit: similiter et Oleum, et ita dividat presbyteris." [164] Similar rubrics are contained in the ancient Pontificals of Constantinople and Silvanectense.[165] The Sixth Provincial Council of Benevento (1374)[166] prescribed that the old oil should be poured into the Sacrarium by way of the baptismal font, and that the *ampullae* be diligently cleansed before refilling with newly-consecrated oil. In 1601 the Congregation of Rites[167] issued a decree commanding that the old oil be disposed of by burning. Since that time until the present day, the practice of burning the old oils upon reception of the fresh supply has been observed thruout the Latin Church.

A final question in regard to the oil arises when the supply begins to run low—and there is danger that it will be exhausted before more oil can be procured. The solution is found in Canon 734, 2, which permits the addition of unblessed olive oil to the diminished supply, but *always* in a smaller quantity than the amount of blessed oil.

This is not the first legislation on the subject. As early as the thirteenth century Innocent III stated: "Non negamus quin oleum non consecratum consecrato possit oleo admisceri."[168] It will be noticed that the Pope made no mention of the amount

---

161 Martene, *De Antiqua Eccles. Disciplina in Divin. Celebrandis Officiis*, cap. xxiii.

162 Constit., Pars II, Capite inscripto "*Quae ad sacramentalia vel ad sacramenta communiter pertinent*"—apud *Acta Eccl. Mediolan.*, t. I, p. 140.

163 Tit. 32, c. 7—apud Catalano, *Rit. Rom.*, t. I, p. 307.

164 Martene, *De Antiqua Eccles. Disciplina in Divin. Celebrandis Officiis*, cap. xxii.

165 Martene, *l.c.*, paragr. iv, n. 1.

166 Tit. III, cap. III, paragr. "*Sed ante;*" Cf. Catalano, *Rit. Rom.*, t. I, p. 71.

167 S. C. R., 7 Sept., 1601—apud Cavallieri, *Opera Liturgica*, tom. IV, cap. 26, *de Sacris Oleis*, Decretum I, p. 199.

168 c. 3, X, *de cons. Eccl.*, III, 40.

that might be added. Later legislation made careful note of the fact that the added oil should be less in quantity than the oil to which it is added. Thus, St. Charles, in the Fourth Provincial Council of Milan[169] ordered the mixture to be made "*guttatim,*" drop by drop, in order to insure the addition always of a smaller quantity.

The Congregation of the Council[170] in 1682, allowed this addition to be made repeatedly, even if the amount of the repeated additions totalled more than the original quantity of blessed oil, provided, of course, that every individual increase of the oil was less than the bulk of blessed oil. This enactment of the Council was re-stated by Pius VI in a constitution,[171] dated May 28, 1793. The Ritual, before its latest revision, allowed the replenishing of the supply of blessed oil with these words: "Id tamen si forte infra annum aliquo modo ita deficiat, ut sufficere non posse videatur, neque aliud benedictum haberi queat, modico oleo non benedicto, in minore quantitate superinfuso reparari potest." [172] The rubric of the latest edition simply repeats the words of the Canon.[173]

As a rule, the bishop should consecrate a sufficient amount at the ceremony on Holy Thursday to supply the diocese for the entire year.[174] It is not allowable to bless a small quantity on that day and immediately afterwards increase the amount by successive additions of unblessed oil. This custom has been condemned twice by the Congregation of Rites.[175] Lawfully, the oil cannot be added unless there is a danger that the supply on hand will give out before the next consecration. There must always exist a *bona fide* necessity.[176]

169 Constitutionum Pars II, cap. "*Quae ad sacramentalia vel sacramenta communiter spectant*"—apud *Acta Eccl. Mediol.*, pars I, t. I, p. 140.

170 Sept. 23, 1682—D. A. by Falise, v. "Oleum," in nota, n. 6; also cf. Quarti, *De Benedict.*, tit. 1, s. 2, dub. 5, n. 13 et 14.

171 Const. "*Sollicitudo Omnium Ecclesiarum,*" responsum 13—"Posse oleo benedicto adjungi non benedictum pluribus vicibus, ita ut oleum adjunctum non consideratum separatim, et in unaquaque admixtione, sit in minori quantitate quam oleum benedictum, quamvis omnibus consideratis omnibus additionibus simul, fiat quantitas major non benedicti; quemadmodum resolutum fuit a S. C. Concilii, 23 Sept., anni 1682" (Bull. Taur. Edit., X, 2623).

172 Tit. V, cap. 1, n. 3—edit. 1913.

173 Tit. V, cap. 1, n. 3—edit. 1925.

174 Woywod, *A Practical Commentary*, I, 628.

175 Dec. 7, 1844, *Patavin.*,—D. A., n. 2883; 28 Jan. 1910—A. A. S., II, 118.

176 Cf. O'Kane, *The Rubrics*, n. 258.

Extreme care must be taken to see that the amount of oil added is less in quantity than the amount already at hand. It is wiser, therefore, to make many additions, rather than undergo the risk of pouring in an amount almost equal to the quantity of consecrated oil. Augustine is slightly confused mathematically when he states: "The mixture should not exceed the proportion of 3 : 2, i. e., only one-third of common olive oil may be added." [177] Strictly speaking, however, the mixture of the oil will not lose its blessing until a greater, or at least, an equal amount of unblessed oil has been added at one time.

The second or third or subsequent additions need not be less than the amount of blessed oil present before the first addition was made. All that is necessary is that the added amount be less in quantity than the amount to which it is added. For example, if originally there remained five ounces of oil, three ounces may be added without imperilling the loss of the consecration. To these eight ounces of oil may be added six ounces more, for even though this is more than the original five ounces of consecrated oil, nevertheless, it is not as large as the sum total of the oil to which it has been added.[178]

Among the older theologians, Zambranus [179] and Quintadvenas [180] held that the oil added to the consecrated oil, whether at once or at various times, should never exceed the amount of original blessed oil. Thus, if sixteen ounces of oil were blessed, the total of additions could never exceed—or even equal—one pound. The argument advanced by Quintadvenas is indeed ingenious:

> "Subjectum hujus benedictionis est illud oleum quod a principio fuit ab Episcopo benedictum; ergo necesse est, ut benedictio conservetur, quod maneat idemmet, quia benedictio non potest esse sine subjecto, nec ad aliud absolute diversum transire; sed quando olei quantitas, etiam in diversis vicibus addita, pervenit ad tantam ex

---

177 *A Commentary*, IV, p. 30. O'Kane notes that in the Collections on Irish Church History, page 122, there is an ordinance drawn up in the middle of the sixteenth century prescribing that the amount of oil added each time shall not exceed one-third—apud *The Rubrics*, n. 257.

178 Cf. De Sainte-Beuve, *De Ext. Unct.*, disp. 3, a. 1, apud Migne, *Curs. Theol. Comp.*, Vol. XXIV, col. 88.

179 *De Cas. Temp. Mortis*, cap. 6, dub. 5, num. 5—quoted by Diana, *Op. Coord.*, t. II, tr. IV, res. IV.

180 *Th. M.*, t. I, tr. 5, singul. 1, num. 4 et sqq.—quoted by Diana, *l.c.*

additis factam, ut si major illa cui facta est additio et initio fuit consecrata; jam non manet absolute idem individuum physicum olei et a principio consecratum, cum vix maneat aliqua pars exigua illius, ob quam duntaxat dici possit non simpliciter, sed secundum quid, idem: ergo in eo non potest manere benedictio, quae conservari non valet, nisi servata identitas subjecti physici.

"Confirmatur primo: quia si oleo consecrato addatur semel seu una vice major pars non consecrati, nullum manet consecratum quia non manet idem individuum physicum; sed idem est, cum diversis vicibus additur major pars non benedicti, ergo nec benedictio manet.

"Confirmatur secundo: nam ideo quando minima pars olei non benedicti miscetur olei benedicti, totum manet benedictum, quia in commixtionibus major quantitas debet in se minorem convertere vel saltem ad sui identitatem trahere et ei communicare suas qualitates: sed hoc fieri non potest cum pars addita est notabiliter major; ergo nec haec poterit participare benedictionem illius. Quod vero major pars olei non benedicti addatur unica vel pluribus vicibus benedicto, non tollit, quod fit major pars."

In refutation of this, Diana [181] quotes an explanation offered as probable by John Uvigers, a professor at Louvain. The theory he offers may be summed up as follows: The mixture of unblessed oil with the blessed oil does not *ipso facto* consecrate the unblessed portion of the mixture. It simply makes it possible that the blessed oil thru such an intermixture be more widely diffused. Although there might be much of the substance still unblessed, nevertheless, every time the thumb would be dipped therein it would touch at least some part of blessed oil.

This is not very satisfactory, but indeed, it is very hard to get a satisfactory explanation of the procedure. How can the mere addition of the same substance in a smaller quantity cause the transfer of a spiritual quality possessed by the original substance to the whole amount? To offer the apothegm: "*Major pars trahit ad se minorem*" does not give an explanation. The knowledge desired is why the greater part transfers its supernatural accidents to the lesser part.

St.-Beuve explained the matter in this fashion. It is the right of the Church to prescribe the rite whereby the oil shall be consecrated. Accordingly, she may, and she has, decreed that the addition of unblessed oil to blessed oil in a minor quantity is really a rite of consecration. "Ecclesia, penes quam est deter-

181 Op. Coord., t. II, tr. IV, res. IV.

minare ritum consecrationis olei, determinavit admixtionem tanquam alterum e ritibus consecrationis.''[182] He rejects the teaching of others who claim that the added oil is blessed thru mathematical contact. Consecration is a spiritual quality; and, therefore, not communicated thru mathematical contact.

However, this opinion can hardly be true. The addition can be made by anybody, bishop, priest, deacon, cleric, or layman. Yet, if this action were a ceremony, a rite of consecration, he who performs it would be the minister. Since only bishops (and priests with apostolic indult) can perform such a blessing validly, it would be necessary to restrict to the bishop this act of adding unblessed oil to blessed oil. Yet there is no evidence of any such restriction in the law, and *de facto* such a thing is rarely done by bishops; indeed, not infrequently is it done by minor clerics.

Catalano[183] gives as the reason why the oil thus added is considered blessed, the will of the Church to extend the prayers of the bishop not only to the oil present before him on Holy Thursday, but also to all the oil which will thereafter be mixed with it. He does not, however, prove that the Church has the power to do this.

---

182 *De Ext. Unct.*, disp. 3, a. 1, quaeres 4—apud Migne, *Cursus Theol. Comp.*, Vol. XXIV, col. 88.

183 *Rit. Rom.*, t. I, p. 309.

CHAPTER XI.

THE RESERVATION OF THE OIL

CANON 946.

Oleum Infirmorum parochus loco nitido et decenter ornato in vase argenteo vel stanneo diligenter custodiat, nec domi retineat nisi ad normam can. 735.

CHAPTER XI.

Holy things are to be treated in a holy fashion. *Sancta sancte tractanda.* Consequently, the Church has prescribed continually a careful custodianship and a respectable repository for the oils used in her sacraments. Immediately after the oil has been consecrated, the bishop commands the priests to guard the chrism and the oil "*attente et fideliter*" under penalty of deprivation of honor.[1]

The Church has a veritable horror of the possibility that the oils may, under any pretext, be diverted to a use other than their proper function in the sacred rites which she has prescribed. Past times saw their application in instances far different than were ever intended. Nefarious practices, such as these, gave origin to stern legislation, threatening dire penalties on those who were tempted to forget the deep reverence due to the oils. Innocent III ordered that careless custodians be suspended from office for three months; and if, thru their negligence, any sacrilege had resulted, punishments still graver were to be inflicted.[2] The particular Councils of Magonza[3] and Arles,[4] both celebrated in 1313, deprived the priest of honor, just as the Pontificale of today. Yet, the seventeenth century had not seen the extirpation of every abuse, for the Thirteenth Council of Beneventano (1656) was compelled to legislate very specifically: "Neque sacra Olea sacerdos laicis ullo modo concedat ne illis abutantur; alioquin laici ipso facto facti sint excommunicati; clerici vero beneficiati suspensione, *beneficiorum privatione ac etiam exilio a civitate et dioecesi mulctentur; non-beneficiati carceris annalis, ac deinde eandem exilii poenam incurrant.*"[5]

---

1 Pontificale Rom., tit. "*Benedictio Olei Cat.*"—"Pontifex jubet presbyteros attente, ut juxta Canonum traditionem, chrisma et olea fideliter custodiant et nulli sub praetextu medicinae vel maleficii tradere praesumant, alioquin *honore* priventur."

2 C. 1, X, *de custod. Euchar., Chrism., et aliorum Sacr.*, III, 44.

3 can. 27—apud Catalano, *Rit. Rom.*, tom. I, p. 74.

4 can. 18—apud Catalano, *l.c.*

5 tit. 49, "*De Officio Parochi,*" n. 35, apud Catalano, *Rit. Rom.*, t. I, p. 76.

The Code is quite detailed in its regulations in regard to the keeping of the sacred oils. It seems especially solicitous about the oil of the sick, for a special canon is inserted to reaffirm the regulation made about the three oils in general in Canon 735. The prescriptions of both canons dove-tail with each other and must be considered together.

The vessel which holds the oil must be made of silver, or at least of lead or tin. "Stannum" was a metal composed of a mixture of lead and silver in Ciceronic times; but in later Latin it acquired the signification of "tin."

This prescription of the Code in regard to the vessel is not new. The Ritual, both before and after its latest revision, coincided with the law of the Code.[6] It was required even before the promulgation of the Roman Ritual, as is evidenced by the enactment of the Councils of Salernitano[7] and Beneventum,[8] ordering that the oils "asserventur in vase argenteo, vel saltem stanneo apte fabrefacto." Baruffaldo[9] notes that gold vessels are not excluded, if the Church is rich enough to afford their purchase. Some authors quoted by him declare the inadvisability of using very pure gold, because it is too soft for practical use. Copper may not be used, for it corrodes and thereby corrupts the oil.[10] Fragile substances, as glass, brick, earthen-ware, marble and tile, are equally unsuitable.[11] Wood is excluded because of its absorptive powers,[12] and brass because of its aptitude to rust and tarnish.[13] Pewter, a mixture of lead, tin and copper, may lawfully be employed.[14]

The vessel itself should be securely closed by means of a detachable cap made of the same metal as the vessel itself.[15] Baruffaldo[16] advises that the cap should be of such a size as to fit only the vessel of the *Oleum Infirmorum*. Some inscription, such as OI or EXTR. UNCT., should be engraved in large

6 Tit. V, cap. 1, n. 3.
7 anno 1579, tit. 32—apud Catalano, *op. cit.*, p. 307.
8 anno 1374, tit. III, cap. 1—apud Catalano, *l.c.*
9 *Ad Rit. Rom. Comm.*, t. I, tit. X, n. 16.
10 De Herdt, *Lit. Prax.*, III, 157; Baruffaldo, *Ad Rit. Rom. Comm.*, l.c. n. 7.
11 De Herdt, *l.c.*, Baruffaldo, *l.c.*
12 Baruffaldo, *l.c.*, n. 18.
13 Baruffaldo, *l.c.*, De Herdt, *l.c.*
14 *Amer. Eccl. Review*, vol. XXXI, p. 373.
15 *Amer. Ecc. Review, l.c.;* Maringola, *Institut. Liturg.*, vol. 1, p. 343.
16 *Ad Rit. Rom. Comm.*, tom. I, tit. 27, n. 46.

characters on the side of the vessel—and it is well to have a corresponding inscription upon the cap.[17]

As a general rule, each church has a large vessel for each oil. For daily use smaller vessels may be used; and may be separate from one another or conjoined. This is explicitly allowed by the Ritual in regard to the oils required in Baptism;[18] and commentators extend this to the oil of the sick.[19] O'Kane notes that in missionary countries the three vessels are usually joined together, making a cylinder about three inches in length. Each compartment is distinct and is marked with its proper letter.[20] In the United States the chrism is marked SC or S. CHR., the Oil of the Catechumens as SO or OC, and the Oleum Infirmorum as OI.

Some absorbent substance should be placed in the smaller vessels in order to prevent the oil from spilling. Cotton is admirable for this purpose and is usually used. Instead of cotton, lint may be employed, and likewise shreds of silk or a small sponge. All of these absorb the oil very readily, and quite as readily yield it at the slightest pressure of the thumb.[21]

The vessel of oil should be encased in a burse of leather,[22] which is lined with purple silk. Burses for the smaller vessels should have attached double silken strings, purple in color, so that they may be suspended from the neck of the priest.[23] The base of the burse, Baruffaldo advises,[24] should be broad and stiff, so that it can stand upright, thus holding the vessel of oil in its correct position.

When not in use the oil should repose in an *armarium* or

---

17 Baruffaldo, *l.c.*, n. 45; Amer. Eccl. Review, *l.c.;* O'Kane, *The Rubrics*, n. 262.
18 Tit. II, c. 1, n. 51.
19 O'Kane, *The Rubrics*, n. 262.
20 *Op. cit.*, n. 261.
21 Baruffaldo, *Ad Rom. Rit. Comm.*, tit. X, n. 22.
22 *Rit. Rom.*, tit. V, cap. 2, n. 2; *Amer. Eccl. Review*, vol. XXXI, p. 373.
23 Heuser, *The Parish Priest*, p. 94; Baruffaldo, *op. cit.*, tit. 27, n. 47-48.
24 *L.c.*

ambry. St. Charles called it a "*ciborium,*"[25] while the Council of Ravenna (1312) termed it "*sacristia.*"[26] It should be made of strong wood, square in form, and as large as is needed.[27] Purple silk should line the inside walls.[28] A little door, tightly closing, should guard the entrance to the ambry, which must be kept under lock and key.[29] Finally, there should be an inscription upon the outside of the door denoting the contents (e. g., "OLEUM INFIRMORUM").

The obligation of keeping the oil under lock and key is very ancient. In 1122 the Synod of Oxoniensis ordered this safeguard for the oils.[30] A century later, Innocent III prescribed this in regard to the chrism and the Eucharist.[31] The Council of Magonza, celebrated in 1310, ordered the keeping of the oil "sub fideli custodia, clavibus adhibitis."[32] St. Charles, in the Fourth Provincial Council of Milan,[33] assigned the keeping of the key to the rector personally, ordering him to relinquish it to no one but another priest who needed the oil for a sick-call. The new Code gives the same command, as is evidenced by the express terminology of canon 735. The pastor is to keep the oils "*sub clavi diligenter.*" DeHerdt[34] notes the advisability of having two keys, but he directs that both of them be held by the rector.

The armarium is to be kept in the church as a general rule. Its most suitable place is upon the side wall of the church on the gospel side of the high altar (or altar where the Blessed Sacra-

---

25 III Prov. Conc. Mediol., cap. "*Quae ad Sacramentalia et Sacramenta pertinent*"—apud *Acta Eccl. Mediolanen.*, pars I, tom. I, page 97. N. B. St. Charles certainly did not mean the tabernacle by this word. This is clear from the legislation he enacted in the IV Prov. Council of Milan (capite inscripto "*Quae ad SS. Euchar. Sacramentum pertinent*"—apud *Acta Eccles. Mediolan.*, pars IV, tom. I, p. 143). There his enactment ordered that the tabernacle wherein the Blessed Sacrament was preserved "vauum etiam sit a reliquiis, vasculo Olei Infirmorum, atque inani alio vase."

26 rub. vii—Harduin VII, 1364.

27 Maringola, *Institut. Liturg.*, t. I, p. 343; Baruffaldo, *Ad Rit. Rom. Comm.*, t. I, tit. 27, n. 42.

28 Baruffaldo, *l.c.*

29 Baruffaldo, *l.c.*

30 can. 24; cf. Catalano, *Rit. Rom.*, t. I, p. 74.

31 c. 1, X, *de custodia Euchar., Chris. et al. sacr.*, III, 44.

32 Mansi, XXV, 329.

33 Constit. pars secunda, cap. "*Quae ad sacramentalia et sacramenta pertinent*"—apud *Acta Eccl. Mediolan*, p. I, tom. I, page 140.

34 *Lit. Prax.*, III, 157.

ment is kept), so that it will be a participant in the rays of light that shine from the tabernacle lamp.[35] It should be hung at such a height that the ordinary man can open the door without stooping or without using a step or a ladder.[36] According to the *Caeremoniale Episcoporum*[37] the oil of the sick should have a special ambry of its own. The reason for this is that the oil of the sick should be kept in the church proper, while the other two oils may be placed in the baptistry (which is sometimes a separate building) or in the baptismal font. Thus the Synod of Ferrara declared: "Fenestellam propriam, atque ad hoc unice praeparatam, habere debet Sanctum Oleum Infirmorum, quam nonnulli vocant Armarium. Propria ista debet esse haec fenestella in parte Ecclesiae ad cornu Evangelii seu in quo adsit Tabernaculum cum Sanctissima Eucharistia."[38] A further reason for placing the oils near the altar where the Blessed Sacrament is kept is the convenience it affords when it is necessary to bring both at once on sick-calls.

The holy oils may certainly not be kept within the tabernacle.[39] They may be placed, however, in a drawer beside the tabernacle or even in the very framework of it.[40] It is not strictly commanded by the Code that the ambry should be hung on the gospel side of the altar of the Blessed Sacrament. The words "*in ecclesia*" do not confine the locality of the ambry to any particular part of the church. The Sacred Congregation of Rites permitted their repose in any becoming place, "sive in cornu Epistolae, sive in cornu Evangelii.[41] Even the sacristy is not excluded as a location of the ambry. At first blush it may seem to be prohibited. Canon 1172 certainly excludes the sacristy as part of the church; and the law of the Decretals[42] mentions both the oil and the Blessed Sacrament in the same enactment and requires that both should be kept in the

35 O'Kane, *The Rubrics*, n. 855; Baruffaldo, *Ad Rit. Rom. Comm.*, t. I, tit. 27, n. 40.

36 Baruffaldo, *op. cit.*, l. c., n. 42.

37 lib. 1, c. 6, § 2.

38 apud D. A., vol. IV, p. 283—Comm. ad decr. 2650, qu. 3.

39 S. C. EE. et RR., 3 Maii, 1693, apud Cavallieri, *Opera Liturgica*, t. IV, c. 6, decr. 13, n. 1.

40 O'Kane, *The Rubrics*, n. 856.

41 S. R. C., *Ariminen.*, 16 Jun. 1663—D. A., n. 1260.

42 c. 1, X, *de Custod. Euchar., Chrism. et al. Sacr.*, III, 44.

church. Since the Blessed Sacrament's place is in the tabernacle of the altar, it would seem to follow that the oils should likewise be kept in the church proper. But Canon 1172, however, deals with "odiosa," and as a result demands a very strict interpretation. Furthermore, the insertion of the phrase "in ipsa ecclesia" makes impossible the more generous interpretation of "ecclesia" so as to include the sacristy. *"In favorabilibus"* the sacristy is considered part of the church. All authors allow the permissibility of fulfilling the Sunday precept by hearing Mass from the sacristy. Furthermore, in virtue of Canon 1269, 3, the Blessed Sacrament itself can be removed (for a serious reason approved by the Ordinary) from the tabernacle at night and put in a safer place. This "safer place" may surely be the sacristy. Moreover, this very canon that we are treating, permits the transfer of the oils under certain conditions even to the rectory. As a consequence, the argument from analogy seems sufficient to allow the erection of the ambry in the sacristy.[43]

"Nec domi retineat nisi ad normam can. 735."

The latter part of the canon forbids the keeping of the oils in the rectory without permission of the Ordinary obtained for a just and sufficient reason. There have been several decrees of the Congregation of Rites on this question. In 1826 it condemned an existing custom of having the oils in the house for reasons of convenience, except in the parishes where the rectory was situated at a great distance from the Church.[44] In 1872 the same congregation declared that the fact that the rectory was separate from the church was not sufficient cause to keep the oils at home; and ordered an observance of the decree of 1826.[45]. This decree was in turn confirmed in a reply given to the Bishop of Compostella who had asked whether the custom existing in the rural parishes of his dioceses of keeping the oils in the rectory might likewise be extended to city par-

---

43 Cf. Blat, *Comm. Text.*, lib. III, pars I, n. 14.

44 S. R. C., *Gandav.*, 16 Dec. 1826, *ad tertiam facti speciem*—D. A., n. 2650.

45 S. R. C., *Toletana*, Aug. 31, 1872 ad V—D. A., n. 3276; A. S. S., XII, 308.

ishes.[46] A second confirmation of the decree of 1872 was made two years later, when the Holy See declared that the inconvenience of summoning sleeping servants to open the church's doors for night calls was not enough to allow a transfer of the oils from the church to the parish house.[47] In every case the Congregation has refused to relax the strictness of the law, admitting an exception only in the single case of great distance from the church.

The Church always remembers that her sacraments are holy things and must be treated with the utmost reverence. Though this be so, she remembers, too, that they are "propter homines" always. Hence, whenever there is danger that the interests of her children may be imperilled by unnecessary delay in the administration of such an important sacrament, she has allowed the feasibility of serving her children to mellow the firmness of her prescriptions. Thus Canon 735 allows the oil to be kept in the house, not alone when it is a great distance from the church, but when any necessity or just cause exists in a particular place. The pastor, however, is not the judge of the seriousness of the reason, but must submit it to the Ordinary for his approval and consent. Blat[48] and Ferreres[49] imply that when necessity is present, the Ordinary's permission is not required, whereas if a grave cause for the transfer of the oils exists, it should be passed upon by the bishop. Other authors, like Vermeersch-Creusen[50] and Woywod,[51] mention no such distinction. Accordingly, if the necessity is foreseen to be short-lived, Blat's opinion may be safely acted upon. If, on the other hand, it is known that the necessity will be of long duration, or if it is uncertain whether it is a case of real necessity, it is wiser and safer to obtain the Ordinary's permission.

A necessity can arise from many causes. A destruction of the church by fire or storm would surely be a necessity.

---

46 S. R. C., *Compostellana,* 15 Nov. 1890, ad II—D. A., n. 3739; A. S. S., XXIII, 636.

47 S. R. C., *Laudenen.,* 23 Jun. 1892, ad VII —D. A., n. 3779: A. S. S., XXV, 114-15.

48 *Comm. Text.,* lib. III, p. I, n. 14.

49 *Comp. Th. M.,* II, 836.

50 *Epit.,* II, 19.

51 *A Practical Commentary,* I, n. 630.

Danger of irreverence to the oils when left in the church or sacristy would also constitute a "necessity." Rome preferred to permit the keeping of the oils in the priest's house rather than to leave them in a sacristy accessible to non-Catholics.[52]

A just cause would be present when the rectory is situated at a considerable distance (not necessarily a great distance) from the church.[53] Just how far this distance must be depends largely on local circumstances. If the time necessarily consumed to reach the church is ordinarily enough to put the priest to serious inconvenience or imperil the opportune reception of the sacrament on the part of the sick, the distance is sufficient to obtain permission to preserve the oils in the rectory. Other good reasons would be the frequency of emergency calls, as in times of plague or in parishes wherein accident hospitals are situated.[54] Besides the existence of the just cause, there must also be had the permission of the Ordinary, as the canon requires. Blat [55] notes that it is quite enough if the permission be tacit "seu ex factis ejus deducta circa illam causam."

What, then, can be said of the custom existing almost everywhere in the United States of keeping the oil in the rectory? It is certainly general, and by no means confined to any particular dioceses, provinces or regions.[56] In view of the line of decisions given by the Congregation of Rites, it would be rash to assert that this custom would be approved, except, of course, where special reasons exist. Moreover, in the opinion of a writer in the *American Ecclesiastical Review*,[57] this custom is altogether unlawful. However, as Augustine notes,[58] it is not formally reprobated by the text of the canon. Perhaps, too, the contention of Blat, that a tacit permission of the bishop suffices, may avail to some extent to excuse our priests.

It is wisely noted by O'Kane [59] that the same reason for keeping the oil of the sick in the priest's house will not suffice

---

52 S. C. P. F., (C. G.—*Helvetiae*) 7 Mar. 1805—Coll., n. 685.
53 Cf. Vermeersch-Creusen, *Epit.*, II, 19; O'kane, *The Rubrics*, n. 267.
54 Ferreres, *Comp. Th. M.*, II, 836; Hanley, *Treatise on Sacr. of Extr. Unct.*, p. 10.
55 *Comm. Text.*, lib. III, pars I, n. 14.
56 Augustine, *A Commentary*, IV, page 31.
57 vol. XVIII, p. 430.
58 *L.c.*
59 *The Rubrics*, n. 267.

for that of keeping the chrism with it, much less the oil of the catechumens.[60] In rare instances only will a priest be called upon to use them outside the baptistery. Sudden baptisms, performed privately, require chrism if handy, according to the prescriptions of Canon 759, 1; but the Oleum Infirmorum is rarely used except when the child is brought to the church. The exceptional case where, by permission of the Ordinary, solemn baptism may be administered outside the baptistery (Can. 776, § 1, 2°), is too infrequent to justify the retention in any other place than the baptistery of the oils used in the ceremony.

When the oils are removed to the house, the rubric and the canon must be observed in regard to the "locus decens."[61] For this purpose it is advisable to procure an ambry similar to those erected in the churches. If this is not done, the compartment used must be clean and suitable for the purpose.[62] "Servandum itaque est religiose," warns Van der Stappen,[63] "non cum aliis suppellectilibus et domesticis utensilibus; sed in propria et speciali capsula, ac semper sub sera." Hanley[64] is of the opinion that a drawer in the priest's desk will suffice. It stands to reason that a drawer thus employed should not be cluttered with profane articles, although it would hardly be wrong to preserve therein other sacred things, such as relics, &c.

The possibility of emergency calls will occasionally raise the question of the permissibility of removing the oils from their repository to a more convenient place. If the interest of souls is at stake, surely a relaxation of the law can be temporarily presumed. This is deducible from a decision of the Holy See in 1893 which tolerated the custom of transferring the oil of the sick from its ambry in the church to a suitable place near arenas where bull-fights were being held.[65] At the

---

60 There can be hardly any reason whatsoever for bringing the oil of the catechumens or the holy chrism along with the oil of the sick on sick-calls. Such a custom is altogether without excuse. Cf. O'Kane, *op. cit.*, n. 911; article by "Peregrinus Gasolinus," in *The Acolyte*, vol. II, n. 8, p. 11.

61 S. R. C., *Gandav.*, 16 Dec. 1826, ad tertiam facti speciem—D. A., n. 2650.

62 Heuser, *The Parish Priest*, p. 94.

63 *Sac. Lit.*, t. IV, Q. 216.

64 *Treatise on the Sacrament of Extreme Unction*, p. 10.

65 S. Poenitent., 19 Sept., 1893—A. S. S., XXVI, p. 447.

same time it was noted that such a custom must not be tolerated if it is known that it promotes the sport, or seemingly approves it in any way. *A fortiori* no such transfer of the oils may be made by agreement (*ex condicto*).

Another case of temporary emergency arises when a pastor expects a sick-call during the night. Older authors fell into much discussion about this case. Barbosa [66] holds a comparatively stern opinion: "Non bene agere parochum timentem de nocte se vocandum pro infirmo periculoso, si vespere ferat oleum ad suum cubiculum, ut vocatus expeditius vadat; vel si de nocte reversus ab unctione infirmi, oleum retineat domi usque mane; nullum tamen credit mortale peccatum contrahere citra scandalum vel periculum alicujus irreverentiae." Alphonsus [67] and Scavini [68] concur in this view, if there is no danger that the pastor will arrive too late thru the inconvenience of procuring the oils from the church. Gobat [69] is somewhat more liberal. He admits the lawfulness of keeping the oils immediately at hand for the sick call, but he does not excuse from all fault if the oils are not returned to the church immediately after their use, unless inclement weather prevails. Later authors make no division of the night into the period prior to the call and that subsequent to the call. Genicot-Salsmans says simply that it is permissible to bring the oils to the house "in casu transeunte quo citius noctu accurri possit ad infirmum qui brevi inungendus videtur."[70] Blat [71] speaks in similar fashion; and this opinion may be safely followed.

In these altogether individual instances the permission of the Ordinary for this temporary removal of the oil is by no means required. The law contemplates the retention of the oil "per modum habitus," and does not refer to cases of this kind. "Jure nihilominus," De Amicis writes,[72] "asservatio in domo prohibita quae est habitualis intelligitur, haud illa quam ali-

66 *De Offic. et Potest. Parochi,* pars 2, cap. 22, n. 44.
67 *Th. M.,* VI, 730.
68 *Th. M.,* III, 533.
69 *Moral.,* Tract. VIII, n. 931-2.
70 *Inst. Th. M.,* II, 421.
71 *Comm. Text.,* lib. 3, pars I, n. 14.
72 *Caeremoniale Parochorum,* n. 198, 2.

quando excusare necessitas potest; sacramenta enim propter homines Christus Dominus instituit."

A final word should be said of the practice of many priests in the United States of carrying with them continually the Oil of the Sick. There is no doubt that such a practice would be permissible in places where the priest is *habitually* in danger of being called upon to administer the sacrament in cases when delay is fatal. Circumstances such as these arise in times of plague, in emergency hospitals or at mining camps. Missionaries who have stations far away from their permanent post are often compelled to carry the oils with the rest of their paraphernalia when they visit these missions. These conditions are exceptional indeed, although they are not unheard of in our land. Where they exist, priests may, without scruple, carry on their persons continually the oil of the unction. Rules and rubrics were made for normal times, and do not bind under extraordinary circumstances.

But what can be said of priests who do this in large cities and flourishing dioceses, where missionary privileges can hardly be called into justification? The question was answered in the *Ecclesiastical Review,* and is quoted here at length:

> "The law prescribes both the reservation of the Holy Oils in an abode separate from his own and the solemn manner of administering the same. 'Habeat igitur parochus loco nitido, &c. Oleum infirmorum,' etc., and then adds by ways of indicating the exception to this reservation and solemn treatment: 'Quodsi longius iter peragendum, aut etiam equitandum sit, vel alias adsit periculum effusionis, vas olei sacculo aut bursa inclusum ad collum appendat ut commodius et securius perferat.' The words 'ut commodius et securius perferat' imply that the Church yields something for the sake of convenience as well as necessity. Her decisions are quite in harmony with this spirit of tolerance, although she never permits us to lose sight of the fact that reverence and the observance of ordinary rules of decorum must not be overridden by mere custom or the negligence which human infirmity sometimes styles 'convenience,' and which is not the same as the 'commodius' of the rubrics. [Here the decision of the Congregation of the Rites, *Gandaven.*, 16 Dec. 1826—D. A., n. 2650—is quoted in full.] In judging, therefore, whether a priest may keep the Holy Oils in his coat-pocket habitually in order that he may be ready at all times to administer the sacrament promptly, it is not so much *his convenience*

that he has to consult as rather the convenience of the people for whose benefit he holds his charge.

"In view of the not infrequent calls made upon priests in America to assist the dying in railroad accidents and other emergencies, when there is no likelihood that the local priest would be on hand, the question of distance and opportunity must be taken more leniently than in well-settled Catholic communities in Catholic countries, where such demands are rarely made upon a priest. Rubricists like Van der Stappen recognize even for Belgium and other Catholic countries certain exceptions. 'Excipitur,' says the latter author, 'casus infirmi periclitantis dum parochus probabile praevidet quod in morte vocatus ad conferendam Sanctam Unctionem praesto non foret, ut promptus accurrat ad illam morituro ministrandum.' This precaution may be applied, we think, in a wider sense by priests on a journey when they are out of reach of the ordinary ministrations of the Church. And in large cities much allowance must be made for a priest who feels he is acting in the interest of souls when he keeps his oil-stocks within constant reach, showing his reverence in other ways. For the rest, bishops and other superiors may well regulate such usages for their localities, as they are the judges of what necessity and the salvation of souls demand within the limits of their jurisdiction."[78]

Since the above has been written the danger of accidents has increased alarmingly. Automobiles daily take a toll of victims; and the feverishness of our commercial and social life demand fast-flying trains at the expense of safety. Certainly the arguments of the writer avail *a fortiori* in the present day.

Yet if this reason is not sufficiently convincing to some for an habitual carrying of the oil upon their person, it should, nevertheless, be enough to justify it in some particular and temporary instances. It will be permissible, for instance, for a priest to bring the oil of the sick with him on every visit to a hospital not well supplied with priestly attention. Railroad and automobile journeys are other examples of the possibility of meeting emergency calls for the administration of this last sacrament. How far local conditions permit the habitual carrying of the holy oil depends largely on the judgment and discretion of the priest, who will always keep in mind the law of his Ritual and of the Code, which strictly prohibits such practices under normal conditions.

---

78 Vol. XLVIII, (1913), p. 459.

CHAPTER XII.

THE RITE OF ADMINISTRATION

CANON 947

1. Unctiones verbis, ordine et modo in libris ritualibus praescripto, accurate peragantur; in casu autem necessitatis sufficit unica unctio in uno sensu seu rectius in fronte cum praescripta forma breviore, salva obligatione singulas unctiones supplendi, cessante periculo.

2. Unctio renum semper omittatur.

3. Unctio pedum ex qualibet rationabili causa omitti potest.

4. Extra casum gravis necessitatis, unctiones ipsa ministri manu nulloque adhibito instrumento fiant.

CHAPTER XII.

I. The Mode of Administration.

I. *The Ordinary Mode.*

1. *Unctiones verbis ordine et modo in libris ritualibus praescripto accurate peragantur:*

The Code has left to the last canon of the title the consideration of the actual confection of the sacrament, i. e., the application of the proximate matter to a subject simultaneously with the pronouncement of the form. The history and discussion of other ritualistic modes of administration have been disposed of in Canon 937, so that we may address ourselves immediately to the confection of the sacrament as performed in the Latin Church according to the Roman Ritual.

"*Unctiones.*"

In his decree to the Armenians, Eugene IV not only mentioned the places of unction, but also the reasons why they were anointed. "*In his locis ungendus est* [infirmus] : *in oculis propter visum, in auribus propter auditum, in naribus propter odoratum, in ore propter gustam vel loquutionem, in manibus propter tactum, in pedibus propter gressum, in renibus propter delectationem ibidem vigentem.*"[1] St. Thomas[2] had advanced these same reasons in his writings, adding with Dionysius the Carthusian:[3] "Omnis autem nostra cognitio a sensu ortum habet; et quia ubi est in nobis prima origo peccati, ibi debet medicina[4] adhiberi, ideo inunguntur loca quinque sensuum." The learned Cathusian further remarks: "Et propter appetitum a quibusdam renes unguntur, et propter vim motivam pedes, tanquam instrumenta ejus praecipua."

---

1 Const. "*Exultate Deo,*" (In Conc. Florentin.), 22 Nov., 1439—paragr. 14, C. I. C. Fontes, n. 52.

2 *Suppl.* q. 32, a. 5 & 6.

3 *Comm. in IV Lib. Sent.*, dist. 23, q. 3, paragr. "*Insuper.*"

4 al. *unctio.*

Prior to the Code the Ritual prescribed seven anointments, but the revision of the Ritual "ad normam Codicis" omits the unction of the loins, in accordance with the second paragraph of this canon. It is understood, of course, that one priest only is to administer the sacrament, except in the unusual circumstances mentioned in the treatment of Canon 938, 1.[5]

The canon makes three requirements in regard to the performance of the unctions. They must be done with the *words,* in the *order* and after the *manner* prescribed by the Ritual. Each requirement will receive a separate consideration.

A) *Verbis.*

The form prescribed by the Ritual for the various unctions reads thus: *"Per istam sanctam unctionem et suam piissimam misericordiam indulgeat tibi Dominus quidquid per* (here the name of the sense anointed is inserted) *deliquisti."* The identical words are used for each anointing excepting the change of the name of the sense. There is serious obligation to use this form, even in a case where an equally valid form might be substituted. Such a change would violate the prescription of the Council of Florence [6] and the rubrics of the Roman Ritual. Thus Benedict XIV [7] notes: "Injungendum est parochis ut formam adhibeant in Rituali praescriptam, quae certe sine gravi flagitio, non potest privata auctoritate immutari."

Just how much of this prescribed form is essential has been mooted much by theologians. To leave any of it out is, of course, illicit, but no theologian holds the absolute essentiality of all the words. There is much difference of opinion, however, as to what is absolutely essential, and also as to what words, though not absolutely essential, can be omitted without grave sin.

Perhaps the most liberal of all is the opinion of Juenin,

---

5 Cf. *supra,* chap. iii, p. 91 sqq.

6 Const. *"Exultate Deo,"* (In Conc. Florentin.), 22 Nov., 1439—paragr. 14—C. I. C. Fontes, n. 52.

7 *De Syn. Dioc.,* l. 8, c. 2, n. 2.

who holds that the only essential words are *"Indulgeat tibi Deus."*[8]

Perin [9] and Sambovius [10] feel that "quidquid deliquisti" is amply implied in the word "indulgeat," but that the action of the minister should be expressed. Hence for them the essence of the form consists in the words "Per istam unctionem indulgeat tibi Deus" (*Dominus*). To this opinion De Sainte-Beuve [11] and more recently, Pesch,[12] adhere. Kenrick,[13] D'Annibale,[14] Salmanticenses [15] and Bucceroni [16] indicate that the opinion that the phrase *"quidquid deliquisti"* is necessary seems more probable. The majority of theologians, however, insist explicitly or implicitly that this clause is absolutely essential to the form.[17]

In the phrase "Per istam sanctam unctionem," the word "sanctam" is generally conceded to be non-essential. It is

---

8 *De Sacramentis in Genere et in Specie,* diss. VII, *"De Ext. Unct.,"* qu. 4, concl. 2, quaeres 2. N. B., Juenin uses the word *"Deus"* for *"Dominus."* Such minor changes are found often in the older authors, as *"hanc"* for *"istam," "remittat"* or *"parcat"* for *"indulgeat."* They do not change the sense, and, therefore, do not affect our question of what words are essential. The Catechism of the Council of Trent (*De Ext. Unct.*, n. 6), though recognizing the identity of signification, nevertheless urged uniformity even of wording.

9 *De Ext. Unct.*, art. 1, quaeres 8.

10 *Tract. de Ext. Unct.*, disp. IV, a. 3.

11 *De Ext. Unct.*, disp. IV, art. 3—apud Migne, *Cursus Theol. Comp.*, vol. XXIV, col. 98.

12 *Prael. Dogm.*, VII, n. 532.

13 *Th. M.*, III, *"De Ext. Unct.,"* cap. unic., n. 4.

14 *Summ. Th. M.*, III, 415.

15 *Cursus Th. M.*, tom. I, cap. 2, punct. 4, n. 30.

16 *Inst. Mor.*, pars. II, vol. III, n. 865.

17 Cf. LaCroix, *Th. M.*, l. 6, pars 2, n. 2097; *Homo Ap.*, (S. Alph. Lig. auctore) tr. 17, cap. 1, n. 5—also cf. *Th. M.*, VI, 711; Diana, *Opera Coord.*, tom. II, tract. IV, *"De Ext. Unct."* res. 15; Nugno, *Addit. ad III part.*, tom. II, q. 29, a. 9, concl. 4; Suarez, d. 40, sec. 3; Coninck, *De Sac. et Censuris*, disp. 19, *"De Ext. Unct.,"* dub. IV; Gobat, *Moralium*, tr. 8, n. 800; Tamburini, *Th. M.*, tom. II, lib. 6, *"De. Ext. Unct.,"* cap. I, paragr. 3, n. 2; Laymann, *Th. M.*, Lib. V, tr. VIII, cap. III, in fine; Elbel-Bierbaum, *Th. M.*, III, P. VIII, Conf. IX, n. 195; Illsung, tr. 6, d. 7, n. 4; Sporer-Kazenberger, *Suppl. Theol. Sacr.*, c. 2, n. 72; Babenstuber, *Ethica Supernaturalis*, tr. 8, P. 6, disp. 7, a. 2, n. 11; Mastrio, *Th. M.*, disp. XXII, *"De Ext. Unct.,"* q. 2, a. 2, n. 27-8; also more recent theologians as AErtnys, *Th. M.*, II, 359; Noldin, *De Sac.* 436; Tanquerey, *Th. D.*, III, n. 774; Genicot-Salsmans, *Inst. Th. M.*, II, 418; Arregui, *Th. M.*, n. 662; Ballerini-Palmieri, *Opus Th. M.*, vol. V, Tr. X, Sect. VI, *"De Ext. Unct.,"* n. 21; Vermeersch, *Th. M.*, III, 654; Ferreres, *Comp. Th. M.*, II, 838; etc.

found in the short form used in cases of necessity;[18] but it is omitted in the form specified by the Council of Florence[19] and by the Council of Trent.[20] Ballerini-Palmieri[21] thinks that "istam" is not required for validity, and Suarez[22] is very dubious about its necessity. To them the specific unction spoken of is sufficiently determined by the action of the priest at the time the form is being pronounced. However, practically all other theologians demand the use of this demonstrative, and even Ballerini advises against its omission in practice.

A fortiori the entire phrase "per istam unctionem" is generally held to be absolutely necessary for validity. There are some dissenting voices. Juenin, as noted above, Arcudius[23] and Drouven[24] deny any such necessity for this phrase in the form. Juenin asserts that there is no need to express the proximate matter in this sacrament any more than in Penance or in Orders, where there is no mention of the action of the minister. Arcudius claims its non-essentiality on the ground that it is not expressed in the Greek form, where it would be found if at all essential. Drouven enumerates both of these reasons as the basis of his opinion.

The common teaching, however, is confirmed to some extent by the insertion of the phrase in the formula given by the Holy Office in 1906 for cases of necessity.[25] It cannot be argued with finality that this insertion settles the question, for the very evident reason that this brief form contains two words, "sanctam" and "Amen," which no author claims to be essential.

The phrase "per suam piissimam misericordiam" has been the cause of much dispute. It is generally taught that "piis-

---

18 *Rom. Rit.*, tit. V, cap. I, n. 21 (edit. "*Ad normam Codicis*," 1925).

19 Const. "*Exultate Deo*" (in Conc. Florentin.) 22 Nov. 1439, paragr. 14. Denziger-Bannwart, in the *Enchiridion* (n. 700), includes "sanctam" in the form announced to the Armenians by the constitution of Eugene IV. He is evidently mistaken, for it is not found in the works he quotes as sources, viz., Mansi (XXXI, 1058); Harduin (IX, 440B); Baronius, *Annales Ecclesiastici* (anno 1439—vol. 28, p. 290), &c. Neither is it found in the "*Bullarum, &c., R. P. Taur. Edit.*," tom. V, p. 50, nor in the excerpts taken therefrom for the "*Fontes*" (n. 52).

20 Sess. XIV, *De Ext. Unct.*, cap. 1.

21 *Opus Th. M.*, vol. V, Tr. X, sect. 6, n. 21.

22 D. 40, s. 3, n. 13.

23 *De Concordia Ecclesiae Occident.*, lib. 5, cap. 2.

24 *De Re Sacramentaria*, lib. 7, qu. 3, *in fine.*

25 A. S. S., XXXIX, 273; Cf. *Rit. Rom.*, tit. V, cap. 1, n. 21 (ed. 1925).

simam" pertains in no way to the essence of the form. Nugno [26] and Bellarmine [27] claim that the rest of the phrase, "per suam misericordiam," is needed for validity, because thru these words the principal cause of the sacrament is explained. Coninck [28] is inclined to favor this opinion; Roncaglia [29] and Kenrick[30] admit its probability, while Suarez [31] hesitates to come to a decision. However, by far the more common and more probable opinion maintains that the whole phrase is altogether unnecessary. The imploring of God's mercy is implied sufficiently in the deprecative form of "Indulgeat." Since the issuance of the approved form for cases of necessity, this more probable opinion has practically become a certainty. While it cannot be held conclusively that every word inserted by the Holy See in the short form is necessary, yet it is deducible that discarded words are not required for validity. As a consequence it can be safely taught that the whole phrase "per suam piissimam misericordiam" does not pertain to the validity of the form.

"Indulgeat tibi Dominus" is certainly essential. The substitution of "parcat," "remittat," or even "sanet" for "indulgeat" does not interfere with the validity (as the Catechism of the Council of Trent notes, *De Extr. Unct.*, n. 6). "Tibi" is required to determine the subject in whose favor the "oratio fidei" is being said. "Dominus" and "Deus" are interchangeable in as far as the essence of the form is concerned, but either one must be said, else the form is nullified.[32]

The word "Amen" at the end of the form is considered unessential by every one. In the present rite it is to be said by the priest,[33] but anciently it was in some rites a response made by the attendant or the sick man.[34]

---

26 *In Addit. ad III p. D. Thom.*, tom. 2, q. 29, a. 9, concl. 4.

27 *De Sacramentis, "De Ext. Unct.,"* lib. 1, c. 8, apud *Opera Omnia*, vol. III.

28 *De Sac. et Censur.*, disp. 19, De Ext. Unct., dub. 4.

29 *Univers. Theol. Mor., "De Ext. Unct.,"* q. 3.

30 *Th. M.*, III, De Ext. Unct., cap. unic., n. 4.

31 Disp. 40, sect. 3, n. 14.

32 Cfr. note 9 of this chapter. It is undoubetdly sinful to substitute "Deus" for "Dominus;" but the question here has only to do with the validity of the change.

33 Vigourel, *A Synthetical Manual of Liturgy*, n. 169, footnote 2.

34 *"Ordo ad Inungendum Infirmum ex Rituali Augustano,"* ed. 1587, apud Daniel, *Codex Litcurgicus*, vol. I, p. 318.

The question of the necessity of mentioning each particular sense for validity was greatly controverted. Diana,[35] Pitigianus,[36] Babenstuber,[37] Tamburini[38] and Laymann[39] hold that the expression of the sense anointed is certainly essential. D'Annibale,[40] Bucceroni[41] and Pesch[42] speak of this opinion as the more probable one. So strongly did its advocates propound it that even in cases of necessity (as will be seen later in our treatment of this canon), all authors required the mention of the senses in the general form. However, many grave theologians thought the mention of the senses to be unessential for validity. Among these were men such as Caramuel,[43] Gobat,[44] De Sainte-Beuve,[45] Salmanticenses,[46] Billuart,[47] AErtnys[48] and Elbel-Bierbaum.[49] Their argument was based on the contention that no mention of the senses is found in the Greek form; that in the Latin form the effect was sufficiently signified by the other words of the form together with the actual unction of the sense; and that Confirmation's unction, though it must be made on the forehead, does not have a form which mentions the place of anointing. This opinion has been raised to a certainty by the short form published in the decree of the Holy Office in 1906 and contained in the rubric of the Ritual.[50] Not even a general reference to the senses is found in it.

To omit anything which is of necessity for validity in the form, of course, nullifies the sacrament. If this is done deliberately, a serious sin of sacrilege is committed. It is also

---

35 *Op. Coord.*, tom. II, tr. 4, *de Ext. Unct.*, res. xv, n. 4.
36 *Comm. in lib. quart. Sent.*, tom. 2, dist. 23, qu. unic., art. 4, dub. 4.
37 *Ethica Supernatur.*, tr. 8, pars 6, disp. 7, a. 2, n. 12.
38 *Th. M.*, tom. II, lib. 6, De Ext. Unct., cap. 1, parag. 3, n. 2.
39 *Th. M.*, lib. 5, tr. 8, c. 3, *in fine.*
40 *Summ. Th. M.*, III, 415.
41 *Inst. Mor.*, Pars. II, vol. III, n. 865.
42 *Prael. Dog.*, VII, 532—Pesch does not agree with the opinion himself, but confesses it to be the more common opinion.
43 *Fund. Th. M.*, vol. III, Fundam. 68, *Substantia Extremae-Unctionalis*, p. 270.
44 *Moral.*, Tract. VIII, n. 800.
45 *De Ext. Unct.*, disp. IV, art. 3—apud Migne, *Cursus Theol. Compl.*, vol. XXIV, co. 98.
46 *Cursus Theol. Mor.*, tr. 7, c. 2, n. 32.
47 *Summa S. Thom.*, "*De Ext. Unct.*," disp. unic., art. 3, pet. 1.
68 *Th. M.*, II, 359.
49 *Th. M.*, III, P. VIII, Conf. IX, n. 195.
50 Tit. V, cap. I, n. 21.

grievous to omit those portions of the form which are only probably unessential, though more probably essential. It is not allowed to abandon the more probable opinion in favor of a probable one in matters pertaining to the administration of the sacraments.[51]

This canon, however, goes further. It orders the unctions to be made with the words prescribed in the Ritual whether they be essential or unessential. Hence, it can be stated with Laymann[52] that not even a single word can be omitted *"sine scelere."* Grave deordination of the wording is, of course, seriously sinful, but lightness of matter is likewise admissible. The omission of the words *"Sanctam," "piissimam"* and *"Amen"* is generally considered to be but venial.[53] Suarez,[54] Gobat[55] and Berengo[56] thought that omission of "sanctam" was grave; but their opinion has little probability today. To omit "istam" is considered a serious sin, even by those who doubt its necessity for validity, as Suarez[57] and Ballerini-Palmieri.[58]

Theologians are divided on the gravity of the omission of the phrase "per suam piissimam misericordiam." Lehmkuhl,[59] Bucceroni,[60] Gobat,[61] Diana,[62] La Croix,[63] Berardi,[64] Vermeersch,[65] Kenrick[66] and others proclaim the gravity of this omission. They do so, not on the ground that such a phrase is essential, but rather because it is a notable violation of an

---

51 S. C. S. Off. 2 Mar. 1679—Denziger-Bannwart, *Ench.*, n. 1151.
52 *Th. M.*, lib. V, tr. VIII, cap. III, in fine.
53 Cf. Genicot-Salsmans, *Inst. Th. M.*, II, 418; Sebastiani, *Summ. Th. M.*, n. 509; Vermeersch, *Th. M.*, III, 656, ad III; Bucceroni, *Inst. Mor.*, pars II, vol. III, n. 865; Ballerini-Palmieri, *Opus Th. M.*, vol. 5, Tract. X, *de Sac.*, sect. 6, *De Ext. Unct.*, n. 21; Berardi, *Prax. Conf.*, II, n. 4997; &c.
54 D. 40, s. 3, n. 13.
55 *Moral.*, Tr. VIII, n. 800.
56 *Enchiridion Parochorum*, n. 113.
57 D. 40, s. 3, n. 13.
58 *Opus Th. M.*, vol. V, tr. X, de Sac., sect. VI, *de Ext. Unct.*, n. 21.
59 *Th. M.*, II, 719.
60 *L.c.*
61 *Moral.*, n. 800.
62 *Op. Coord.* tom. II, tr. 4, *De Ext. Unct.*, res. 16 and 17.
63 *Th. M.*, lib. VI, Pars. 2, *De Ext. Unct.*, n. 2097.
64 *Prax. Conf., II*, n. 4997.
65 *Th. M.*, III, 654.
66 *Th. M.*, III, *De Ext. Unct.*, cap. unic., n. 4.

ecclesiastical precept. Others, however, like Genicot-Salsmans,[67] Arregui,[68] Sebastiani [69] and Ballerini-Palmieri,[70] hold this deordination in the form as slight. Of course, this is no sin at all when left out when the sacrament is given in case of necessity, for the short form does not contain this phrase.

A similar controversy has arisen about the gravity of omitting the mention of the sense which is being anointed. Those who contend that the sin thus committed is grave are Konings,[71] Sebastiani,[72] D'Annibale,[73] Vermeersch,[74] Ballerini-Palmieri,[75] La Croix,[76] &c. On the other hand some authors hold that the deliberate omission is, at least probably, nothing more than venial. Among these are Gobat,[77] Genicot-Salsmans [78] and Arregui.[79]

Vermeersch [80] calls attention to a point that may have escaped many: "Qui sensum specialem non designaverit, nihil quidem omittit quod sacramento sit essentiale, sed sacramentum quasi totum simul administrare videtur. Quare qui plures sensus, nullum nominando, sed repetendo formam unxerit, videtur quasi pluries sacramentum iterare. Et si specialis sit efficacia ad extinguenda peccata quae per singulos sensus commissa sunt, infirmum illa peculiari utilitate privat." But this observation comes to naught when it is remembered that the Greeks anoint several times yet make no mention of the sense that is being anointed in their form. It can hardly be claimed that each unction constitutes a distinct sacrament in that rite. Furthermore, the determination of the words to a specific sense can be done by the very act of anointing such an organ. Those who hold the theory of Kern [81] have no trouble in overcoming this

67 *Inst. Th. M.*, II, 418.
68 *Summ. Th. M.*, n. 662.
69 *Summ. Th. M.*, n. 509.
70 *Opus Th. M.*, vol. V, Tract. X, Sect. VI, n. 21.
71 *Th. M.*, n. 1503.
72 *Summ. Th. M.*, n. 509.
73 *Summ. Th. M.*, III, n. 415—*probabilius.*
74 *Th. M.*, III, 654.
75 *Opus Th. M.*, l.c.
76 *Th. M.*, lib. VI, Pars. II, de EU, n. 2097.
77 *Moral.*, n. 800.
78 *Inst. Th. M.*, II, 418.
79 *Summ. Th. M.*, n. 662.
80 *Th. M.*, III, 654.
81 *Tract. de Ext. Unct.*, P. 323-30.

difficulty, for, according to Kern's solution, it is the priest's intention which determines whether the effect is to be produced by a single unction or by several anointings.

To omit the phrase "quidquid deliquisti" is surely a mortal sin. It is held by most theologians to be essential, for otherwise, the signification of "indulgeat" is not sufficiently determined. As Scavini notes,[82] "indulgere" can have several other meanings, such as "obsequi," "consentire," "facile concedere," "plus aequo remittere." Hence its deliberate omission seriously imperils the validity of the sacrament and entails the guilt of mortal sin for the perpetrator.

Older authors considered the contingency of the inadvertent substitution of "dereliquisti" for "deliquisti." Gobat,[83] after treating the matter at some length, decides that the sacrament is to be repeated. By no stretch of symbolism or hyperbole can "derelinquere" be made synonymous with "deliquisti." The opinion of Gobat is accepted by others who have considered this case, such as Elbel-Bierbaum,[84] Clericatus,[85] Kazenberger [86] and LaCroix.[87] As a consequence, when such a thing occurs, whether consciously or inadvertently, the sacrament should be absolutely repeated. Of course, the deliberate substitution of this word for the prescribed verb is undoubtedly a mortal sin.

It is quite necessary that the form which corresponds to each sense be applied to that particular sense and no other. Hence, when anointing the eyes, it would vitiate the unction to implore the remission of sins committed thru the sense of hearing. Elbel-Bierbaum considers a case where the priest forgot to anoint the hands, and when anointing the feet used the form "quidquid per tactum," &c.[88] If the priest has not left the man, Elbel-Bierbaum demands that the unction of the hands be supplied, "quia juxta omnes dum fieri facile potest, sacramenta debent rite et integre administrari." If, however, he has left the sick man, this author thinks he need not return if it

82 *Th. M.*, III, 528; cf. Billuart, *Summa S. Thom.*, "*De Ext. Unct.*," diss. unic., a. III.
83 *Moral.*, tr. 8, n. 811.
84 *Th. M.*, III, Pars VIII, conf. IX, n. 210.
85 *Decisiones Sacramentales*, "*De Ext. Unct.*," dec. 68, n. 19.
86 *Suppl. Theol. Sacr.*, c. 2, n. 72.
87 *Th. M.*, lib. VI, pars II, *De Ext. Unct.*, n. 2097.
88 *Th. M.*, III, Pars VIII, Conf. IX, n. 205.

is difficult or liable to provoke scandal, except when the man has received no other sacrament. If the patient, however, is easy of access, the defect should be remedied. Since the promulgation of the new Code, it would seem that his return is hardly obligatory. Only one unction is required for validity, and furthermore, the sense of touch is anointed by the unction of the feet as well as by that of the hands.

B) *Ordine.*

The second prescription of the canon demands the several unctions of the sacrament be performed in the order given by the Ritual.[89] Accordingly the eyes are anointed first,[90] and very fittingly too, for, as St. Ambrose[91] says, they are the watchguards of the senses and the windows of the soul. Some ancient Rituals commenced the unctions with the anointment of the ears.[92] In the Roman Ritual, however, the ears come in the second place, the nose next, then the lips, the hands and finally the feet.

If the sense-organs are double, both are to be anointed, commencing with the organ on the right side of the sick man.[93] The nose, as shall be seen later, may receive either a single unction on the tip, or an unction on each nostril. The mouth or lips are to be anointed once.

That any change in the order of these unctions does not affect the validity of the Sacrament is conceded by all. Hence, if the unctions cannot be commenced upon the eyes without grave inconvenience, it is certainly allowable to start the rite by applying the oil to another sense.

To change the prescribed order of unctions without such necessity is thought by some to be a serious sin, by others to be only venial. Kenrick,[94] St. Alphonsus[95] and Sebastiani[96]

89 Tit. V., cap. 2, n. 8-12.
90 *Rit. Rom.*, l.c., n. 8.
91 Cf. *Examer.*, l. 6, cap. 9—M. P. L., 14, 266.
92 Cf. Ritual of Church of Soissons apud Martene, *De Antiq. Eccl. Rit.*, l. 1, c. 7, a. 4, Ordo XIII; the Pontifical of Constantinople, apud Martene, *l.c.* Ordo XVII.
93 Cf. De Herdt, *Lit. Prax.*, III, 200.
94 *Th. M.*, III, *De Ext. Unct.*, cap. unic., n. 5.
95 *Th. M.*, VI, 708.
96 *Summ. Th. M.*, n. 513.

hold an inversion of the order of anointments to be seriously sinful. It is, they contend, a notable change, in the traditional usage of the Church. AErtnys [97] agrees with this opinion, but allows lightness of matter, as, e. g., when the order of the unction between only two senses is inverted. The great majority of theologians do not coincide with this view.[98] Such a change is only accidental, they claim, and consequently only slightly wrong, unless indeed, as Ballerini-Palmieri [99] wisely notes, such a thing is done out of contempt or with the intention of starting a new rite.

The complete omission of the unction of a sense is certainly a mortal sin; and there is hardly any dispute about the gravity of the omission of the anointment of one of the organs where the sense is double, and where both organs can be conveniently reached.[100] However, since the validity is affected in no way by the omission of the unction of one of the twin organs, a sufficient cause will permit the priest to be content with the unction of either one of the organs. Such a cause appears when the man cannot be easily turned, or when bandages cannot be removed from the organ without great inconvenience, &c.[101]

The prescription ordering the organ on the right of the sick man to be anointed first in these double-unctions is not gravely binding. It surely does not create any grave deordination of procedure.[102]

C) *Modo.*

The third and last requirement made by this canon is that the unctions be made in manner and fashion prescribed by the Ritual. This entails an examination into the procedure of administering the sacrament proper, and the unction of each particular sense deserves a word of individual attention. Hence

---

97 *Th. M.*, II, 357.

98 Cf. Suarez, disp. 40, s. 2, n. 9; Lehmkuhl, *Th. M.*, II, 720; Noldin, *De Sac.*, 435; Genicot-Salsmans, *Inst. Th. M.*, II, 417; Vermeersch *Th. M.*, III, 653; Ferreres, *Comp. Th. M.*, II, n. 835, quaer. 8; &c.

99 *Opus Th. M.*, vol. V, tr. X, sect. 6, n. 19.

100 Cf. Vermeersch, *Th. M.*, III, 653; AErtnys, *Th. M.* II, 357, quaeres 2; Lehmkuhl, *Th. M.*, II, 720. However, see Sebastiani, *Summ. Th. M.*, n. 513.

101 Genicot-Salsmans, *Inst. Th. M.*, II, 417.

102 Cf. Genicot-Salsmans, *Inst. Th. M.*, II, 417; Noldin, *De Sac.*, n. 435; Sebastiani, *Summ. Th. M.*, n. 513.

the treatment of this question will follow the order of the rubrics of the Ritual.

> "Deinde, intincto pollice in Oleo sancto, in modum crucis ungit infirmum in partibus hic subscriptis &c." (*Rit. Rom.*, tit. V., cap. 2, n. 8.)

The vessel of oil should be held firmly by the priest in his left hand during the performance of the unctions, unless there be an acolyte present to hold it. Baruffaldo [103] advises the use of a purificator wrapped about the hand to absorb any oil that may be spilled. O'Kane [104] notes, however, that there will be little need of such a precaution if the oil is soaked in cotton.

The priest should dip his right thumb into the vessel, forcing the cotton to yield the oil upon the fleshy part and not upon the nail.[105] Then raising his thumb to the sick man he makes the unctions with oil gathered thereon. The nail should not be so long that the oil may get beneath it,[106] nor so sharp that it will scratch the patient.

The rubric demands that the unction be made in the form of a cross. "Crucis signum adhibetur," writes Baruffaldo,[107] "in cunctis Sacramentis ministrantibus, quia cum ortum suum habeant a Christi sanguine in Cruce effuso, non melius exprimi potest eorum fons et origo."

The practice of making the unction in the form of a cross is very old. It is found in the ancient *Liber Sacramentorum* of St. Remigius of Rheims.[108] It existed also in the monasteries of Cluny, as the third book of Burchard tells us.[109] Similarly very many rituals in the collections of Martene [110] and Lounoi [111]

---

103 *Ad Rit. Rom. Comm.*, tom. I, tit. 28, n. 65.

104 *The Rubrics*, n. 925.

105 Cf. O'Kane, *l.c.*, Baruffaldo, *l.c.* nn. 66-7; De Amicis, *Caeremoniale Parochorum*, n. 203, 10.

106 Baruffaldo, *op. cit.*, l.c., n. 67.

107 *L.c.*, n. 69.

108 apud Launoi, *Op. Omnia*, tom. I, p. 489.

109 apud Launoi, *l.c.*, p. 493.

110 Ordines I, III, IV, IX, X, XII, XV, XVI, XVIII, XIX, XXI, XXII, XXVII, XXIX, apud *De Antiq. Eccl. Rit.*, lib. I, cap. vii, art. IV.

111 Pontifical of Cambrai—apud *Op. Omnia*, t. I, p. 496; Manuscript from the Dominican Library of Paris—*l. c.*, p. 498; Pontifical of Laon,—*l.c.*, p. 501; the Manuals of the Churches of Vienne (1500)—*l.c.*, p. 503; Châlons-sur-Marne (1529)—*l.c.*, p. 511; and Amiens—*l.c.*, p. 515.

contain this prescription. Catalano[112] likewise found a similar rubric in the Codex of Beauvais.

The crosses are to be made with the thumb by drawing first a line downwards from the place anointed and then another line across it at right angles from left to right of the priest.[113] Not to make the unction in the form of a cross does not affect the validity, of course, and hence in a case of necessity it need not have careful attention. Outside of urgency, however, its neglect is a venial sin.[114]

Ad oculos.

The right eye should be the first organ anointed, with the unction of the left eye following immediately afterwards before the form corresponding to the sense of sight has been completed.[115] It is advisable to distribute the words of the form so that the first unction will have been completed by the time "unctionem" has been reached and the second unction before the form has been completed.[116] The Roman Ritual has only one cross marked, although there are to be two unctions, each in the form of a cross.[117]

No special distribution of the words of the form is prescribed by the rubric in these double anointings of the same sense. Moreover, the cross found in the Ritual between the penultimate and ultimate syllables of "Unctionem" does not signify that the priest is there to pause, complete both unctions, and then continue with the form. The anointing should be performed while the words are being said without any interruption.[118] With this in view, O'Kane[119] recommends a slow recital of the form, so that there may be ample time to make both unctions.

The eyes should be closed, if possible, and according to most

---

112 *Rit. Rom.*, t. I, p. 333.

113 Cf. O'Kane, *The Rubrics*, n. 829; DeHerdt, *Lit. Prax.*, III, 200, 3; De Amicis, *Caeremon. Paroch.*, 203, ad 10.

114 Cf. Genicot-Salsmans, *Inst. Th. M.*, II, 417; O'Kane, *The Rubrics*, n. 925.

115 *Rit. Rom.*, tit. V, cap. I, n. 18.

116 O'Kane, *The Rubrics*, n. 927.

117 O'Kane (*l.c.*), notes that the Ritual of Liege has two crosses. St. Charles, likewise, marked two crosses in his "*Ordo ad Ministrandum Sac. Ext. Unct.*"—apud *Acta Eccl. Mediol.*, t. I, p. 606.

118 Cf. De Herdt, *Lit. Prax.*, III, 200.

119 *The Rubrics*, n. 931.

authors, the unction should be made upon the eyelids.[120] Others like De Herdt[121] and Falise[122] direct that the unction should be on the eyebrows. They have the weight of ancient custom behind them. The Ritual of the Church of Cambrai,[123] orders that the anointing be done "in superciliis juxta angulos oculorum." A rubric of similar nature is found in the Pontifical of the Monastery of Gemmeticensis.[124] A double unction "in superciliis et subciliis juxta angulos oculorum" was commanded by the Ritual of the Monastery of St. Remigius of Rheims.[125] In practice, either opinion may be followed, for an unction in either place is equally valid.[126] However, if the eyes cannot be closed, or if the eyelids are too tender to anoint, the unctions can be made on the eyebrows or below the eyes. Bucceroni[127] and Scavini[128] recommend that in these cases the old rubric of the Ritual of Cambrai be followed by anointing on the eyebrow "juxta angulos oculorum." Van der Stappen,[129] directs the unction to be made beneath the eyes.

> "Minister vero, si est in Sacris, vel ipsemet Sacerdos, post quamlibet unctionem, tergat loca inuncta novo globulo bombacii, vel rei similis, eumque in vase mundo reponat, et ad ecclesiam postea deferat, comburat, cineresque projiciat in sacrarium." (*Rit. Rom.*, tit. V, c. 2, n. 9.)

When Extreme Unction is given in lands where the prescriptions of the Ritual are carried out *adamussim*, one or even several ministers accompany the priest on his mission to the sick room.[130] In this country, however, and, as O'Kane notes,[131] in Ireland, custom has established that the priest goes on sick calls

---

120 Cfr. O'Kane, *The Rubrics*, n. 927; Catalano, *Rit. Rom.*, tom. I, p. 333; Van der Stappen, *Sac. Lit.*, t. IV, q. 219; De Amicis, *Caeremoniale Parochorum*, n. 203, 14; Pighi-Ferrais, *Liturgia Sacerdotalis*, n. 555; Heuser, *Parish Priest on Duty*, n. 97; Scavini, *Th. M.*, III, 529; &c.

121 *Lit. Prax.*, III, 201.

122 *Lit. Pract. Comp.*, sect. V, cap. V, n. 9.

123 apud Martene, *De Antiq. Eccl. Rit.*, l. I, c. 7, a. 4, Ordo XVII.

124 apud Martene, *l.c.*, Ordo I.

125 Launoi, *Op. Omnia*, t. I, p. 489.

126 Cfr. Wapelhorst, *Comp. Sac. Lit.*, n. 290, 6; De Amicis, *Caeremoniale Parochorum*, n. 203, 14.

127 *Inst. Mor.*, p. II, vol. 3, n. 868.

128 *Th. M.*, III, n. 529.

129 *Sac. Lit.*, t. IV, q. 219.

130 Cf. tit. V, c. 2, n. 2.

131 *The Rubrics*, n. 928.

unaccompanied by any acolytes, or other ministers. If nevertheless there is a man in major orders assisting him in his ministrations, such a one should wipe off the unctions after the priest has anointed. This rubric is stricter than the practice of older days. A rubric of the Ritual of Châlons-sur-Marne[132] reads: "Et debet esse aliqua persona ad detergendum dictas cruces cum stuppis, et in qualibet Cruce accipiat stuppas novas, candelis accensis." And later in the same Ritual: "Lavat sacerdos, unctione peracta, manus suas cum sale et aqua. Similiter *ille* vel *illa, qui,* vel *quae extersit cruces de stuppis,* quae debent custodiri et reservari inter duas scutellas ligneas, et reponi in quodam armariolo in Ecclesia, et de eisdem facere cineres pro die Cinerum, vel recondi in terra sancta." It is evident that even a woman might have been employed for this purpose, although today practically all authors say that under no circumstances is a woman to act even in a minor capacity in the administration of this sacrament.[133]

A fresh pellet of cotton or similar substance should be used for each form. Hence where the sense is double, the same cotton is to be used for wiping off both anointments.[134] Thus the Council of Salernitano prescribed: "Eadem vero stuppa seu bombice singula loca non ungantur, sed in qualibet membrorum specie mutetur."[135]

The unction should be wiped off as soon as the form is completed. In the double senses, therefore, both unctions should be made before the cotton is applied.[136]

If there is any danger of one of these organs coming in contact with the bed clothes or with the pillow—and this is especially true in the case of the ear,—then it is a laudable practice to wipe off the first unction before the second anointing is made.[137] The Ritual of Toulon incorporates this recommendation in its rubrics.[138]

---

132 apud Martene, *De Antiq. Eccl. Rit.*, l. I, c. 7, a. 4, Ord. XXVII.
133 Cf. e. g. Ballerini-Palmieri, *Opus Th. M.*, vol. V, tr. X, sect. VI, n. 34.
134 Cf. *Rit. Rom.*, tit. V, cap. 2, n. 1.
135 Tit. 32, cap. 6, (anno 1579)—Catalano, *Rit. Rom.*, t. I, p. 333.
136 O'Kane, *The Rubrics*, n. 928; De Herdt, *Lit. Prax.*, III, 200.
137 Cf. O'Kane, *The Rubrics*, n. 928; Falise, *Liturg. Pract. Comp.*, pars. II, sec. V, cap. 5, n. 9, p. 669.
138 *Dictionnaire des Ceremonies*, Art. "Ext. Unct.," n. 25.

Cotton need not necessarily be used for wiping off the unctions. The rubric allows the substitution of any "res similis." Older rituals ofter prescribed flax or linen. The preparation of "linum aut stuppam" was ordered by the Ritual of Liege, edited in 1553,[139] and the Ritual of Châlons-sur-Marne[140] and was permitted by the Council of Salernitano in the legislation just noted.

When there is no minister present in Sacred Orders the priest shall wipe off the oil himself. After use, each pellet should be laid upon another plate or put into a little pocket or bag. Such a pocket is often found in the burse itself, but it should be well closed, so that the cotton will not touch the oil-stock.[141] Baruffaldo[142] for this very reason insists upon the use of a separate bag or burse to carry home the cotton. Into this special burse (or into the pocket of the same burse) should also be placed the bread crumbs with which the priest washes his hands at the end of the anointings.

The cotton is to be burned and the ashes thrown into the sacrarium. The Ritual of Châlons-sur-Marne permitted the ashes to be used on Ash Wednesday[143] but such is certainly not allowable now. According to the rubric the cotton should be burned at the Church. De Herdt[144] notes that in many places there is a custom sufficiently common to permit the burning of the cotton and bread at the sick man's house. Heuser[145] acknowledges the lawfulness of this; but differs from De Herdt in regard to the disposition of the ashes. The former insists on the fulfillment of the rubrical prescription, whereas De Herdt thinks no further attention need to be paid to the matter after the cotton has been thrown into the fire. Wapelhorst[146] allows DeHerdt's disposal of the cotton if it is inconvenient to bring it to the church. Pighi-Ferrias[147] is more generous that De

139 apud Martene, *De Antiq. Eccl. Rit.*, l. I, c. 7, a. 4, Ordo XXVIII.
140 apud Martene, *l.c.*, Ordo XXVII.
141 O'Kane, *The Rubrics*, n. 928.
142 *Ad Rit. Rom. Comm.*, t. I, tit. 28, n. 76.
143 Martene, *De Antiq. Eccl. Rit.*, l. I, c. 7, a. 4, Ordo XXVII.
144 *Lit. Prax.*, III, 204.
145 *The Parish Priest on Duty*, p. 100.
146 *Comp. Sac. Lit.*, n. 290, paragr. 7.
147 *Liturgia Sacerdotalis*, n. 556; "Bombacium et quidquid ad abstersionem adhibitum fuerit, relinqui potest familiaribus infirmi, ut in ignem projiciant."

Herdt, for he permits the priest to leave to the family of the sick man the duty of throwing the bread and cotton into the fire. Berengo [148] also allows this. Consequently it may be done without hesitation, if the priest is certain that the family will fulfill their charge.

Ad aures.

The Pontifical of Prudentius, Bishops of Troyes, and the Pontifical of Cambrai [149] order that the ears be anointed "deintus." An old Codex of the Church of Noyon [150] contains a rubric which specifies the unction "ad aures, infra et supra." Still different was the direction of the Codex Victorinus [151] to make the crosses of oil "in aures intus et foris." However, the universal practice today is to anoint the ears on the lobes or lower extremities. [152] Baruffaldo [153] gives as the reason the facility with which the oil can be wiped from the lobes in comparison with the hollow of the ear.

The distribution of the words here have no special regulations. They may be distributed in any way provided the two unctions be performed during their pronouncement. It is interesting to note that the Ritual of the Church of Soissons, edited in 1530, had a distinct form for each ear.[154]

Ad nares.

The Pontifical of St. Prudentius of Troyes,[155] the Pontifical of Cambrai [156] and the Manual of the Church of Verdun [157] direct the unction to be made on the tip of the nose. The Ritual of St. Remigus of Rheims says the anointing should be done "in summitate et subtus."[158] St. Charles in his *"Instructiones"*

---

148 *Enchiridion Parochorum,* P. II, n. 114.
149 Martene, *De Antiq. Eccl. Rit.,* l. I, c. 7, a. 4, Ordines II & XVI.
150 Martene, *l.c.,* Ordo X.
151 Martene, *l.c.,* Ordo XIX.
152 Cf. O'Kane, *The Rubrics,* n. 930; Heuser, *The Parish Priest,* p. 98; Baruffaldo, *Ad Rit. Rom. Comm.,* t. I, tit. 28, n. 78; Van de Stappen, *Sac. Lit.,* t. IV, q. 219, &c.
153 *L.c.*
154 apud Launoi, *Op. Omnia,* tom. I, p. 513.
155 Martene, *De Antiq. Eccl. Rit.,* l. I, c. 7, a. 4, Ordo II.
156 Martene, *l.c.,* Ordo XVI; also apud Launoi, *Op. Omnia,* tom. I, p. 497.
157 apud Launoi, *l.c.,* p. 524.
158 apud Launoi, *l.c.,* p. 489.

placed two crosses in the formula to be used for the nose, thus implying that a double unction was to be made.[159]

Even today authors differ whether one or two unctions are to be made. Baruffaldo,[160] Falise,[161] Lehmkuhl,[162] Bucceroni[163] and Sebastiani[164] wish a double unction. O'Kane[165] calls this the more common opinion; and in the Ritual of Toulon it is expressly prescribed.[166]

On the other hand De Herdt[167] and De Amicis[168] permit only one unction to be made.[169] This single unction is placed at the juncture of both nostrils in the tip of the nose.

On the other hand the double unction, of course, would be made by anointing each nostril on the side, or, as Baruffaldo[170] expresses it, "ad narices quae sunt nasi alae laterales."

As a consequence of this dispute many authors simply mention that a single or a double unction is permissible.[171] The local custom should be followed; and if there is no unity of custom, either manner of procedure is entirely licit.

Ad os, compressis labiis.

The differences in the forms of the ancient rituals are very interesting. The sense of taste received no mention in some. Thus the Pontificale Anglicanum[172] prescribed this form: "Ungo labia ista consecrati olei medicamento, ut quicquid otiosa vel criminosa peccati locutione, divina clementia miserante expietur hac unctione. Per Dom." &c. The identical words are found

159 apud *Acta Eccl. Mediol.*, pars. IV., "*Instruct. Extr. Unct.*," paragr. "*Ordo Ministrandi*"—tom. I, p. 606.
160 *Ad Rit. Rom. Comm.*, tom. I, tit. 28, n. 79.
161 *Lit. Pract. Comp.*, sec. 5, cap. 5, n. 9, page 669.
162 *Th. M.*, II, 720 and footnote.
163 *Institut. Theol. Mor.*, pars II, vol. 3, n. 868.
164 *Th. M.*, n. 513.
165 *The Rubrics*, n. 932.
166 apud *Dictionnaire des Ceremonies*, Art. "*Ext. Unct.*," n. 25.
167 *Lit. Prax.*, III, 201.
168 *Caer. Paroch.*, n. 203, n. 14.
169 Cf. Bissus E., n. 244, paragr. 18.
170 *L.c.*, N. B. It is curious to note that the very reason that Baruffaldo gives (*l.c.*) for a double unction, namely, to prevent the provocation of a sneeze, is the one of the reasons DeHerdt gives for a single unction.
171 Cf. Wapelhorst, *Comp. Sac. Lit.*, n. 290, 6; Pighi-Ferrais, *Lit. Sacerdotalis*, n. 555; Heuser, *The Parish Priest*, p. 98; Van der Stappen, *Sac. Lit.*, t. IV, q. 219.
172 Martene, *De Antiq. Eccl. Rit.*, l. I, c. 7, a. 4, Ordo I.

in the form of the Pontifical of Prudentius of Troyes,[173] while five other rituals in Martene's collection [174] contain no prayer for forgiveness of the sins of taste. On the other hand, in the Ritual of the Church of St. Mary Magdalen near Le Mans the form commemorates the sense of taste.[175] Two other forms are worthy of notice: that of the Church of Liege,[176] and that of the Ordo Romanus X.[177]

The unction of the mouth is to be made with the mouth closed and should extend over both lips. If this is impossible, an unction on either lip will suffice.[178] When the mouth is wide open in unconscious patients, the priest should not attempt to close it, for such a thing is likely to interfere with the breathing and harm the patient.[179] If there is any danger of infection, as in cases of hydrophobia or mouth cancer, the unction can be made very carefully on any part of either lip, or an instrument may be used. Only one unction is to be made, even if but one lip is anointed. Van der Stappen[180] in this case recommends the upper lip or a place near the lips.

Ad manus:

The unction of the mouth is followed immediately by the unction of the hands. In this anointment a distinct difference of place is made between priests and others. "Manus vero," reads the rubric [181] "quae reliquis infirmis interius ungi debent, Presbyteris exterius ungantur."

No Rituals in Martene's collection which date back beyond the twelfth century prescribe this distinction. Thus the Ritual of Prudentius of Troyes simply instructs the unction of the

---

173 Martene, *l.c.*, Ordo II.

174 Ordines XIX, XX, XXI, XXIII, XXV.

175 Martene, *l.c.* Ordo XXVI.

176 Martene, *l.c.* Ordo XXVIII; "Per istam unctionem et suam piissimam misericordiam indulgeat tibi Dominus quidquid deliquisti per gustum et illicitum sermonem. Amen."

177 apud Mabillonius, *Musei Italici*, tom. II, n. 33: "Per istam sanctam unctionem et suam piissimam misericordiam parcat tibi Dominus quicquid linguae vel oris vitio deliquisti."

178 Cf. Vermeersch-Creusen, *Epit.*, II, 231; Van der Stappen (*Sac. Lit.*, t. IV, q. 219), prefers the lower lip in this case.

179 Baruffaldo, *Ad Rit. Rom. Comm.*, tom. I, tit. 28, n. 80. Cfr. also O'Kane, *The Rubrics*, n. 934; DeHerdt, *Lit. Prax.*, III, 204 & 80-1.

180 *L.c.*

181 *Rit. Rom.*, tit. V, cap. 1, n. 17.

hands to be made "exterius."[182] A similar rubric is found in the Ritual of Cambrai.[183] Since the twelfth century very many rituals have made this distinction in the anointing of hands. Some of these directed a double unction of each hand—upon the palm and the back—for laics, while directing that priests should be anointed with a single unction only—on the back of the hands. Thus the Ritual of Châlons-sur-Marne (1529)[184] has the following rubric: "Item super manus et infra; si vero sit sacerdos, ungatur tantum extra." Similar rubrics are found in the *Codex Floriacensis,*[185] the *Codex Domini Desmarais*[186] and the Ritual of Amiens.[187]

A larger number of Rituals, however, corresponded in their prescription to the present Roman Ritual. Thus those who were not priests received a single unction on the palm of each hand, while men in priestly orders were anointed on the back of the hand.[188]

Durandus in the "*Rationale Divinorum Officiorum*"[189] speaks of the distinction made in favor of sacerdotal hands; and St. Charles twice stresses the mode of procedure in this unction in his Instructions, "De Extrema Unctione."[190]

An opinion no longer tenable was advanced by Paludanus[191] and Rubeus.[192] It is positively wrong, they taught, to anoint priests on the back of the hands. The sacerdotal character bespeaks no impeccability as to sins of touch, and since the centre of touch is rather in the palms of the hands than in the back, priests as well as laymen should be anointed on the palm. There is no incongruity arising from the former unc-

---

182 Martene, *De Antiq. Eccl. Rit.*, lib. I, cap. 7, art. 4, Ordo II.
183 Martene, *l.c.*, Ordo XVI.
184 Martene, *l.c.*, Ordo XXVII.
185 Martene, *l.c.*, Ordo XXI.
186 Martene, *l.c.*, Ordo XXIII.
187 edited 1541—apud Launoi, *Op. Omnia,* tom. I, p. 578.
188 Cf. *Rituale Ecclesiae Aeduensis*—apud Launoi, *l.c.*, p. 576; The Rituals of Rotomagi, edited in 1544, 1586 and 1611—apud Launoi, *l.c.;* Chartres, 1489 and 1544—apud Launoi, *l.c.*, p. 577; Meaux, 1596—Launoi, *l.c.*, p. 577; Orleans (1581)—Launoi, *l.c.;* Vannes (1596)—Launoi, *l.c.*, p. 577; Rheims (1504, 1530 & 1585)—Launoi, *l.c.*, p. 578.
189 Lib. l. c. 8, n. 25.
190 *Acta Eccl. Mediol.*, pars IV, tom. I, pp. 602-3 & 606.
191 *Comm. in Lib. IV Sent.*, dist. 23, q. 3, a. 3, concl. 5.
192 *Comm. in IV Sent.*, dist. 23.

tion in ordination because there is no question of a sacerdotal anointing in this sacrament. It is simply the application of the oils to the physical sources of sin, i. e., the senses.

Of course, such a view is no longer valid. The explicit regulation in the Church's liturgy has made it obligatory to draw a distinction between the unction of the hands of priests and those of other sick people. Deacons and lower clerics do not receive the unction as priests, but bishops do.[193]

The reason for the difference of procedure has not been officially declared, and liturgists are not in unison in regard to its explanation. St. Charles Borromeo,[194] Barbosa,[195] the Ritual of Bressanone,[196] Van der Stappen [197] and Vermeersch-Creusen [198] ascribe it to the unseemliness of anointing the exact part of the hands that has already been anointed in ordination by a bishop. Baruffaldo [199] offers quite a different reason. Priestly dignity, he says, distinguishes the priest from other men. Consequently, a different unction would serve to conjure up in the priest the consciousness of his superior dignity, and thus move him to a greater sorrow for his sins. The hands are the most becoming place to make this change of procedure in anointing. Hands, hallowed by the constant contact of the body of Christ, should never have been sullied. An unction made upon them in a different place than upon the rest of men would call the subject's attention especially to the sins of his hands, which for him should be a cause of deeper sorrow and repentance.[200] De Herdt [201] gives both reasons for the distinction. Those who hold the former reason may have trouble explaining away the new regulation which directs that the single unction in cases

---

193 Cf. O'Kane, *The Rubrics*, n. 934.

194 "*Instructiones de Ext. Unct.*," apud *Acta Eccl. Mediol.* pars. IV, tom. I, p. 602-3.

195 *De Off. et Pot. Parochi*, pars II, cap. 22, n. 32.

196 paragr. 8, apud Baruffaldo, *Ad Rit. Rom.*, tom. I, tit. 27, n. 110.

197 *Sac. Lit.*, t. IV, q. 219.

198 *Epit.*, II, 231.

199 *L.c.*, n. 113.

200 Baruffaldo (*l.c.*) notes the rather impractical advice given by Molina, in his "*Instructiones pro Sacerdotibus.*" This worthy author was wont to say that the hands of priests were so venerable that they should be at all times gloved, lest they touch anything defiled.

201 *Lit. Prax.*, III, 201.

of emergency be put upon the forehead, which has been anointed by chrism by the Bishop in Confirmation.

Ad Pedes:

The final unction in the present discipline is that of the feet. The history of the unction affords us no definite idea of the part of the feet that should be anointed. As in the other unctions, the Rituals of the several Churches reveal wide variances of practical procedure in anointing the feet.

The Ritual of the Church of Chartres [202] contains this very peculiar rubric: "Ungatur infirmus . . . sub plantis pedum inferius, si sit certus de morte; et si dubitetur de morte, fiat supra pedes." A double unction was directed to be made upon the soles and upon the insteps by Pontifical of Sens[203] and the *Codex Domini Desmarais*.[204] A single unction "super pedes" was prescribed by the Rituals of Amiens[205] and Châlons-sur-Marne, [206] while St. Charles,[207] ordered the unction to be done "in plantis."

As a result there is a difference of opinion among liturgists as to the proper place of anointment. Castaldus,[208] Baruffaldo,[209] Billuart [210] and Dens [211] favor the instep as the more proper place. Thus reverence prompts Dens [212] to give as the reason of his preference "ne sanctum oleum pedibus calcari videatur." On the contrary Catalano [213] and St. Alphonsus Liguori[214] think that the soles of the feet are the proper places to be anointed, because it seems more conformable to the form, "quidquid per gressum deliquisti."

---

202 edited 1489, 1544 & 1604—apud Launoi, *Op. Omnia*, tom. I, p. 577.
203 Martene, *De Antiq. Eccl. Rit.*, lib. I, cap. 7, a. 4, Ordo XV.
204 Martene, *l.c.*, Ordo XXIII.
205 Martene, *l.c.*, Ordo XXIV.
206 Martene, *l.c.*, Ordo XXVII.
207 "*Instructiones de Extr. Unct.*," apud *Acta Eccl. Mediol.*, pars. IV, tom. I, page 606.
208 Lib. 2, s. 14, c. 10, n. 7.
209 *Ad Rit. Rom. Comm.*, tit. 28, n. 84.
210 *Summa S. Thom.*, *De Ext. Unct.*, a. 2, Observanda 6.
211 *Tract. De Ext. Unct.*, N. 3, p. 23.
212 *L.c.*
213 *Rit. Rom.*, tom. I, p. 335.
214 *Th. M.*, VI, 711.

After years of dispute the question was put for a decision to the Holy See. On August 27, 1836, the Sacred Congregation of Rites [215] decided that nothing new was to be introduced. As a consequence each one should follow the custom of his particular locality[216] If there is no custom established, a priest is free to follow either opinion. In his decision as to the place to anoint, it may be well for him to note that touching of the soles often causes a tickling sensation in the patient, which at times may be very distressing. An anointment on the instep will prevent any such inconvenience.

Authors agree that if any difficulty is found in anointing the part of the foot demanded by the local custom, it is perfectly permissible to anoint any other convenient part.[217]

> "Si quis autem sit aliquo membro mutilatus, pars illa proxima inungatur, eadem verborum forma." (*Rit. Rom.*, tit. V, cap. 1, n. 19.)

Occasionally a priest will be called to anoint a man who is lacking one or more of the sense organs that should be anointed. The mode of procedure in such a contingency has been settled by the Roman Ritual. Its prescription is in accordance with the common teaching of the Doctors of the School.[218] All of them held, that even if the member had been permanently mutilated since birth, an unction was beneficial, because, as St. Thomas described,[219] "quamvis non habeant membra, habent tamen potentias animae quae illis membris debentur, saltem in radice, et interius peccare possunt per ea quae ad illas partes pertinent, quamvis non exterius."

Hence, when a member is obtruncated or lacking in any way, the nearest part to it is to be anointed. De Herdt thinks that this is also to be done when the member is bandaged or covered

215 *Rhedonen.*, ad 1—D. A., n. 2743; "Anne, ultra pedum pars superior, inferior quoque ungenda sit in Sacramento Extremae Unctionis? R. Nihil innovetur."

216 Cf. Vermeersch-Creusen, *Epit.*, II, 231.

217 Cf. O'Kane, *The Rubrics*, n. 936.

218 Cf. St. Thomas, *Comm. In IV Lib. Sent.*, ad dist. 23 libri quarti, q. 2, a. 3, quaestiunc. 3; St. Bonaventure, *Comm. in Lib. IV Sent.*, dist. 23 libri quarti, a. 2, quaest. 3, concl., paragr. 4, n. 4; Diana, *Op. Coord.*, tom. II, tr. III, res. 48; Naldus, *Summa*, verb. "*Mutus,*" n. 3 & verb. "*Ext. Unct.,*" n. 8.

219 *L.c.*

so that it cannot be touched.[220] This would be of especial value in hospitals, and in accidents where a man's hands or feet may be pinned under fallen walls, &c.

A quite different predicament would occur if the man were found to have redundant members, as for example, three hands or three feet. In this case Baruffaldo [221] decides that those organs are to be anointed which are collocated in the natural *situs* of the body, so that, "*dempto membro superfluo,*" the body can be said to be complete and well organized. O'Kane [222] and De Herdt [223] allow the suggestion of Baruffaldo, and also assert as an alternative the lawfulness of anointing the members most in use in such people. The method of procedure when a person has been blind, deaf or dumb since birth was much discussed by the older theologians. The Ritual of Paris [224] contained the rubric: "In infirmis ab ortu caecis vel surdis nulla fit oculorum auriumve unctio nullaque his sensibus respondens forma pronuntiatur." Natalis Alexander [225] agrees with this disposition of the question and notes that those who have been mute from birth may be anointed on the lips, but the words "*et locutionem*" must be omitted from the form. La Croix[226] places in the class of those perpetually insane, and hence incapable of receiving Extreme Unction, all persons who have had the misfortune of being deaf, dumb and blind since birth. When, however, the three afflictions are not simultaneously present in the same individual, he allows his admissibility to this sacrament.[227] Most of the theologians and liturgists realized that men blind or deaf or mute since birth could easily sin through inordinate desires for the possession of such powers. Accordingly they directed that these organs were to be anointed in such men just as in

220 *Prax. Lit.*, III, 200, 7.
221 *Ad Rit. Rom. Comm.*, tom. I, tit. 27, n. 119.
222 *The Rubrics*, n. 893.
223 *Lit. Prax.*, III, 200, 7.
224 apud Dens, *Theol. Mechlinensis*, "*De Ext. Unct.*," N. 4, page 27.
225 *Th. D. et M.*, lib. 2, "*De Ext. Unct.*," c. V, reg. 7.
226 *Th. M.*, Lib. VI, p. II, n. 1875.
227 *Op. cit.*, lib. VI, pars. II, n. 2084.
228 "*Instructiones de Ext. Unct.*," *Acta Eccl. Mediol.*, pars IV, tom. 1, p. 604.

those who actually had the use of them. St. Charles says[228] "Caecis, surdis, mutis, paralyticis, quamvis eo sensu, vel videndi vel loquendi vel ambulandi, semper caruerint, [Extrema Unctio] praebebitur; peccare enim potuerunt per internas potentias, quibus ea membra respondent." Catalano,[229] Diana,[230] St. Thomas,[231] St. Bonaventure,[232] St. Alphonsus[233] and Salmanticenses[234] all insist on the unction of these organs though never used from birth.

The latter opinion has become universally accepted today. All recent liturgists instruct that the unction of such senses be done, on their proper organs if they are present, and if not, on the nearest places.[235] Vermeersch-Creusen[236] notes that if one of the members of a twin sense is altogether missing, (e. g., an arm cut off at the shoulder) it is quite sufficient to anoint the remaining organ. If the sense has not two organs, or if both organs are completely obtruncated, the nearest place is to be anointed, *salva semper modestia.*

II. Mode of Anointing in Case of Necessity.

In casu autem necessitatis sufficit unica unctio in uno sensu seu rectius in fronte cum praescripta forma breviore, salva obligatione singulas unctiones supplendi, cessante periculo.

The ordinary rite of administration of Extreme Unction is somewhat elaborate and requires not a little time to perform it. Yet it often occurs that the priest reaches a person so shortly before death that it is quite impossible to fulfill this elaborate ceremonial. From the times of the Scholastics this question of giving the sick man the benefit of the sacrament without imperilling its validity has beset theologians.

229 *Rit. Rom.*, t. I, p. 320.
230 *Op. Coord.*, tom. II, tr. III, res. 48.
231 *Suppl.*, q. 32, a. 7.
232 *Comm. in Lib. IV Sent.*, dist. 23 libri quarti, a. 2, q. 2, concl., paragr. 4, n. 4.
233 *Th. M.*, VI, 732, 3.
234 *Cursus Th. M.*, tr. 7, c. 2, p. 3, n. 23 et 24.
235 Cf. De Herdt, *Lit. Prax.*, III, 200, 7; O'Kane, *The Rubrics*, n. 893; De Amicis, *Caeremoniale Parochorum*, n. 203, 12; Pighi-Ferrais, *Liturgia Sacerdotalis*, n. 556, &c.
236 *Epit.*, II, 231.

The Scholastics held generally that the unction of the five senses was necessary. Their problem was to prove that the unction of the entire body was unessential; and they did not endeavor to investigate whether the unction of the five senses was absolutely required for the validity of the sacrament. The senses were viewed by them as the roots of sin, and therefore their anointment seemed so appropriate that they considered it as divinely ordained.[237] Later theologians wholeheartedly subscribed to this opinion, giving it so bright a hue of external probability that it could not be ignored. Thus Bellarmine [238] declared that the opinion maintaining the validity of a single unction was "singularis et ideo minus tuta." Gregory of Valencia [239] and Gonet [240] joined their names to this array of authority on the question.

To gather definitely the opinion of Suarez on this question is rather difficult. In one place [241] he seems to favor the opinion asserting the validity of a single unction, while later in his works[242] he considers the question whether the unctions of five senses sufficiently express the effects of the sacrament. He decides that they do, because they are the roots of sin, and although there can be other sins of the intellect, yet "nihil est in intellectu quod non prius fuerit in sensu."

The Scholastics, no doubt, looked at the question from an "*a priori*" standpoint. When theologians who studied the positive arguments in this question appeared, the opinion gained weight that only a single unction with a general form need be applied. Some of the pioneers were Sylvius,[243] Serarius, S. J.,[244]

---

237 Cf. St. Thomas, *Suppl.*, q. 32, a. 5 et 6; St. Bonaventure, *Comm. in lib. quart. Sent.*, dist. 23, a. 2, q. 3; D. Soto, *Comm. in lib. quart. Sent.*, dist. 23, q. 2, a. 3, &c.

238 *De Ext. Unct.*, lib. unic., c. 10.

239 *Comm. Theol.*, tom. 4, disp. 4, q. 3, p. 2.

240 *Clypeus Theol. Thomist.*, tom. VI, *De Ext. Unct.*, disp. I, a. 2, n. XXX.

241 D. 40, sec. 3, n. 16: "Non videtur de essentia hujus sacramenti, ut in illis partibus unctio fiat; Jacobus enim solum dicit: '*Ungentes eum,*' quod verbum sufficienter compleretur ungendo infirmum in corpore, in capite, &c."

242 D. 41, sect. 2, n. 13.

243 *In Suppl.*, q. 32, a. 6, quaest. 2.

244 *Tract. de Ext. Unct.*, cap. 7.

Becanus,[245] Estius,[246] Natalis Alexander,[247] Juenin,[248] De Sainte-Beuve [249] and Tournely.[250] Their researches into the various Ordines of administration, ancient and contemporary, proved a useful corrective and saved them from asserting the sweeping conclusions of the Scholastics.

Later theologians recognized the probability of both opinions, with the consequence that the liceity of a single unction was admitted when the prescribed mode of anointing could not be carried out. Thus the Pastoral of Mechlin, approved by the Academy of Louvain, and issued in 1589, announced: "In morbis contagiosis, et peste grassante, ut periculum vitetur, sufficit inungi sensus organum magis ad unctionem expositum ac detectum, dicendo: 'Per istam sanctam unctionem, et piissimam suam misericordiam indulgeat tibi Deus quicquid per visum, auditum, ordoratum, gustum et tactum.' "[251] The Apostolic Nuncio to Belgium and Germany, Octavius Frangipano, extended this shortly afterwards to the diocese of Cologne [252] and the Manuals of the Churches of Cambrai and Arras approved the very same procedure.[253] Tournely[254] cites the Ritual of Paris which contained the following rubric: "Si non possit super infirmum fieri, nisi unica unctio, ungatur oculus vel aliud sensuum organum, et ceteris precibus praetermissis, dicatur: 'Per istam sacri Olei Unctionem, et suam piisimam misericordiam, indulgeat tibi Deus quidquid peccasti per sensus.' " Launoi [255] points out a similar rubric in the Ritual of Châlons-sur-Marne, edited in 1605.

---

245 *Summ. Theol. de Sac. in Specie,* c. 27, q. 7.

246 *Comm. in lib. quartum Sent.,* dist. 23, paragr., 14, tom. 4, page 295-6.

247 *Th. D. et M.,* tom. I, lib. 2, c. 5, reg. 6.

248 *De Sac. in Genere et in Specie,* diss. 7, q. 3, cap. 2, concl. 2 & 3.

249 *Tract. de Ext. Unct.,* disp. 3, a. 2; apud Migne, *Curs. Theol. Comp.,* vol. XXIV, col. 98.

250 *Prael. Theol.,* tom. II, "*De Ext. Unct.,*" q. 2, a. 2 in fine.

251 apud Natalis Alexander, *Th. D. et M.,* tom. I, lib. 2, c. 5, reg. 6.

252 Cf. Bened. XIV, *De Syn. Dioc.,* l. 8, c. 3, n. 4.

253 apud Natalis Alexander, *l.c.*

254 *Prael. Theol.,* t. II, *De Ext. Unct.,* q. 2, a. 1.

255 *Op. Omnia,* tom. I, p. 576.

It is to be noted that the third Council of Mechlin, held in 1607, decreed that "infecti morbo contagioso instar aliorum aegrotorum inungantur saltem in altero organo singulorum sensuum." When the legislation went to the Holy See for confirmation, the Roman Correctors struck out this prescription,[256] thereby giving an inkling of the unwillingness of the Holy See to condemn an opinion which eventually it confirmed by inserting it in its Code of Canon Law.

Moved by a solicitude that the patient at the point of death should receive the sacrament with as much certitude as possible, theologians devised various expedients to be used in shortening the time required for anointing. Thus St. Alphonsus[257] urged the priest to hurry through the unction of the five senses under one general form. Some suggested the anointment of the five senses on the head (anointing the cheeks for the sense of touch), and the use of a general form. In regard to the form, St. Alphonsus [258] cautioned an explicit mention of the senses, rather than a general formula such as "quidquid per sensus deliquisti." Likewise he recommended the placing of the word "*deliquisti*" before the mention of the five senses, since it was probable that the mention of them was not essential, while that of "*deliquisti*" was. But with all their solicitude, the theologians never failed to recognize the probability of the opinion which maintained the sufficiency of a single unction; and in case of absolute necessity they permitted it to be put in practice.

The validity of the single unction when made in a case of necessity, was generally considered to be doubtful, and consequently, if time permitted, the sacrament was to be conditionally repeated in the ordinary fashion. The expression of the condition in this instance was given as "Si nondum es hoc Sacramento refectus."[259] No theologian dared to declare the conditional repetition unnecessary, for the opposite opinion holding only the validity of the five-fold unction was "antiquior, communior, et tutior, ideoque omnino sequenda."[260]

---

256 Cf. Dens, *Theol. Mech.*, "*Tract. De Ext. Unct.*," N. 4, p. 28.
257 *Th. M.*, VI, 710.
258 *Th. M.*, VI, 710.
259 Cf. Scavini, *Th. M.*, III, n. 434; Heuser, *The Parish Priest*, p. 101; &c.
260 D'Annibale, *Summ. Th. M.*, n. 414.

While theologians were propounding their arguments and conclusions, the Holy See stood silently by, waiting for the opportune time to make a decision on the question. When asked in 1754 whether a single anointing would suffice, the Congregation of the Holy Office avoided the question.[261] It was not until April 25, 1906, that it declared in case of necessity a single form sufficed.[262] This decree contained nothing explicit about the sufficiency of a single unction, although this is easily deducible from the single form. The new Code removes all rational and irrational doubt by an express declaration to this effect.[263]

In casu autem necessitatis.

In every case of necessity, no matter whence it arises, the shorter form of Extreme Unction can be employed. Necessity is surely present when a man's expiration is feared before the longer rite might be completed. Similarly, when it is doubtful whether a man is alive or not, as contemplated by Canon 941, it is safe to employ this briefer mode of administration.

Various other cases of necessity are propounded by authors. Vermeersch-Creusen [264] declares that necessity can arise from the peril of contagion. Accordingly when serious danger threatens the health of the priest if he should dally too long in the sick room, he may leave after a single unction has been performed. In times of pestilence such danger is constantly present, and Extreme Unction may be imparted to all in this quicker fashion.[265] Another instance would occur in the case where the sacrament has to be administered to a large number of sick people and it is feared that some may not receive the sacrament

---

261 S. C. S. Off., *Algeriae*, 11 Jul. 1754—apud Coll. S. C. P. F., n. 596, footnote.

262 S. C. S. Off., apud Coll. S. C. P. F., n. 2233; A. S. S., XXXIX, 273.

263 Cfr. *Ephemer. Liturg.*, vol. XX, p. 451; *Razon y Fé*, vol. XVI, p. 236; *Il Monitore*, vol. XIX, p. 231, &c.

264 *Epit.*, II, 231.

265 Cf. Alphonsus, *Th. M.*, VI, 710; Clericatus, *Decisiones Sacramentales*, "*De Ext. Unct.*," dec. 66, n. 9; Benedict XIV, *De Syn. Dioc.*, l. 13, c. 19, n. 39.

in good time, or perhaps not at all, if the longer formula is persolved [266] in each case. In time of epidemics, or on the battlefield such instances must not be infrequent. Wapelhorst [267] cites an extraordinary railroad accident as an example of this necessity.

Other cases can be easily imagined. Thus, if a priest had but a limited time assigned to him by hospital authorities wherein he must perform all his ministrations, it may often be necessary to be content with but a single unction, especially when many patients have to be visited and attended. A similar case of necessity would occur, if during an operation a man would suddenly fall into danger of death and the work of the surgeons would be seriously, if not fatally, delayed, were they to suspend progress until the entire rite was performed. Thus, too, the brief formula may be employed when the patient is in danger of death from an internal cause so imminently that an operation is immediately urgent.

Necessity will be at hand too, when scandal would arise from the employment of a lengthy formula. In maternity cases it is sometimes wise for a priest who must attend a woman in the throes of parturition to retire from the scene as soon as possible. Likewise the conditional anointment of a man who up until the last moment of consciousness refused the sacraments [268] may often have to be done very judiciously, and even secretly, with a single unction, in order to avoid any scandal to the bystanders. Those who feel justified in anointing non-Catholics conditionally in virtue of the probable opinion announced in the Commentary on Canon 940, may often have to resort to a secret unction. Lastly, the presence of a physical obstacle preventing access to the ordinary places of unction will suffice for the lawful employment of the brief form.[269]

---

266 Cf. *Modo Practico,* cap. ix—O'Kane, *The Rubrics,* n. 900.

267 *Comp. Sac. Liturg.,* n. 292.

268 Cf. *supra,* chap. vii, p. 241 sqq.

269 Vermeersch-Creusen, *Epit.,* II, 231.

Sufficit unica unctio.

For the first time in the legislation of the Church the sufficiency of a single unction has been explicitly declared. As noted before, the decree of the Holy Office in 1906 allowing a single form furnished a very rational basis for this deduction, as did also two decisions of the Holy Office since that time in regard to supplying the unctions.[270] But the precise declaration was not forthcoming until the promulgation of this Canon in the Code.

A single unction is sufficient, the Canon declares. Consequently, a single unction is valid; and in case of necessity is also licit. The force of "*unica*" is noteworthy. It dispels any doubt that might arise as to the number of unctions necessary if the organs of the sense anointed were double. Now it is clear that an unction on either of the two organs is all that is required.

"*In uno sensu seu rectius in fronte.*"

No particular sense is specified to receive this single unction. It may be made on any of them with equal validity and liceity. However the Code suggests that it be done upon the forehead, "quia in capite sita est cogitationis sedes ac centrum nervorum sensuum."[271]

"Rectius" has the force of "consultius," i. e., "more properly," or "more becomingly." It is nothing more than a counsel, arising from the fitness of anointing the seat of all the senses. Surely, however, the wish of the Church should be acceded to unless some obstacle prevents it. Such an obstacle can be present physically, for example, when the man's head is entirely bandaged, when he is lying beneath an engine with only feet protruding, &c. In such contingencies the unction can be made on any organ that can be reached. The canon specifies only the unction of a particular sense; and since the sense of touch is diffused throughout the entire body, any place anointed

---

270 S. C. S. Off., 31 Jan. 1907; 9 Mar. 1917; Cf. A. A. S., IX, 178.

271 Blat, *Comm. Text.*, lib. 3, pars. I, n. 292.

can be said to be an unction of the sense of touch. Thus Tanquerey says that the unction can be made "in pectore aut scapulis."[272]

Moral obstacles may also prevent an unction on the head. Thus in the two instances given as cases of moral necessity, viz., the unction of one who refused the sacraments up until the moment of unconsciousness and the administration of this sacrament to a dying non-Catholic, it was noted that it would often be necessary to avoid scandal by imparting the sacrament secretly. Secrecy may be more insured by an unction on the hand rather than on the forehead. Thus, if a priest were cautiously to open his oil stocks in his pocket, dip his thumb therein, and afterwards touch one of the hands of the sick man, it would be enough. What would seem to the bystanders only a mark of friendliness on the part of the priest might be for the sick man the means of his salvation.

Finally, a word should be said about a place of unction in the case of a man beheaded. Since, as O'Malley[273] notes, it is always probable that such a man does not die at once, conditional administration of the sacrament can, and, at times, even must, be made in accordance with the prescription of Canon 941. But where is the cross of oil to be placed in such a case? It is very uncertain whether the soul is resident in the trunk or in the head. The only solution is to anoint both parts of the body once. The unction upon the head should be made upon the forehead, if feasible, whereas the unction of the trunk can be made upon the hand or any other convenient place. In the case where either the head or the trunk is not obtainable, it is clear that the priest should anoint the part of the body at hand.

"Cum praescripta forma breviori."

The form prescribed is found in the latest edition of the Roman Ritual.[274] It is identical with that given in the decree

---

272 *Th. D.*, III, 769.

273 *Ethics of Med. Homicide*, p. 83.

274 Tit. V, cap. 1, n. 21.

275 A. S. S., XXXIX, 273; Coll. S. C. P. F., n. 2223.

of the Holy Office in 1906,[275] and reads thus: "Per istam sanctam unctionem indulgeat tibi Dominus quidquid deliquisti. Amen."

If the single unction is employed, this form must accompany it by virtue at least of the ecclesiastical precept. Hence any mention of the senses, or other variations, though not invalidating, are prohibited.

"Salva obligatione singulas unctiones supplendi, cessante periculo."

Since the judgment of man in regard to the proximity of death is very fallacious, it is very often the case that the patient lives long enough after the single anointment that he would have survived even the administration of the longer rite of unction. Hence if the patient is still alive in such cases as these, the canon orders the omitted unctions to be supplied.

Prior to the decision of the Holy Office in 1906, this had been demanded by practically all theologians. They looked on this second ceremony as a surer confection of a sacrament that was but doubtfully administered before. Hence this second administration was always done conditionally, because of the probable validity of the prior rite.

The decree of the Holy Office in 1906 caused the theological kettle to boil over. The force of the term "sufficit" in the decree was the matter of much discussion for a period of ten years at least. Very many theologians held that the sacrament was pronounced valid when conferred with this short form (and single unction), with the consequence that no further anointings were to be done, even if the patient survived for a time. Proponents of this teaching were Noldin,[276] Lehmkuhl,[277] Gennari,[278] Micheletti,[279] and writers in the *Ephemerides Liturgicae,*[280] *Revue Theologique Français,*[281] *L'Ami du Clergé*[282] and

276 *De Sac.*, 452, edit. VII (1908).

277 *Th. M.*, II, 719, edit. XII (1914).

278 *Il Monitore Eccl.*, XIX, 231-2.

279 *Summa Th. Past.*, p. 110.

280 anno 1906, p. 451.

281 anno 1906, p. 408.

282 anno 1908, p. 13; anno 1911, p. 736; anno 1912, p. 640.

The Irish Ecclesiastical Record.[283] Practically all of these men declared positively unlawful any further unction of the senses passed over in the short form.

On the other hand some theologians allowed, though did not insist upon, the performance of the rite in the longer fashion after the single unction had been used. Thus Vermeersch wrote in the *Periodica* in 1911:[284] "Quodsi peracta summaria ista unctione tempus superfuerit, consuetae singulorum sensuum unctiones sub longiore forma peragere non negleget [sacerdos]."

Similarly, Ferreres[285] held: "Sed si tempus post peractam hanc unicam unctionem supersit, videntur fieri posse sensuum unctiones cum forma singulis propria ad pleniorem sacramenti significationem exprimendam." Tanquerey [286] agreed with these opinions: "Ad integritatem vero sacramenti eas [i. e., unctiones in singulis sensibus] perficiendas esse sub conditione, quam alii aliter sentiant."

Modified and cautious statements like these did not betray the settled conviction of Slater [287] and the Redactor of the *Acta Sanctae Sedis* [288] on this matter. These men contended that there was no definite settlement of the question made by the Holy See. What the decree decided was the sufficiency of the words required for the form, leaving as much in doubt as ever the validity of confection with a single unction. Hence the entire rite was to be repeated conditionally upon a man who survived for a sufficient length of time after receiving the sacrament thru a single unction.

Father Slater's arguments are interesting. In the first place, he draws an analogy from the sacrament of Penance.

---

283 Cf. Query and argument by "Religiosus" and the reply of M. J. O'Donnell, Vol. VI, fifth series (1915), pp. 525-8; also article by M. J. O'Donnell, Vol. VII, fifth series (1916), pp. 28-43.

284 vol. III, p. 242 (58).

285 *Comp. Th. M.*, II, 683, edit. quart. (1909).

286 *Brev. Syn. Th. M.*, n. 1260, edit. 1911.

287 *Th. M.*, vol. II, p. 235, edit. 1908; also I. E. Record, vol. VI, fifth series, Dec. 1915, pp. 567-74.

288 Comment. on the decree of the Holy Office, Apr. 25, 1906, in *Acta S. S.*, XXXIX, 275-6.

There is much dispute, he notes,[289] about the exact words essential for the form of absolution. Some think "Ego te absolvo" is sufficient while others claim that "absolvo a peccatis tuis" is required. Suppose then a bishop should ask the Holy See for a determination of what form should be used in case of necessity. In answer to this, let us presume that the Holy Office declares that "Ego te absolvo a peccatis tuis" is quite sufficient (*sufficit*). Surely if a priest used this formula of absolution to a man in extreme danger who has not made a manifest confession, all that the priest knows is that the form was valid. He is still in ignorance in regard to the validity or invalidity of the reception of the sacrament—for this depends upon the placing of the matter as well as the form. Consequently the same thing must be argued in regard to the decision of the Holy Office about Extreme Unction. All the decree asserts is the sufficiency of the words of the form, without even insinuating the sufficiency of a single unction.

This argument is certainly not without weight. It can be reasonably claimed that several unctions—and indeed the unctions of the five senses—might easily be made while this single form was being said, thus uniting, as the old theologians advised, all the anointments under a single formula.

The other arguments advanced by Slater are not so happy. He claimed that, even if the decree of the Holy Office implied the use of a single unction, the question was not finally settled, for such decisions are neither infallible nor irrevocable. It is hardly edifying, to say the least, to find his contention based on the supposed falsity of a decision which represents the highest authority outside infallibility to which a Catholic can appeal. If not infallible, these decisions are certainly authoritative.

Furthermore he advances an argument from authority, asserting that Noldin, Ferreres, Vermeersch, Tanquerey and the Redactor of the *Acta Sanctae Sedis* (all as quoted above) agree with him. However, with the exception of the Redactor an exact identity of opinion cannot be claimed. Vermeersch, by using "non negleget," took little pains to emphasize his instructions, and his failure to adduce any reason makes his statement appear

289 apud I. E. Record, *l.c.*, p. 570.

all the more half-hearted. Ferreres and Tanquerey are in unison with Slater in regard to the practical thing to be done, but certainly not for the same reason. Slater looked upon the sacrament conferred with a single unction as only probably valid and he demanded the conditional repetition by the longer form, when possible, in order that the "tutior pars" would have been cared for even in such a case. Ferreres said the subsequent unctions were to be made *"ad pleniorem sacramenti significationem exprimendam."* Moreover, the halting expression that he employs, *"videntur fieri posse,"* can hardly be taken as an indication of stable conviction on one side or the other. Tanquerey taught that the unctions were to be made *"ad integritatem sacramenti."* Evidently he maintained the validity of the single unction; but viewed the additional anointings as completing the sacrament. It is strange that he ordered this "completion" to be made "sub conditione." If the first sacrament were incomplete, the "completion" should be made absolutely.

The most peculiar procedure of all is Slater's attempt to show that Noldin does not oppose him. Noldin [290] wrote: "Si sacramentum in periculo mortis unica unctione collatum fuerit, postea *cessante periculo,* nihil repetendum vel supplendum est." Slater [291] remarks on this passage: "Of course when the danger has ceased, when the sick person is no longer in danger of death, nothing should be repeated or supplied." Apparently he interprets Noldin's phrase "cessante periculo" to imply the passing of all danger. Yet within the very next paragraph he adopts a very different rendering of the identical phrase used by the Redactor of the *Acta Sanctae Sedis* in his comment on the decree. "Sed, *cessante periculo,"* wrote the Redactor,[292] " . . . sub conditione repetendae singulae unctiones in singulis sensibus, sub suis particularibus formis" &c. No reason is assigned for these contrary interpretations of this very same phrase, with the result that one argument counterbalances the other, and effects nothing.

Argumentation such as this between theologians lasted until 1917. One camp continued to hold the position that the first

290 *De Sac.*, 452, edit. VII (1908).
291 I. E. Record, vol. VI, fifth series, Dec. 1915, p. 573.
292 A. S. S., XXXIX, 275-6.

unction was but probably valid and that, consequently, a second and conditional administration was to be done as soon as possible. The other phalanx of authority refused to recede from its contention that the validity of the first unction was so certain that even a conditional repetition was positively wrong. Both sides failed to take into consideration the possibility that, even if the single unction were valid, the separate anointings should be supplied when they have not already been employed.

This omission is easily explainable. No other sacrament demands such a repetition of omitted rite. If one of the triple ablutions prescribed for solemn baptism is omitted, for example, it is seriously wrong to supply it later with a separate form. Secondly, liberal views, holding the subsequent application of omitted unctions to be altogether illicit, were widespread even in the Eternal City, where the vigilance of the Vatican promptly prohibits erroneous opinions on such important issues.

At any rate, in 1917 both camps of theological thought were thoroughly surprised by a decision of the Holy See. The unctions, the decree announced, which were to be supplied accord- to a former decree, dated January 31, 1907, were to be done absolutely and not conditionally.[293]

Theologians had known nothing of the decree of 1907, else the differences as to the mode of procedure after the application of a single unction would not have arisen. The decree itself was never published, and probably known to very few outside the members of the Congregation of the Holy Office. Cardinal Gennari, the Prefect of the Congregation of the Council, and in almost daily contact with the Cardinals of the Inquisition, held a diametrically opposite opinion.[294] Moreover, the edition of the Ritual in 1913, although, as the decree of approbation puts it, "novissime recognitum, auctum et diligenter revisum a

293 A. A. S., IX, 178: S. C. S. Off., 9 Mar. 1917—"An administrato Sacramento Extremae Unctionis in casu necessitatis unica Unctione in fronte adhibita, per verba 'Per istam sanctam unctionem indulgeat tibi Dominus quidquid deliquisti. Amen,' cessante periculo, unctiones, ad tenorem Decreti 31 Jan. 1907, supplendae, sub conditione adhibendae sint vel non?

R., Negative ad 1am partem; affirmative ad 2am."

294 *Il Monitore Eccles.*, xix, p. 232: "Dunque se l'ammalato dura in vita dopo l'unzione abbreviata, non devono ungersi gli alteri membri; ma debono solo supplersi le preghiere non recitate."

Sacra Rituum Congregatione," contains nothing more than the unabridged decree of 1906.

In absence of the decree of 1907, theologians found themselves in deep difficulty when trying to exegete the true meaning of the decree of 1917. One solution could be obtained by emphasizing the phrase "*sub conditione,*" while another would result from stressing "*Adhibendae.*" The former would yield the unlawfulness of the subsequent unctions; the latter would imply that the unctions were to be supplied absolutely.

Theological minds were therefore in a quandary. The Irish Theological Quarterly[295] refused to make a decision. The American Ecclesiastical Review[296] reversed its interpretation within a few months, first holding that nothing was to be repeated and afterwards maintaining the absolute performance of the omitted unctions. In this confusion on the correspondents of the *Ephemerides Liturgicae* sent to that publication the following query: "Quid de novo decreto S. Officii (die 9 Martii, 1917) de Sacramento Extremae Unctionis in casu necessitatis? Multi periti apud nos non possunt interpretari responsionem S. Officii, et nemo scit aliquid de decreto citato diei 31 Januarii 1907." Without stating the source of its information, this journal published the decree of 1907. Presumably it is authentic. As given by the periodical,[297] the decree reads: "Feria v die januarii, 1907, Suprema S. Congregatio S. Officii a S. M. Pio PP. X. hujus resolutionis approbationem retulit: 'SSmus D. N., ne in posterum dubium oriantur, ita reformari jussit decretum de die 25 aprilis, 1906; "Sufficere formam '*Per istam sanctam unctionem indulgeat tibi Dominus quidquid deliquisti. Amen.*' Si vero infirmus supervixerit, suppleantur singulae unctiones et orationes." ' "

The fact that this decree was not published had the effect of frustrating its purpose. It amended the decree of 1906 "*ne in posterum dubium oriantur,*" yet the unamended form was incorporated in the Ritual of 1913.[298] Why the Roman authori-

---

295 Vol. XII (1917), p. 274.

296 Vol. LVI, p. 620; vol. LVII, pp. 196-8.

297 Anno 31, num. 8, p. 437.

298 Tit. V, cap. 1, n. 20.

ties did this is difficult to say. Without a knowledge of the reasons which prompted them to such a course, it would be imprudent, if not impudent, to criticise their action.

The promulgation of the Code shortly after the decision of 1917 brought to an end a discussion which would have otherwise assumed great proportions. A single unction with a single form suffice, the Code says, but there must be a supply of the unctions omitted.

None of the theories advanced before 1917 exactly hit the truth. The recommendation of Tanquerey would have been correct, had he omitted the words "sub conditione"—which at best were a very illogical insertion on his part. Ferreres came very near the truth when he inclined to the belief that the subsequent unctions were to be done absolutely. All he announced was, however, only an optional supplying of these omitted anointings. But there is still a difference between what is lawful and what is of obligation. Not only may the supplementary unctions be made, but they *must* be done, if there is time.

Strictly speaking, the Code has wrought no change in the mode of procedure determined by the decisions of 1906, 1907 and 1917. Practically, however, it has ended the disputing of theologians which resulted from a lack of knowledge of the decree of 1907. Thus all theological minds must change their views, while Rome continues in the steady tenor of its ways.

Since the Code, the manner of action is clear. If the patient continue to live after he has been anointed with the brief form, all the unctions prescribed by the longer rite are to be supplied. Every unction of the longer rite should be made, whether the first unction was made on the forehead or on a sense organ. The first unction is an anointment of the subject *simpliciter,* the second is an unction of the particular part of the individual. The first unction was made, not to obtain the particular graces resulting from the unction of an individual sense, but to receive the effect of the complete sacrament. Consequently, even if anointed before, the sense organ should receive its proper unction (with its particular form) when the anointings are being supplied.

The supplementary rite is to be done absolutely, in accordance with the decree of 1917. "Sapienter," writes Vermeersch-

Creusen, [299] "respondit S. C. S. Officii, 9 Mar. 1917, unctiones istas supplendas esse absolute, non condicionate. Condicionata enim administratio priorem dubiam fuisse supponeret: quod admitti nequit."

Immediately we are precipitated into another difficulty. Is the "supplying" a repetition of the sacrament or not? If it is, how can it be reconciled with the second paragraph of Canon 940, forbidding readministration in the same danger of death? If it is not, what is the meaning and the effects of the "supplied" unctions?

Various replies are possible. Taking for granted that the supplying of the unctions is really a second bestowal of the sacrament upon the sick man, three theories can be advanced. They can be briefly outlined as follows: When a patient rallies, the danger of death in which he is then placed has changed from an "imminent" danger to a "normal" or "ordinary" one. Consequently this second sacrament is given in a new danger of death—and Canon 940 is not violated.[300]

This theory labors under some difficulties. The "ordinary" or "normal" danger is hardly a new and distinct peril. At most, it is a modified form, a partial recession, of the former jeopardy. Hence the principle of Canon 940 must be violated. Furthermore, suppose the necessity which caused the use of the short form was due, not to a proximity of death, but to a moral urgency. Suppose, too, that the opportunity presents itself to confer the longer rite, yet in the meantime the patient has not rallied but has been sinking gradually toward the end. In such a case surely there is no new danger of death, yet just as surely the unctions must be supplied. The inadequacy of this theory becomes apparent.

A second explanation fares better. It appeared in the *Il Monitore Ecclesiastico* [301] and has been adopted as an alternative explanation by Sabetti-Barrett.[302]

---

299 *Epit.*, II, 231.

300 Cf. I. E. Record, vol. XI, fifth series, p. 295; O'Kane, *The Rubrics*, n. 899.

301 vol. XXIX, p. 166.

302 *Th. M.*, p. 799.

The prescription of Canon 940, 2, applies only when the sacrament is conferred with the full rite. Consequently it is licit to administer the sacrament twice in every occasion where the brief form has been used, even if the patient be in the same danger of death. "Il precetto di non iterare l'estrema unzione," wrote the Il Monitore, "vale quando si e conferita nella sua piena integrità, non già quando si è dovuta ridurre al minimum necessario." This procedure then is an exception to Canon 940 made by the Code itself.

This theory certainly escapes the difficulties of the first. There is only one thing against it—and that is the seemingly decisive character of the wording of Canon 940. Not the faintest hint of a conditional prohibition appears therein; there is no room made for an exception.

Another explanation is mentioned as possible by Fr. O'Donnell in The Irish Ecclesiastical Record.[303] The obligation of "supplying" the unctions arises only when the danger has ceased—"*cessante periculo.*" This must be interpreted to mean after *all* peril has ceased, with the consequence that the administration is not repeated during the same danger. While this escapes the prohibition of paragraph 2 in Canon 940, it runs counter to the prescription of paragraph 1 of the very same canon. *Incidit in Scyllam qui vult vitare Charybdin.* A patient out of danger altogether is no longer a valid subject of the sacrament. Any attempt to anoint at that time would certainly be inefficacious, to say nothing of being sacrilegious.

Besides these theories which presuppose that the sacrament is twice conferred, there are two others which teach that the first unction is simply supplemented by the longer rite, so that the two unctions comprise one moral action. Thus far the two theories agree, but they differ widely in their explanation of the reason for "supplying" the unctions and the effects thereof.

Ferreres [304] is a typical exponent of one of these theories. He teaches that the unctions of the second rite are required by the Church for the fuller expression of the signification of the

---

303 vol. XI, Fifth series (1918), p. 295.

304 *Comp. Th. M.*, II, 838.

sacrament. In other words, they are nothing more than ceremonies, designed to make the subject realize in a better way the true effects of the sacrament. They have no results "*ex opere operato.*" They can be compared to the ceremony of the ordination Mass, where the bishop says to the ordinands: "Accipite Spiritum Sanctum. Quorum remiseritis peccata, remittuntur eis," &c. Since the candidates are already priests, they have already received the power of remitting sins. They receive nothing more by this supplementary ceremony. It is not sacramental in its nature, but merely explanatory of a sacramental effect previously received.[305] Such is also the doctrine of Kern,[306] and was accepted by the Ecclesiastical Review [307] when Ferreres' interpretation of the rite was called to its attention. Genicot [308] is evidently with this group, although his statement is none too positive. "Unctiones absolute supplendae sunt," he writes, "saltem ad ritum consueto modo complendum." Lehmkuhl [309] can be included within this circle of authority. According to him the first unction only has a sacramental effect; the repeated unctions, however, stimulate the dispositions of the sick man and result in the production of a more complete effect of the sacrament. O'Kane[310] joins in this view, thus completing a galaxy of authority that cannot be ignored.

The other theory offers a far different explanation. According to its proponents, the separate unctions constitute the integrity of the sacrament. The essential graces are conferred by the single unction; but the sacrament has also certain actual graces which are peculiar to it alone. These actual graces are produced in proportion to the fulness with which they are expressed. Hence the supplementary unctions are commanded so

---

305 Cf. Ferreres, *Razon y Fé*, vol. XLVIII, pp. 85 & 236: "En la ordinación sacerdotal, cuando el Obispo, concuida la Misa, dice a los ordenandos: 'Accipite,' . . . . &c., no les confiere la potestad de absolver, sino que ésta la recibieron cuando los hizo sacerdotes, que fué antes de la Misa que acaban ellos de celebrar, consagrando juntamente con el Obispo. Aquellas palabras sirven para explicar major la potestad ya recibida en virtud del sacramento."

306 *Tract. de Ext. Unct.*, p. 328.

307 vol. LVII, p. 198.

308 *Inst. Th. M.*, II, 417.

309 *Th. M.*, II, 718, 3.

310 *The Rubrics*, n. 899.

that the recipient will have the benefit of the minor sacramental effects which result from the anointments of the particular senses. By these unctions the sacrament is perfected, not repeated. From them its integrity results, not only its fuller significance. They are not mere ceremonies; they have a sacramental essence. "Sunt actiones vere sacramentales," says Sabetti-Barrett,[311] "non sunt sacramentale quid, nam ne verbum quidem in responso S. Officii habetur de usu sacramentalis, nec de mutata natura actionis quae est materia ipsa sacramenti." Thus Extreme Unction can be compared in this respect to the Eucharist. With the consumption of either species, the sacrament is fully received. When it is received under both species, the grace received from the first is increased, accidentally and in a minor degree, but none the less "ex opere operato." In similar fashion the effects occur in Extreme Unction. As Vermeersch [312] puts it: "Novis tamen unctionibus significatio iteratur, et novus titulus gratiae ponitur, sive gratiae ejusdem si dispositio manserit eadem, sive amplioris si subjectum sit perfectius dispositum."

Those who favor this theory are likewise a formidable host. The principal names on its roster are those of Noldin,[313] Vermeersch,[314] Tanquerey-Quevastre,[315] and Quinn.[316] Sabetti-Barrett [317] gives it as an alternative to a theory noted before, which maintains the true repetition of the sacrament. In general, their conclusions on this point are traceable to their opinions of the unity of this sacrament.

No matter what theory is accepted, the practical procedure is the same. If there is time and occasion to supplement the short form with individual unctions of the senses, it is binding upon the priest by virtue of this canon to do so. Not to comply would be a serious sin, for it not only violates an ecclesiastical precept in grave matter, but also deprives the subject of a grave

---

311 *Th. M.*, p. 799.
312 *Th. M.*, III, 651.
313 *De Sac.*, 431.
314 *Th. M.*, III, 651.
315 *Brev. Syn. Th. M.*, n. 1260.
316 *Some Aspects of the Dogma of Extreme Unction*, p. 80-2.
317 *Th. M.*, p. 799.

thing due to him in justice. If the ceremonies in the baptismal rite, which are surely only sacramentals, must be supplied *sub gravi,* certainly these unctions, which are probably part of the sacrament, must constitute grave matter. A proportionate cause however will excuse from this obligation, just as in the case of the baptismal ceremonies.

The duty of supplying the unctions rests in justice upon the pastor of the parish. Hence if another priest has anointed *ex caritate* with the short form, the "supplying" of the unctions can be left to the pastor. It must be noted, however, that it is not lawful for any priest to use the short form except in case of necessity. But when this contingency does occur, the supplying of the unctions may be left to the ordinary minister of the sacrament, if he is at all obtainable. If the single unction is given because of the patient's supposed proximity to death, it will be advisable to continue with the unctions immediately without informing the pastor. A delay may be fatal. If, on the other hand, the necessity was moral and not physical, it is better for the priest to notify the parish priest and leave things in his hands.

If the patient was anointed with the brief form in one parish, and transported, by ambulance for example, to another, the pastor of the second parish is bound to complete the anointings, if time and other circumstances permit. The duty of caring for the sick in his parish rests on the "*parochus loci*" and not upon the pastor of the sick person.[318]

There is hardly any divergence of opinion on the exegesis of the words "*cessante periculo.*" They are interpreted to mean the recession of that urgency which forced the use of a single unction, but not to such an extent that the subject has passed beyond all danger of death. Thus Genicot[319] writes: "Cessante *urgentia* seu periculo." Ferreres[320] and Tanquerey-Quevastre[321] consider as equivalent the phrase "Si tempus supe-

---

318 Cf. canons 468, 1 and 938, 2.

319 Genicot-Salsmans, *Inst. Th. M.*, II, 417.

320 *Comp. Th. M.*, II, 838.

321 *Brev. Syn. Th. M.*, 1260.

rest." Vermeersch[322] suggested that it would have been better, if the clause "*non* cessante periculo" had been used. Under no circumstances can it be taken to mean the cessation of all danger in the patient, for then he would no longer be "in mortis periculo ob infirmitatem."

There is a difference of opinion as to the amount of time that may lapse between the single unction and its supplementary rite. Genicot,[323] in pursuance of the theory that the supplied unctions are merely ceremonial, contends that the obligation of supplying them ceases after they would fail to signify what they were intended to express, viz., the full signification of the sacrament. Hence the lapse of a notable period of time (one hour, in the opinion of Genicot) would suffice to relieve a priest from this obligation.

Vermeersch[324] admits this as a reasonable interpretation of the canon. He does not favor it, however. He inclines toward the belief that the unctions may be supplied at any time within the duration of the identical danger of death. Since these unctions are sacramental in character (as he alleges with Noldin), their execution is never without some avail, no matter how great the interval between the single unction and this subsequent rite. Furthermore, he notes, the specific efficacy which these individual unctions have because of the peculiar actual graces conferred by them is not to be discounted. "Quod si res ita se habent," he concludes *l.c.*, "suppletio omissae unctionis semper utilis esse potest, ac proin facienda videtur."

Either theory may be safely followed; and even though one adopts the view of Genicot in theory, it will not be wrong for him to use in practice the more generous view of Vermeersch. It may also be noted that, if there is still time remaining after the supplying of the unctions, the prayers of the Ritual, prescribed for recitation when conferring Extreme Unction ordinarily, should be recited.[325]

---

322 *Th. M.*, III, 651.

323 *Inst. Th. M.*, II, 417.

324 *Th. M.*, III, 651.

325 Cf. *Rit. Rom.*, tit. V, c. 1, n. 12; Blat, *Comm. Text.*, lib. III, p. I, n. 292.

The practical course to be followed can be summed up briefly:

1. If there is no danger that the patient will die before the completion of the entire formula as found in the *Rituale*, all the rubrical prescriptions should be carried out accurately.

2. If it is feared that the patient will die before the rite can be completed, yet not before the unction of the senses can be carried out, the priest will commence with the anointings.[326] Moral necessity may also compel this, for example, when there is a danger of contagion, or when the work of the surgeons upon the patient will not brook delay. If, however, the priest has the time and opportunity after anointing thus, he should say the prayers prescribed by the Ritual, first those which follow the unctions, and later, those which are preparatory to the anointing.

3. If through a mistake in judgment the longer rite of unction has been commenced, only to have the patient seemingly die before its completion, at least the unctions remaining should be quickly performed conditionally, as has already been said in the treatment of Canon 941.[327] It is even in this case quite lawful to add the prayers of the Ritual.[328]

4. If, due to physical obstacles or other causes, all the senses cannot be anointed, the priest shall proceed to anoint as many as he can. If afterwards he finds that the obstacle has been removed, he shall anoint the senses that he has omitted.[329] The supposition here is that the priest can get in no way close to the organs which should receive the oil, as in the case where a man's head is wholly bandaged, &c. It is to be noted, however, that if he can get near to the place of unction, he may anoint the nearest part—provided, of course, it is reasonably contiguous to the sense organ prescribed for the unction. When this unction is done, nothing need be repeated.

326 *Rit. Rom.*, tit. V, cap. n. 12.

327 Cf. *supra*, chap. vi, p. 221 sq.

328 Cf. *I. E. Record*, vol. XI, Fifth Series, p. 296 (art. by M. J. O'Donnell).

329 Cf. Vermeersch-Creusen, *Epit.* II, 231.

5. When there is danger that the patient will succumb before the completion of the longer form could be reached, it is permissible to anoint one organ of sense, or preferably the forehead, pronouncing simultaneously the short form. This may also be done when the necessity is moral as well as physical. If the patient still lives after this brief rite, the unctions are to be supplied on the individual senses absolutely.

6. Where there are many to be anointed and it is feared that some will die before the longer form can be performed in each case, all should be anointed first with a single unction. Then the individual unctions should be supplied on those still alive, starting, naturally, with the subjects nearest to death. If some survive even after this, the prayers should be supplied as in the other cases, except that the plural number should be used instead of the singular.[330]

7. Supplying of the unctions in cases where the brief formula has been used may be done as long as the identical danger of death continues. A priest is not to be blamed, however, who feels himself freed from all obligation on this score after an hour has intervened without presenting an opportunity to perform the subsequent rite.

8. The right and the obligation of supplying the unctions belong exclusively to the pastor of the place where the man lies sick.

9. When the unction is conditionally given by a single form, as e. g., in cases of apparent death, the unctions should not be supplied until the subject has given signs of life. Until that time there is no cessation of the urgency which prompted the short form.[331]

---

330 *Rit. Rom.*, Tit. V, cap. I, n. 22.
331 Amer. Eccl. Review, LXIX, p. 303.

II. The Unction of the Reins.

Unctio renum semper omittatur.

Besides five forms for the unctions of the senses and another for the anointing of the feet, the Roman Ritual contained until its revision in 1925 a seventh form for the anointing of the reins. It was identical with the other forms except, of course, for the specific mention of the sins of the flesh. Thus it read: "Per istam sanctam unctionem et suam piissimam misericordiam indulgeat tibi Dominus quidquid *per lumborum delectationem* deliquisti. Amen." This unction, the rubric told us, was to be performed only upon men; "sed renum unctio in mulieribus, honestatis causa, semper omittitur."[332] Even in men the omission of this anointment was allowed when the sick man could not be conveniently moved.[333] Finally instructions were given that neither in men nor in women should any other part of the body be anointed in substitution for the unction of the reins.[334]

Authors differed as to the exact place of unction. Van der Stappen[335] mentions three different modes of making this anointment. The renal region is situated in the back between the lowest ribs and the hip or haunch bone (*ossa coxalia*). Hence a single unction made in the middle of the back upon the lumbar vertebrae (i e., the spinal column at the height at which the priest's cincture encircles him) would suffice for the unction of both reins, and was consequently permissible. Likewise a double unction, one on the right and the other on the left of the spinal column in this region was permitted. Some authors taught that a single unction on either side of the spine sufficed. In these two latter cases the anointings could be made immediately by the side of the lumbar vertebrae, or in the middle of the renal region on each side of the spine, or on the side of the body.[336]

---

332 Tit. V, cap. 1, n. 15, edit. 1913.

333 Rit. Rom., *l.c.*

334 Rit. Rom., *l.c.*

335 *Sac. Lit.*, tom. IV, Q. 219, n. 7.

336 Cf. De Herdt, *Prax. Lit.*, III, 201; Wapelhorst, *Comp. Sac. Lit.*, n. 290, 6; De Amicis, *Caerem. Paroch.*, n. 203, 14 (g).

The unction of the reins was hardly universal at any time. Of the thirty rituals given by Martene[337] only two are found to contain a form for the reins.[338] The older, the *Codex Regiae Bibliothecae* (Francorum), dates back no further than the latter part of the fourteenth century, while the other is the Ambrosian Ritual edited in 1645 by command of Caesar Montius, then archbishop of Milan. Launoi's collection [339] reveals a similar omission in many ancient rituals and codices.

It did exist in many localities, however. The Sixth Provincial Council of Benevento, held in 1374, prescribed this unction. These organs, the Council wrote,[340] "loco genitalium, quibus maxime in hominibus culpa contrahitur et perpetratur, et venialis et mortalis, inunguntur propter foeditatem membri, propter quam natura rationalis erubescit cogitare; et ideo absit quod Oleum Sanctum debeat ibi opponi."

Many rituals of the fifteenth and sixteenth centuries ordered the unction of the reins for men and that of the umbilicus for women.[341]

In view of this rather widespread practice, it is hard to account for the denunciations of Victorelli made by Baruffaldo[342] and Catalano [343] because he recommended this procedure in regard to women.[344]

The Council of Salerno, celebrated in 1579, did not allow this unction to be made upon women, but permitted an unction upon the reins of men, if the sickness did not prevent it.[345] If the unction of the reins could not be made, it was lawful to substitute for it an unction of the breast. The appearance of the

---

337 *De Antiq. Eccl. Rit.*, lib. I, cap. 7, a. 4.
338 Ordines XXIV and XXV.
339 *Op. Omnia*, t. I, p. 574 sqq.
340 Tit. 8, cap. 4—Catalano, *Rit. Rom.*, t. I, p. 336.
341 This prescription is found in the following Rituals of Launoi's collection (apud *Op. Omnia*, t. I, p. 574 sqq.): Coutances (1494), Uzès (1500), Lisieux (1505 & 1522), Paris (1504, 1542 & 1581), Clermont (1518 & 1525), Nîmes (1533), Magalonesis (1533), Abrincensis (1539), Limoges (1555), Noyon (1560), Bordeaux (1561), Lucon (1584), Nantes (1592), Poitiers (1584), Maleacensis (1584), Vannes (1596), Bayeux (1611).
342 *Ad Rit. Rom. Comm.*, tom. I, tit. xxvii, n. 109.
343 *Rit. Rom.*, t. I, p. 319.
344 *Tract. de Sancto Ext. Unct. Sacram.*, p. 62, (edit. 1609).
345 Tit. 32, *de Sac. Ext. Unct.*, cap. 6—Catalano, *Rit. Rom.*, t. I, p. 319.

Roman Ritual shortly afterwards corrected this regulation in regard to substituting one part of the body for another.[346]

Gradually, however, the custom of anointing the reins fell into desuetude. Benedict XIV [347] witnesses to its omission in many places in his day. Van der Stappen [348] states that it was never general in Belgium. France had many local rituals which omitted this custom, and some of these even prescribed the unction of the breast instead.[349] In the Ritual published for the use of the English clergy,[350] the unction of the reins was not mentioned. Kenrick[351] and the "*Excerpta ex Rituali,*" published at Baltimore in 1860, reveal the fact that the practice of anointing the reins had never been in vogue in the United States.

It is not without reluctance that the Holy See abandoned this rite. This is evidenced by a reply given to the Archbishop of Utrecht by the Sacred Congregation of Rites in 1858.[352] His Grace had asked permission of the Holy See to permit the omission of this unction in his archdiocese. In answer the Sacred Congregation wrote:

> "Quod vero attinet ad renum unctionem quam in administrando Sacramento extremae Unctionis nunquam in ista dioecesi Amplitudo Tua adhibitam fuisse testatur, et quam idcirco postulat ut in Rituali Romano omitti permittatur, visum est Sacrae Congregationi nullam prorsus, sive in hac sive in alia quacumque re, suppressionem vel immutationem in Rituali induci oportere, sed illud voluit integre et fideliter imprimi, prout a Paulo V editum et a Benedicto XIV recognitum et castigatum fuit. Quod si unctio renum inusitata istic hactenus fuit, declaravit S. Congregatio patienter se laturam si singularia istius Diocesis adjuncta impediant quominus illico et universim ad praxim unctio isthaec deducatur; insimul tamen ardentissimum votum suum expressit, ut, curante Amplitudine Tua et docentibus parochis, paulatim et sensim sine sensu disponantur fideles ad istam quoque specialem unctionem in extremo agone recipiendam, juxta Ritualis Romani praescriptiones."

Since that time there has been a gradual leniency shown

346 Cf. Tit. V, cap. 1, n. 15.
347 *De Syn. Dioc.*, l. 8, c. 3, n. 2.
348 *Sac. Lit.*, t. IV, Q. 220.
349 *Dictionnaire des Rites Sacres*, art. "*Extrême Onct.:*" Resume d'un grand de Rituels, par Beuvelet.
350 Richardson, Derby, 1856.
351 *Th. M.*, III, "*de Ext. Unct.*," cap. unic., n. 5.
352 Aug. 14, 1858—D. A., n. 3075: A. S. S., III, 612.

by the Holy See. It had always been allowed to omit the unction when there was any danger to the patient. Other concessions had been granted in unusual circumstances. For example, it was the custom in China that missionaries should perform the unction of consumptives and others sick with lingering diseases in a public fashion in the church or chapel after Mass. Naturally the presence of so many people caused much embarrassment to the patient and to the priest. Disturbances among the crowd itself were not infrequent, because of the finicky customs of the locality.[353] Consequently, it was graciously granted that the omission of the unction of the reins was allowable when the sacrament was conferred "in coetu fidelium." Later, the Holy See permitted the omission of the unction simply because of long-standing custom. Thus in 1897 Leo XIII authorized the extirpation of the unction in the diocese of Bruges for the selfsame reason that it had been denied to the Archbishop of Utrecht forty years before.[354] The path to a general prohibition of the unction was paved by the concession of this indult.

Under the new regulation it is not only lawful to omit the unction of the reins, but it is a positive sin not to omit it.[355] It brings into sharp relief the Church's power over individual unctions; and it is, at least to some extent, an argument against those who held that the separate unctions were divinely ordained as the essence of the sacrament. Those who hold with Kern [356] that the sacrament has a unity of indivisability, wherein the intention of the minister determines the time at which the principal effect will be produced during the anointings, will see that the minister must not extend his intention to the seventh unction. At the very latest, he must intend that the effect will be produced after the unction of the feet. Those who hold with Quinn [357] will have to look upon this prohibition as

353 "Quando autem pro renum unctione peragenda in viris laxantur et elevantur vestes, statim multi, maxime mulieres, rubore suffunduntur, et velociter aufugiunt propter gentis mores"—S. C. P. F. (C. P. pro Sin.) 21 Sept., 1843—*Sutchuen.*—Collectanea, n. 968.

354 Cf. *Collationes Brugenses,* II, 1897, pp. 601-603.

355 I. E. Record, Fifth Series, vol. XI (1918), p. 289.

356 *Tract. de Ext. Unct.,* pp. 323-331; Cf. *supra,* chap. I, s. VI, p.

357 *Some Aspects of the Dogma of Extreme Unction,* pp. 74-82.

an exercise of the Church's power to neglect a minor sacramental effect for sufficient reasons.

At any rate, to anoint the reins now is probably a grievous sin. It would resurrect a rite that the Holy See wishes to remain dead. It constitutes a serious insertion into the sacramental rite, resulting in a direct violation of this canon and a grave deordination of the Ritual's prescriptions.

III. The Unction of the Feet.

Unctio pedum ex qualibet rationali causa omitti potest.

The unction of the feet was rarely regarded as an essential unction. Nevertheless, it was widely practiced, and did not fall into desuetude like the unction of the loins. Whenever the Ritual called for the unction of five senses, the anointing of the feet generally followed. However, exceptions existed in some localities. Two of Martene's Ordines[358] do not include the unctions of the feet, although that of the five senses is explicitly required. Evidently it was not done in particular localities at the time of St. Alphonsus, for he writes "Unctio vero pedum non est de necessitate sacramenti, ut communiter dicunt Pal., &c. . . .; unde dicunt in hac unctione pedum servandam esse consuetudinem Ecclesiarum."[359] De Herdt[360] seems to imply the same thing, when he says "Ubi Rituale [Romanum] est in usu, pedum unctio omitti nequeat."

Many difficulties have been encountered in carrying out this prescription of anointing the feet. Peculiar local conditions have given rise to situations wherein this unction could not be easily performed. Missionaries in China had a very difficult time in persuading women of that land to permit their feet to receive the oils. It was only after long and sedulous instruction that these people viewed the sacredness of the rite

358 Ordo XI (*Codex Regiae Bibliothecae*) and Ordo XVIII (*The Pontifical of Constantinople*)—*De Antiq. Eccl. Rit.*, l. 1, c. 7, a. 4. N. B. The former speaks of additional unctions upon the "membra convenientia." The feet may or may not be included. At any rate, unction of the feet is not specified in particular. The Pontifical of Constantinople is content with prescribing the anointing of the five senses.

359 *Th. M.*, VI, 710, 2.

360 *Lit. Prax.*, III, 200 ad 9.

in such a light that they put aside their false modesty. The Synod of Sutchuen, held in 1803, announced that this instruction had been so successful that no missionary should leave out this salutary unction, even in the case of women recently converted.[361] If any murmuring or scandal was feared in a particular case, the Synod instructed the priest to enlighten the patient on the true meaning and internal sanctity of the rite and urge her to put away the barrier of false shame that was preventing her from the reception of these special graces. The bystanders were also to be taught the holiness of this action performed by a priest administering a sacrament so beneficial to the patient. When this instruction had been made, the sacrament was to be administered only to those who acquiesced. If, on the other hand, a danger might arise from scandal given to the infidels, the sacrament was to be administered, but the unction of the feet should be omitted. Likewise the Ritual of Passau[362] exempted from unction the feet of women in parturition or suffering from a flow of blood.[363]

In England the omission of the unction of the feet was allowed when the patient was a woman in a public hospital or infirmary, and the priest feared scandal or comment. Such leave was granted explicitly by the English Ritual.[364]

Under the present law the unction can be omitted for any reasonable cause. It is a welcome innovation, for it will relieve many scruples in this regard. The omission, however, is not *ad libitum;* there must be at hand a proportionate reason.

Pastoral prudence and hygienics will determine very often whether the unction should or should not be made. A priest need not be too strict in his judgment of the sufficiency of the cause. Numerous examples might be cited. If the patient is in a ward of a hospital, and no screen about the bed; if the patient is a woman, and there is no one present to uncover the feet except the priest; if there is sufficient reason to think that the

361 Cf. Collectanea, n. 1718—footnote, p. 243, vol. II. The decree of this synod was confirmed by the Sacred Congregation for the Propagation of the Faith on July 29, 1822.

362 c. 8.

363 Cf. Elbel-Bierbaum, *Th. M.*, III, Conf. IX, n. 194.

364 Cf. Slater—*Moral Theol.* (third edit.) p. 234.

feet might not have been properly washed before the arrival of the priest; if the patient has shoes and stockings on at the time of unction, or if a woman has her stockings on while confined to bed—these are but a few of the many cases when the unctions of the feet may, and often should, be omitted. Blat[365] adds several more, viz., the displeasure of the patient at this unction, the nature of the disease, e. g., if the feet were gangrenous, and even their uncleanness. Heuser[366] remarks: "The unction of the feet is usually omitted in all cases in which it would expose the patient to grave inconvenience or prove dangerous to the attendants in contagious disease by reason of the delay," etc. Finally it may be remarked with O'Kane[367] that if the local Ritual or the custom of the place allows the omission of this unction in every case, it may be followed. Custom is surely a reasonable cause.

IV. The Use of an Instrument.

Extra casum gravis necessitatis, unctiones ipsa ministri manu nulloque adhibito instrumento fiant.

Altho Extreme Unction—unlike Confirmation—does not strictly require the imposition of hands as part of its proximate matter, nevertheless it is strictly prescribed that the unction be formed by the personal contact of the hand of the minister with the sick person. The Code does not specifically state what portion of the hand is to be employed, but the Ritual[368] orders the thumb to be employed for this purpose. It is generally conceded, however, that to use another finger is at most a venial sin; and any reasonable cause makes such a substitution lawful.[369]

It was not always the case to use the hand immediately in anointing. Thus the Ritual of the Church of Liege[370] contained

---

365 *Comm. Text.*, lib. III, p. I, n. 292.

366 *The Parish Priest*, p. 103.

367 *The Rubrics*, n. 936.

368 Tit. V, cap. 2, n. 8.

369 Cf. Genicot-Salsmans, *Inst. Th. M.*, II, 417: Sebastiani, *Summ. Th. M.*, n. 513.

370 Martene, *De Antiq. Eccl. Rit.*, lib. 1, cap. 7, a. 4, Ordo XXVII.

the rubric: "Pollicem vel virgulam intingit in oleum, &c." La Croix[371] states that many learned men of his day anointed with a small rod. Van der Stappen notes that up until the year 1873, it was done in the Diocese of Mechlin, and that many oil-vessels were so narrow in diameter that it would be physically impossible to insert the thumb therein. Similarly custom had implanted itself in the places which requested decisions of the Holy See on this point.[372]

The new Code allows a substitution only in case of grave necessity. Custom does not justify the matter, as is evidenced by the replies of the Roman Congregation. In 1788 The Propaganda warned the Bishop of Pekin and the Vicar Apostolic of Chan-si not to permit the substitution of a "penicilla" for the hand in the administration of Extreme Unction.[373] Three later decrees of the Congregation of the Rites demanded the extirpation of this custom in various places, asserting that long-standing practice was not a sufficient cause for its continuance. A deviation from the prescribed way was permitted only in cases of necessity.[374]

Almost all the instances of necessity can be placed under the heading: "where there is danger of infection or contagion." Infection would result from direct contact with the skin of the patient; contagion might occur from the proximity of the priest to the sick man. Since, as noted before, the imposition of hands is not required in this sacrament, it is permissible to anoint with an instrument. One anoints when he uses a *virgula* to apply the oil, just as truly as he writes when he uses a pen to form the letter.[375]

Hence in every case of plague or pestilence it is entirely lawful to anoint thru the mediation of an instrument. It is permissible, too, in every case outside of the time of plague

---

371 *Th. M.*, lib. 6, pars 2, "*de Ext. Unct.*," n. 2115.

372 *Sac. Lit.*, t. IV, Q. 218.

373 S. C. P. F., 21 Jun. 1788, Coll. n. 596.

374 Cf. S. R. C., *Portus S. Aloysii*—9 Maii, 1857 ad 2, D. A., n. 3051; *Toletana*—31 Aug. 1872 ad III et IV, D. A., n. 3276; *Colimen.*—12 Jul. 1901 ad VIII, D. A. 4077.

375 Cf. Chapeauville, *Tract. de Necessitate et Modo Ministrandi Sacramenta tempore pestis,* q. 39, quoted by Benedict XIV, *De Syn. Dioc.*, l. XIII, c. 19.

where infection or contagion is reasonably feared. Thus in individual cases of leprosy,[376] syphilis, highly infectious eczema or any other similar cases, such a mediate unction is allowed. The mouth may be anointed in this fashion when the patient has hydrophobia, or other disease where danger lurks in contact of the saliva. In such cases, however, it is quite as well to anoint some part near the mouth with the hand rather than take an instrument for this single unction.[377]

A case of physical necessity can be imagined where the use of the virgula does not arise from danger of infection or contagion. If the patient could only be reached by some small aperture thru which the hand could not be inserted, the instrument may be employed to reach the sick man.

The virgula can be made out of practically any substance. Gold, silver, glass, ebony—any material suitable for use at all suffices. If nothing else is handy, a small twig will be satisfactory.[378] A brush or even a little cotton can be employed. It will be advisable to wrap a bit of cotton tightly about the end of the stick before dipping it in the oil, for the cotton absorbs more oil and assures a better unction.[379]

This cotton can be changed after each unction, thus preventing infection of the oil. If the cotton is not twisted about the end of the instrument, the priest should take care to wipe the instrument carefully with cotton after each unction before it is dipped again into the vessel of oil.[380] If wooden instruments are used they should be employed only for a single unction and burned immediately after the rite is completed.[381] It is highly recommended that a priest should have a separate oil stock for such contagious diseases.[382]

---

376 Cf. Ferreres, *Comp. Th. M.*, II, 836.

377 Cf. O'Kane, *The Rubrics*, n. 926.

378 Augustine, *A Commentary*, IV, 408.

379 Augustine, *l.c.*

380 Cf. O'Kane, *The Rubrics*, n. 296; Heuser, *The Parish Priest*, p. 103; Sylvius, *Addit. ad III p. S. Thomae*, q. 32, a. 3; De Herdt, *Lit. Prax.*, III, 207 ad iii.

381 Cf. O'Kane, *l.c.*

382 Cf. Heuser, *The Parish Priest*, p. 103.

To use an instrument outside of necessity is a grave sin, for it is a radical departure from the unity of procedure established by the Code. La Croix[383] asserted the seriousness of the offense was ascribable to the fact that it was a grave deviation from the universal custom. This custom has now become the written law of the Church.

It is to be remembered that, though such an instrument may be used, it is not of obligation. Many modern authors ask priests to scorn such a resource, not only because they thereby avoid scandal, but also because there is very little danger from the physical contact. The oil itself acts as a preservative, and there is no transfer of infectious germs. Capellman[384] goes to great lengths to expostulate with priests who are tempted to use an instrument when anointing. In the first place, he notes, infections are prevented thru the oil. Ulcers and other open sores upon the sense-organs can be avoided by anointing the proximate parts of the body. Moreover, the use of a "virgula" or "stylus" is often a source of scandal to the bystanders. "Circumstantes certe," he wrote, "neque id sine ratione, mirabuntur et offendentur eo, quod pastor animarum adeo pavidus ac timidus sit, quum eodem in periculo, v. g., a medico sine ullo timore infirmum iterum iterumque manu tangi et apprehendi videant. Quid vero de aegrotis fieret, si medicis etiam tantus contagionis timor inesset? Porro quid de ipsis medicis fieret, si tantum esset contagionis periculum? Patet, ita vulgo homines et interrogaturos et judicaturos esse." As a consequence Dr. Capellman advises a priest to use a separate piece of cotton for each unction. Thereby he avoids the scandal that would occur from the use of a thin rod, and simultaneously protects the oil from an infection which might result from the successive insertion of the thumb into it.

Many other precautions are enumerated by various authors for cases of contagious diseases. All unnecessary touching should be avoided; the priest should not stand between the patient and the fire; special clothing should be worn,

---

383 *Th. M.*, lib. 6, pars 2, n. 2115.

384 *Medicina Past.*, p. 127.

if advised by the physician; and a judicious use of disinfectants should be made. Trust and confidence should fill the priest in the performance of his duty. The Master did not shrink from the leper; other Christs should not flee from a similar situation. The sacramental grace of Holy Orders stimulates the soul of the true shepherd. It is only the hireling "qui videns lupum fugit."[385]

There are two extremes to be avoided. Too many pains should not be taken in the employment of preventives to avoid infection. The more means that are used, the greater the fear of infection becomes and the danger increases.[386] Even prescinding from the element of the supernatural that must surround priests in such situations, the natural protections are quite sufficient to allay inordinate fears and scruples.

Although "optimum remedium est administrare confidenter et intrepide"[387] a priest, on the other hand is very unwise in taking unnecessary risks. Foolhardiness is not to be confounded with intrepidity. Charity to one's self exacts a reasonable care of one's health—and charity to one's neighbor requires that we do not imperil his life by a transfer of germs or in any other way. A priest has no right to expect himself to be welcome at the homes of other sick when he neglects all precautions at a previous attendance upon a person afflicted with a contagious disease. Indeed, in hospitals, if priests refuse or neglect to take sufficient means of disinfection after their visits to contagious wards, they need not be at all surprised at the unwillingness of hospital authorities to permit indiscriminate access to the other patients of the institution. Accordingly in every case he should use the means which they often prepare in all kindness for his safety—not in a meticulous fashion, as though he were full of terror, but thoroughly and conscientiously, as the rational procedure of one who must insure himself against being an agent in the transfer of deadly germs to others under his spiritual care.

---

[385] *John,* X, 12.

[386] De Herdt, *Lit. Prax.,* III, 207 ad iii.

[387] De Herdt, *Lit. Prax.,* III, 207 ad iii.

The happy medium is attained by those who do not spurn natural means or neglect preventive methods to protect their own health and the health of others, and yet who feel no fear or hesitation in attendance upon the most virulent case of contagious disease.[388] Such a priest never forgets the words of the Comforter: "Noli timere . . . Meus es tu. Cum transieris per aquas, tecum ero et flumina non operient te; cum ambulaveris in igne, non combureris et flamma non ardebit in te."[389]

---

388 Cf. Micheletti, *De Past. Animarum*, n. 417 (c); Stang, *Past. Th.*, p. 70.
389 *Isai.*, XLIII, 1-2.

BIBLIOGRAPHY

Sources

Acta Apostolicae Sedis, Romae, 1909-1926.

Acta Ecclesiae Mediolanensis, (2 vols.), Mediolani, 1843.

Acta et Decreta Sacrorum Conciliorum Recentium, (6 vols.), Friburgi, 1876.

Acta Sanctae Sedis, (41 vols.), Romae, 1865-1906.

Acta Synodi Roffensis Tertiae, Rochester, 1914.

Bail, *Summa Conciliorum,* (2 vols.), Petavii, 1723.

Benedicti XIV Bullarium, (13 vols.), Mechliniae, 1827.

Bizzarri, *Collectanea in Usum Secretariae S. C. Episcoporum et Regularium,* Romae, 1885.

Bullarii Romani Continuatio, (14 vols.), Prati, 1844.

Bullarum, Diplomatum, et Privilegiorum Sanctorum Romanorum Pontificum Taurinensis Editio, (24 vols.), Augustae Taurinorum, 1865.

Caeremoniale Episcoporum, Benedicti Papae XIV Jussu Editum et Auctum, Mechliniae, 1867.

Canones et Decreta Concilii Tridentini, Taurini, 1913.

Codex Juris Canonici, Pii X Pontificis Maximi Jussu Digestus, Benedicto Papae XV Auctoritate Promulgatus, Romae, 1917.

Codicis Juris Canonici Fontes, (vol. I-III) Romae, 1923-1925.

Collectanea Sanctae Congregationis de Propaganda Fide, (2 vols.), Romae, 1907.

Concilii Plenarii Baltimorensis II, Decreta, Baltimorae, 1868.

Corpus Juris Canonici, (*Editio Lipsiensis Secunda*), Lipsiae, 1922 (Richter-Friedburg).

Decreta Authentica Congregationis Sacrorum Rituum et Instructio Clementina ex Actis Ejusdem Collecta ab Aloisio Gardellini, in Usum Cleri Commodiorem Ordine Alphabetico Concinnata Opera et Studio Wolfgangi Muhlbauer, (3 vols. and 3 vols. suppl.), Monachii, 1863.

Decreta Authentica Congregationis Sacrorum Rituum Ex Actis Ejusdem Collecta Ejusque Auctoritate Promulgata, sub Auspiciis SS. Domini Nostri Leonis Papae XIII, (6 vols.), Romae, 1898-1911.

Decreta Synodi Dioecesanae Kansanopolitanae Secundae, Atchison, 1912.

DENZIGER-BANNWART, *Enchiridion Symbolorum, Definitionum et Declarationum de Rebus Fidei et Morum, (edit. decimamquartam et quintam)* Friburgi Brisgoviae, 1922.

HARDUIN, Jean, *Conciliorum Collectio Regia Maxima,* (12 vols.), Parisiis, 1715.

HEFELE, Charles, *Conciliengeschichte,* (9 vols.), Freiburg, 1873-1890.

MANSI, Joannes, *Amplissima Collectio Conciliorum,* Paris-Leipsic, (51 vols.), 1759 sqq.

Pontificale Romanum, Clementis VIII ac Urbani VIII, Jussu Editum et a Benedicto XIV Recognitum et Castigatum, Romae, 1890.

Rituale Romanum, Pauli V Pontificis Maximi Jussu Editum, a Benedicto XIV et a Pio X Castigatum et Auctum, Ratisbonae et Romae, 1913.

Rituale Romanum, Pauli V Pontificis Maximi Jussu Editum Aliorumque Pontificum Cura Recognitum atque Auctoritate Sanctissimi, D. N. Pii Papae XI Ad Normam Codicis Juris Canonici Accomodatum, Turonibus, 1925.

Statuta Dioecesis Oklahomensis, Oklahomae (n. d.)

Synodus Dioecesana Prima Habita in Ecclesia Cathedrali ad S. Philumenae In Urbe Omaha, Philadelphiae, (n. d.)

AUTHORITIES

ABELLY, Louis, *Medulla Theologica,* (2 vols.), Parisiis, 1679.

ADAMI, J. G., *The Principles of Pathology,* Philadelphia and New York, 1908.

ÆRTNYS, Josephus, C. SS. R., *Theologia Moralis,* (2 vols.), Tornaci, 1898.

A LAPIDE, Cornelius, *Commentarius in Epistolas Canonicas,* Venetiis, 1717.

ALBERTUS a BULSANO (KNOLL), *Opera Omnia,* Parisiis, 1872.

ALBERTUS MAGNUS, *Opera Omnia*, (38 vols.), Parisiis, 1890-1899.

A MEDIA VILLA (MIDDLETON), *Richardus*,—see Richard Middleton.

Analecta Juris Pontificii, Romae et Parisiis, 1855-1891.

ANTOINE, Paulus Gabriel, *Theologia Moralis Universa*, (6 vols.), Avenione, 1818.

ANTONELLI, Joseph, *Medicina Pastoralis in Usum Confessariorum et Curiarum Ecclesiasticarum*, (3 vols.), Romae, 1920.

ARCUDIUS, *De Consensu Ecclesiae Occidentalis et Orientalis In Septem Sacramentorum Administratione*, Lutetiae Parisiorum, 1672.

ARHANGELSKIJ, Mihail, "*Izslědovanije ob isteričeskom razvitii činosoveršenija Jeleosvjaščenija ot ustanovlenija sego tainstva do izdanija nyněšnjago jego „Posledovanija," s podrobnym izjasnenijem sego poslědnjago*," S.—Peterburg, 1895.

ARREGUI, Antonius, *Summarium Theologiae Moralis*, Bilbao, 1922.

AUREOLUS, *Commentarius in Textum Magistri*, Romae, 1596-1605.

BABENSTUBER, Ludovicus, *Ethica Supernaturalis Salisburgensis seu Cursus Theologiae Moralis*, Augustae Vindelicorum, 1718.

BALLERINI-PALMIERI, *Opus Theologicum Morale*, (7 vols.), Prati, 1893.

BARBOSA, Augustinus, *Pastoralis Sollicitudinis sivi De Officio et De Potestate Parochi Tripartita Descriptio*, Lugduni, 1712.

BARGILLIAT, M., *Droits et Dévoirs des Curés et des Vicaires Paroissaiaux*, Paris, 1919.

Praelectiones Juris Canonici, (2 vols.), Parisiis, 1923.

BARONIUS, Cesare, *Annales Ecclesiastici*, (37 vols.), Barri Ducis, 1864-1883.

BARUFFALDO, Hieronymus, *Ad Rituale Romanum Commentarium*, (2 vols.), Florentiae, 1847.

BECANUS, Martinus, *Summa Theologiae Scholasticae*, Parisiis, 1679.

BELJAEV, A., „*Jeleosvjaščenije*" v „*Pravoslavnoj Bogoslovskoj enciklopediji*," S.—Peterburg, 1904.

BELLARMINUS, Robertus, *Opera Omnia,* (8 vols.), Neapoli, 1872.

BENEDICTUS XIV, *De Synodo Dioecesana,* (2 vols.), Romae, 1806.

Institutiones Canonicae, (3 vols.), Romae, 1784.

BERARDI, Æmilius, *De Parocho Compendium,* Faventiae, 1887.

Praxis Confessariorum, (2 vols.), Bononiae, 1891.

BERENGO, Joannes, *Enchiridion Parochorum,* Venetiis, 1877.

BERTI, Giovanni, *Opus de Theologicis Disciplinis,* (10 vols.), Bassani, 1792.

BILLOT, Ludovicus, *De Ecclesiae Sacramentis Commentarius in Tertiam Partem S. Thomae,* (2 vols.), Romae, 1897.

BILLUART, F. Carolus, *Summa Sancti Thomae,* Parisiis (8 vols.), (n. d.)

BINTERIM, Anton J., *Die Vorzüglichsten Denkwürdigkeiten de Christ-Katholischen Kirche,* Dusseldorf, 1816.

BLAT, Albertus, O. P., *Commentarium Textus Codicis Juris Canonici,* Romae, 1924.

BONAVENTURA, Sanctus, *Breviloquium,* Friburgi, 1881.

Opera Omnia, (8 vols.), Ad Claras Aquas, 1892-8.

BORD, J. B., *L'Extrême Onction,* Bruges, 1923.

BUCCERONI, Januarius, S. J., *Casus Conscientiae,* (2 vols.), Romae, 1913.

Institutiones Theologiae Moralis, (3 vols.), Romae, 1915.

CABASSUTIUS, Joannes, *Juris Canonici Theoria et Praxis,* Lugduni, 1687.

CABROL et LECLERQ, *Monumenta Ecclesiae Liturgica,* (6 vols.), Parisiis, 1900-2.

CAPELLMAN, C., *Medicina Pastoralis,* Aquisgrani, 1890.

CAPPELLO, Felix, S. J., *Tractatus Canonico-Moralis De Sacramentis juxta Codicem Juris Canonici,* (vols. I & III), Taurinorum Augustae, 1921-1923.

CAPREOLUS, Joannes, *Defensiones Theologiae D. Thomae,* Turonibus, 1902-8.

CARAMUEL, Joannis, *Theologia Moralis Fundamentalis,* (4 vols.), Lugduni, 1675-1676.

Casuist, The (5 vols.), New York, 1906-1917.

CATALANUS, Josephus, *Rituale Romanum, Benedicti Papae XIV Jussu Editum et Auctum, Perpetuis Commentariis Exornatum,* (2 vols.), Petavii, 1760.

Catholic Encyclopedia, The (16 vols. and Supplement), New York, 1907-1922.

CAVALLIERI, Joannes Michael, *Opera Omnia Liturgica,* (5 vols.), Venetiis, 1758.

CAVE, Gulielmus, *Scriptorum Ecclesiasticorum Historia Literaria,* Genevae, 1705.

CHELODI, Joannes, *Jus de Personis juxta Codicem Juris Canonici,* Tridenti, 1922.

CLERICATUS, Joannes, *Decisiones Sacramentales,* (3 vols.), Romae, 1757.

COCCHI, Guidus, *Commentarium in Codicem Juris Canonici ad Usum Scholarum,* (7 vols.), Taurinorum Augustae, 1925 (edit. tertia).

COLLET, Pierre, *Institutiones Theologiae Moralis,* Lugduni, 1768.

CONCINA, Daniel, *Theologia Christiana Dogmatico-Moralis,* (10 vols.), Neapoli, 1772-1775.

CONINCK, Aegidius de, *Commentariorum ac Disputationum in Universam Doctrinam D. Thomae De Sacramentis et Censuris Tomi Duo,* Antverpiae, 1619.

DANIEL, Herm. Adalb., *Codex Liturgicus Ecclesiae Universae,* (4 vols.), Lipsiae, 1847.

D'ANNIBALE, Josephus, *Summula Theologiae Moralis,* (3 vols.), Romae, 1892.

DE AMICIS, Petrus, *Caeremoniale Parochorum,* Romae, 1910.

DE AUGUSTINIS, Æmilius, S. J., *De Re Sacramentaria Praelectiones Scholastico-Dogmaticae,* (2 vols.), Woodstock Marylandiae, 1879.

DE LEE, Joseph, *The Principles and Practice of Obstetrics,* Philadelphia and London, 1915.

DE LUGO, Joannes, *De Sacramentis in Genere,* Venetiis, 1718.
Disputationes Scholasticae et Morales (8 vol.), Parisiis, 1868-1869.

DENS, Petrus, *Theologia Mechliniensis,* Mechliniae, 1865.

DENZIGER, Henricus, *Ritus Orientalium,* (2 vols.), Wirceburgi, 1864.

DIANA, Antoninus, *Coordinati Opera Omnia,* (10 vols.), Venetiis, 1728.

Dictionnaire des Ceremonies et des Rites Sacres, Petit-Montrouge, 1847.

DIONYSIUS, Carthusianus, *In Sententiarum Librum Quartum Commentarii Locupletissimi,* Venetiis, 1784.

Opera Omnia, (18 vols.), Monstrolii, 1896-9.

DROUVEN, Renatus, *De Re Sacramentaria Contra Perduelles Haereticos,* (2 vols.), Venetiis, 1772.

DURANDUS, *In P. Lombardi Sententias Theologicas Commentariorum Libri Quattuor,* Venetiis, 1586.

DURANTUS, Joannes, *De Ritibus Ecclesiae Catholicae,* Romae, 1591.

ELBEL-BIERBAUM, *Theologia Moralis per Modum Conferentiarum,* (3 vols.), Paderbornae, 1892.

Encyclopedie de la Theologie Catholique, Paris, 1903.

ESTIUS (Est), Gulielmus, *In Quattuor Libros Sententiarum Commentaria: Quibus Pariter S. Thomae Summae Theologicae Partes Omnes Mirifice Illustrantur,* (2 vols.), Parisiis, 1696.

FAGNANUS, Prosperus, *Jus Canonicum seu Commentarium Absolutissimum in Quinque Libros Decretales,* (4 vols.), Venetiis, 1696.

FALISE, J. B., *Liturgiae Practicae Compendium,* Ratisbonae, 1876.

FANFANI, *De Jure Parochorum Ad Normam Codicis Juris Canonici,* Taurini-Romae, 1924.

De Jure Religiosorum, Taurini-Romae, 1925.

FEIJOO, O. S. B., *Cartas Eruditas, (ed. Rivadeneyra)* Madrid.

FERRARIS, F. Lucius, *Bibliothecae Prompta Canonica, Juridica, Moralis, Theologica,* (8 vols.), Romae, 1885.

FERRERES, Joannes, S. J., *Compendium Theologiae Moralis ad Normam Codicis Juris Canonici, Barcinone,* (3 vols.), (edit., quarta) 1909; (edit. tertia decima) 1925.

Death, Real and Apparent in Relation to the Sacraments, St. Louis, Freiburg, 1906.

FORTESCUE, Adrian, *The Orthodox Eastern Church,* London, 1907.

FRASSEN, F. Claudius, *Scotus Academicus,* (12 vols. in 9), Romae, 1720-1722.

GENICOT-SALSMANS, *Casus Conscientiae,* Bruxellis, 1922.

Institutiones Theologiae Moralis, (2 vols.), Bruxellis, 1921, (edit. nona).

GERSONIUS, Joannes, *Opera Omnia,* (5 vols.), Antverpiae, 1706.

GIHR, Nikolaus, *Die hl. Sacramenten d. Kath.,* Kirche, 1903.

GOAR, *Euchologion sive Rituale Graecorum,* Venetiis, 1730.

GOBATUS, Georgius, S. J., *Operum Moralium, hoc est, Experientiarum Theologicarum, sive Experimentalis Theologiae de Septem Sacramentis,* Duaci, 1700.

GONET, Joannes B., *Clypeus Theologiae Thomisticae Contra Novos Ejus Impugnatores,* (6 vols.), Parisiis, 1876.

GURY-FERRERES, *Casus Conscientiae,* (2 vols.), Barcinone, 1921.

GURY, Joannes, *Compendium Theologiae Moralis,* (2 vols.), Romae, 1873.

HANLEY P. J., *Treatise on the Sacrament of Extreme Unction,* New York, 1907.

HEIMBUCHER, *Die heilige Oelung,* Ratisbonne, 1888.

HERDT, P. J. de, *Sacrae Liturgiae Praxis et Cura,* (3 vols.), Lovanii, 1883.

HEUSER, Herman J., *The Parish Priest on Duty,* New York-Cincinnati-Chicago (n. d.)

HURTER, Henricus, S. J., *Theologiae Dogmaticae Compendium,* (3 vols.), Oentiponte, 1885.

ICARD, Severin, *La Mort Reélle et la Mort Apparente,* 1897.

IGNATIJ, *„O tainstvah jedinoj, svjatoj, sobornoj i apostolskoj cerkvi. Opyt arheologičeskij.“* Sanktpeterburg, 1863.

JUENIN, Gaspare, *Commentarius Historicus et Dogmaticus de Sacramentis In Genere et in Specie,* Venetiis, 1740.

KENRICK, F. P., *Theologia Moralis,* (3 vols.), Philadelphiae, 1843.

KENRICK, F. P. *Theologia Dogmatica,* (3 vols.) Mechliniae, 1859.

KERN, Josephus, S. J., *De Sacramento Extremae Unctionis Tractatus Dogmaticus,* Ratisbonae, 1907.

KING, James I., *The Administration of the Sacraments to Dying Non-Catholics,* Washington, 1924.

KIRCHELEXICON, (12 vols.), Freiburg-Briesgau, 1882-1901.

KONINGS, *Theologia Moralis,* Neo-Eboraci, (n. d.)

KOUDELKA, Charles, *Pastors, Their Rights and Duties,* Washington, 1921.

KOZMA DE PAPI, Carolus, *Liturgica Sacra Catholica,* Ratisbonae, 1863.

LACROIX, Claudius, *Theologia Moralis,* (2 vols.), Venetiis (n. d.)

LAUNOI, Joannes, *Opera Omnia,* (5 vols. in 10), Coloniae Allobrorum, 1731.

LAYMANN, Paulus, *Theologia Moralis,* (2 vols. in 1), Venetiis, 1719.

LEHMKUHL, Augustinus, *Casus Conscientiae,* (2 vols.), Friburgi Brisgoviae, 1902.

Theologia Moralis, (2 vols.), Friburgi Brisgoviae, 1914.

LIGUORI, St. Alphonsus, *Homo Apostolicus,* Augustae Taurinorum, 1879.

Theologia Moralis, (10 vols.), Mechliniae, 1842-1845.

LINGARD, John, *The Antiquities of the Anglo-Saxon Church,* Philadelphia, 1841.

MABILLON, Jean, *Praefationes in Actis Sanctorum Ordinis S. Benedicti in Saeculorum Classes Distributis Praefixae,* Rotomagi, 1732.

MABILLONIUS, Joannes, *Museum Italicum seu Collectio Veterum Scriptorum ex Bibliothecis Italicis,* (2 vols.), Lutetiae Parisiorum, 1724.

MAGISTRETTI, Marcus, *Manuale Ambrosianum,* 1905.

MAKARIJ, *„Pravoslavno-dogmatičeskoje bogoslovije."* Peterburg, 1895.

MALDONATUS, Joannes, *Commentarius in Quattuor Evangelistas,* (2 vols.), Moguntiae, 1862.

MALTZEW, Alexios, *Die Sacramente der Orthodox-katholischen Kirche des Morgenlandes,* Berlin, 1898.

MANY, S., S. S., *Praelectiones de Locis Sacris,* Parisiis, 1904.

MARINGOLA, Aloisius, *Institutiones Liturgicae,* Neapoli, 1864.

MARTENE, Edmundus, *De Antiquis Ecclesiae Ritibus,* (4 vols.), Rotomagi, 1700-6.

MASTRIUS, Bartholomeus, *Theologia Moralis,* Venetiis, 1671.

MATHARAN-CASTILLON, *Asserta Moralia,* Paris, 1920.

MICHELETTI, A. M., *De Pastore Animarum,* Friburgi et Romae, (n. d.).

MIDDLETON, Richard, *Authorati Theologi Ricardi a Media Villa,* Parisiis, 1519.

MIGNE, J. P., *Cursus Theologius Completus,* (28 vols.), Petit-Montrange, 1845-1860.

Patrologia Graeca, (161 vols.), Parisiis, 1858-1864.

Patrologia Latina, (221 vols.), Parisiis, 1847-1870.

MOTHON, Joseph, *Institutions Canoniques a L'Usage des Curies Episcopales, du Clerge Paroissial, et des Familles Religieuses,* (2 vols.), Lille, 1924.

MURPHY, George, *Delinquencies and Penalties in the Administration and the Reception of the Sacraments,* Washington, 1923.

NATALIS, Alexander, *Theologia Dogmatica et Moralis,* (2 vols.), Venetiis, 1705.

NEYRAGUET D., *Compendium Theologiae Moralis,* Ratisbonae, 1851.

NOLDIN, H., S. J., *Summa Theologiae Moralis,* Oentiponte, (3 vols.), (ed. septima) 1908; (edit. quarta decima), 1921.

O'KANE, James, *Notes on the Rubrics of the Roman Ritual,* Dublin, 1922.

O'MALLEY, Austin, *The Ethics of Medical Homicide and Mutilation,* New York, 1922.

PALLAVICINI, Sforza, *Istoria del Concilio di Trento,* (4 vols.), Roma, 1833.

PALMIERI, Dominicus, *Opus Theologicum,* Prati, 1889-93.

PALUDANUS (Peter de Palude), *Exactissimi atque Maxime Probati ac Clarissimi Doctoris Petri de Palude Predicatori ordinis Hierosolymitani quondam patriarchi diguissimi quartus sententiarum liber,* Parisiis, 1518.

PAPPIANI, Albertus, *Doctrina Christiana de Sacramentis Ecclesiae Sacrosanctis Ab Heterodoxorum Erroribus Vindicata,* Florentiae, 1772.

PASCHANG, John L., *The Sacramentals According to The New Code of Canon Law,* Washington, 1925.

PELLICIA, *De Christianae Ecclesiae Primae, Mediae et Novissimae Polita,* (2 vols.), Collonniae, 1829.

PERRONE, Joannes, *Praelectiones Theologicae,* Mediolani et Genevae, 1857.

PESCH, Christianus, *Praelectiones Dogmaticae,* (9 vols.), Friburgi Brisgoviae, 1920.

PETRUS LOMBARDUS, *Quattuor Libri Sententiarum* (Cf. Migne, P. L., 192).

PIERROT, L'Abbé, *Dictionnaire de la Theologie Morale,* Petit-Montrouge, 1849.

PIGHI-FERRAIS, *Liturgia Sacerdotalis,* Veronae, 1907.

PIGNATELLI, Jacobus, *Consultationes Canonicae,* (vols. 10), Coloniae Allogobrorum.

POHLE-PREUSS, *The Sacraments,* St. Louis, 1920.

PRUEMMER, *Manuale Juris Ecclesiastici,* Friburgi Brisgoviae, 1922.

Manuale Theologiae Moralis, (3 vols.), Friburgi Brisgoviae, 1923.

RAHMANI, Ignatius Ephraem II, *Testamentum Domini Nostri Jesu Christi,* Moguntiae, 1899.

REDING, Augustinus, *Theologia Scholastica Universa,* Einsiedeln, 1687.

REIFFENSTUEL, Anacletus, *Jus Canonicum Universum,* (7 vols.), Paris, 1864-70.

REUTER-LEHMKUHL-UMBERG, *Neo-Confessarius Practice Instructus,* Friburgi Brisgoviae, 1919.

ROHLING, Augustinus, *Medulla Theologiae Moralis,* Sti. Ludovici, 1875.

ROPES, James Hardy, *International Commentary on the Epistle of St. James, A Critical and Exegetical Commentary,* New York, 1916.

SABBETTI-BARRETT, *Compendium Theologiae Moralis,* Neo-Eboraci, 1920.

SAINTE-BEUVE, Jacobus de, *Tractatus de Sacramento Extremae Unctionis,* (*apud Migne, Cursus Theologicus Completus,* vol. xxiv.)

SALMANTICENSES, *Collegii Salmanticensis Fratrum Discalceatorum B. Mariae de Monte Carmeli Primitivae Observantiae Cursus Theologiae Moralis,* Venetiis, 1728.

Sanchez, Joannes, *Selectae, Illaeque Practicae Disputationes de Rebus in Administratione Sacramentorum,* Venetiis, 1639.

Sanford, Alexander, *Pastoral Medicine, Revised and Enlarged by a Chapter on the Moment of Death by the Rev. Walter M. Drum,* S. J., New York, 1905.

Sasse, Joannes, S. J., *Institutiones Theologicae De Sacramentis Ecclesiae,* (2 vols.), Friburgi Brisgoviae, 1898.

Scavini, Petrus, *Theologia Moralis Universa Ad Mentem S. Alphonsi M. de Ligorio, Pio IX Pontifici M. Dicata,* (4 vols.), Mediolani, 1869.

Schaaf, Valentine T., *The Cloister,* Cincinnati, 1921.

Schanz, *Die Lehre von der heilegen Sakramenten der Katholischen* Kirche, 1893.

Schell, Herman, *Katholische Dogmatik,* (4 vols.), Paderborn, 1889.

Schmitz, *De Effectibus Extremae Unctionis,* Friburgi Brisgoviae, 1893.

Scotus, Joannes Duns, *Reportata Parisiensia,* Parisiis, 1894.

Sebastiani, Nicolas, *Summarium Theologiae Moralis ad Codicem Juris Canonici Accomodatum,* Taurinorum Augustae, 1921.

Simar, Theophil, *Lehrbuch der Dogmatik,* Paderborn, 1889.

Slater, Thomas, *A Manual of Moral Theology,* (2 vols.), New York, 1908.

Sotus, Dominicus, *Commentarium F. Dom. Soti in Quartum Sententiarum,* (2 vols.), Venetiis, 1575.

Stang, William, *Pastoral Theology,* Brussels, 1897.

Suarez, Franciscus, S. J., *Opera Omnia,* (26 vols.), Parisiis, 1861.

Sylvester, *Summae Sylvestrinae,* (2 vols.), Venetiis, 1601.

Sylvius, Franciscus, *Commentarium in Tertiam Partem S. Thomae Aquinatis,* Venetiis, 1726.

Tamburini, Thomas, S. J., *Juris Divini, Naturalis, et Ecclesiastici Expedita Moralis Explicatio,* (3 vols. in 2), Venetiis, 1748.

Tanquerey, Adrian, *Synopsis Theologiae Dogmaticae ad Mentem S. Thomae Aquinatis Holdiernis Moribus Accomodata,* Romae-Tornaci-Parisiis, (3 vols.), 1921.

TANQUEREY-QUEVASTRE, *Brevior Synopsis Theologiae Moralis et Pastoralis,* Romae-Tornaci-Parisiis, (editions of 1911 and 1920).

TAPPER, Richardus, *Opera,* Coloniae, 1583.

TELCH, Carolus, *Epitome Theologiae Moralis Universae per Definitiones, Divisiones et Summaria Principia,* Oentiponte, 1919.

THOMAS AQUINAS, Sanctus, *Opera Omnia,* (34 vols.), Parisiis, 1871-1880.

Summa Philosophia Contra Gentiles, Parisiis (n. d.).

Summa Theologica, (6 vols.), Romae, 1894.

TOURNELY, Honoratus, *Praelectiones Theologicae de Septem Ecclesiae Sacramentis,* (2 vols.), Parisiis, 1729.

Tractatus de Universa Theologia Morali, (9 vols.), Parisiis, 1743-50.

TROMBELLIO, Joannes C., *Tractatus de Sacramentis per Polemicas et Liturgicas Dissertationes Dispositi,—De Extrema Unctione,* (3 vols.), Bononiae, 1776.

VAN DER STAPPEN, J. F., *Sacra Liturgia,* (5 vols.), Mechliniae, 1911.

VAN ESPEN, Zegerus, *Jus Ecclesiasticum Universum Ceteraque Scripta Omnia,* Venetiis, 1769.

VERMEERSCH, Arturus, S. J., *Theologiae Moralis, Principia, Responsa, Consilia,* (3 vols.), Romae, 1923.

VERMEERSCH-CREUSEN, *Summa Novis, Juris,* Romae, 1918.

Epitome Juris Canonici, (3 vols.), Romae, 1925.

VICTORIA, Franciscus, *Summa Sacramentorum,* Antverpiae, 1572.

VIGOUREL, Adrian, S. S., *A Synthetical Manual of Liturgy,* Baltimore, 1907.

VOIT, Edmundus, *Theologia Moralis,* (2 vols.), Wirceburgi, 1860.

WALDENSIS (Thomas Netter), *Doctrinale Antiqui Fidei,* Venetiis, 1571.

WARREN, F. E., *The Liturgy and Ritual of the Celtic Church,* Oxford, 1881.

WATERWORTH, *Canons and Decrees of The Council of Trent,* London, 1848.

WERNZ-VIDAL, *Jus Canonicum De Personis,* Romae, 1923.

WOYWOD, Stanislaus, O. F. M., *A Practical Commentary on the Code of Canon Law,* (2 vols.), New York, 1925.

PERIODICALS

ACOLYTE, The, Huntington, vol. II (1926).

AMERICAN ECCLESIASTICAL REVIEW, The, Philadelphia, vols. XVIII (1898), XIX (1898), XX (1899), XXII (1900), XXV (1901), XXXI (1904), XXXIII (1905), XXXIV (1906), XLII (1910), XLVIII (1913), LVI (1917), LVII (1917), LVIII (1918), LX (1919), LXI (1919), LXII (1920), LXIX (1923).

ANALECTA ECCLESIASTICA, Romae, vol. VIII (1900).

BRITISH MEDICAL JOURNAL, The, London, Feb. 1914.

CANONISTE CONTEMPORAIN, Louvain, vol. XXX (1907).

DE RELIGIOSIS ET MISSIONARIIS SUPPLEMENTA ET MONUMENTA PERIODICA, Brugis, vol. III (1911).

EL CRITERIO CATHOLICO EN LAS CIENCIAS MEDICAS, Barcelona, May to Aug., 1903.

EPHEMERIDES LITURGICAE, Romae, vols. V (1891), XX (1906), XXI (1907), XXXI (1917).

ETUDES FRANCISCAINES, Paris, tome V, No. 25, (Jan. 1901).

HOMILETIC AND PASTORAL REVIEW, The, New York, vols. XXII (1922), XXVI (1926).

IL MONITORE ECCLESIASTICO, Roma, vols. VI (1895), XIX (1907), XXIX (1916).

IRISH ECCLESIASTICAL RECORD, The, Dublin, (Fifth Series), vols. VI (1915), VII (1916), XII (1918).

IRISH THEOLOGICAL QUARTERLY, The, Dublin, vols. II (1907), XII (1917).

JOURNAL OF EXPERIMENTAL MEDICINE, The, New York, vol. XVI (1912).

JOURNAL OF THE AMERICAN MEDICAL ASSOCIATION, Chicago, July 6, 1912 (vol. LIX, No. 1), Jan. 9, 1915, (vol. LXIV, No. 2).

L'AMI DU CLERGE, Langres, vols., XXX (1908), XXXIII (1911), XXXIV (1912).

NOUVELLE REVUE THEOLOGIQUE, Tournai, vol. XXXI (1899).

PHILADELPHIA PUBLIC LEDGER, Jan. 3, 1923.

PRESSE MEDICALE, LA, Paris.

RAZON Y FE, Madrid, vols. VIII (1903), IX (1903), XVI (1906), XLVIII (1917).

REVUE BENEDICTINE, Abbaye de Maredsous, vol. XIII (1896).

REVUE CATHOLIQUE DES EGLISES, vol. II, (1905).

REVUE D' HISTOIRE ET DE LITTERATURE RELIGIEUSES, Paris, vol. X (1905).

REVUE THEOLOGIQUE FRANCAIS, Toulouse, 1906.

THEOLOGISCH-PRAKTISCHE QUARTALSCHRIFT, Linz, vols. LXIX (1916), LXXI (1918), LXXIX (1926). (This is quoted in the footnotes as the Linzer Quartalschrift).

WASHINGTON POST, The, March 10, 1926.

ZEITSCHRIFT FUR KIRCHENGESCHISCHICHTE, Gotha, vol. XX (1900).

INDEX

Facultas Juris Canonici

Universitas Catholica Americae

Washingtonii

1925-1926

No. 32

DEUS LUX MEA

THESES

QUAS

AD DOCTORATUS GRADUM

IN

JURE CANONICO

Apud Universitatem Catholicam Americae

CONSEQUENDUM

PUBLICE PROPUGNABIT

ADRIANUS HIERONYMUS KILKER

SACERDOS ARCHIDIOECESIS

PHILADELPHIENSIS

JURIS CANONICI LICENTIATUS

HORA XI A. M. DIE XXVII MAII A. D. MCMXXVI

JUS CANONICUM

XXXIV. De Superiore Potestatem Coactivam Habente 2220-2225
XXXV. De Remissione Poenarum 2236-2240
XXXVI. De Absolutione Censurarum 2252-2254
XXXVII. De Natura et Divisione Excommunicationis 2257-2258
XXXVIII. De Effectibus Excommunicationis 2259-2267
XXXIX. De Definitione et Divisione Interdicti 2268-2269

ROMAN LAW

Justinian Law

XL. Slavery—Modes and Effects
XLI. Release from Slavery
XLII. The Effects of Release
XLIII. "Affines Servi"
XLIV. Citizens—Who are Citizens and How Citizenship Is Acquired
XLV. Loss of Citizenship
XLVI. Modification of Personality
XLVII. "Cura et Tutela"

Institutes of Gaius

XLVIII. Modes of Manumission
XLIX. Rights of Citizenship
L. Loss of Citizenship

INTERNATIONAL LAW

LI. The Nature of International Law
LII. Sources of International Law
LIII. The Drago Doctrine
LIV. The Extraterritoriality of Vessels
LV. The Monroe Doctrine
LVI. Spheres of Influence
LVII. Treaties—Purpose and Scope
LVIII. Diplomatic Agents: Immunity
LIX. Extradition
LX. Piracy

Vidit Facultas:

PHILIPPUS BERNARDINI, S. T. D., J. U. D., Decanus.
H. LUDOVICUS MOTRY, S. T. D., J. C. D., a Secretis.

Vidit Rector Universitatis:

✠THOMAS J. SHAHAN, S. T. D., J. U. L., L. L. D.

VITA

Adrian Jerome Kilker was born in Girardville, Pennsylvania, on August 21, 1901. He attended the public schools of that town, graduating from High School in 1916. In September of the same year, he entered the Seminary of Saint Charles Borromeo at Overbrook and eight years later was ordained to the priesthood by His Eminence, D. Cardinal Dougherty.

In September, 1924, he matriculated at the Catholic University of America at Washington, and registered in the School of Canon Law. At the end of the academic year of 1924-25, the degrees of Bachelor and Licentiate in Canon Law were conferred upon him. In partial fulfillment of the requirements for the degree of Doctor in Canon Law, he wrote and published this dissertation on Extreme Unction.

www.ingramcontent.com/pod-product-compliance
Lightning Source LLC
LaVergne TN
LVHW050300080826
844660LV00012B/665

* 9 7 8 0 8 1 3 2 2 2 2 2 6 *